Dear Michael,
    Wishing I could Be
the kind of author you are!
        Russell

Excerpts from Reader Comments

"You have made your constitutional points emphatically. This is a timely, informative, courageous, historical contribution."

Alfred J. Schweppe, distinguished jurist, treaty expert, American Bar Association

". . . one of the greatest frauds of our time as well as one of the least intelligent strategic decisions of any U.S. Administration since our founding."

John K. Singlaub, Maj. Gen. USA (Ret.), Former Chief of Staff, U.S. Army, South Korea

"I only wish that those responsible for the Treaties had had the chance to read this book back in 1977."

Philip M. Crane, U.S. Representative, House Ways and Means Committee

"This book presents to the American people the 'other side of the story' which has been 'spiked' by the media."

Gordon Sumner, Jr., Lt. General, USA (Ret.), Ambassador at Large, Latin America

". . . how President Carter succeeded in flouting the will of the American people in the Panama Canal giveaway."

Reed Irvine, Chairman, Accuracy in Media

". . . one of the sorriest chapters in our history . . . how we were trapped into this suicidal blunder. . . ."

Steven D. Symms, U.S. Senator, Committee on Finance

"The finest, most authentic book written about the tragic giveaway of the Panama Canal — a despicable deed by craven men."

Meldrim Thomson, Jr., Former Governor of New Hampshire

"Every so often there comes an American patriot with the courage and integrity to speak the truth to his countrymen. . . ."

Jesse Helms, U.S. Senator, Committee on Foreign Relations

Complete comments are on the last pages of the book.

Ambiguity haunted the entire Panama Canal treaties process, negotiations, ratification and implementation. It was not necessarily a failure to communicate — but a determination to transfer the Canal whatever the cost and with or without a meeting of minds. Diametrically opposing views prevailed:

Americans say they would support the Treaties if . . . "the Treaties provided that the United States could always send in troops to keep the Canal open to ships of all nations." As you know, the Treaty of Neutrality and the recent Statement of Understanding provide the United States this right.
— President Jimmy Carter, letter to Senator Ted Stevens, R-Alas., November 5, 1977

In order to have intervention, there has to be a reason to intervene. If some day this intervention does arise, it will find a country that does not want to be intervened. And if the intervention is to defend the Canal, what they may get is the impossibility of traffic through it.
— General Omar Torrijos, statement to *La Prensa* newspaper, Panama, December 14, 1980

. . . expeditious passage means that our ships can go to the head of the line.
— U.S. Secretary of State, Cyrus R. Vance, testimony before the Senate Foreign Relations Committee, September 26, 1977

. . . expeditious passage for U.S. warships does not mean privileged passage and the concept of privileged passage is rejected. If the Gringos with their warships say, "I want to go first," then, that is their problem. We cannot go that far.
— Dr. Romulo Escobar Bethancourt, Panamanian chief negotiator, press conference, Panama City, August 24, 1977

THE PANAMA CANAL TREATIES SWINDLE
Consent to Disaster

by G. Russell Evans

In collaboration with

PHILLIP HARMAN

Chairman, Committee for Better Panama
and United States Relations

Introduction by Admiral Thomas H. Moorer
U.S. Navy (Ret.)

Signal Books
201-C East Main Street
Carrboro, NC 27510

LIBRARY OF CONGRESS CATALOGING-IN-PUBLICATION DATA

Evans, G. Russell
The Panama Canal Treaties Swindle
3rd printing

1. Panama Canal — History – Treaties
2. U.S. Constitution — Separation of Powers
86-062370

ISBN: 0-930095-00-6

To Anne

ACKNOWLEDGMENTS

The following individuals contributed to the development of our story and to the completion of the manuscript, some extensively and some in minor ways. Their inputs are acknowledged with gratitude.

Charles W. Adair, former U.S. Ambassador to Panama
Efrain Angueira, U.S. intelligence officer
Gustave Anguizola, author and lecturer
Nicolas Ardito-Barletta, President of Panama
Arnulfo Arias, former three-times President of Panama
Charles H. Breecher, former State Department treaty specialist
Allan C. Brownfeld, columnist
Clayton Burwell, attorney
Dick Clark, former U.S. Senator
Scott Cohen, Staff Director, Senate Foreign
    Relations Committee
Thomas M. Constant, Colonel, USA (Ret.), member Consultative Committee,
    Panama Canal
Ryan Conway, Associate Legislative Assistant to Senator Alan Cranston
Alfredo Costellanos, Treaties language specialist
Philip M. Crane, U.S. Representative
Robert E. Dalton, Assistant Legal Adviser for Treaties, State Department
Sam Dickens, Colonel, USAF (Ret.)
William L. Dickinson, U.S. Representative
Robert Dockery, former staff official in charge of Treaties for the Senate Foreign
    Relations Committee
Herbert W. Dodge, former State Department Foreign Service Officer
John M. Fisher, President, American Security Council
Robert P. Griffin, former U.S. Senator
Herbert J. Hansell, former Legal Adviser, State Department

George W. Hansen, U.S. Representative
William C. Hansen, Colonel, USAF
Phillip Harman, Chairman, Committee for Better Panama & U.S. Relations
Margaret Hayes, Western Hemisphere Specialist, Senate Foreign Relations
  Committee
Jesse Helms, U.S. Senator
Ashley C. Hewitt, Jr., Political Counselor, U.S. Embassy, Panama
Sherman Hinson, Panama Desk, State Department
Norvill Jones, former Chief of Staff, Senate Foreign Relations Committee
Jerry Jordan, attorney
Michael Kozak, Deputy Legal Adviser, State Department
Demetrio B. Lakas, former President of Panama
James P. Lucier, Chief Legislative Assistant to Senator Jesse Helms
Thomas C. Mann, former Assistant Secretary of State for Inter-American Affairs
Richard McCall, former Deputy Staff Director, Senate Foreign Relations
  Committee
James McClellan, former Chief Counsel and Staff Director, Senate Subcommittee
  on Separation of Powers
James McKenna, Chief Legislative Aide to Representative George Hansen
Fernando Manfredo, Deputy Administrator, Panama Canal Commission
Boris Martinez, former Colonel and Chief of Staff, Panamanian National Guard
Ralph G. Mendenhall, senior Panama Canal Pilot
Terrence Modglin, former Staff Director, House Subcommittee on the Panama
  Canal
Thomas H. Moorer, Admiral, USN (Ret.), former Chairman, Joint Chiefs of Staff
John M. Murphy, former Chairman, House Committee on Merchant Marine and
  Fisheries
Dwight G. Osborne, senior Panama Canal Pilot
Robert O. Pastor, former staff assistant, National Security Council under President
  Carter
Carl Perian, former Chief of Staff, House Committee on Merchant Marine and
  Fisheries
Robert W. Porter, Jr., General, USA (Ret.), former Commander-in-Chief, U.S.
  Southern Command
William T. Pryce, Deputy Chief of Mission, U.S. Embassy, Panama
Marco Robles, former President of Panama
William D. Rogers, former Assistant Secretary of State for Inter-American Affairs
Alison Rosenberg, Legislative Assistant for Foreign Affairs, Senate Foreign
  Relations Committee
Amado Sanjur, former Colonel and Chief of Staff, Panamanian National Guard
Alfred J. Schweppe, attorney
Ramiro Silvera, former Colonel and Chief of Staff, Panamanian National Guard
John K. Singlaub, Maj. General, USA (Ret.)
W. Cleon Skousen, author and lecturer
Charles Stevenson, Legislative Aide to Senator Joseph R. Biden, Jr.
Cesar Napoleon Suazo, former Maj. General, Nicaraguan National Guard
Gordon Sumner, Lt. General, USA (Ret.)
Steven Symms, U.S. Senator

C. M. Talbott, Lt. General, USAF (Ret.)
Meldrim Thomson, Jr., former Governor, New Hampshire
Herbert D. Vogel, Brig. General, USA (Ret.)
John Wallace, senior Panama Canal Pilot
John C. "Rufus" Webb, Jr., author and publisher

PREFACE

The one thing that made possible the "surrender" of the Panama Canal, against the will of the American people, was the awesome power of the U.S. presidency. Indeed, Harry Truman once said, not even the might of Genghis Khan, Augustus Caesar or Napoleon could compare with it.

It was not the President's power of pandering persuasion or his agonizing doggedness in accumulating the votes of 68 Senators for "Advice and Consent"—it was his *assumed* power, seized to ratify unilaterally and with impunity, for the United States, Treaties that had by-passed vital requirements of the U.S. Constitution and the Vienna Convention on the Law of Treaties. Thus, in effect, he dictated final approval without Senate concurrence.

President Jimmy Carter traveled to Panama to ratify the Panama Canal Treaties on June 16, 1978 and accepted, without the consent of the Senate, Panama's last minute counter-reservation that nullified U.S. rights to defend and keep open the Canal unilaterally, rights that presumably had been guaranteed by the DeConcini reservation and without which the Senate would never have agreed to the Treaties.

Consequently, the U.S. Senate had consented to one version of the Treaties and the Republic of Panama to another. We call it *The Panama Canal Treaties Swindle: Consent to Disaster* because it deprived Americans of their property under false pretenses and set the stage for future confrontation.

Five identifiable swindles and four smoking guns were discovered—all based on obscuring U.S. rights for the security of the Canal, rights that Panama never agreed to from beginning to end. One of the most shocking discoveries was President Carter's admission, in his book of memoirs four years after the fact, that he told Omar Torrijos, Panama's dictator, to write his own reservation as to U.S. intervention. Other irregularities involved basic constitutional procedures: (1) the failure to permit the House of Representatives to participate in the treaty phase for the disposition of U.S. property (Article IV); and (2) the failure to abrogate the old treaty as a "Law of the Land" (Article VI) and in accordance with *Jefferson's Manual*. These inconveniences were brushed aside in favor of legislative efficiency, thereby avoiding challenges in the House of Representatives.

Our purpose is to document the Canal swindle. In this complicated story, repetition of important issues is considered necessary to maintain perspective and relevance to the deception being explained. In this respect, clarity is preferred to sophistication. Reiteration, moreover, reinforces our polemic. The other side has been elegantly covered in the writings of Messrs. Carter, Zbigniew Brzezinski, Henry Kissinger, Sol Linowitz, William Jorden and others seeking to rationalize the wisdom of relinquishing sovereign rights in a strategic area under unstable conditions.

The Treaties are the product of non-observance of the constitutional system of checks and balances by the Legislative, Executive, and Judicial Branches—each of which failed at critical junctures along the way. The failure to produce legal Treaties has paved the way for future conflict where Americans will have no alternative but to use force to uphold their legitimate interests. Charges by Panama of misdeeds on the part of Teddy Roosevelt and the Frenchman, Bunau-Varilla, will be dwarfed in future history by denouncements of the Carter-Torrijos fraud.

Panama has long been called "the land of endemic revolution and political turmoil." On June 7, 1977, two months before the Treaties were unveiled, Torrijos was telling Latin American journalists:

> We want the Canal because it belongs to us and we never give up our rights. If the U.S. doesn't turn it over, I can assure them that the Canal and the Zone will be without water, without lights, and without a Canal and without Gringos, in very short order.

On September 27, 1985, the Napoleonic commander of Panama's *Guardia*, Manuel Antonio Noriega, threw out the president he had selected the year before and installed another in order to save himself from a criminal investigation in connection with murder and drug trafficking. Brig. General Noriega, the opportunist, panders to potential winners such as Nicaragua's Daniel Ortega and Cuba's Fidel Castro. U.S. strategists can find no comfort in developments that threaten the Canal's security long before 1999, the transfer date.

The oath of office to "preserve, protect and defend the Constitution" is vastly more important than U.S. property or territory. The Constitution is our national treasure. Daniel Webster said in 1832, "... if these columns fall, they will be raised not again." The invasion of the Executive into Legislative prerogatives is unacceptable precedent. If unchallenged, it will return to haunt future leaders down the years, long after the Panama Treaties may have faded from memory.

Acknowledgments: Special recognition goes to my collaborator, Phillip Harman, Chairman of the Committee for Better Panama and U.S. Relations, whose exhaustive studies developed parts of our story never before publicized: the coup against Arnulfo Arias, the mysterious Efrain Angueira, and many details of the various swindles.

Alfred J. Schweppe, the distinguished Seattle jurist, helped nail down slippery treaty points; he reviewed the manuscript for legal propriety and constitutional accuracy. Eminent attorneys Clayton Burwell of Washington, D.C. and Jerry Jorden of Dallas checked our constitutional arguments. Thanks for the donations of time and expertise.

Research was facilitated by the staffs at Norfolk's Old Dominion University, Kirn Memorial Library, and Lyman Beecher Library, and at Williamsburg's Marshal-Wythe Law Library of the College of William and Mary.

The "Acknowledgments" section identifies 66 individuals who contributed to our story.

Especially I am grateful for the patience and support of my wife Anne—from start to finish my partner in turning out this manuscript—critic, proofreader and inquisitor.

G.Russell Evans

Norfolk, Va.
August, 1986

CONTENTS

INTRODUCTION

This book deserves close study by all Americans interested in the vital geo-strategic importance of the Panama Canal to the security of the United States in particular, and of the Western World in general. As the author unfolds this tragic story step by step, in accurate and precise detail, Americans will be appalled at what actually took place. They will have extreme difficulty believing that the Executive and Legislative Branches of the U.S. Government would foster such non-Treaties and swindle on our nation despite the clear indication that the vast majority of the American people were strongly opposed to this obvious giveaway.

On the day the vote was taken, the halls of Congress were stacked with letters from concerned citizens opposing the Treaties. Unfortunately, 68 Senators from both sides of the aisle chose to ignore the fact that the American people have a basic instinct for survival and recognize political antics when they see them. Senators Baker, Percy, Mathias, Church, Pell, Sarbanes, and Biden, along with their colleagues, did not carve a very good niche in history for themselves by their ill-advised votes for these Treaties.

It was clear from intelligence reports that Panama fitted in the grand scheme of the Soviets to project Marxism into the Caribbean through the Cuban connection. In short, we were faced with a Torrijos-Castro-Breshnev Axis. Moreover, Torrijos had frequent contacts with Castro.

The Panamanians were prepared to play hard ball. On the return flight from Washington following the Treaties signing ceremonies in September 1977, Torrijos called Castro on the radio as he overflew Cuba and congratulated him on the success of his "revolution." During a visit to Panama, Senators Howard Baker and Jake Garn received a threatening briefing from Torrijos's strong man, Brig. General Manuel Antonio Noriega, who is currently in command of the Panamanian Defense Force (formerly the National Guard).

I testified before Committees of both the Senate and House of Representatives several times. It was quite clear throughout that very few of the members of Congress had any concept of the long range implications of these Treaties on the security and prosperity of the United States. Rather, they chose to deal in emotional and ideological levels. Repeatedly, the point was incorrectly made that Panama had been "colonized" by the United States.

Love, hate and fear were frequently advanced as reasons for disposing of the Canal and even paying the Panamanian Government to take it. The arguments by Senators, who should have known better, went something like this: "If we give the Canal to Panama, everyone will love us; if we don't give it away, everyone will hate us; and besides if we don't surrender it, the radicals in Panama will destroy the Canal." Of course, none of these arguments is valid.

There were several negative points associated with these hearings that the Senate failed to explore: (1) Very senior officials in the Carter Administration stated publicly that the Treaties would not cost the American taxpayer one cent. In matter of fact, they will cost many millions of dollars for years to come and this was obvious from the outset. (2) Panama was paying about 48% of its annual budget just to pay interest on debts. The question arises, what special interests had visions of recovering bad loans by Treaties designed to pass Canal toll revenues to pay off bank loans? (3) In 1978, Panama stood at the bottom of the list in the State Department evaluation of human rights in Central and South America. Nevertheless, the Carter Administration, which prided itself on emphasizing human rights, was so obsessed with giving away the Canal that it chose to overlook the violations in Panama, and thus resorted to "selective morality."

The impact of the Panama Canal Treaties made clear for all to see as soon as Congress passed the enabling legislation which made the Treaties operative. Castro went into action and was strongly supported by Torrijos, his admirer. Panamanian aircraft were used to fly arms from Cuba to Panama, and then from Panama to Nicaragua to aid the communist Sandinistas. In May 1979, the Central Intelligence Agency summarized Castro's intentions this way:

> The Castro regime apparently concluded by at least last fall (after signing of the Panama Canal Treaties) that prospects for revolution in Central America over the next decade or so had markedly improved largely because of the weakened position of Nicaragua's Somoza and the ripple his removal would have on other countries in Central America. As a result, Cuba has intensified its attempt to unify insurgent groups not only in Nicaragua but in El Salvador and Guatemala as well.

So, there you see all. Today, because of our failure to stand fast in support of the principles expressed in the Monroe Doctrine and to retain full control of the greatest maritime gateway of the world, we are in very serious trouble in Central America. The Congress seems determined to thwart President Reagan on every move and we even have the sad spectacle of Congressional leaders trifling with treason, and flouting the Logan Act, as they jointly write a letter to the Communist chief of Nicaragua and assure him of their support in opposing the Administration of their own country.

And what about Panama today? Nine years after the signing of the Treaties very little has changed. The Canal machinery is the worse from wear, poverty is rampant, and the national debt is still very large. Panama had not had an election in 16 years although one was held in May 1984.

Presidents have moved in and out like pinch hitters but the real power rests, as always, with the Commander of the National Guard, the dedicated Marxist, Brig. General Noriega. Perpetual instability is the state of affairs in Panama. It is a dangerous environment in which to position one of our most valuable strategic and economic assets.

McLean, Virginia

Thomas H. Moorer, Jr.
Admiral, U.S. Navy (Ret.)
Former Chairman,
Joint Chiefs of Staff

Despite the serious ambiguities accepted by both countries, President Carter and Panamanian Ambassador Gabriel Lewis Galindo react in the White House Oval office on April 18, 1978 to the news that the second Panama Canal Treaty had been approved by the U.S. Senate. From the left are Carter, U.S. negotiators Sol Linowitz and Ellsworth Bunker, and Lewis
(AP/Wide World Photos)

· 1 ·

THE FIRST DOMINO IN LATIN AMERICA

The spirit of the Panama Canal in the early 1900s was the spirit of America: young and confident, and with a determination that knew no bounds. No sacrifice, no hardship was too great for the heroes digging the long-sought Canal across the Isthmus of Panama.

Indeed, this was the spirit of the young engineer in charge of the rock-crushing plant at Ancon in early 1910, one J. A. Loulan by name, in cheerfully recounting his frequent 2 a.m. emergency calls: "We worked from that time until breakfast to get the engine back, and were satisfied to know that the accident did not delay operations at the crusher. Not a man on the force was late getting back to work after four hours of strenuous extra night duty."[1]

Such "inconveniences" were the rule, not the exception; and they epitomized this great success story. Another engineer told of being called two or three times a night, adding, "We are well paid, and we owe it to our country to make whatever sacrifice the work demands. And after a month or two we get out of the habit of feeling that it is a sacrifice."

Visitors to the site of the Big Ditch were commonplace and stories of the dedicated Americans spread around the globe. One of the European visitors exclaimed, "It was a delight for me from beginning to end to see the magnificent type of American manhood at work and the pride taken by every worker in the project."[2]

Of course, the character of every project is set at the top. So it was with the Canal's Chief Engineer, George Washington Goethals, who was summoned to the scene of the disastrous slide at Cucaracha one Sunday morning in 1913. "Whatever are we going to do now?" he was asked. After calmly lighting a cigarette, Goethals answered, "Hell, dig it out again!"[3]

And indeed it was dug out again, many times, as Colonel Goethals "made the dirt fly." This Army officer's genius and the sweat of the American, Jamaican, and other diggers produced an engineering symphony, later described by the distinguished author and historian, Captain Miles P. Duval, Jr., USN (Ret.), who wrote in his book, *And the Mountains Will Move* (Greenwood Press, 1968):

Culebra Cut, when seen from one of its high banks in the cool of the tropical night, is a sight that can never be forgotten. Red and white bank lights pulsate at each turn in the channel. Green range lights, marking the center line of the reaches of the Cut, guide vessels as they slowly pass. There is profound silence and calm, disturbed only by the whistle signals of vessels rounding turns in the Cut, the rustle of leaves in the light breeze, or the euphonious sounds of insects, birds, and animals — the symphony of the jungle.[4]

But alas, all did not continue harmonious. Some sixty years later, the qualities that produced this wonder of the world gave way to doubt and a mea culpa complex that eventually surrendered this great waterway to the unstable dictatorship of the Republic of Panama. This was done by means of long-sought treaties: The Panama Canal Treaties of 1977. Moreover, the loss of the Canal has been called the first domino in Latin America.

The Treaties were the product of non-observance of the constitutional system of checks and balances. Among the arguments for surrendering sovereign rights over United States territory and giving away taxpayers' property, and paying Panama to take it, were pleas for justice and Hemispheric good will. Moreover, it appeared, during the extended debates, the strongest argument was that Senators should put aside their own best judgment and vote for the Treaties in order to avoid a "devastating blow to the prestige of President Carter."

At one point, former Senator Robert P. Griffin, R.-Mich., lamented, "In my judgment it was ironic and rather sad that, when the crunch came, the strongest argument for the treaty was the weakness of the President."[5]

But, these arguments were superficial when compared with the reasons advanced by Congressman Ron Paul, R.-Tex., who warned his colleagues on June 21, 1979 about doing business with Panama's dictator, Omar Torrijos, on behalf of the banking interests with their "insatiable greed." He said:

Insane as it seems to most Americans, I believe it is understandable just how this all came about. International blackmail, power politics and an insatiable greed for the money of the world all played a part in this transaction. The biggest hoax was the excuse that the Treaties were necessary because of some benevolent conviction on the part of the American politicians. If this were so, the continued financing and indirect control of the Canal would not have been sought after and maintained.[6]

Mr. Paul, of course, was speaking about "a third party's interest in the Panama Canal" — i.e., the megabanks with their ancillary, the Trilateral Commission, that international consortium of bankers, businessmen and world leaders dedicated to a "more equitable world order." Rather frightening, he said, was the "boldness of those who once kept secret the relationship between the ruling politicians and the big banking and big business interests." Moreover, the open press, such as *U.S. News & World Report,* were publicizing the connection of President Carter, and many of his advisers, to the Chase Manhattan Bank, David Rockefeller and the Trilateral Commission.

At the time of the Treaties in 1977, Panama had bank debts of almost $3 billion, most of which had been incurred by Torrijos who, in turn, had provided a loosely regulated "haven" for his creditors, the international bankers. Eventually, almost 40 percent of Panama's budget was needed for debt service to New York banks who, in turn, needed a "solvent" Torrijos in order to protect their bad loans as well as their privileged banking paradise. The Panama Canal was the solution — and Representative Paul stated, "These Treaties were undoubtedly written by the banking and big business interests of Wall Street."

During the 1979 debates on the implementing legislation for the Panama Canal Treaties, Mr. Paul asked, "Why did the politicians not act like politicians?" and vote the way the overwhelming majority of the people wanted them to vote if the politicians were to "maintain their jobs." He answered his own question:

But with the Panama Canal Treaty vote, things were different. I believe this vote reflects just who is owned and controlled by the Establishment: that is, the big money and the big business interests of the world.

· · · · ·

I believe, in reality, the Canal is now "owned" by fascist-oriented, international banking and business interests and is merely managed by the Marxist-oriented Torrijos dictatorship, with the bills being paid by the American taxpayers — a rather sad set of circumstances. Further confirmation of this unlikely partnership of business interests and a left-wing dictatorship is the fact that the controversial Marine-Midland Bank has become "partner" with the Hong Kong and Shanghai Banking Corporation, whereby this Far Eastern bank will purchase 51 percent of the stock of the New York-based bank. Interesting indeed, since it is the Marine-Midland Bank that acts as the sole agent for the Panamanian Government for all its banking dealings in the United States. Sol Linowitz was a director of this same bank prior to his becoming the chief negotiator for the United States in working out the details of the new Treaties.

Representative Paul documented "backdoor advantages" for other business interests such as the Export-Import Bank, the Agency for International Development, and the Overseas Private Development Corporation — all of which were to subsidize the Panamanian Government to the tune of $300 million, a largesse which, he predicted, will ultimately be laid on the American taxpayers. He concluded:

The passage of the Panama Canal Treaties represents one of the saddest events in the history of the United States.

It seems absolutely incredible that the strongly expressed will of the American people could be thwarted with impunity by the Establishment, big banks and big business.

Moreover, this power that dictated the disposition of the Panama Canal is a power even more frightening than the power of the presidency itself. Its servants were not bound by the restraints of the U.S. Constitution and international law, and, in obedience, transferred the Canal in what was called "the worst fraud ever perpetrated on the United States Senate and on the American people."

By way of orientation for the reader: the first two chapters of the story of the Canal swindle define and identify the main points at issue, and provide an historical background and introduction to the principal characters. Thereafter, the details are developed and documented.

ALLEGATIONS OF UNCONSTITUTIONAL TREATIES

The new Treaties transferred sovereignty of the Canal Zone and the Canal to Panama on October 1, 1979. Ownership of the Canal and U.S. installations will be transferred on December 31, 1999. This is the date when all U.S. bases in Panama are to be closed and all military forces removed. The entire Canal operation will then be the sole province of Panama and any U.S. presence, even temporarily, will be at the sufferance of the Panamanian government in accordance with its interpretations of the Treaties, interpretations that differ considerably from those of the United States.

Serious allegations were made after the Treaties were ratified that they were unconstitutional and illegal because: (1) Panama's instruments of ratification contained a reservation that denied U.S. unilateral rights to keep the Canal secure and that had not been submitted to the Senate for approval; (2) ratification procedures were contrary to requirements of international law, i.e., the Vienna Convention on the Law of Treaties, in that substantive changes had not been agreed to by both parties; and (3) non-resident aliens were assigned as U.S. officials to the Panama Canal Commission.

Unfortunately, the American people have not been told about these serious charges of impropriety. But they have not forgotten the Canal debates of 1976-79. The loss of the Canal was one of the most discussed foreign affairs issues in the history of the Congress. Millions of Americans wrote to their Senators and to newspaper editors protesting the giveaway of the Canal. The ultimate outcome generated disbelief, frustration, and unbridled condemnation on the part of many citizens, most of whom never quite knew how the Canal was lost.

On June 23, 1983 one of President Ronald Reagan's closest friends and advisers, Senator Paul Laxalt, R.-Nev., appeared before Senator John P. East's Subcommittee on Separation of Powers where he made a statement questioning the validity of the Treaties. At this hearing, expert witnesses and substantial documentation brought into question the constitutionality of the Treaties. Moreover, new evidence, never before publicized by the media, was presented and labeled by the witnesses "swindles" and "smoking guns." Much of this evidence, they asserted, had been covered up or stonewalled.

Who made these claims? They were made by the late Dr. Charles H. Breecher, distinguished jurist and former treaty specialist with the State Department; Dr. Herbert W. Dodge, another former State Department treaty official; and Phillip Harman, Chairman of the Committee for Better Panama and United States Relations, intelligence operative and student of Panamanian affairs for several decades, also an adviser to Ronald Reagan at one time.

Presenting the State Department's case at Senator East's hearing was Robert E. Dalton, Assistant Legal Adviser for Treaty Affairs. Mr. Dalton contended that Panama's counter-reservation did not alter either nation's rights or duties and therefore, did not constitute a change in meaning — hence, he concluded, the Treaties are valid.

Therein lies the disagreement. A brief preliminary historical accounting may help place the situation in context.

A series of unpleasant incidents involving sovereignty and flag-flying in the Canal Zone helped induce President Lyndon Johnson to announce on September 24, 1965 that the basic 1903 Hay-Bunau-Varilla Treaty with Panama would be abrogated and that U.S. rights of sovereignty in the Canal Zone would be relinquished.[7] Thereafter, all negotiations proceeded in that direction.

Sovereignty, of course, is the bedrock foundation for defending and operating the Canal; and it has been surrendered. Now, if it desires to do so, Panama could nationalize the Canal at any time with the full authorization of the United Nations Charter. This situation gravely threatens America's southern flank, particularly in view of the Soviet and Cuban incursions into the Caribbean area.

On at least three counts, the surrender of rights of sovereignty by the United States assured the inherent weaknesses of the Canal Treaties of 1977. First, the Torrijos dictatorship that accepted the Treaties was not elected by the people of Panama and was not a constitutional regime; and therefore, any future administration, not having ratified the Treaties, could reject them and refuse to recognize the guarantees of U.S. defense rights over the Canal. Second, it is an historical fact that treaties are broken whenever either nation finds it advantageous to do so.

The third weakness of the Treaties is that Panama could nationalize the Canal under current provisions of international law which allow any nation to expropriate foreign-owned property within its borders. Moreover, the United Nations Charter says no nation can use force to prevent such expropriation. Since the Canal would remain U.S.-owned property until the year 2000 in territory over which Panama has sovereignty, it is subject to the threat of expropriation and nationalization.

When the Treaties were being negotiated and debated in 1977 and 1978, Ronald Reagan warned at least three times about the dangers of treaties that could nationalize the Canal, as reported by his executive secretary, Helene Von Damm in her book, *Sincerely, Ronald Reagan* (Berkeley Publishing Corporation, 1980). Apparently, no other President, or future President in this case, had ever publicly recognized the threat of expropriation.

Mr. Reagan drew a parallel with Egypt's Gamal Abdel Nasser's nationalization of the Suez Canal on July 26, 1956:

In other words, if we relinquish our present right (of sovereignty over the Canal) — as the Treaties would do — Panama could expropriate the Canal any time after they went into effect, and we could not even use the forces stationed there to resist. Remember the case of the Suez Canal, when Nasser, in violation of his treaty, seized the British installations. When they threatened the use of force, even the United States joined the Soviet Union and others in forcing them to back away and let Nasser keep the Canal.

The 1977 Treaties gave Panama sovereignty over the Canal Zone, eventual ownership and virtually everything else ever asked for. The original 1903 Treaty was also beneficial: It guaranteed Panama's independence from Colombia and assured other advantages for the new nation — and for the United States, it granted a 10-mile wide Zone for the purpose of constructing a canal for civilization, an area in which the United States was granted rights of sovereignty.

Panama, the land of "endemic revolution and endless political turmoil," was once a jungle and disease-ridden province of Colombia. In the 57 years preceding the 1903 Canal Treaty with the United States, there had been 53 revolutions, rebellions, or other outbreaks in the area.[8] In view of such upheaval and strife, the United States, under President Theodore Roosevelt, knew that unless political stability and governmental control were permanently maintained in the Canal Zone, it would be useless to try to construct and operate a canal.

Roosevelt and the Panamanian leaders seeking independence from Colombia in 1903 understood these requirements which necessarily became the foundations of the basic Canal Treaty of November 18, 1903 in the clear-cut and unconditional provisions granting complete and exclusive rights of sovereignty over the Canal Zone to the United States in perpetuity. Indeed, the United States could not afford to undertake such an enterprise without these absolute guarantees — and Panama itself could not afford to do less than grant "full control of both the Zone and the Canal itself to the United States."

The Panamanians were extremely pleased with their new nation, new found independence, and new friend in the United States. There were no questions about sovereign rights in the beginning, nor about other provisions. They were reveling in the warm glow of freedom and self-determination. On December 2, 1903 the provisional government of Panama ratified the Treaty. The U.S. rights of sovereignty were clearly stated in Article III of the Treaty:

The Republic of Panama grants to the United States *all the rights, power, and authority* within the Zone mentioned and described in Article II of this agreement and within the limits of all auxiliary lands and waters mentioned and described in said Article II *which the United States would possess and exercise if it were the sovereign* of the territory within which such lands and waters are located *to the entire exclusion of the exercise of the Republic of Panama of any such sovereign rights, power, or authority*. (Emphasis added)

Shortly thereafter, Panama's Secretary of Government, Tomas Arias, again recognized U.S. sovereignty and jurisdiction in a diplomatic note to the United States, dated May 25, 1904:

The government of Panama considers that upon the exchange of ratification, on February 26, 1904, of the Treaty for opening the inter-ocean Canal across the Isthmus of Panama, *its jurisdiction ceased over the Zone.*[9] (Emphasis added)

One of the American statesmen most quoted out of context on the matter of U.S. rights of sovereignty over the Canal Zone was William

Howard Taft, who, as Secretary of War and later as President, had held responsible positions during the construction of the Canal longer than any other high official. At a banquet given by the President of Panama on November 16, 1910 in Panama, President Taft made a clear statement of policy under which the Canal Zone had been acquired. It was significant:

We are here to construct, maintain, operate, and defend a world canal, which runs through the heart of your country, and you have given us the necessary sovereignty and jurisdiction over the part of your country occupied by that Canal to enable us to do this effectively.[10]

President Taft was reasserting and reemphasizing the rights of sovereignty; they were indisputably established.

In 1903 the Frenchman Philippe Bunau-Varilla, former engineer for the French Canal Company, had helped the Panamanians win American support for their independence movement. Subsequently, the Panamanians made him their negotiator "to adjust a treaty for the canal construction by the United States." Some Panamanians later criticized this selection, but it was their own doing, with their own junta (the provisional government).

As for Theodore Roosevelt, he always felt the grant of the Canal Zone to be one of his greatest accomplishments. Nonetheless, he too was criticized for interceding to prevent Colombia from putting down the Panamanian revolution. Even so, it was bloodless, and Panama had its long-sought independence — the United States its long-sought canal route.

Nor did President Roosevelt escape the admonition of the U.S. Minister to Bogata, James T. DuBois, in a letter to Secretary of State Philander Chase Knox dated September 30, 1921 (*sic.*, 1912):

From 1810 to 1903 Colombia was the best friend the United States had south of the Rio Grande. . . . Nine years ago this was all changed suddenly and unexpectedly when President Roosevelt denied to Colombia the right to land troops upon her own soil to suppress a threatened revolt. . . . The confidence and trust in the fairness of the United States, so long manifested, has completely vanished.

Mr. Knox, as a Democratic Senator from Pennsylvania earlier, had debated at length the 1903 Treaty as a member of the Senate Judiciary Committee. Mr. Roosevelt had an entirely different view of the acquisition of the Canal Zone:

ACQUISITION OF THE CANAL ZONE

. . . We did our duty by the world, we did our duty by the people of Panama, we did our duty by ourselves. We did harm to no one save as harm is done to a bandit by a policeman who deprives him of his chance for blackmail. The United States has many honorable chapters in its history, but no more honorable chapter than that which tells of the way in which our right to dig the Panama Canal was secured and of the manner in which the work itself was carried out.[12]

Later, ex-President Roosevelt wrote to his friend, W.R. Thayer, "You could no more make an agreement with the Colombian rulers than you could nail currant jelly to a wall — . . . The people of Panama were a unit in desiring the Canal and in wishing to overthrow the rule of Colombia."[13]

The Canal benefited the new nation of Panama immensely. But as often happens with great relationships, erosion set in as Panama's demands increased. A 1936 treaty marked the beginning of the surrender of U.S. rights of sovereignty affecting the Canal, especially rights of eminent domain within the Republic of Panama in matters relating to defense and sanitation. A 1955 treaty surrendered additional rights and U.S. property, including $24 million worth of freight yards and passenger stations of the Panama Railroad.[14]

These capitulations caused withdrawal of U.S. activities to the Canal Zone and serious impairment in defense and Canal operations. Most costs, of course, were borne by U.S taxpayers. But even more important, future bargaining chips with the Panamanians had been given away.

A number of events followed the 1955 treaty in what appeared to be well-regulated and ordered sequences, orchestrated by a State Department determined to transfer the Canal. Some of the main events were these: the formal display of the Panamanian flag in the Canal Zone beginning in 1960; the 1965 decision by President Johnson to surrender sovereignty and to terminate the old treaty; the 1971 Senate abrogation of U.S. canal rights in Nicaragua; and the 1974 Kissinger-Tack Statement of Principles, the forerunner of the 1977 Treaties.

Unfortunately, these 1977 Treaties are ambiguous concerning U.S. involvement in safeguarding the Canal in case its security is threatened, since different versions were agreed to by each party. Panama did not intend, in its new "partnership relationship" with the United States in operating and defending the Canal, that its sovereignty would be infringed for any reason. This premise caused the ambiguity that continued through-out negotiations, and that still exists.

The Hay-Bunau-Varilla Treaty by which the United States acquired the right to construct, own and operate the Canal in 1903 was very specific in Article XXIII about employing force when necessary:

If it should be necessary at any time to employ armed forces for the safety and pro-tection of the Canal, or ships that make use of the same, or the Railroad and auxil-iary works, the U.S. shall have the right at all times and at its discretion to use its police, land and naval forces or to establish fortifications for these purposes.

Similar clear-cut U.S. defense rights were embodied in the DeConcini reservation to the 1977 Treaties but these rights were voided by a last-min-ute counter-reservation submitted by Panama, a reservation that the U.S.

Senate did not vote upon. Failure to submit this measure to the full Senate for advice and consent was an important part of the Panama Canal swindle.

This allegation and other charges of wrong-doings presented at the 1983 hearing before the East Subcommittee extend to the President of the United States, as well as to the Department of State and, in some respects, to the leadership of the United States Senate.

The United States negotiators of the Panama Canal Treaties appear to have proved the maxim: "Yield to all and you will soon have nothing to yield" (Aesop).

THE INVOLVEMENT OF THE PRESIDENT OF THE UNITED STATES

In his testimony before the Senate Subcommittee, Dr. Breecher characterized the circumstances surrounding the transfer of the Canal as "the worst fraud ever perpetrated on the United States Senate and on the American people" for the reason that both nations had not accepted the same versions of the Treaties. The fact that President Carter and his State Department did not properly alert the Senate leadership to the last minute Panamanian counter-reservation constituted fraud that resulted in the uncontested Exchange of Protocols and the subsequent "transfer" of the Canal.

Breecher used Articles 2.1 (d) and 20.2 of the 1969 Vienna Convention on the Law of Treaties to substantiate his assertion that the Treaties had *not* been ratified in international law and therefore, did not go into effect on October 1, 1979. In adding their three paragraph long "understanding," which was actually a reservation, the Panamanians nullified the DeConcini reservation under which the United States had permanently the right to use independently, with or without Panama's consent, military force in Panama to keep the Canal open and operating.[15]

International law (the Vienna Convention) states: " . . . a reservation requires acceptance by all the parties" (Article 20.2). Since the United States did not accept Panama's reservation ("understanding"), which is a further amendment to the text of the Treaties, there are no Panama Canal Treaties in international law.

This rudimentary application of international treaty law is known as "boilerplate" to Foreign Service Officers. Its application to the Canal Treaties was reinforced by the letter of Herbert J. Hansell, State Department Legal adviser, to Senator John J. Sparkman, Chairman of the Foreign Relations Committee, saying:

This will confirm our previous advice to you . . . that under United States law substantive amendments and reservations to the Panama Canal Treaties put forth by Panama that would affect United States rights or obligations under the Treaties cannot be accepted by the United States unless approved by the President and the Senate.[16]

The subsequent failure of the President and the State Department to notify the Senate of the inconsistencies between the DeConcini reservation and Panama's counter-reservation constitutes a breakdown in the constitutional requirement for advice and consent. This was a main concern expressed by Senator East at his Subcommittee hearing. It involves oaths of office to protect and defend the Constitution.

Other constitution-related matters in the surrender of the Canal included: the by-passing of the House of Representatives in the treaty negotiations transferring U.S. territory and property; and the alleged unrestrained and direct negotiating of some Senators with the Panamanian Head of Government, thereby jeopardizing the separation of powers mandated by the Constitution.

Our objective, then, is to present a documented and understandable story of the facts, circumstances and conflicts in the transfer of the Canal and of the activities of the elected and appointed political officials involved — all looking toward positive action by the Congress and the Executive Branch for negotiating constitutional and legal Treaties or reasserting U.S. sovereignty over the Canal Zone and the Canal which, under international law, as explained at the East hearing, are still the properties of the American people.

In breaking down the Canal swindle into component parts, it can be said that there were five swindles, all considered serious and each apparently saving the Treaties at one time or another. Each swindle is briefly identified as follows:

Swindle Number One was the most serious: The failure of the State Department to explain adequately to the Senate leadership and to the 15 members of the Foreign Relations Committee Panama's last minute three paragraphs of counter-reservation that nullified the DeConcini reservation, authored by Senator Dennis DeConcini, D.-Ariz. Consequently, the Senate never voted on this major change. These paragraphs were available at some time during the two month period between the Senate vote on the second treaty (April 18, 1978) and the Exchange of Protocols (June 16, 1978). Alas, they were either glossed over or covered up. Since most members of the Foreign Relations Committee were attorneys, one of them would certainly have recognized the devious language, if he had seen it, and asked for a two-thirds vote of approval by the Senate. In which case, rejection was virtually certain — hence, no Treaties that day.

Swindle Number Two was the failure to use the Clements Clause in the 1977 Treaties. This clause guaranteed U.S. defense rights and was a major part of the earlier 1975 draft neutrality treaty. Since the Panamanians had always opposed unilateral U.S. rights for defense of the Canal, the Clements Clause was quietly removed, apparently by the State Department. If it had been included in the 1977 Treaties, the Panamanians would undoubtedly have voted disapproval in their October 23, 1977 plebiscite — hence, no Treaties that day.

Swindle Number Three was the stonewalling of the request of Senator Robert P. Griffin, R.-Mich., to President Carter on March 16, 1978, the day of the Senate vote on the Neutrality Treaty, for information concerning Panama's rejection of U.S. defense rights. If the Senate had had this information in time, both the Treaties and the DeConcini reservation would have failed — hence, no Treaties that day.

Swindle Number Four was the failure to require a second plebiscite in Panama to ratify the Neutrality Treaty which had been substantially amended by the addition of the DeConcini reservation. The late Senator Dewey F. Bartlett, R.-Okla., attempted to remedy this defect, but his Reservation Number 4 was tabled by a vote of 60 to 37 on March 16, 1978, the day the Senate approved the Neutrality Treaty, thanks to the Senate leadership which, in effect, curtailed debate. If the Panamanians had been allowed to vote in a second plebiscite, they would have undoubtedly rejected the amended Treaty because of the hated DeConcini reservation — hence, no Treaties that day.

Swindle Number Five involved another parliamentary move in the Senate to avoid another challenge by Senator Bartlett for a second plebiscite in Panama to consider both Treaties which had been substantially amended since the first plebiscite. This time Bartlett's Reservation Number 3 was again tabled, this time by a vote of 63 to 35, on April 18, 1978, the day the Senate approved the final treaty. Again the Panamanian people had not voted on the U.S. defense guarantees provided by the DeConcini reservation. The Senate leadership again opposed further delay. And again, if the Panamanians had voted, they would have undoubtedly turned down the Treaties in a second plebiscite — hence, no Treaties that day.

Each of the five swindles is based solely on one issue: the guaranteed U.S. rights to defend and keep the Canal operational. Unfortunately, Panama never agreed to this at any phase of the negotiations or ratification. The U.S. representatives tried in many ways to paper over Panama's objections but, in the end, these differences always surfaced.

Repeated efforts by the author and Phillip Harman, the Chairman of the Committee for Better Panama and United States Relations, and by others too of course, to obtain information and clarification regarding the handling of Panama's three paragraphs of counter-reservation and the circumstances of the five swindles have been met in most instances with stonewalling and with what might justifiably be characterized as cover up. Nonetheless, much evidence is available. This evidence and the apparent suppression of other facts plus a series of personal interviews during November 1983 in Washington, D.C. — all combine to form the story of the Canal swindle.

DRAMA IN THE UNITED STATES SENATE

The climax, the greatest thrill for President Carter, was evidently the Senate vote on the first treaty, the Neutrality Treaty. This was the treaty that had been "saved" by the DeConcini reservation that set forth in plain language the U.S. rights to defend the Canal against all threats. Indeed, the Senate would *not* have consented to the Treaties without the DeConcini reservation. Perhaps Mr. Carter considered this vote to be a test of the prestige of his presidency.

On a gloomy Thursday afternoon in the Spring of 1978, President Carter sat expectantly in the White House office of Susan Clough with other aides, Zbigniew Brzezinski, Hamilton Jordan and Jody Powell. He was clenching his fists as he anxiously waited to tick off the Senate vote on the Neutrality Treaty from the radio reports.[17]

Meanwhile, at the other end of Pennsylvania Avenue, the Senate Majority Leader, Robert C. Byrd, D.-W. Va., was quoting Shakespeare about a "tide in the affairs of men which, taken at the flood, leads on to fortune." He was in high spirits as he called upon his colleagues to vote on the first of the two Panama Canal Treaties. "The Rubicon of decision on the Treaties is about to be crossed," he intoned.[18]

The hour was 3:45 p.m. and after 22 days of rehearsal and debate on the Senate floor, the cast was ready and the stage was set for high drama: galleries filled, crowded Senate chamber, excitement in the air. History was being made. Outside, under glowering skies, sleet, snow and a biting March wind added to the theatrics.

This drama of March 16, 1978 was also payday: the pay-off for exhausting and prolonged campaigning for the controversial Treaties, perhaps the most contentious issue before the U.S. Congress in a hundred years. Later, Mr. Carter was to write in his memoirs, "I thanked God when we got the 67th vote. It will always be one of my proudest moments, and one of the greatest achievements of the United States Senate."[19]

Zbigniew Brzezinski described the moment in his own memoirs, *Power and Principle* (Farrar-Straus-Giroux, 1983): "He sat there . . . and finally banged his fists together when we got the required 67th vote. It was a moment of genuine elation and relief."[20]

As for the U.S. Senate, it was an unusual achievement against the difficulties of obscure treaties and an adamant constituency. Nonetheless, after the "Advice and Consent" vote of 68 to 32, one over the required two-thirds, the Minority Leader, Republican Howard H. Baker, Jr. of Tennessee, joined the celebration, exhilarating, "In a word, Mr. President, the Senate of the United States has comported itself well."

Many have credited Baker more than any other person with the victory since many other Senators followed his lead. However, other Republican Senators were less enthusiastic about the outcome: for example, Robert P. Griffin of Michigan stated, "This instrument called a treaty is a mask of ambiguities." Malcolm Wallop of Wyoming recalled the story of the emperor's new clothes: People pretend he's dressed for the ball when "our little emperor is as naked as he can be."[21]

At 4:27 p.m. the 67th "aye" had been cast by Gaylord Nelson, D.-Wis., who later, incidentally, lost his bid for reelection in 1980. Paul Hatfield, D.-Mont., had been the 67th Senator "converted" to the Treaties, followed by a recalcitrant Howard W. Cannon, D.-Nev. Both voted "aye" and later, both lost bids for reelection.

Other Senators had been groomed as backups. One was the veteran Jennings Randolph of West Virginia, ready to support the Treaties for the party's sake, but faced with a problem: He had a tough reelection fight coming up. So, on the first roll call, he simply "passed," saving his no vote for the next round after the Treaties had safely arrived.

Altogether 35 Senators who voted "aye" are no longer in the Senate, 24 having been defeated at the polls and 10 retired, and one died in office. Appendix A is a roll call of Senators who voted to transfer the Canal, the asterisks marking those no longer serving.

Approximately one month after his first vote, the basic treaty was approved by the same one vote margin, on April 18, 1978 — but not without difficulty and acrimony. Nonetheless, President Carter had won a hard fought and exhilarating political victory. To be sure, within 15 months of his inauguration, he had produced ratified and approved Panama Canal Treaties after the preceding 14 years of on-again off-again negotiations under 4 administrations. Moreover, this victory climaxed a near lifetime drumbeat of bickering, burning and agitating in Panama to run the Gringos out.

CRITICAL MOMENTS PRECEDE SENATE VOTE

The events leading up to President Carter's great political success with the Treaties were just as unique and intriguing as the drama of ratification itself, perhaps even more so. The mysterious action in dropping the Clements' Clause (specifying clear-cut U.S. defense rights) from the draft 1977 Treaties left a void that was not acceptable to many Senators. The *1975* draft treaty had included this important defense clause but, for some reason, it had been deleted from the 1977 draft. Some feel this was the work of the State Department whose representatives believed it was not acceptable to the Panamanian negotiators.

In its place was substituted Article IV in the Neutrality Treaty, a co-equal and parallel-action-type statement designed to "maintain the regime of neutrality" but with no specific language for unilateral defense rights.[22]

In an attempt to correct this problem with the Senators who rejected Article IV, the President and Omar Torrijos, the dictator and Head of State of Panama, met in Washington on October 14, 1977 and issued their famous Statement of Understanding, which later became a part of the Neutrality Treaty in the form of two leadership amendments. This pleased the Panamanians who voted approval of the Treaties shortly thereafter in their plebiscite of October 23, 1977 — but it did not satisfy the group of Senators who had originally questioned the ambiguous provisions relating to U.S. rights. The leadership amendments did *not* resolve this ambiguity because, again, specific U.S. defense rights were omitted.

As a consequence, the same Senators still objected and the first treaty, the Neutrality Treaty, seemed doomed. President Carter, then, on March 9, 1978 asked Senator Dennis DeConcini, D.-Ariz., for help.[23] It was given. And within a few days, the DeConcini reservation was before the Senate being debated pro and con. This reservation in plain language guaranteed U.S. unilateral rights *in Panama* to defend and to keep the Canal open.

But it was *not* acceptable to Panama and Mr. Carter wrote in his diary for March 15, 1978 that General Torrijos "was planning to . . . reject the Treaties outright because of some language that DeConcini insisted upon."[24]

On the following day, March 16, 1978, the Senate gave its "Advice and Consent" to the Neutrality Treaty after voting its approval also of the DeConcini reservation. During the course of the debate on March 16, Senator Griffin asked for information on reports of Panama's rejection of U.S. defense rights — and Senator Bartlett, in turn, called for a second plebiscite in Panama so that the people could vote on the substantial changes that had been incorporated into the Treaties by the Senate amendments.

Senator Griffin's request was stonewalled by the White House until the next day, after the vote had already been taken. This has been classified as one of the swindles. Senator Bartlett's reservation was tabled and this has been called another swindle. That is to say, the action, or lack of action, taken in both cases could be characterized as swindles or frauds, i.e., "in law, intentional deception to cause a person to give up property or some lawful right."[25]

(Later, on April 18, 1978, during the debate on the second and final treaty, Senator Bartlett had a similar experience. He introduced another resolution (reservation) concerning the failure of Panama to hold a second plebiscite so its people might consider the new terms. This too was quickly tabled. It was the fifth swindle.)

Nonetheless, swindle or no swindle, the first step had been highly successful: The Senate had approved the first treaty, the Neutrality Treaty, with the DeConcini reservation intact. President Carter had reason to breathe easier — that is, until he heard from Torrijos. The Panamanians were far from satisfied.

An example of the Panamanian attitude at that time was disclosed at a news conference on March 17, 1978, the day after the Senate had approved the Neutrality Treaty with the DeConcini reservation guaranteeing U.S. defense rights in Panama. The following news item was typical of those that appeared in the Panamanian press:

NEGOTIATORS ESCOBAR, ROYO HOLD PRESS CONFERENCE

Romulo Escobar Bethancourt and Aristides Royo, who were part of Panama's treaty negotiating team, met this afternoon with the local press to report on the status of the new Panama Canal Treaties which are midway in the process of ratification by the United States.

Escobar indicated that a reservation such as the one presented yesterday by Senator Dennis DeConcini and approved by the Senate *may oblige Panama to present its own reservations when the instruments of ratification are exchanged.*[26] (Emphasis added)

Romulo Escobar Bethancourt had been Panama's chief negotiator. He was announcing that Panama might "present its own reservation" in order to nullify U.S. rights in the DeConcini reservation. This basic disagreement continued to threaten.

HOW THE SECOND TREATY WAS SAVED

One evening in early April 1978 — midway between the times of the Senate's approval of the first and second treaties — Mr. Carter was having a problem. It was Torrijos. Carter's diary entry, in gentle language, touched upon a very critical moment in ratification.

President Carter's version of the Canal transfer is contained in his memoirs, *Keeping Faith* (Bantam, 1982), which also includes a number of diary entries. Four years after the fact, in the chapter titled "Jimmy Carter is Giving Away Our Canal," he recorded an interesting chronology, much of it not previously made public. His diary entry for this Friday evening, April 7, 1978, was revealing:

We discussed the Panama problems that have arisen because Torrijos is sending letters around indicating that he might renounce the Treaties. We decided to review the options for him, which are very good ones. The fact is that the text of the treaty expresses our nonintervention commitment. This is repeated in the OAS and UN Charters, which we certainly would not renounce, and ultimately, if Torrijos wants to, *he can issue a reservation about his understanding of what the Treaties mean* on intervention in the internal affairs of Panama. . . . (Emphasis added) — *Diary, April 7, 1978.*[27]

Mr. Carter was very anxious about the fate of the Treaties. At issue, of course, as always, was whether the United States *did* or *did not,* under the proposed Treaties, have the unilateral right, with or without Panama's consent, to use military power or whatever force was necessary to intervene, if need be, to keep open the Canal should it be closed or to defend it should it be threatened. This principle was the crux of the transfer arrangements. Torrijos had at no time sincerely accepted this principle. Nonetheless, he wanted the Canal.

President Carter's suggestion to Torrijos that he issue his own reservation about his understanding seemed to be the perfect solution. Moreover, Mr. Carter was echoing Bethancourt's earlier announcement that the DeConcini reservation "may oblige Panama to present its own reservation when the instruments of ratification are exchanged."

Torrijos readily accepted Carter's solution; and his "own reservation" appeared in the form of the three paragraph counter-reservation that was not submitted to the U.S. Senate and that became a part of the Panamanian instruments of ratification. The net result was a drastic change in the meaning of the Treaties, completely contrary to what the Senate voted on. Moreover, Dr. Breecher called this "the most substantive change" imaginable and contrary to the accepted standards and requirements under international law.

These considerations are an important part of our story. They are also the subject of Dr. Breecher's statement, Appendix B.

The Panamanians drafted their final three paragraphs with care. And while Torrijos was waiting in the wings with them, another drama was unfolding on the far side of the stage. It was the American plan to placate further the Panamanians and the undecided Senators: the preparation of another so-called leadership amendment — this time to the second and final treaty. It now seems clear that the authors of this new leadership amendment (Senators Robert C. Byrd, Frank Church and Paul Sarbanes; William D. Rogers, former Assistant Secretary of State; Deputy Secretary of State Warren Christopher; and Panamanian Ambassador Gabriel Lewis Galindo) did not know that Torrijos had his own solution.

Two days later this leadership amendment became a reservation to the second treaty, the Panama Canal Treaty. For Panama, it was supposed to remove the "imperialistic claws" of the DeConcini reservation. For the undecided Senators, it was supposed to "soften" the language of the DeConcini reservation without changing its meaning.[28]

Actually, it merely emphasized the principle of nonintervention "in the internal affairs of the Republic of Panama" but it did not address or mention unilateral U.S. rights for defense. The Panamanians believed the DeConcini reservation had been voided and the U.S. Senators evidently considered that it had not. They voted concurrence on April 18, 1978.

Strangely, even after he won the Canal, Omar Torrijos publicly announced that he had given orders for the National Guard "to attack and blow up the Canal if the Senate had rejected our agreement." Said General Torrijos, if the Treaties had been rejected, "we would have started our struggle for liberation, and possibly tomorrow the Canal would not be operating any more."[29]

But, of course, the Treaties were not rejected. And, Carter was exuberant that, instead of being enemies at war over a closed or damaged Canal, we would be allies with Panama, with both nations committed to a "partnership in operating this crucial waterway."

The perceived loss of the Canal has facilitated further erosion of the Monroe Doctrine, as the Soviets and their surrogates increase their adventures in the Western Hemisphere with impunity and regularity. Apparently, Mr. Carter chose to discount these threats as he strove to transfer the Canal to Omar Torrijos, a friend and admirer of Cuba's Castro.[30]

Without a doubt, foreign policy has changed, perhaps the assertion of values too, from the America of days gone by. For example, sixty years ago the U.S. Secretary of State and later Chief Justice, Charles Evans Hughes, was confronted with a comparable problem regarding the Canal Zone. He declared to Panama that it was absolute futility "to expect an American administration, no matter who it was, any President or any Secretary of State, ever to surrender any part of rights which the United States had acquired under the treaty of 1903."[31]

Furthermore, Mr. Hughes was keenly aware of the threat and of the linkage between the Canal and the Monroe Doctrine, adding:

I believe that the sentiment of the American people is practically unanimous that in the interests of our national safety we could not yield to any foreign power the control of the Panama Canal, or the approaches to it. . . .So far as the region of the Caribbean Sea is concerned, it may be said that if we had no Monroe Doctrine, we should have to create one.

Interestingly, "the sentiment of the American people (remained) practically unanimous" in 1977-78 against yielding control of the Canal to any foreign power, according to many opinion polls. Nonetheless, this 1923 policy statement by Secretary Hughes is in sharp contrast to the 1978 policy that meekly yielded control to a foreign power.

A few months earlier, in October 1976, Candidate Carter had declared during his presidential campaign, "I would never give up control of the Panama Canal Zone."[32] And he added, "I would never lie to you."

Nevertheless, within a few days of his inauguration, President Carter initiated the "top priority" — his words — in his foreign policy program: the negotiation of a new treaty with Panama based on the Kissinger-Tack agreement of February 7, 1974, the progenitor of the 1977 Treaties which not only yielded "complete control" but paid the Panamanians for the privilege. Therefore, one of Mr. Carter's first official acts ignored a solemn campaign promise not to give up control of the canal. For the preceding three years, the Kissinger-Tack Statement of Principles had stood on the public record and its most basic premise was to surrender control and sovereignty over the Canal Zone. When Mr. Carter announced that the new treaties would be based on this agreement, many supporters were shocked.

Moreover, he was unable to sell the Treaties to the Senate for advice and consent without the secretive three paragraph Panamanian counter reservation which the Senate never had a chance to evaluate or vote on. This was called a swindle, a fraud, by Dr. Breecher who said, "That fraud was committed by pretending in their respective instruments of ratification, the U.S. and Panama had agreed to the same treaty text," whereas in reality, this simply was not so.[33]

Mr. Carter called the transfer of the Canal, epitomized by the passage of the Neutrality Treaty, "one of my proudest moments." Others have called it "one of the saddest chapters in our history": this deliberate loss of a vital asset and irreplaceable monument to American pride, ingenuity and generosity, indeed, the Key to the Western Hemisphere.

Edmund Burke said in a speech (1775) to the British Parliament: "Magnanimity in politics is not seldom the truest wisdom; and a great empire and little minds go ill together." Another British statesman, Benjamin Disraeli, said, "Nations have no friends, only interests."

· 2 ·

THE EVOLUTION OF
TWO SETS OF TREATIES

A meeting of minds was never quite achieved regarding the American role on the Isthmus of Panama. Former Panamanian President Harmodio Arias said, "Whatever faults or shortcomings Spanish Americans may have . . . they are extremely jealous of foreign encroachments on their sovereign rights. . . ." Earlier, American diplomat John Bassett Moore had stated, "The United States, in undertaking to build the canal, does a work not only for itself but for the world."

This basic difference was never resolved and the two sets of Panama Canal Treaties of 1977 was the inevitable result of decades of bickering over rights of sovereignty—with the United States conceding bit by bit until the Canal was gone.

Were the interests of the United States served in capitulating to the pressures for surrendering the Canal, particularly to an unstable government of proven communist sympathies? In matter of fact, the late self-appointed Brig. General Torrijos and his successors have systematically aided the insurgents in Central America by the transshipment of war supplies and by the use of training facilities.[1] Moreover, the Canal is proving to be a valuable asset to the communist-backed revolutionaries in the area, most of them terrorists.[2]

The former ease of operation and control of the Canal by the United States has been supplanted by the Panama Canal Commission with joint management in accordance with the new Treaties. In relinquishing control and sovereignty, Admiral Thomas H. Moorer, USN (Ret.) and former Chairman of the Joint Chiefs of Staff, told the Senate Subcommittee on

Separation of Powers some seven months before the Senate agreed to the Treaties: "In military affairs there is no substitute for ownership of territory and the ability to control or deny the waters or air space." As to surrendering the Canal, Admiral Moorer warned, "U.S. security as well as U.S. prosperity would be placed in serious jeopardy" and "the Canal Zone could become the satellite base of an adversary."[3]

Complicating the loss of this military asset is the hazard of two sets of Treaties. (1) Panama's version contains three paragraphs of counter-reservation that legally deny unilateral U.S. rights to come in to reopen or defend the Canal; and (2) the U.S. version does *not* contain Panama's counter-reservation but does countain the DeConcini reservation that authorizes legal intervention to open or defend the Canal. Parenthetically and in order to keep the record straight, Panama's version *does* include the DeConcini reservation but it then proceeds to nullify the DeConcini reservation with its ingenious three paragraphs denying unilateral U.S. rights. Incidentally, without the DeConcini reservation, a survey taken in 1983 proved that the 1978 Senate Majority Leader Robert Byrd could not have mustered the required two-thirds vote.

As a consequence of these differences, Panama and the United States did not agree, in their respective instruments of ratification, to the same text of the Treaties. Therefore, under international law there was no meeting of minds and no ratification. Hence, no valid Treaties. Dr. Breecher made these points in his deposition before the Senate Subcommittee on Separation of Powers. Appendix B is a portion of Dr. Breecher's testimony.

Moreover, when the Treaties were being debated, confusion was the order of the day. At times, there seemed to be six treaties instead of two: Carter's versions of the two Treaties, Panama's versions and the Senate's versions.

Ambassador Sol M. Linowitz, the U.S. co-negotiator, said in reference to understandings and reservations, "It is what a statement does, not what it is called, that is important." This is also what Article 2.1 (d) of the 1969 Vienna Convention on the Law of Treaties says.

At one time, Zbigniew Brzezinski, the President's National Security Adviser, tried to liven things up with a history mini-quiz: "Who was the first President, while in office, to travel abroad?" he asked members of the press corps. When his "pupils" failed, the "teacher" answered, "Taft, in 1909. He went to Panama." Later, editors found the treaty salesman wrong on two counts: It wasn't Taft, it was Teddy Roosevelt; it wasn't 1909, it was 1906. But it *was* Panama; T.R. went to Colon.[4]

So much for clarifications by the "experts."

As for the issues, they are simple. An examination of the instruments of ratification reveals the difference: Panama accepts and repeats verbatim the DeConcini reservation and then adds its counter-reservation to cancel it. The U.S. instruments do *not* contain Panama's counter-reservation. In not obtaining the Senate's consent to the counter-reservation, the U.S. treaty handlers made a mistake and assured flawed Treaties.

Why? Panama's counter-reservation states in unequivocal language that the United States can use military force in Panama *only* in self defense pursuant to Articles 1 and 2 of the Charter of the Organization of American States—and *only* "in a manner consistent with the principles of mutual respect and *cooperation*. . . ."[5] (Emphasis added)

This means, of course, if Panama decides not to cooperate, the United States has no legal right to use military force to reopen a closed Canal, if such action becomes necessary. Then, confrontation and probably a cacophony of anti-Americanism. Moreover, the legal President of Panama, Dr. Arnulfo Arias Madrid, ousted from office in 1968 by a military *coup d'état,* stated upon returning from exile on June 10, 1978, "These Treaties will be the seeds of future bloodshed between our two countries."

THE DeCONCINI RESERVATION V. PANAMA'S THREE PARAGRAPHS

The discordant note that continued to sour the harmony of ratification of the Treaties was the U.S. insistence on clear-cut future U.S. defense rights. Specifically, it was the DeConcini reservation that was upsetting President Carter on April 7, 1978 when he wrote in his diary that Torrijos was about to "renounce the Treaties." Mr. Carter apparently decided to plant a "seed" by suggesting that Torrijos write his own reservation. Ultimately this developed into the three paragraph counter-reservation.

Perhaps the "seed" was unnecessary. At any rate, it reinforced the statement made by Panama's chief negotiator, Romulo Escobar Bethancourt, to the Panamanian press on March 17, 1978 that the DeConcini reservation "may oblige Panama to present its own reservations when the instruments of ratification are exchanged." Of course, Panama did present its own reservation.

A comparison of the DeConcini reservation with Panama's counter-reservation (three paragraphs) shows the conflict. The DeConcini reservation, in plain language, guarantees unilateral U.S. rights:
U.S. INSTRUMENT—NEUTRALITY TREATY
PANAMANIAN INSTRUMENT—NEUTRALITY TREATY
(b) Conditions
(1) Notwithstanding the provisions of Article V or any provision of the Treaty, if the Canal is closed, or its operations are interfered with, the United States of Amer-

ica and the Republic of Panama *shall each independently* have the right to take such steps as each deems necessary, in accordance with its constitutional procedures, *including the use of military force in the Republic of Panama,* to reopen the Canal, as the case may be.[6] (Emphasis added)

Torrijos and his government from the beginning did not accept the concept of U.S. intervention for defending or reopening the Canal, unless specifically invited. Their sovereignty was to be inviolable—a requirement the U.S. negotiators and ratifiers never owned up to. Torrijos prepared his instruments of ratification carefully. He repeated the DeConcini reservation verbatim, as is customary in order to avoid misunderstanding, and then added his own three paragraphs of counter-reservation which became the *last word.* It *was* the last word. The U.S. Senate never officially saw this handiwork and, of course, never voted on it in order to discharge its constitutional obligation to advise and consent on all treaties.[7]

Herewith are Panama's three (unnumbered) paragraphs of counter-reservation that *nullified* the DeConcini reservation. Consequently, these paragraphs are *not* part of the U.S. instruments of ratification, and therefore, *not* a part of the U.S. version of the Treaties:

PANAMANIAN INSTRUMENT—NEUTRALITY TREATY
(*not* in the U.S. instrument)
The Republic of Panama agrees to the exchange of the instruments of ratification of the aforementioned Neutrality Treaty on the understanding that there are positive rules of public international law contained in multilateral treaties to which both the Republic of Panama and the United States of America are Parties and which consequently both States are bound to implement in good faith, such as Article 1, paragraph 2 and Article 2, paragraph 4 of the Charter of the United Nations, and Articles 18 and 20 of the Charter of the Organization of American States.

It is also the understanding of the Republic of Panama that the actions which either Party may take in exercise of its rights and the fulfillment of its duties in accordance with the aforesaid Neutrality Treaty, including measures to reopen the Canal or to restore its normal operation, if it should be interrupted or obstructed, will be effected in a manner consistent with the principles of *mutual respect* and *cooperation* on which the new relationship established by that Treaty is based.

The Republic of Panama declares that its *political independence, territorial integrity, and self-determination* are guaranteed by the unshakeable will of the Panamanian people. Therefore, the Republic of Panama *will reject, in unity and with decisiveness and firmness,* any attempt by any country to intervene in its internal or external affairs.[8] (Emphasis added)

A close examination of these paragraphs, which were not accepted by the United States, is in order. The first paragraph is something of a smoke screen. It is misleading and unnecessary to the Treaties, and is "clever lawyer's obfuscation at its worst," according to Dr. Breecher in his Senate testimony.

Breecher explained to Senator East, "The fact the United States and Panama have adhered to the Charters of the United Nations and the OAS, multinational treaties, does not prevent the U.S. and Panama to make a later treaty among themselves in partial derogation of the provisions of the OAS treaty only and that is exactly what the DeConcini reservation is—a very limited exception, applicable to the U.S. and Panama only under special circumstances. . . ."[9]

Moreover, the referenced Article 18 of the OAS Charter binds the American states "not to have recourse to the use of force, except in the case of self defense." Of course, both the U.S. and Panama subscribe to this article but that does not conflict with the rights of individual states to make treaties among themselves for their own "special circumstances." Consequently, these OAS and UN regulations have nothing to do with the Panama Canal Treaties.

The second paragraph in Panama's counter-reservation is clear in requiring that "measures to reopen the Canal or to restore its normal operation" will be effected in accordance with the "principles of mutual respect and cooperation," i.e., if Panama agrees to cooperate. Therefore, Panama reserves to itself the right *not* to cooperate, in which case: disagreement, confrontation and a potential danger to the security of the Canal.

This second paragraph deserves closer examination. Our concern about the fundamental meaning of "cooperation" and the withholding of Panama's three paragraphs from the Senate prompted interviews with a number of officials involved with the Treaties. The interviews were conducted in November 1983 in Washington, D.C.

One involved Michael G. Kozak, Deputy Legal Adviser of the State Department, who was an Assistant Legal Adviser at the time of the Treaties and who had worked on them since 1971. In our discussion at the State Department on November 21, 1983, Mr. Kozak observed in regard to "cooperation" and its application: "If either party has to take action . . . it will be done in a manner consistent with the principles of mutual respect and cooperation upon which the Treaties are based . . . and that again, is not terribly important. . . ."

His answer to our specific question about U.S. rights if Panama, for any reason, closed the Canal and refused to permit U.S. action to reopen it, was inclusive: ". . . This is talking about that, as with any treaty, that any action will be taken in that treaty . . . should be in accord with the entire treaty and if mutual respect and cooperation and so on is a principle, you should give effect to that principle . . . but you take your treaty rights in a manner consistent with those principles."[10]

Earlier, on November 15, 1983, our interview with Robert Dockery, the former staff official in charge of the Treaties for the Senate Committee on Foreign Relations, produced the following responses about mutural cooperation: "The whole foundation of the new agreement is a partnership arrangement . . . and from what we know today, that partnership arrangement has worked very well." In respect to Panama's instruments of ratification with the unchallenged three paragraphs, he said, "This is signed by the President of Panama, we did not agree to that . . . all we have agreed to is what is signed jointly by the President of the United States and the President of Panama. . . ." In response to our question as to why the Treaties should not be perfectly clear on rights and responsibilities, Mr. Dockery stated, "What you're asking for, is, for the most part, impossible."[11]

We asked Dr. James McClellan, the former Chief Counsel of the Senate Subcommittee on Separation of Powers, about these three paragraphs in our interview on November 15, 1983, the same day we talked with Dockery. His view was that the Senate should have voted on them, "There was never any debate in the Senate as to whether these three additional paragraphs altered the meaning of the Treaties . . . and the intent of the paragraphs is quite unclear because the Senate did not have a chance to debate the entire document."[12]

In considering the views of Messrs. Kozak and Dockery, the question may be asked: Why negotiate treaties at all if implementation of rights depends on "mutual respect and cooperation?" As to Mr. Dockery's observation that the President of Panama had signed the instrument of ratification, this is not true, of course, as Omar Torrijos, the Head of Government, signed. This was unconstitutional because Article 163 of the 1972 Constitution of Panama authorizes "the President of Panama alone . . . to enter into international treaties"—and the President was Demetrio B. Lakas.

As to the "partnership arrangement's (working) very well," one might note that Panama received a generous settlement and also, there has been no crisis of a closed Canal. Therefore, the partnership has not been tested under emergency conditions.

In regard to Mr. Dockery's assertion to the effect that each nation need not agree with the contents of the other's instruments of ratification, this view is not consistent with Articles 2.1 (d) and 20.2 of the Vienna Convention on the Law of Treaties.

The third paragraph of Panama's counter-reservation is also clear: Americans and Panamanians are put on notice that Panama will reject with force any U.S. military action used without Panama's "cooperation," and further, that Panama "reserves to itself the right to do so because it would regard an independent U.S. decision as interference in Panama's internal and external affairs."[13] Moreover, the third paragraph reinforces the other two, emphasizing Panama's territorial integrity, and firmly rejecting any other country's interference for any reason.[14]

In what appears to be further obfuscation, we note that the first two paragraphs of Panama's counter-reservation are repeated verbatim in the Protocol of Exchange, *but* not the third paragraph about the "unshakeable will." The Protocol, of course, is the document transmitting the instruments of ratification and is signed by both heads of state. It is *not*, however, a part of the Senate's advice and consent responsibility.

To restate the issue: Panama's unilateral counter-reservation altered the legal effect of the DeConcini reservation because Panama made clear that any United States effort to reopen a closed Canal would have to be in self-defense (Article 18 of the OAS Charter) and *only* with Panama's "cooperation." Moreover, "the unshakeable will of the Panamanian people" would reject with decisiveness any such intervention, according to Panama's assertions in the very last words of the Treaties.

The specific *differences* between the treaties ratified by the United States and those ratified by Panama are marked in Appendix C, containing the texts of the Protocol of Exchange and the instruments of ratification of both countries. Vertical lines in the page margins identify portions of the Protocol and instruments to which the U.S. Senate never gave its "Advice and Consent."

These are substantive changes and they voided U.S. rights in the DeConcini reservation. Moreover, unlike all other phases of the Treaties process, these changes were *not* made public until the day of ratification in Panama, June 16, 1978. Then it was too late for complaints. The Treaties became a *fait accompli*.

An incident that portends future aggravation occurred on January 20, 1982 when 3,000 dock workers struck against the Panama Port Authority, paralyzing the loading and unloading of ships at each end of the Canal.[15] This unilateral action demonstrated that Panama can close the Canal.

If a similar incident should happen again and cause the Canal to be closed for an extended period of time, would Panama "cooperate" by permitting U.S. military forces to reopen the Canal? Or, not "cooperate" and call upon her Third World allies to help stop U.S. forces from crossing picket lines?[16]

Without a doubt, there are two sets of Panama Canal Treaties, both verbatim in every detail except one: the United States right for unilateral action, if necessary, to defend the Canal and to keep it open and operating. As officialdom neatly wrapped up the Treaties with signed Protocols in Panama on June 16, 1978, the first domino in Latin America had fallen.[17]

THE EROSION OF RIGHTS BEGAN EARLY

A number of milestones mark the road to the Panama Canal Treaties of 1977, the agreement that finally "surrendered" U.S. rights of sovereignty and control and that will turn over some $10 billion worth of American property at the end of the century. One of the first *milestones* was a dramatic voyage around South America that served to crystalize the idea for an isthmian canal—under United States control.

At the beginning of the Spanish-American War, the services of the battleship *Oregon* were needed off Cuba, but she was in the Puget Sound Navy Yard in the state of Washington, 13,000 miles away. Her 79 day voyage to Santiago Bay via Cape Horn drew the attention of the world which anxiously awaited the outcome of the war. The world also realized that if the Oregon could have cut across the Isthmus of Panama her time and distance would have been halved and possibly, the war itself affected.[18]

This event intensified the urgency for a transoceanic waterway. The U.S. Congress went into action. The Hay-Bunau-Varilla Treaty of 1903 was the end product of a desultory series of diplomatic disappointments. Eventually, this 1903 Treaty was also the beginning of a long series of incidents aimed at returning to Panama ownership, sovereign rights and control over the Canal Zone and the Canal. These "incidents" are the milestones to the abrogation of the 1903 Treaty and to the new 1977 Treaties. The text of the 1903 Treaty is contained in Appendix D.

At first the Panamanians were happy. The provisional government asked for a consensus from all *cabildos* (town councils) and everyone by unanimous vote applauded the 1903 Treaty. Significantly, this was a time before the National Assembly was organized.[19] These grass roots resolutions of approval demonstrated that virtually all the people of Panama were pleased with the arrangements. However, this fact is rarely mentioned by historians and others who deplored the "scandalous negotiations" by the North Americans.

Another incident neglected by historians was the May 13, 1909 letter from Panamanian President Domingo de Obaldia to Philippe Bunau-Varilla stating, in part: ". . . our peoples will keep eternally engraved in their memory your fruitful services and will put in a preeminent place the names of Amador and your own. The national gratitude gives them the title of Benefactor of Panama."[20] (Dr. Manuel Amador was the first President of Panama.)

Nonetheless, Bunau-Varilla had an ulterior motive for his "fruitful services": He was a stockholder in the New Panama Canal Company and stood to benefit financially once a treaty with the United States was ratified. A parallel could be drawn with the Linowitz-Rockefeller banking connection to the 1977 Treaties with one exception: In 1903 the U.S. taxpayer was not the victim.

Moreover, wrote John Major in the Spring 1984 *Diplomatic History* (pp.115-23), Bunau-Varilla had help in drafting the 1903 Treaty, i.e., it was not his work alone as long alleged. Assistance came from Senator John Tyler Morgan, D.-Ala., Secretary of State John Hay and from several American draft treaties on the subject. Thus, the historical record is improved, but the fact of a legitimate treaty remains, albeit done in the diplomatic style of the day. So, Panama's complaints about "that dapper Frenchman" and U.S. postage stamps, among other things, began early on but such haggling did not alter the fact of sovereign rights and a legal treaty.

A few months after the 1903 Treaty was ratified, the first problem involving sovereignty arose: It was the new U.S. Dingley Tariff Act that placed high duty rates on everything coming into the Canal Zone, including goods from Panama. This restricted Panama's economy because the only real customer in the area was the Canal construction company. Secretary of War Taft called the tariff law "an unfortunate mistake in our policy."[21]

Another irritant was postage rates: 2¢ in the Canal Zone versus 5¢ in Panama to send a letter to the United States. These problems and others were conscientiously investigated by Mr. Taft who was sent to Panama by President Roosevelt. Thereafter, an Executive Order was issued to correct them. In addition, several "extras" were added, for example, a 6-mile long highway from Panama City into the countryside. Currency irregularities were also adjusted.[22]

Teddy Roosevelt intended to have good relations. Moreover, he assured the Panamanians that the Canal Zone would not become a competing government in their midst and that it was not intended to injure their businesses or reduce their prestige as a nation. Among his "instructions" to Taft were the following:

The United States is to confer on the people of Panama a very great benefit by the expenditure of millions of dollars in the construction of the Canal. But this fact must not blind us to the importance of so exercising the authority given us under the Treaty with Panama as to avoid creating any suspicion, however unfounded, of our intentions in the future.

We have not the slightest intention of establishing an independent colony in the middle of the State of Panama, or of exercising any greater governmental functions than are necessary to enable us, conveniently and safely, to construct, maintain, and operate the Canal under the rights given us by this Treaty. Least of all do we desire to interfere with the interest and prosperity of the people of Panama.[23] (Emphasis added)

Nonetheless, in order to support the thousands of workers on the Canal project, it became necessary to set up commissaries to supply food and other essentials. The Panamanians did not have the facilities to do this, and they resented the "incursion" into their local economy. Even so, the U.S. government, of necessity, continued the commissaries and expanded them into general merchadising, even luxuries. This was needed to attract and hold quality and skilled employees essential to the construction of the Canal.

In his *Panama Odyssey* (University of Texas Press, 1984), author William J. Jorden does not recognize (p.24) the importance of complete U.S. autonomy within the Canal Zone, e.g., postal service, custom houses and other support services, in order to control all matters that might directly or indirectly relate to "digging and running a canal." This was a very dangerous job, cutting a canal through a malaria-infested jungle and through the Continental Divide in a land noted for its instablility and political turmoil. Complete jurisdiction was legal, justified, and necessary. Moreover, sovereign rights had been granted. What was wrong with exercising them?

Conflicts between the "two side-by-side communities" were inevitable even after the Canal was opened. The old problems continued to cause discontent: business competition, tariffs, commissaries, and job opportunities. New ones cropped up also, particularly the Treaty rights for acquisition by the United States of additional land and water areas needed for the operation and defense of the Canal. As before, the sovereignty question was part of virtually every dispute.

Indeed, sovereignty and the Gringo presence were important in every political campaign also. As Panama developed her own national identity and economy, the attacks against U.S. policies increased. In fact, this was a "way of life for aspiring politicians."[24]

The differences in interpretation of sovereignty caused much of the anti-American feelings. Accordingly, at one point, Secretary of State Hay tried to mollify the Panamanians by stating that "titular sovereignty" remained with them.[25] Whether right or wrong, this assertion did have the effect of diluting U.S. jurisdiction and enlarging the Panamanian concept of residual rights.

Nevertheless, in 1924, Secretary of State Hughes made a forthright statement on the U.S. position on sovereignty. He told the Panamanians that the United States "could not and would not enter into any discussions affecting its full rights to deal with the Canal Zone under Article III of the Treaty of 1903 as if it were the sovereign of the Canal Zone to the entire exclusion of any sovereign rights or authority on the part of Panama."[26] Apparently, Mr. Hughes never doubted secure U.S. rights of sovereignty—and the record shows, the Panamanians did not argue with him.

Beginning with World War I, United States planners realized that the Canal Zone and the Canal were great strategic assets—not only for the rapid transfer of naval power from ocean to ocean but also for base sites to protect the Caribbean sea lanes and the southern flank of the United States. Soon it was recognized as the key to the defense of the Western Hemisphere. Accordingly, U.S. policy during the period 1903-1930 was to hold firm to positive U.S. jurisdiction in the Canal Zone under the 1903 Treaty and to legal U.S. ownership of the territory purchased from individual owners and squatters.[27]

During this period the attorneys of the State Department depended on their own interpretations of the 1903 Treaty to resist Panama's pressures for changes and, within the bounds of legal rectitude, were able to rationalize whatever goals the White House desired in the Canal Zone.[28]

Several decades later, in handling the 1977 Treaties, the State Department Legal Advisers were working the other side of the issue—this time, they were attempting to rationalize White House goals for transferring the Canal and Canal Zone to Panama.

PANAMA ASSUMES 'GIANT KILLER' ROLE

Panama continued its assault on the 1903 Treaty. And in 1926, another *milestone* was reached: A new treaty was negotiated and, although never ratified, it was a breakthrough, a precedent. After considerable agitation and many meetings, the new treaty was ready, proposing to modify some of the terms of the old one and expand others.[29]

No major changes were to be involved however. Significantly, Article I recognized the "grants" made in the 1903 Treaty and prescribed methods of passing title to all property acquired by the United States. There was no argument about sovereignty, ownership or title or perpetuity. All this was to come later. Indeed, Dr. Ricardo J.Alfaro, President of the Republic of Panama and Chief Negotiator in 1926, said that Panama stood by "all her obligations and recognized" U.S. rights of sovereignty.

Relatively minor proposals included new roads and bridges, commissary store operation, sanitation and quarantine enforcement, currency, and cooperation in time of war or other threat to the Canal. Article XIII emphasized that nothing in the proposed 1926 treaty would limit or restrict terms of the 1903 Treaty.

Nonetheless, the Panamanian National Assembly refused ratification because of insufficient concessions made by the United States and the U.S. Senate took no action. The fact that negotiations had been conducted at all signified a change from "big stick" diplomacy toward more of a "good neighbor" policy.

Earlier, in 1922, this change in U.S. diplomacy was also manifested when the United States patched up its differences with Colombia regarding the 1903 Panamanian revolution. Under terms of the Thompson-Urrutia Treaty, Colombia was paid $25 million indemnity for the loss of Panama, its former province, in return for Colombia's promise to recognize the independence of Panama. Hence, this argument was settled and the United States at "its expense conferred another invaluable bonus on Panama."[30]

The next *milestone* on the way to surrendering sovereignty was the 1936 Hull-Alfaro Treaty, a direct outgrowth of President Franklin D. Roosevelt's Good Neighbor Policy. The Panamanians had requested negotiations for a new treaty immediately after Mr. Roosevelt announced in 1933 his intentions of improving relations in Latin America. The message for the 1936 Treaty was unmistakable: The 1903 Treaty was not impregnable.[31]

Moreover, a total of 14 concessions were made in the 1936 Treaty, among them three changes involving sovereignty: First, the defense of the Canal would be shared by Panama; no longer would defense be the sole reponsibility of the United States. Second, Article I of the 1903 Treaty, providing that the United States would guarantee the independence of Panama, was deleted and Panama, 33 years later, was to be on her own as an independent nation. The third major change was the abolition of U.S. rights to intervene in the Republic of Panama to preserve order. Thenceforth, Panama would be solely responsible for law and order outside the Canal Zone.

Other significant changes in 1936 included more dilutions of sovereignty: The United States gave up its right to take, at its own discretion, any additional areas outside the Zone that might be needed for the defense and operation of the Canal. Thenceforth, Panama's consent would be necessary. In another change, the United States relinquished its authority under Article VII of the 1903 Treaty to acquire property in Panama City and Colon by eminent domain when necessary for Canal operations and sanitation in the Canal Zone. Thenceforth, such properties would have to be bought.

Other changes in the 1936 Treaties included increasing the annual payment to Panama from $250,000 to $430,000, reflecting the devaluation of the U.S. dollar since 1903. The new agreement covered some aspects of community and commercial problems: Residence in the Canal

Zone and the privilege of using the U.S. commissaries were restricted primarily to employees of the United States and their families. Moreover, no new businesses were to be opened in the Canal Zone unless directly related to the operation and defense of the Canal.[32]

Neither nation was anxious to ratify this 1936 Treaty—Panama because the Treaty did not concede enough and the United States because it conceded too much and further eroded control and rights of sovereignty. Even so, with war clouds gathering over Europe and uncertainties about the intentions of Nazi Germany in Latin America, the Treaty was ratified in 1939.[33]

At the beginning of World War II, the United States came to regret surrendering its 1903 Treaty rights for acquiring areas in Panama needed for defense of the Canal. Indeed, the surrender of defense base rights was another *milestone* on the way to loss of the Canal. As negotiations for base rights with Panamanian President Arnulfo Arias dragged on, an exasperated Philip Bonsal of the State Department observed that "practical considerations should prevail over theoretical ones." Uncharacteristically, for a Foreign Service Officer, Bonsal was implying that the United States should take over sites for defense bases, with or without Panama's consent.

Arias' successor, Ricardo de la Guardia, installed in the presidency after Arias had left the country without proper permission, signed the Defense Sites Agreement on May 18, 1942, but not before U.S. forces had moved in to occupy the necessary sites. This action was authorized, however, by a 1939 exchange of notes that permitted emergency action.[35]

By this time, the United States had met most of Panama's demands for compensation and agreed to surrender the bases one year after the war ended. Moreover, Panama used the military bases issue to gain other concessions.

Panama demanded prompt evacuation of all bases one year after Japan's surrender. The United States stalled past the September 1, 1946 "deadline" and finally an agreement was proposed for postwar bases. Nonetheless, amid general turmoil and riots, Panama's National Assembly voted disapproval on December 22, 1947 based on the minority report of Jose Dominador Bazan and Rogelio Robles.[36]

President Harry Truman, angered at this development, then ordered all U.S. personnel back into the Zone within 48 hours, except those manning the Rio Hato air base, and Panama took over the bases.

Denison Kitchel in *The Truth About the Panama Canal* wrote:
If any one is puzzled today over the brashness with which diminutive Panama stands up to one of the world's two superpowers and makes "or else" demands, a

look back at these military base confrontations will supply part of the answer. For it was then that Panama took on "Jack the Giant Killer" role that has characterized her attitude towards the United States. . . .[37]

This defeat for the United States over the military bases in Panama was another *milestone* on the way to the 1977 Treaties. It was also a part of the pattern. The Greek philosopher Aristotle observed, three centuries before Christ, that gratitude soon grows old.

The Panamanians had bested the Americans and had satisfied their nationalistic fervor but, in the process, had dealt a severe blow to their economy. The Yankees' dollars and generous habits were being withdrawn; and with the departure of all U.S. troops by February 1, 1948, many Panamanian workers at the defense sites had lost their jobs.[38]

The "land of endemic revolution and political turmoil" continued its historic role and beween 1948 and 1952 there had been five chief executives. Colonel Jose "Chichi" Remon, the former commander of the National Guard, was inaugurated President in October 1952. The following year, Remon's negotiators travelled to Washington to open new treaty talks with the representatives of the new American President, Dwight D. Eisenhower. Panamanian negotiator Octavio Fabrega damned the 1903 Treaty in a fiery speech before he left Panama:

Fifty years of the Bunau-Varilla treason will soon be observed, fifty years in which the people have been under the yoke of an enslaving treaty. No Panamanian signed that treaty, no Panamanian seal was affixed to it. The treaty was signed twice by the United States. Panama gave away the monopoly of the treasure of its geographic position in that treaty. Panama has not received adequate compensation for the sacrifices it has made and is making here at the Canal.[39]

Among the 21 new Panamanian demands were the following: (1) restore Panama's sovereignty over the Canal Zone; (2) reduce the duration of the 1903 Treaty to 99 years; (3) fly the Panamanian flag wherever the U.S. colors are displayed in the Canal Zone; and (4) give Panama 20% of the Canal's gross receipts with a minumum payment of $5 million per year.

These four demands were rejected by Eisenhower's negotiators, but a number of concessions were made in the treaty that followed, the Chapin-Fabrega Treaty of 1955, which was also another *milestone* toward the surrender of the Canal.[40] A few of the concessions included: upping the annuity from $430,000 to $1,930,000; terminating U.S. treaty rights to regulate sanitary conditions in Colon and Panama City; and transferring $25 million worth of U.S. property in those cities to Panama. Other concessions were made on taxes, wages, benefits, and commissary privileges.

Panama's National Assembly was not happy with the treaty of 1955, some members complaining that Panama's sovereignty had not been satisfied. Nonetheless, others noted the application of the old aphorism, "the harder one shakes the Yankee tree, the greater the number of plums to be gathered."[41]

'FLAG WAR' SIGNALS MAJOR CONCESSIONS

In 1958 the agitation over flying the Panamanian flag in the Canal Zone erupted with high school and university students launching "Operation Sovereignty." Demonstrations and riots continued intermittently, resulting in a number of injuries and considerable property damage.

This was the forerunner of another event which became an important *milestone* on the road to loss of the Canal: It was President Eisenhower's capitulation on the flag issue near the end of his second term in office.[42] His Executive Order of September 17, 1960, directing that Panama's flag be flown alongside the Stars and Stripes at Shaler Triangle, touched off demands to fly the flag anywhere in the Canal Zone, even at the mastheads of ships transiting the Canal, and exacerbated the intermittent "Flag War" of 1958-1964.

President Eisenhower wanted "visual evidence that Panama does have titular sovereignty over the region." Nonetheless, for the preceding 57 years only the Stars and Stripes had flown over the Canal Zone, pursuant to sovereign rights granted in the 1903 Treaty "to the entire exclusion" of any sovereign rights by Panama. Perhaps Eisenhower was thinking of the NATO alliance whose members' flags were flown at the headquarters building. Certainly the Canal Zone was not analogous to NATO.

Representative Armistead I. Selden, Jr., D.-Ala., in the House debate of February 2, 1960 said, "For all practical purposes, 'titular sovereignty' is meaningless unless . . . the United States decides to relinquish possession of the Canal Zone." He added that Panama's flag in the Zone "will be interpreted . . . as an erosion of U.S. sovereignty . . . the formula for wrenching further concessions from the United States."[43] On the other side of the argument, with some apparent trepidation, Walter Judd, R.-Minn., thought no harm would result "if we go along with the Panamanians' desire to fly their flag" in the Zone. Later events proved Selden absolutely right about "wrenching further concessions," and Judd wrong.

So, on that day, the House of Representatives voted overwhelmingly, 382 to 12, against displaying Panama's flag in the Zone. It was a non-binding "sense of the House" resolution, amended to withhold appropriated funds that might be used to erect flagpoles or otherwise facilitate display of Panama's flag. Eisenhower circumvented this restriction by using emergency funds under his own control after the Congress had adjourned.

William Jorden (*Panama Odyssey*) labeled the opponents of the measure to permit flying Panama's flag in the Zone as "superpatriots" and the leader of the House opposition, Congressman Daniel J. Flood, D.-Pa., as "irrepressible" in this victory over the erosion of U.S. sovereign rights. Moreover, Jorden wrote that the House itself was a place "where whim and passion often prevail over detached judgment" (p. 30). Many Americans would not agree; 97% of their representatives had voted to preserve traditional interests.

In 1960, the following twelve Congressmen voted to grant Panama's request to fly its flag in the U.S. Canal Zone: *Richard Bolling, D.-Mo.; Frank M. Coffin, D.-Me.; Cornelius E. Gallagher, D.-N.J.; *Byron L. Johnson, R.-Colo.; Walter H. Judd, R.-Minn.; *Robert W. Kastenmeier, D.-Wisc.; William H. Meyer, D.-Vt.; Adam Clayton Powell, Jr., D.-N.Y.; James M. Quigley, D.-Pa.; *Henry S. Reuss, D.-Wisc.; *Frank Thompson, Jr., D.-N.J.; Stewart L. Udall, D.-Ariz. The asterisk (*) indicates five Congressmen who voted in 1979 to implement the Canal Treaties, when 232 voted *for* the Treaties. The remaining seven Representatieves were no longer in the Congress. Notably, in 1960, 382 had opposed even the flying of Panama's flag in the Zone, a drastic change in mood in 19 years.[44]

Despite the setback in Panama's interests in 1960, President John F. Kennedy promised Panama's new President, Roberto "Nino" Chiari, "a complete reexamination . . . with respect to Isthmian canal facilities," but left unchallenged Chiari's claim that "Panama has basic sovereignty" in the Zone. A "secret" memorandum led Chiari to believe a new treaty had been promised. The issue was kept "secret" because the public would have been outraged. Even so, it was JFK who took the first step toward the 1977 Treaties. The pressure paid off for Chiari.

On January 1, 1963, Kennedy expanded Eisenhower's "flag order" with an Executive Order that Panama's flag be flown everywhere in the Canal Zone where the U.S. colors were displayed. This was another *milestone*. Sites were designated, but this was not enough.

A "Flag Riot" began on January 9, 1964 when Balboa High School students marched from Ancon down the steps of the Canal Company administration building on to their school flag pole a few blocks away for the purpose of hoisting the American flag, in defiance of the Canal Zone Governor's order. Since this was not one of the designated sites, Zone police stopped the students, told them they could hold up the flag and sing the national anthem, but not to hoist the flag.

When Panamanian students marched into the Zone to hoist their own flag, a scuffle started and the Panamanian flag was accidentally torn. This was the spark that ignited three days of rioting and bloodshed and that eventually caused President Chiari to break diplomatic relations with the United States. Order was restored only after 20 Panamanians and 5 Americans had been killed. Property damage was about two million dollars.[45] Substantial evidence proved that the continuing roits and violence were communist-led and inspired. Moreover, they had made careful preparations for the use of fire bombs and small arms.[46]

The "Flag Riot" was a test for the new American President, Lyndon Johnson, according to Thomas C. Mann, former Assistant Secretary of State for Inter-American Affairs. Mann was confidant and adviser to Johnson through 1966. During an interview on October 20, 1984, Mr. Mann expressed his view that "the flag incident was a prelude to the shoot out that followed." He added, "It was all stimulated by the National Guard and the government which was a creature of the Guard. It was all laid on to see what Johnson would do."

He continued, "We had a lot of new revolutionaries in Washington at that time, right after the Kennedy assassination, and it was peace at any price in Panama and anything Panama wanted was okay as long as we didn't defend ourselves." Moreover, he noted, the National Guard had been in control in Panama ever since the nation had been founded and suddenly, when rioting and bloodshed erupted, the Guard leaders decided they could not maintain order.

The next major *milestone* was Lyndon Johnson's announcement on March 21, 1964 that one of his presidential goals would be to recognize "the fair claims of Panama," including, he said, the renegotiation of the 1903 Treaty, surrender of U.S. sovereign rights in the Canal Zone, and a spectacular plan for a sea level canal.[47] These proposals shocked the public who, according to a 1964 poll, opposed by a six to one margin any more concessions to Panama.[48] Undoubtedly, deep in the American conscience lay a strong resistance to giving up the Canal.

Concessions had been the rewards for the violence and threats that had always characterized Panama's efforts to reclaim the Canal Zone from the beginning. This was a program with highly successful results. While claiming not to respond, the fact is, President Johnson reacted boldly in Panama's favor. In Panama, Chiari had continued the pattern of turbulence and violence, and Torrijos later perfected it. Will the Panama of the future use the same technique to obtain any future "rights" it may perceive under the 1977 Treaties, whether justified or not?

An outgrowth of the negotiations initiated by Mr. Johnson's bold "solution" was the study, "Panama Canal Issues and Treaty Talks," in March 1967 by the Center for Strategic Studies, Georgetown University,

Washington, D.C. and containing both a majority and minority report by the 9-member panel.

The mission of the panel of "practicing experts" on the Panamanian situation was "to make an independent investigation of the issues and to draw up conclusions . . . to help resolve the unsettled questions."

MEMBERS OF THE PANEL

Joseph S. Farland, Chairman—U.S. Ambassador to Dominican Republic, 1957-1960; to Panama, 1960-1963.

Major General William A. Carter, USA (Ret.)—Deputy Director, Project Analysis Division, Inter-American Development Bank; Governor of the Canal Zone, 1960-1962.

Jules Davids—Professor of American Diplomatic History, Georgetown University.

Donald Marquand Dozer—Professor of Latin American History, University of California, Santa Barbara, California; State Department, Division of Research for American Republics and the Historical Division, 1944-1956.

Eleanor Lansing Dulles—Professor of Government, Georgetown University; State Department, 1942-1962.

Victor C. Folsom—Vice President and General Counsel, United Fruit Company.

Major General K. D. Nichols, USA (Ret.)—Consulting engineer; District Engineer, Manhattan District, 1942-1947; General Manager, A.E.C., 1953-1955.

Covey T. Oliver—Professor of International Law, University of Pennsylvania; U.S. Ambassador to Colombia, 1964-1966.

Vice Admiral T. G. W. Settle, USN (Ret.)—Formerly Commander, Amphibious Forces, U.S. Pacific Fleet; service in Caribbean, Asiatic and European waters, including transportation, shipping and navigational affairs.

The majority report accepted as a *fait accompli* the President's announced intentions to relinquish sovereign rights and to abrogate the 1903 Treaty, and then, proceeded to make recommendations that appeared, in some repects, to give priority to Panama's desires, such as: additional economic benefits for Panama whose "principal natural resource" is after all the Canal; early agreement on the terms of the new treaties because of the upcoming Panamanian national elections (May 1968); and the prompt negotiation of three treaties to cover: (1) abrogation of the 1903 Treaty; (2) a second canal or improving the present one;

and (3) a new base-rights and status-of-force agreement. Other recommendations of the majority included: defense of the Canal should continue to rest with the United States; plans for a new or improved canal should be flexible; and increased publicity should "impress upon the people of the hemisphere the multiple benefits received by them from successful U.S. operation of the Canal."

The minority report by the late Professor Donald M. Dozer and the late Vice Admiral T. G. W. Settle, U.S. Navy, (Ret.), did not accept President Johnson's statement "that purports to abrogate a treaty which has been constitutionally ratified and to relinquish sovereign control over legally acquired territory of the United States." The minority report made recommendations to terminate the present negotiations and hold Panama accountable for the maintenance of law and order; withdraw arrangements for shared management; reassert the validity and force of the 1903 Treaty, including rights of sovereignty over the Canal Zone; as a condition for resumption of negotiations, require Panama's agreement for revocation of certain concessions made to Panama in the Treaties of 1936 and 1955; and proceed with improvement of the existing Canal in accordance with the Terminal Lake-Third Locks Plan.

The minority members of this study panel warned that Panama's independence, which had been guaranteed by the Hay-Bunau-Varilla Treaty had, since World War II, been endangered by crises fomented by communist-oriented agitation and further, that the Canal's security had been compromised by the United States' relinquishing important rights and controls. By progressively relinquishing its authority in the Canal Zone, Dozer and Settle added, the United States has furthered "the long-range communist objectives of gaining control of the strategic waterways of the world."

Even so, the majority report of this important study reflected the give-in complex that had always characterized dealings with Panama; this was also another *milestone* toward surrender.

Moreover, in the Preface to this study, the Director of the Center for Strategic Studies, retired Navy Admiral Arleigh Burke, a former Chief of Naval Operations, seemed to endorse the majority report in acceding to Panama's demands, with minimal concern for U.S. strategic and economic interests. For example, of the five questions posed in the Preface, none addressed the relationship between U.S. sovereign rights over the Canal Zone and national security. Therefore, instead of an "independent investigation," the study appeared to be a rationalization for President Johnson's announced intention of virtual surrender. That is, the panel had a "stacked deck."

Continuing this give-in complex, the U.S. Congress itself established an important *milestone* on the road to surrendering U.S. interests in the Caribbean: On February 17, 1971 the Senate voted 66 to 5 to terminate the Bryan-Chamorro Treaty of 1914 in another puzzling action that unnecessarily weakened U.S. defenses on the southern flank. The fact is, in 1914 the United States paid Nicaragua $3 million for "exclusive proprietary rights" to construct a canal through Nicaragua and for 99 year leases on the Corn Islands in the Caribbean and for a future base on Nicaragua's Pacific coast on the Gulf of Fonseca.[49]

Although the United States had never exercised any of these treaty rights, it *had* paid out $3 million of taxpayers' money which the Nicaraguans had long ago spent. Even so, the State Department urged termination of this treaty because the proposed canal route "had been discarded" by the Atlantic-Pacific Interoceanic Canal Study Commission and the treaty itself was "an irritant" to the Nicaraguans.[50]

Senator Strom Thurmond, R.-S.C., countered that the developing troubles in the Caribbean made the base rights in Nicaragua extremely important, and particularly so should the balance of power be adversely affected in that area. Mr. Thurmond continued his argument against abrogating this 1914 Treaty:

Finally, Mr. President, it will not go unnoticed in the world that an important precedent has been set here. The treaties give the United States the right to exercise her sovereignty and laws on the Corn Islands and on the naval base. We have similar rights in the U.S. Canal Zone in the Isthmus of Panama. When the Panamanians see that we have given up such rights in Nicaragua without a whimper, they will be ever *so much more adamant that we must give up our rights in the U.S. Canal Zone*. Little notice has been given to this treaty today in the United States, but I submit that it will be big news in Panama.

To sum up then, this treaty of abrogation is just another building block in the edifice designed by the State Department's architects of retreat and surrender. The main object of these policymakers appears to be to rationalize defeat and *to invent tedious excuses for not exercising our just rights and powers*. The ratification of this treaty today will contribute to the undermining of our authority and leadership, and I shall cast my vote nay.[51] (Emphasis added)

Only five Senators voted to retain U.S. rights in Nicaragua, rights that had been negotiated and paid for. The Senators were Harry F. Byrd, IND.-Va., Norris Cotton, R.-N.H., Edward Gurney, R.-Fla., Strom Thurmond, R.-S.C., and John Tower, R.-Tex. In view of developments in Central America in the 1980s, U.S. bases in Nicaragua would have been invaluable. Again, the Senate failed to protect U.S. interests, capitulating at the first sign of "irritation" in a treaty freely accepted by Nicaragua and concerning which, the U.S. had met all terms. The Secretary of State presiding over the surrender of U.S. base rights in Nicaragua was Henry Kissinger who later was prominent in planning the "surrender" of the Panama Canal.

But considerably more was involved than the arbitrary loss of potentially valuable bases in Central America, myopic and irresponsible though this forfeiture may have been. There was also the matter of constitutional propriety: The Senate had acted on its own in abrogating the Bryan-Chamorro Treaty (1914) without the participation of the House of Representatives, whereas, Article VI of the Constitution makes "Treaties . . . the supreme Law of the Land" along with laws enacted pursuant to the Constitution.

Therefore, just as laws are repealed by legislative acts (both Houses of Congress) so must treaties be terminated in the same manner. *Jefferson's Manual of Parliamentary Practice* could not be clearer: ". . . an act of the legislature alone can declare them [treaties] infringed and rescinded" (paragraph 599). Indeed, this was the procedure since 1798 and the Library of Congress's authoritative publication, *The Constitution of the United States of America, Analysis and Interpretation* (1973), so finds and promulgates many historical examples.

On February 17, 1971, however, Senate Majority Leader Mike Mansfield was in a hurry—call it "legislative efficiency" or "political expediency" or "rule by consensus," but it was not in accordance with the Constitution. Senator Strom Thurmond, R.-S.C., protested "the unseemly haste with which this matter was taken up," noting with alarm that "the Senate had little or no opportunity to study the matter before unanimous consent was obtained" to proceed to a vote.

Thus, the argument can be made that the Bryan-Chamorro Treaty (1914) remains in force because constitutional procedures were not observed. The same argument, and others, apply to the Hay-Bunau-Varilla Treaty (1903) granting the Canal Zone and rights of sovereignty in perpetuity to the United States. The Constitution was by-passed in both cases and by 1978, this serious aberration was accepted by the political expediters as "settled diplomatic practice."

The consequences of such "efficiency" were soon evident. In 1983 the Soviet Union was reported to be locating earth-moving equipment in Nicaragua for the apparent purpose of constructing a canal across that country. The then-U.S. Ambassador to the United Nations, Jeane Kirkpatrick, stated, "The canal [in Nicaragua] is part of the Soviet master plan to move as rapidly as possible for the protection of their military power in the Western Hemisphere."

Henry Kissinger took a big step toward relinquishing sovereignty in the Canal Zone with his proposal to President Richard Nixon for the "possibility of a termination formula." Mr. Nixon signed National Security Decision Memorandum 131 on September 13, 1971, thereby providing U.S. negotiator Robert Anderson with flexibility for a new treaty with the Panamanians. Eventually Anderson left government service, but NSDM 131 had laid the groundwork for Dr. Kissinger's next step.

THE KISSINGER-TACK STATEMENT OF FALSE PREMISES

The next major *milestone* was the Kissinger-Tack Statement of Principles, signed in Panama on February 7, 1974 by U.S. Secretary of State Kissinger and Panamanian Foreign Minister Juan Tack, Appendix E. Mr. Tack was the author of this "Statement of Principles" and had tried unsuccessfully to get Secretary of State William P. Rogers to sign it previously on July 10, 1973.

Appendix F tabulates significant dates in the formulation of the Treaties, beginning with the Kissinger-Tack Statement of Principles of 1974.

In this agreement, which became the framework of the 1977 Canal Treaties, Kissinger alleged in 3 of the 8 "principles" that the Canal Zone was Panamanian territory,[52] a false premise and one that presumed to set aside the historic rulings by the U.S. Supreme Court and the Fifth Circuit Court of Appeals that the Canal Zone was U.S. territory. Unfortunately, Kissinger's misstatements went largely unchallenged and, of course, became the bases for later negotiation and misunderstanding. They also weakened the U.S. negotiating position.

In matter of fact, the United States exercised both rights of sovereignty and ownership over all areas in the U.S. Canal Zone. Dramatic proof of ownership was presented on March 11, 1978 before the Senate Subcommittee on Separation of Powers, under Chairman James B. Allen, D.-Ala., when sample crates of fee simple titles to 3,598 tracts of land were carted into the hearing room as evidence.[53] This display of ownership and the previous Court rulings on sovereignty and territory should have settled all arguments.

The allegations by the U.S. Secretary of State that the Canal Zone was "Panamanian territory" were climatic to the State Department's decades-long subtle undermining of U.S. jurisdiction—and had no foundation in fact. Kissinger chose to ignore the landmark clear-cut decisions of U.S. courts.

The first such case was *Wilson v. Shaw*, 204 U.S. 24, in which the U.S. Supreme Court in 1907 heard a lawsuit seeking to restrain the Secretary of the Treasury from paying out funds for the construction of the Canal on grounds that the United States did not have title. The unanimous court found:

The Hay-Bunau-Varilla treaty (1903) with Panama, ceding the Canal Zone was duly ratified. Congress has passed several acts to provide a temporary government;. . . . These show a full ratification by Congress of what has been done by the Executive. Their concurrent action is conclusive upon the Courts. It is too late in the history of the U.S. to question the right of acquiring territory by treaty.

Quoting Articles II and III of the 1903 treaty granting in perpetuity "all the rights, powers and authority" as "if it were sovereign," the Court concluded:

It is hypercritical to contend that the title of the United States is imperfect, and that the territory described does not belong to this nation, because of the omission of some of the technical terms used in ordinary conveyances of real estate. . . . Alaska was ceded to us forty years ago but the boundary between it and the English possessions east were not settled until within the last two or three years, yet no one ever doubted our title to this Republic of Alaska.[54]

Another major case reinforced these findings of the 1907 Supreme Court. In 1971 the U.S. Circuit Court of Appeals for the Fifth District in *United States v. Husband R. (Roach)*, 453 F.2d 1054 (1971), a case involving the relationship of the Canal Zone and the Canal Zone government, found:

. . . Congress has complete and plenary authority to legislate for an unincorporated territory such as the Canal Zone. . . . The Canal Zone is an unincorporated territory of the United States.[55]

In an effort to determine something about the authority for and the ramifications of Kissinger statements that the Canal Zone was "Panamanian territory," a total of some 74 letters, including copies, were sent to U.S. officials by Phillip Harman, Chairman of the Committee for Better Panama and United States Relations. The following questions were asked:

—Has the *Wilson v. Shaw* (1907) decision that the Canal Zone is U.S. territory been rescinded?

—If not, can Secretary of State Henry Kissinger overturn a ruling of the U.S. Supreme Court?

—If not, what is the penalty for alleging in an official document that the *Wilson v. Shaw* (1907) decision has been rescinded?

—What U.S. government agency will assume jurisdiction for possible violation of U.S. law in cases similar to this, including possible violation of oath of office to protect and defend the U.S. Constitution?

These questions, or similar ones, were asked of President Gerald R. Ford, the Secretary of State, the nine Justices of the U.S. Supreme Court, the Legislative Attorney of the Library of Congress, and several members of the Congress. The Deputy Clerk of the Supreme Court answered that the *Wilson v. Shaw* decision stood, but that the Court could not advise about possible violations of the law. Apparently no one wished to challenge Secretary Kissinger or to address a basic constitutional question involving separation of powers.

Even so, during our interview on November 14, 1983, William D. Rogers, former Assistant Secretary of State, supported Kissinger's assertion that the Canal Zone was Panamanian territory, calling it "a good interpretation of the 1903 Treaty." In light, however, of the Court rulings, the proofs of ownership of 3,598 tracts of land, and Article III of the 1903 Treaty giving the U.S. the rights of sovereignty, Kissinger's "interpretation" is not supportable. Later, Mr. Rogers said, "I wouldn't question they [the State Department] tried to overrule the Supreme Court."[56]

Others disagreed with Kissinger and Rogers. For example, Representative Philip M. Crane, R.-Ill., author of *Surrender in Panama* (Dale Books, 1978), said on November 18, 1983 during our interview:

I think Henry Kissinger . . . demonstrated an appalling lack of understanding of history of the circumstances whereby we acquired sovereign control of that portion of land on each side of the Canal . . . that was American territory . . . and earlier Courts held that to be true. It was indeed U.S. Territory and after 1903 it was never Panamanian territory.[57]

Former Senator Dick Clark, D.-Iowa, and Representative George V. Hansen, R-Ida., also did not agree with Kissinger's action in proclaiming the Canal Zone to be Panamanian territory. During our interview with Mr. Hansen on November 18, 1983, he stated:

We have found a lot of people in high positions conveniently making assumptions for their own purposes, contrary to fact and established points of law. Just because Kissinger or anyone else makes such statements doesn't make it so.[58]

THE LINOWITZ REPORT

The Kissinger philosophy carried over to the Linowitz Report, the final *milestone* before reaching the 1977 Canal Treaties. Officially titled "The Americas in a Changing World," this study was issued October 29, 1974 by the Commission on United States-Latin American Relations. The chairman and founder of the Commission was Sol M. Linowitz, later to become a co-negotiator of the Panama Canal Treaties. A key member of the Commission was William D. Rogers, later destined to help construct the leadership amendment to the Panama Canal Treaty (the second treaty approved), an amendment, Mr. Rogers said, that had, in effect, neutralized the U.S. unilateral rights in the DeConcini reservation.

Among the assumptions on which the Linowitz Report is based: "The

United States should change its basic approach to Latin America and the Caribbean." Mr. Linowitz's Commission of 23 members also included W. Michael Blumenthal, Secretary of the Treasury under President Carter; the Reverend Theodore Hesburgh, President of the University of Notre Dame; and Nicholas deB. Katzenbach, a former Deputy Director of the Federal Bureau of Investigation. The following statement is evidently their evaluation of the Monroe Doctrine:

Dramatic transformations within Latin America and the Caribbean, major developments in the wider international arena, and significant changes in the terms on which this hemisphere relates to the rest of the world, all have undermined the assumptions which governed U.S. policy in the Americas from the Monroe Doctrine through the Good Neighbor policy to the Alliance for Progress and its successor, the Mature Partnership. We strongly believe that the policies which the United States has inherited from the past—including many of their most basic assumptions and goals—are inappropriate and irrelevant to the changed realities of the present and the trends of the future.[59]

This statement not only suggests the obsolescence of the Monroe Doctrine but could also be interpreted as bidding for change in the U.S. Constitution, perhaps a document inappropriate "to the changed realities of the present and the trends of the future." Is the "Mature Partnership" the substitute for the Monroe Doctrine and would it do the job done by the Monroe Doctrine? Probably not, considering the incursions into the Western Hemisphere since the Linowitz Report was issued. Even so, the United States' success in Grenada in 1983 was, in many respects, an application of the Monroe Doctrine, though not called by name. Nonetheless, the world accepted it.

The Monroe Doctrine was apparently not a consideration for Mr. Linowitz who in May 1983 was urging a "recognition of the fact that some relative loss of U.S. influence is to be expected in a . . . changing world, and that the risks of intervention considerably outweigh those of a more restrained policy." He added through his Inter-American Dialogue Group, in effect, that Russia can nicely be persuaded to "keep Latin America out of the East-West conflict" and further, that "the dangers to the Western Hemisphere are political and economic, not military."[60]

These observations, almost a decade later, are consistent with the Linowitz Report of 1974. As to the dangers to the Western Hemisphere, hardly anyone might successfully dispute that they are indeed "political and economic." However, history proves that military backup is essential when countering the communists' imposition of their own brand of "political and economic" solutions, i.e., against the will of the people.

Two of the major recommendations of the Linowitz Report were perhaps predictable: (1) Prepare and ratify a new Panama Canal treaty based on the Kissinger-Tack Statement of Principles. And (2) reduce personnel and operations in the Canal Zone and transfer the United States Armed Forces Southern Command from the Canal Zone to the continental United States.[61]

Later, on December 26, 1976, a second Linowitz Report was issued, again recommending "justice for Panama." The Executive Director of this second Linowitz Commission was Dr. Robert Pastor, who, a few weeks later as a member of President Carter's staff, would submit the National Security Council memorandum that recommended, in effect, that the Canal be turned over to Panama. This initiated the new negotiations.[62]

Therefore, when President Carter assumed office in January 1977, he had two Linowitz Reports and the Kissinger-Tack Statement to guide his Central American policies. He combined these with the "Zimbabwe Solution," believing that human rights and social justice would follow—even with socialism (state capitalism). The collapse of Central America ensued.[63] Unfortunately, even with the Administration of Ronald Reagan, much of the "Zimbabwe Solution" still stood at State.

The road to the surrender of the Canal led in the same direction from the first milestone to the last—always toward more concessions and loss of sovereign rights and control to Panama. Particularly since World War II, the Panamanians had baited the United States, often feigning martyrdom and mistreatment. Few opportunities were missed; and national tantrums eventually gained for Panama virtually everything she ever wanted from the United States, culminating finally in two different sets of Panama Canal Treaties.

From the day of the discovery of Panama by Spanish explorer Rodrigo de Bastidas in 1501, the great strategic and economic value of a ship canal was recognized. Now, almost five centuries later, the American-built Canal passes to Panama, the former province of Colombia whose Great Liberator, Simon Bolivar, said in 1815:

That magnificent portion [of America], situated between the two oceans, will in time become the emporium of the universe. Its canals will shorten the distances of the world, and will strengthen the commercial ties of Europe, America, and Asia.[64]

*Major Amado Sanjur, third from left, relaxes at
the Fort Amador Officers' Club, U.S. Canal Zone
in late 1966, with fellow National Guard Officers:
Major Juan Bernal, far left; Major Alejandro
Araúz, far right: and Major Omar Torrijos, second
from right. Other officers were from the United
States, El Salvador, Taiwan, Guatemala and Chile.
On December 15, 1969, Sanjur mounted an
unsuccessful coup against the military dictatorship
of Torrijos. (Collection of A. Sanjur)*

· 3 ·

'TORRIJOS . . . LIKELIEST MAN TO DO THE JOB'

During the Bolsheviki Revolution of 1917, John Reed, the American reformer, was outside Petrograd careening along in a truck filled with *grubit* bombs. He wrote, ". . . Vladimir Nicolaivitch (Lenin) bellowed to me about the internationalization of the Panama Canal. . . ." Lenin was echoing instructions of the All-Russian Executive Committee: "All straits opening into the inland seas, as well as the Suez and Panama Canals, are to be neutralized."[1]

When the Suez Canal was nationalized in 1956, the Panamanians declared their situation analogous and sought to participate in the settlement conference. Although denied a seat, they did publicize their crusade for sovereignty over the Canal Zone.[2] The Soviets mounted a campaign for shifting control and ownership of the Canal to some international body. A number of U.S. officials also heralded this "internationalization" as the Panama Canal solution. They were backing Lenin's solution.

In due time the Neutrality Treaty of 1977 established the Canal's "internationalization," and Lenin's goal was achieved. Romulo Escobar Bethancourt, Panama's negotiator, reinforced the concept of neutrality by declaring that no U.S. warships would get priority passage.[3] This assertion was contrary to the Treaty; but perhaps Bethancourt meant priority handling was illegal because Panamanians had not approved it by plebiscite, as constitutionally required.

U.S.-Panama relations worsened after the Suez crisis, despite U.S. efforts at reconciliation. President Eisenhower permitted display of Panama's flag in the Zone in September 1960, touching off more demonstrations in which Cuban revolutionaries exerted "considerable influence."[4] President Kennedy's Alliance for Progress in 1961 provided generous aid; but Panama pressed for more concessions until Kennedy in 1962 authorized Panama's flag to be flown at 16 additional locations. The *New York Times* reported, ". . . tensions can be eased but . . . repeated concessions have increased them."[5]

JOHNSON SETS POLICY
FOR SURRENDER OF CANAL

The progenitor of the 1977 Treaties was President Johnson's letter of March 21, 1964 to the Organization of American States, announcing his intention to "come up with any solution that is fair," even as riots continued in Panama. On January 9, 1965, McGeorge Bundy, the National Security Adviser, promulgated Johnson's new Canal policy: plan a sea level canal; provide a new treaty for the present canal; and include adequate defenses. Perhaps Mr. Johnson visualized his legacy as a sea level canal. His capitulations, however, constituted a shocking reversal of U.S. policy.[6]

In September 1965 he announced far-reaching plans to abrogate the 1903 Treaty, surrender U.S. sovereign rights, and terminate any new treaty on a specific future date. Simultaneously, President Marco Robles was advising the Panamanians. Failure to mention U.S. constitutional requirements for treaties and U.S. territory may have misled Panamanians who, for the most part, were accustomed to one-man rule. In this manner the die was set for future negotiations, and Ellsworth Bunker's statement of the previous year about bargaining with no preconditions suddenly became meaningless.

Americans were unprepared for such commitments. And Johnson's goal for "discharge of our common responsibilities" posed problems: (1) Panama's claim to sovereignty clashed with U.S. base rights, and (2) a joint command was fraught with control questions. Johnson assured U.S. Senators that his plan was sound, while Robles was guaranteeing his supporters that Panama would have unequivocal sovereignty in the Zone.

Panama's objective of total control was incompatible with the U.S. requirement for a secure Canal under U.S. control. This impasse confronted Johnson's new negotiator, Robert B. Anderson, a fellow Texan and former Secretary of the Treasury. After two years the negotiators proposed the 1967 draft treaties, very similar to the 1977 Treaties: a basic treaty to transfer the Canal; one for defense; and a third for a sea level canal. Provisions were considered generous.

Although initialed by U.S. Secretary of State Dean Rusk and Panama's Foreign Minister Galileo Solis, the draft treaties failed, as explained by Phillip Harman, an experienced intelligence operative:

This is what happened; I was there. The National Assembly was controlled by Arnulfo Arias's party and refused to act, as they considered the government of President Robles spurious because of irregularities in the 1964 election when Arias lost to Robles.[7]

Arias did not want Robles, his political enemy, to have the honor of ratifying new treaties. "Politics," said Robles during a September 9, 1984 interview, adding that Panamanians objected to the proposed treaties because "most people thought we did not have sovereignty and not enough economic benefits."

This failure to obtain ratified treaties may have influenced Mr. Rusk's statement to the Senate Foreign Relations Committee on October 14, 1977 to the effect that the more democratic the government in Panama the harder to get treaties. Immediately after the 1967 treaties failed, a military coup ousted elected President Arias, and shortly thereafter installed the Torrijos dictatorship which in due time ratified the 1977 Treaties.

DID THE UNITED STATES WANT A COUP AGAINST ARIAS?

Considerable evidence suggests that the State Department preferred a dictatorship: (1) A U.S. Army Corps of Engineers draft position paper of February 16, 1968 concluded that "a strong military dictator" was needed for new Canal treaties. (2) Dean Rusk suggested as much in his testimony. (3) The U.S. Southern Command's liaison officer, Efrain Angueira, knew about the coup in advance.

Mrs. Rose Marie Aragon told the Senate Foreign Relations Committee on October 12, 1977 that her husband, journalist Leopoldo Aragon, had seen the Army position paper:

In 1971 Leopoldo was assigned to Panama. . . . he was shown a Corps of Engineers draft position paper dated February 16, 1968. That paper noted that popular opposition had rejected the 1967 Canal treaties . . . and concluded that a new treaty could not be passed in Panama except under a strong military dictatorship. Mr. Rusk said the same thing, almost to a word, when he testified. . . . This paper recommended *Torrijos as the likeliest man to do the job.* (emphasis added)[8]

Secretary Rusk had testified earlier before the House Armed Services Committee, and on October 14, 1977 told the Senate Foreign Relations Committee:

Opponents of these Treaties object to . . . arrangements with a dictator. . . . I would suggest that the more democratic the government in Panama, the more insistent they would be on a prompt and fundamental change . . . regarding the Canal.[9]

Both witnesses were indicating that a dictator might get results. Said Senator Robert P. Griffin, R.-Mich., "There is the chance that Torrijos will 'ratify' these changes by himself"[10]—meaning the changes the Senate had approved but Panamanians had not voted on. This came true. No plebiscite was held, and Torrijos *did* "ratify" by himself.

Seven years earlier, on July 10, 1970, two high Canal Zone officials called the Torrijos regime "more stable" than previous ones. The hearing record of the House Subcommittee on Inter-American Affairs is laced with "security deletions" in the testimony of Maj. General Walter P. Leber, the Canal Zone Governor, and General George R. Mather of the Southern Command. The context of the deletions suggests "Torrijos as the likeliest man." On October 15, 1984 General Leber declined to comment on the draft position paper or on speculation that the U.S. might have preferred a Torrijos dictatorship over an Arias democracy.

The role of Efrain Angueira was intriguing. On the night of the coup against Arias, October 11, 1968, he was entertaining seven senior Guard officers in his home. They were Amado Sanjur, Omar Torrijos, Juan Bernal, Federico Boyd, Humberto Jimenez, Luis Nentzen-Franco, and Ramiro Silvera, according to Sanjur's sworn statement of September 17, 1981. Silvera confirmed on November 4, 1984 that Angueira knew about the coup which, he said, was initiated by Major Boris Martinez, *not* Torrijos. Sanjur said, "The conversation moved immediately to the coup and its execution, and everything seemed ready now that the Southern Command was backing the coup through Efrain Angueira. . . ."[11]

Access to Angueira's records, under the Freedom of Information Act, was denied by the Army Intelligence and Security Command as endangering national security. Angueira stated in interviews in 1984 that he "was not able to discuss that meeting because it is still classified."[12] However, in January 1986, he said he warned his "Agency," under Maj. General Chester L. Johnson, U.S. Army, of the coup 48 hours in advance. Dr. Arias was not alerted.

On the day of the coup, Dr. Hildebrando Nicosia, associate of Dr. Arias, contacted Angueira but nothing was said about the pending coup.[13] All top U.S. officials were out of the country that day: Ambassador Charles Adair and General Leber were in Washington; General Robert Porter Jr., Commander U.S. Southern Command, was in Paraguay.

The Harman Committee asked eleven officials involved with Panama at the time of the coup why Arias was not alerted. Six replied. Dean Rusk had "no advance warning," nor did General Johnson. An interesting answer came from General Porter in his September 3, 1981 letter:

My headquarters had received earlier reports that the *Guardia* might move against Dr. Arias. . . . Nothing had developed. I was in Paraguay at the time of the coup. From my investigation . . . I decided the move by Torrijos and his command was sparked by the decision of Arias to discharge all officers who participated in the earlier overthrow of his government.

Perhaps General Porter had inadequate intelligence information: Torrijos had no command; he was a staff officer. Martinez had troops and executed the coup, *not* Torrijos. Moreover, Arias could not discharge officers who had earlier overthrown him because the officers in 1968 were too young in 1951 to have led an uprising—and Arias was *impeached* in 1951, not ousted by a coup. General Porter said on October 6, 1984 that he knew of no U.S. policy that preferred a dictator for Panama.[14]

Neither did former Ambassador Adair. William E. LeBrun, head of the Canal Security Office, and Covey T. Oliver, former Assistant Secretary of State, were not informed of a coup threat. But said Dr. Oliver, "Any American knowing of a planned coup on Arias *should have executed the U.S. foreign policy* by passing on the information" (his emphasis).[15]

Walter W. Rostow, former assistant to President Johnson, disclaimed knowledge of any "alleged session with the liaison officer (Angueira)," adding, "I have recently talked with an exceedingly knowledgeable man on this matter. . . . He says flatly that no such meeting took place.[16] Could that "knowledgeable man" be William Jorden, author of *Panama Odyssey?* Both he and Rostow were at the Lyndon Baines Johnson Library in 1981, Jorden busy with his book. At the time of the Angueira meeting in 1968, Jorden had no duties with Panama, but the CIA station chief, J. Foster Collins, did. When Jorden became Ambassador to Panama (1974-78), he had access to the CIA files. So, presumably, Rostow could turn to Jorden right there at the LBJ Library.

Two former *Guardia* Chiefs of staff emphasized that the meeting with Angueira did indeed take place: Amado Sanjur described details in his notorized statement and again when interviewed on July 31 and August 31, 1984. Boris Martinez reported the meeting in a *La Prensa* interview on October 10, 1980.[17] Angueira himself acknowledged the meeting.

Recapping our evidence, the following points are pertinent:

- Senior Guard officers were at Efrain Angueira's home during the coup against Arias, discussing the takeover.
- U.S. authorities chose to ignore Angueira's timely warning and allowed Arias to be ousted by the coup.
- Torrijos eventually emerged as dictator and "likeliest man to do the job" as predicted by the Corps of Engineers position paper.

- Rusk, Mather, and Leber apparently defended the dictatorship in their congressional testimony.

PRELUDE TO THE 1968 COUP

Arnulfo Arias lost his third presidency on October 11, 1968 to a coup after eleven days in office—Panama's 28th government in 65 years. Dr. Arias, a graduate of Harvard Medical School, was generally pro-American, though at times unpredictable. In the barrios, he was El Hombre, the last of the great *caudillos*. He had complained about the 1967 treaties, but he supported them anyway, probably a political position to impress the Americans. Major Boris Martinez, *Guardia* commander of the David, Chiriqui garrison, engineered the *coup d'etat*.

Most writers, including William Jorden in *Panama Odyssey,* credit Torrijos with the coup.[18] But, Torrijos and six other officers were celebrating with Efrain Angueira in the Canal Zone at the time. Interviews with Sanjur, Martinez, and President Robles establish that Martinez led the coup, and further discussions developed details apparently never before disclosed.[19] The three principals of the coup that established the dictatorship that eventually took the Canal were Martinez, Sanjur, and Torrijos, the latter killed on July 31, 1981 in a plane crash.

Mr. Jorden wrote the Torrijos story, obviously embellishing the folk hero image. The following story of the coup is from the coup survivors, Martinez and Sanjur, and from Phillip Harman: *Guardia* officers feared that Arias would dilute their power. Martinez and Torrijos were to go to remote posts. *Guardia* commander Bolivar "Lilo" Vallarino was seen as the key to stability, a constitutionalist. Said Sanjur, "The only way the Guard could survive was to keep Vallarino" who since 1952 had permitted no coups, but who in October 1968 was about to retire.[20]

A number of apparent discrepancies in the Jorden book were disturbing to Martinez and Sanjur. For example, they were not present at the August 1968 meeting to plot against Arias (p.127). Nor was Sanjur a member of Torrijos's combo social group (p.129). And Martinez did not attend a plotting session in September at Vallarino's home (p.130), nor an 11:00 p.m. meeting on October 11 where Torrijos was alleged to be trying to form a civilian government (p.136). Besides Martinez and Sanjur, others discounted claims that Vallarino ever plotted a coup, including Angueira, Adair, Porter, and Robles.

Major Martinez had a popular following in the *Guardia,* and commanded a large detachment of troops in contrast to Torrijos who, as a staff officer, had no soldiers. Martinez had the power. He reported patriotic motives for his coup, saying he had declined half a million dollars, one month prior to Arias's inauguration, to install Raul "Lul" Arango as President when propositioned by Arango's son "Baby."

Convinced that the *Guardia* might be reduced to provincial police posts and worried about a coup, Major Amado Sanjur on October 10, 1968 met privately with the cabinet officer having *Guardia* jurisdiction, Justice Norberto Zurita, urging him to keep Vallarino as Commandant in order to avoid a *coup d'état:*

After some time reasoning, he told me my recommendation was a very wise one, made without selfish motives, and he would leave Vallarino in. . . . But it was another story the next day.[21]

The next day was the day of the coup, preceded by announcements of transfers of 56 *Guardia* officers, including Torrijos to El Salvador, Martinez to Chitre, and Sanjur to Colon. At noon, Vallarino retired, Jose Maria Pinilla succeeded him and retired three hours later. Bolivar Urrutia then became *Guardia* commander. But foremost in the minds of the officers was not their new general, but their new President and what he intended to do. Urrutia complained to the American Embassy about Arias's failure to keep promises. His answer, relayed from Washington, was U.S. support for constitutional processes. The Embassy obviously believed the threat of a coup had passed.[22]

MARTINEZ DECIDES ON COUP

As General Vallarino was leaving his retirement party, he told Martinez, "Leave things the way they are." In turn, Torrijos stopped Martinez, "Boris, I beg you, do something to stop my transfer." *Guardia* officers were worried about their careers. Martinez decided at that moment, 2:00 p.m., October 11, 1968, to take action, "I decided on this coup to avoid bloodshed, to use military assistance for a real democracy." He proceeded to the airport detachment and won support of the officers there:

They all knew my plan for a coup against the communists. So, there was never any plan for a coup against Arias. It was my plan, the one against the communists.[23]

Martinez assigned Major Federico Boyd and Lt. Pablo Garrido to secure transportation and communications, to take over *Guardia* headquarters in Panama City, and to execute other details of his plan. At 5:00 p.m. he took off in his Cessna for David to prepare his troops.

Torrijos and Demetrio B. Lakas, later appointed President by Torrijos, were suspicious of Martinez, but nonetheless proceeded to Angueira's home in the Canal Zone, where with other officers, they gossiped about the coup. Sanjur recalled this affair and, with Martinez, described the coup

Major Boris Martinez, Panamanian National Guard, is pictured shortly before instigating his coup d'etat against President Arnulfo Arias Madrid on October 11, 1968. A few months later, Lt. Colonel Omar Torrijos seized power from Martinez and continued as Panama's military dictator until his death on July 31, 1981. (Collection of B. Martinez)

that was in progress without Torrijos's participation. When *Guardia* headquarters were reported secure, the party broke up. Martinez found out what happened next from his officers:

Lakas took Torrijos to a block ahead of Guardia headquarters, but had to put a pistol to his chest because Torrijos was afraid to go in, even though the building had been secured by the cavalry.[24]

The U.S. Army commander in Panama, General Johnson, confirmed that Martinez, "the strong one," led the coup, adding, "Torrijos, as would become his nature, seems to have been filled with doubt and reluctance to act, but was overcome by Martinez."[25]

Martinez, when assured of his troops' loyalty, called from David, telling Torrijos not to support Arango for President and "wait for me." At 4:00 a.m. on October 12, Martinez landed at Tocumen and rushed into Panama City. His story continues:

We did the coup for the people. My solution was Pinilla as President and Urrutia Vice President until elections. I was in complete charge. Torrijos and Lakas seemed paralyzed with fear. I don't know what happens in crisis; people panic and beg for solutions.

The Jorden story in *Panama Odyssey* is different: Angueira is not named, but is called a "U.S. agent," implying a CIA man. Angueira was the Southern Command's intelligence official assigned to liaison duties with the *Guardia*. The alleged Torrijos bravado during the coup (pp.133-35) and quieting Angueira with a bottle of whiskey, said Martinez, "were fabrications to make Omar look good."

After Pinilla and Urrutia were elevated to the junta, Colonel Aristides Hassan became *Guardia* commander. He was soon succeeded by Torrijos with Martinez as Chief of Staff. Although in a secondary role, Martinez was the leader. Torrijos spent his days drinking while the Chief of Staff tried to form a provisional government. These circumstances were confirmed by Sanjur.

Mr. Jorden describes a Torrijos adventure, obviously told by Torrijos, but quite different from the story by Martinez who was also present. First, the Jorden account: A few days after the coup, Torrijos met with General Johnson at Ft. Amador to assure him that democratic elections were planned. Members of Torrijos's "small entourage" are unnamed—unusual since *Odyssey* anecdotes are usually specific. Enroute, U.S. guards angered Torrijos by asking for identification. Fearful of being kidnapped and suspicious that Johnson favored Arias, Torrijos rushed from the general's quarters and "sped to the exit gate" where the sentries stopped him again. Grabbing his submachine gun, Torrijos said, "Come ahead, you sons of bitches," and drove away.[26]

Martinez's account, confirmed in some detail by Sanjur, is in his own words:

Angueira called me and said General Johnson wants to talk. I went with Torrijos and Angueira, with Torrijos driving Angueira's car. We had no problem at the gate. Then suddenly, an MP car stopped us and two MPs with pistols searched us police fashion. We were unarmed and in civilian clothes. I said, "Angueira, this is way you treat friends?" We showed IDs and they let us alone. Angueira said we should rush to the general's house. I said, "I cannot talk with him after this. . . . So, please Angueira, drive us home." Torrijos said nothing at all. Angueira took over the car and that was the end of that.[27]

MARTINEZ IS HANDCUFFED AND GAGGED

Relations deteriorated between the two new leaders. "Torrijos was not doing anything," complained Martinez. Lt. Colonel Juan Bernal came to Martinez early one Sunday morning with an urgent message from *Guardia* officers, "We don't like Torrijos's drinking; get rid of him or we will." When confronted, Torrijos became emotional, "I promise to try, give me another chance."[28]

During the succeeding weeks, Martinez continued his efforts to explain the revolution and its goals to the people. "I tried to get Omar to be the main speaker," said Martinez, "but he was short on ideas and couldn't communicate." This situation precipitated an ugly climax brought on by a television broadcast on Friday evening, February 21, 1969.

Once again, Mr. Jorden's account, evidently through the eyes of Torrijos, differs sharply from that of Martinez and Sanjur. First, the *Odyssey* version (pp.142-43): Martinez's TV appearance was alleged to be unauthorized and insubordinate; and, "Torrijos had not been consulted." Martinez was placed in "protective custody."[29]

The Martinez story was corroborated by Sanjur: Torrijos *wanted* the economic program presented on TV and agreed that Martinez should do it. Present at the station were Torrijos, Sanjur, Martinez and five other *Guardia* officers. Martinez continued:

We needed to explain to the people and Torrijos agreed I should do it. Omar and most of the staff were there. People in Panama saw that. So, it is not true Torrijos did not know; he was there.[30]

Over the weekend, Torrijos made plans. Early Monday he sent for his Chief of Staff. When Martinez entered, he was blackjacked, and bound and gagged:

Silvera slugged me from behind. I remember Omar's big eyes; he didn't want to look at me. . . . I waited there handcuffed one hour. Then, we were put into a DC-3 and flown to Miami via Jamaica.

Also taken into "protective custody" for the flight into exile were *Guardia* officers Humberto Ramos, Federico Boyd, and Humberto Jimenez.

On hand to meet the plane in Miami were Ambassador Roberto "Chato" Aleman and Fernando Manfredo, later a Deputy Canal Administrator, offering Martinez a job—even Aleman's. "Tell Torrijos no," said Martinez. "He took away my career, but not my pride."

When asked in a 1984 interview why the *Guardia* officers sided with Torrijos on February 24, 1969 when he was exiled, Martinez said:

Too much honesty if I stayed. . . . I'll give you an example: Free license plates went to Guard officers; the Commandant gave them to friends and family. Once I found three in my desk. I told them we had to pay. This was a little dishonesty but it was just one reason they backed Torrijos.

Apropos Martinez's concern in 1969: On October 31, 1985, a report from Panama alleged that the *Guardia* under Manuel Antonio Noreiga was "taking much of the millions from U.S. aid and installing the majors and colonels in absolute luxury."

TORRIJOS SURVIVES COUNTERCOUP

Amador Sanjur was the next Chief of Staff. He attended meetings between Torrijos and Communist Party leaders to promote "communist businesses in Panama." One such conference in early 1969 included brother Moises "Monchi" Torrijos, Efrain Reyes-Medina, and Cleto Sousa at a time when Omar was under treatment for neurosis. Eventually, known communists, said Sanjur, held policy positions in the government: Adolfo Ahumada, treaty negotiator, became Minister of Government and Justice with jurisdiction over the *Guardia*. Juan Materno Vasquez became President of the Supreme Court. And Romulo Escobar Bethancourt, the chief treaty negotiator, headed the Electoral Tribune and the University of Panama, as Chancellor.[31]

Sanjur was a captain during the 1964 Flag War and observed communists creating problems so the U.S. Army could be blamed. Ambassador Ellsworth Bunker, in his report to the OAS, confirmed that communists were indeed involved. However, Mr. Bunker denied this influence during his August 1979 testimony before the House Committee on Merchant Marine and Fisheries in supporting implementation of the Canal Treaties. Chairman John M. Murphy, D.-N.Y., then produced the damning 15-year old OAS report.[32]

Guardia influence in Panamanian politics is, and has been, virtually supreme—often turbulent. A reliable source in October 1985 reported the

liquidation of "people who protest the Noriega Administration." A Panamanian newspaper on November 1, 1985 carried a story of Noriega's hos-
pitalization for hysteria.[33] Fernando Manfredo said on August 3, 1984 that
his friend Sanjur had led a countercoup in 1969 "to keep Panama from
going too far leftward under Torrijos."[34]

Sanjur's countercoup originated on December 14, 1969 while Torrijos, Lakas and *Guardia* officers Ruben D. Parades and Rodrigo Garcia
were playing the horses in Mexico. Back in Panama, Lt. Colonel Ramiro
Silvera and Lt. Colonel Luis Nentzen-Franco were urging Sanjur to stage a
coup and implement a real civilian government. Said Sanjur later:

Our coup was for Pinilla to be President *in fact* and to consolidate power with a
friendly Guard. We wanted free elections and free unions. Torrijos opposed. He
had communists in government and too much power as dictator. Also, I didn't like
the drug traffic through Panama. We announced that we would have early democratic elections. Next, Pinilla telephoned our Ambassador in Mexico City, Alejandro Remon, and told him Torrijos would be the Ambassador. It was Pinilla who
called, not me, as incorrectly written in the Jorden book. Omar called when he got
to David and told me to surrender.[35]

Silvera wanted to sack Torrijos whereas, a few months earlier, he was
helping Torrijos sack Martinez. Silvera had quarreled about the dictatorship, but, he said later, "This coup was a mistake. Pinilla was recognized as
President. He fired Torrijos and appointed me Guard commander."[36] His
promotion was short-lived, as a raging Torrijos mounted his own countercoup in a matter of hours.

"The real reason for Torrijos's successful return to Panama," said Sanjur, "was (President Anastasio) Somoza of Nicaragua," who provided him
with an aircraft after his party had flown to San Salvador from Mexico in a
rented plane on December 15, 1969.[37] This was strange. Somoza was helping Torrijos, and Torrijos was supplying arms to the communist Sandinistas for Somoza's overthrow. Torrijos's role at that time in subverting
Central American nations was documented by Lt. General Gordon Sumner,
U.S Army (Ret.), in congressional testimony on June 7, 1979 in connection
with implementing the Canal Treaties.[38]

By the time Torrijos reached Panama City, Sanjur, Silvera, and Franco
had been jailed by some of the same *Guardia* officers who had backed the
coup. Said Sanjur, "I don't think they liked losing power and privileges to a
civilian government." Six months later, on June 8, 1970, after considerable
solitary confinement and hardship, they escaped from the Carcel Modelo
jail, using a counterfeit key provided by *Guardia* Private Jose Gonzales,
eventually landing via the Canal Zone in Hoboken, N.J. on July 3, 1970
aboard the U.S. merchant vessel *Export Aid*.

After Sanjur's attempted countercoup, Torrijos placed Pinilla under house arrest, removed him from the presidency, and appointed Demetrio B. Lakas who then served almost ten years, the longest of any Panamanian President. On October 11, 1979, Aristides Royo was appointed. There had been no election in over eleven years. The Panama Treaties had been ratified under the dictator Torrijos, the "likeliest man to do the job."

KISSINGER ABOLISHES U.S. SOVEREIGN RIGHTS

With Martinez and Sanjur deposed, Torrijos settled in to run the country. The National Assembly was no problem; Martinez had abolished it the day after the coup. Torrijos notified the Nixon Administration that the 1967 treaties were rejected; and Panama returned to a no compromise position, inspired no doubt by the U.S. Senate's termination in 1971 of the Bryan-Chamarro Treaty that granted proprietary U.S. rights for a canal in Nicaragua. "Now," warned Senator Strom Thurmond, R.-S.C., "Panama will be ever so much more adamant that we give up our rights in the U.S. Canal Zone."[39] He was correct.

Robert Anderson's 9-year tenure as U.S. negotiator was marred by Panamanian intransigence and impatience with U.S. procedures. For example, on June 29, 1971, Fernando Manfredo called U.S. constitutional procedures "crass internal political requirements" contradicting U.S. foreign policy. He was objecting to "Advice and Consent" by the Senate. Later, Torrijos told U.S. Ambassador Robert Sayre that unless he got a treaty soon, the masses might "recover by force what we have been unable to achieve by negotiation."

At the instigation of Henry Kissinger in 1973, President Nixon appointed 79-year old Ellsworth Bunker as chief U.S. negotiator. Mr. Bunker, the pragmatist and veteran diplomat with ties to the Council on Foreign Relations and Foreign Policy Association, had served as Ambassador to Argentina, Italy, India, Nepal, Vietnam, and the OAS. His special mission in 1962 resulted in the loss of West New Guinea's independence to Achmed Sukarno's communist government of Indonesia. John Foster Dulles, President Eisenhower's Secretary of State, had laid the groundwork. Anti-Americanism and communism seemed to increase in countries where Bunker served.[40]

Shortly after Dr. Kissinger became Secretary of State, word was leaked that the United States might relinquish rights in the Canal Zone in order to gain a solution. Many private groups saw the threat to the Canal and began alerting the public, among them the Veterans of Foreign Wars, the Canal Zone Non-Profit Public Information Corporation, and the Emergency Committee to Save the Canal.[41]

Bunker made two quick trips to Panama in late 1973 to prepare for the "promptest possible negotiations."[42] He was also setting the stage for Kissinger's triumph on February 7, 1974 in signing the Eight-Point-Pact with Panama's Foreign Minister Juan Tack. Three of the eight points in this Statement of Principles, however, incorrectly alleged that the Canal Zone was Panamanian territory.[43] Thus, Secretary Kissinger purported to abolish single-handedly U.S. sovereign rights granted by the 1903 Treaty and confirmed by U.S. courts. Nonetheless, Kissinger's Pact remained as the basis for the 1977 Treaties.

Kissinger did not enter the Canal Zone on this his first trip, nor did he confer with the Governor or the Commander, U.S. Southern Command. He sought good will and won thunderous applause at the Legislative Palace in asserting, "The Panamanian territory in which the Canal is situated shall be returned to Panama; and I hereby commit the United States to complete the negotiations as quickly as possible." Kissinger had increased the pressure for fast action and cast the U.S. Congress as a rubber stamp. He spent the remainder of his five-hour visit with a National City Bank official, Gene Gerard. Once again he proved the efficiency of his "new diplomacy." Torrijos was pleased, too, "There wasn't anything more to ask for."

Kissinger's generosity was based on his concept of linkage which, in this case, was the managed use of force and counterforce so that benefits would flow to all concerned as long as everyone abided by the agreements. Therefore, he reasoned, giving Panama a big stake in the new treaties would inspire her to observe all terms for the mutual profit of both nations.[44]

Most Americans and members of Congress were unprepared for such lone ranger diplomacy and its astonishing Eight-Point-Pact for surrendering the Canal and its protective framework of U.S. territory. Also at issue was the constitutional procedure for disposing of territory (Article IV), as requiring action by both Houses of Congress. Dr. Donald M. Dozer, a leading authority on Latin America, wrote:

As recently as 1972 . . . the Canal Zone has been declared by the U.S. Supreme Court and other U.S. courts . . . to be "unincorporated territory of the United States" over which "Congress has complete and plenary authority." Questions involving the status of the Canal Zone therefore, lie outside the purview of the President's power under the treaty clause of the Constitution . . . A President, if acting in pursuance of the Constitution, cannot make treaties on subjects which are denied constitutionally to him or which lie within an area which he may not enter.[45]

Strom Thurmond and 38 other senators sponsored a resolution on March 28, 1974 opposing any termination of U.S. sovereign rights in the

Canal Zone. Prior to the Kissinger-Tack Principles, Mr. Thurmond had advised both Kissinger and Bunker that U.S. sovereign rights were "not negotiable." In signing the Pact, Kissinger was charged with an "egregious blunder" in committing the United States when there was no assurance that the Senate would support abrogation of sovereignty.[46]

President Ford sent out emissaries to win support. Bunker told the Rainer Club in Seattle, "We no longer can — nor would we want to be— the only country in the world exercising extra-territoriality on the soil of another country." This statement was unfair, incorrect, and worse, it was inflammatory.

An astute observer of the Canal controversy was Thomas C. Mann, a former Assistant Secretary of State. He wrote in 1975:

For 50 years the efforts to reconcile differences have been fruitless. Panama has followed the tactic of making demands, obtaining such concessions as feasible, and then making an entirely new set of demands . . . I do not believe it would serve U.S. interests to make additional concessions since there can be no safeguard against a new set of demands.[47]

Prior to the 1976 presidential elections, Mr. Ford told the Joint Chiefs of Staff to "go along with the State Department and stop rocking the boat." He appointed a deputy negotiator for defense, Lt. General W.G. "Tom" Dolvin, U.S. Army (Ret.), and issued National Security Decision Memorandum 302, strengthening defense positions and authorizing two sets of treaties. To the end, Ford favored transferring the Canal.

Phillip Harman had briefed President Ford on Panama in 1973 and thereafter, through his secretary, Mildred Leonard. He also briefed Ronald Reagan, who subsequently used the information in his speeches. When candidate Carter began winning primaries in March 1976, the Harman group approached and suggested briefings on Panama and the Canal. Efforts to reach Carter through his advisers, Matt Schaeffer, Charles H. Kirbo, and Jack Watson were futile.

Dr. Winston Robles, Director of the Panamanian Commission for Human Rights, was aghast that the United States would make a treaty with Torrijos, "condemning future generations to live under a dictator." He added:

In 1968, Panamanians found themselves under the brutal rule of one of the most corrupt and arbitrary dictatorships . . . Following the coup, the University of Panama was closed for a year, political parties were banned, newspapers and radio stations were seized, and all media controlled. Many Panamanians are tortured, incarcerated, murdered or simply disappear. . . .

Arrests are made on the grounds of "insults to the General" or "disrespect to authorities" because of private conversations. . . .

The government, its officers and friends are involved in all kinds of illegal business. The involvement of high ranking officers in drug traffic is well known. . . . Today, the military are the social, political, and economic aristocracy of a country in bankruptcy.[48]

And President Carter, despite his campaign pledge never to give up "practical control," caved in after the votes were in. He would be doing business with Omar Torrijos; and 51 years of negotiations had ended. Mr. Carter was the "likeliest man to do the job" for the United States, and Torrijos proved himself the "likeliest" for Panama.

Before a packed house on September 7, 1977 in the Hall of the Americas of the OAS Head-quarters, Washington, D.C., President Carter and General Omar Torrijos signed the Panama Canal Treaties with the OAS Secretary-General, Alejandro Orfila, center, observing. In the far background, left to right, are U.S. Negotiators Sol Linowitz and Ellsworth Bunker, face obscured, and Panama's Negotiators Romulo Escobar Bethancourt and Aristides Royo, who later became titular President of Panama under Dictator Torrijos. (Official OAS photo)

· 4 ·

'MAJOR MILITARY DEFEAT FOR THE UNITED STATES'

The new President's first order of business was to "correct an injustice"—his words. He had won on pledges of justice, integrity and good will. His thoughts were on justice for Panama primarily, it appears, and his promise to Americans "never [to] give up practical control of the Canal" was quickly scrapped. He had told the voters during the campaign that "sovereignty was not at issue." Events were to prove, however, that sovereignty was the most important issue of all. Later, in his memoirs, he wrote, "Nevertheless, I believed that a new treaty was absolutely necessary. . . . Our failure to take action after years of promises under five Presidents had created something of a diplomatic cancer. . . ."[1]

The decision to accede to Panama's demands for the Canal had been formulating through 51 years of negotiating—reinforced by Panamanian school and university textbooks teaching the "injustices" of the 1903 Treaty, and by a U.S. diplomacy that failed to take a stand for America's interests. Nonetheless, most people refused to believe the Canal would be lost. They had elected a President who had promised not to surrender "control" and who had said many times, "I'll never lie to you."

A series of interlocking developments reinforced President Carter's decision in early 1977 to move quickly into negotiations to complete the Treaties: (1) In October 1974, the first Linowitz Report, prepared by the Commission on United States-Latin American Relations, recommended "negotiating a new Canal treaty with Panama." (2) In November 1976, Linowitz and David Rockefeller of the Chase Manhattan Bank, after consulting with Torrijos in Panama, recommended that the Linowitz Report be part of the foreign policy plans of the newly elected Carter. (3) On December 26, 1976, a second Linowitz Report recommended "justice for Panama," a concept promptly endorsed by the Council on Foreign Relations. (4) In January 1977, Zbigniew Brzezinski, Carter's National Security Adviser, appointed Robert Pastor, a former Linowitz deputy, to "take charge of the Panama situation." And (5) on January 21, the day after inauguration, Pastor handed Brzezinski a National Security Memorandum that recommended "concluding new canal treaties with Panama."[2]

Dr. Brzezinski approved this memorandum and passed it on to President Carter who, after conferring with Henry Kissinger, gave it the go-ahead, i.e., negotiations were to begin at once.

NEGOTIATORS WITH CONFLICTS OF INTEREST

The appointments of Ellsworth Bunker and Sol M. Linowitz as chief negotiators for the 1977 Treaties assured an experienced American team, well versed in Panama's problems and responsive to State Department policies on Central America. Moreover, Mr. Bunker had been negotiating with Panama for the preceding three years; and Linowitz's law firm, Coudert Brothers, had had continuing involvements in Panama and Central America.

Mr. Carter's objectives for his presidency included, among other things, justice for Panama, human rights, social justice everywhere and a de-emphasis of U.S. military strategic considerations. Certainly surrender of the U.S. operated Panama Canal was an important part of this latter goal. Overall, his approach suggested a "proclivity for global disengagement."

Political observers noted, at the beginning of the negotiations with Panama, a temporizing accommodation that characterized the Carter foreign policy in general. Indeed, it was a mood well suited to surrender in dealing with the tough Latin negotiators. Columnist Kevin Phillips expressed the shift toward internationalism in this manner:

Many of Carter's foreign policy aides, such as Zbigniew Brzezinski, have written openly and boldly about their beliefs in the obsolescence of individual nation-states and "national" interests. By this yardstick, the Panama Canal is merely a vestigal bit of our imperialist past that must be sacrificed for our multinational organizational future.[3]

Earlier, Assistant Secretary of State Hewson Ryan had referred to the Canal Zone as "the last remnant of imperialism."[4] This seemed to exemplify the State Department's position. Nonetheless, it was incorrect and an unfair representation of American interests.

Remarks by U.S. negotiators were equally disturbing. Bunker said, "The United States does not own the Panama Canal Zone" and Linowitz called the Zone a "colonial enclave . . . which has caused bitter resentment." Of course, the U.S. Supreme Court and the Fifth Circuit Court of Appeals had ruled otherwise, classifying the Canal Zone as "unincorporated U.S. territory." And the United States never had a colony.

The appointment of Mr. Linowitz was for a six months period only, ending August 10, 1977; thereafter, he served as adviser. In that way, no Senate confirmation hearing was required and no potential conflicts of interest could be aired. As expected, his credentials were compatible with the President's policies and objectives, and clearly he was the right man to complement the State Department zealots. Moreover, his business and government acumen was a great asset for the negotiations to come. His background was extensive.

In 1966 Mr. Linowitz was the United States Representative to the Organization of American States with the rank of Ambassador and also, U.S. Representative on the Inter-American Committee of the Alliance for Progress. Previously, he had been chairman of the Commission on United States-Latin American Relations, a private group promoting the State Department's objectives in Panama and encouraging abandonment of the U.S. leadership role in the Western Hemisphere.[5] Another credential was his service on the board of directors of the Center for Inter-American Relations, one of whose objectives included transferring the Canal to Panama. Mr. Linowitz's qualifications for transferring the Canal to Panama were unique.

His banking connections were also unique. At the time of his appointment as negotiator, he was reported to be a member of the executive committee of the Marine-Midland Bank of New York, a participant in overdue loans of some $115 million to Panama. Under pressure from Senator Jesse Helms, R.-N.C., he resigned from this banking group.[6] At one time, he was a registered agent (number 2222) of the communist government of Chile's Salvador Allende. On February 1, 1977, as treaty negotiations were about to begin, Linowitz was an agent (number 2440) of Colombia, next door to Panama and, of course, interested in the Canal![7]

He was a long time member of the internationalist Council on Foreign Relations and the Foreign Policy Association.

With such interests, and his key role in the future of the Canal, he attracted attention. Reed Irvine of Accuracy in Media suggested that he might not be the best choice as a negotiator: He cited a 1971 case in which Linowitz's law firm, Coudert Brothers, with a $2,000 per month retainer fee, was advising Allende on confiscating American-owned copper mines.

The Chilean Marxist leader decided on a $774 million assessment. When the U.S. threatened to cut foreign aid, Linowitz complained of "unilateral" action. He resigned his job with Allende when the Justice Department ruled he would have to register as a foreign agent.[8]

In his letter to President Carter, Senator Helms asked about the legal propriety and breach of good faith in the six-months-only appointment of Linowitz—an appointment that required no Senate investigation and confirmation. Both Senators Helms and James A. McClure, R.-Ida., demanded hearings. None were held. Mr. Helms asked the obvious question of his colleagues on the Senate floor:

Is it beyond reason that members of the banking fraternity involved in Panama are looking to the proposed surrender of U.S. sovereignty and territory in the Canal Zone as a way of propping up the Torrijos regime and providing increased revenues to his government? Is it not fair to ask whether the short-range interests of those financial institutions might not be subordinated to the long-term interests of the United States?[9]

Senator Helms was referring to the interests of the banks in the outcome of the negotiations under the Bunker-Linowitz team. These institutions had heavy financial stakes in the survival of Omar Torrijos, who had begun his dictatorship in 1968 with bank debts of $150 million that had mushroomed by 1977 to almost $3 billion.[10] In trying to attract financial support, Torrijos had made Panama a banking sanctuary, with tax advantages, gold trading, and a sort of financial free port devoid of restrictive banking regulations. His obligations could be amortized with tolls from the Canal, a source of revenue that always tantilized some of Panama's leaders. In 1977, Panama's economy was in shambles, public spending out of control, and labor costs so high that Panamanian products were not competitive on the world market. Enter Ambassadors Bunker and Linowitz to prepare treaties that were bound to have a profound impact on the economy and bank investments.

THE UNITED STATES V. A 'STACKED DECK'

The 1977 negotiations were quite different from the preceding 21 years of bargaining. The United States had nothing to trade, having already conceded eight major points in the 1974 Kissinger-Tack Statement of Principles, as follows: (1) abrogation of the 1903 Treaty, (2) prompt transfer of jurisdiction to Panama, (3) Panamanian sovereignty over the Canal Zone, (4) a fixed termination date for the new treaties, (5) increased economic benefits for Panama, (6) joint defense of the Canal, (7) joint operation of the Canal until termination of the treaties, and (8) provisions for enlarging the Canal.[11]

The U.S. situation in 1977 was virtually the antithesis of the position in 1964 when Mr. Bunker told the OAS that each government was free to discuss anything without "the insistence of one of the parties on a precondition. . . ." Thus, after 13 years of pressure, the Panamanians had achieved their major goals even before sitting down at the negotiating table, and could thereafter concentrate on additional benefits. It was a "stacked deck." At one point, negotiator Bethancourt was demanding $5 billion for continued use of the Canal by the United States and for "rental" of military bases.[12]

The American and Panamanian negotiators began their work on February 13, 1977, a scant three weeks after President Carter took office. The scene was the tropical island of Contadora, some 30 miles off Panama's Pacific coast. The Panamanian representatives included Romulo Escobar Bethancourt, the fiery left-leaning educator; Nicolas Gonzalez-Revilla, the new foreign minister; and Edwin Fabrega Velarde, Jaime Arias and Adolfo Ahumada, the latter another leftist.

The American team also had five members, headed up by Ambassadors Ellsworth Bunker and Sol Linowitz with State Department regulars, Richard Wyrough and S. Morey Bell. The Defense Department representative was Lt. General Welborn G. "Tom" Dolvin, U.S. Army (Ret.).

But the Contadora rounds were short-lived when the Panamanians rejected U.S. ideas on neutrality and defense. The negotiators went home and the next session was a secret one in New York City at the Century Club on West 43rd Street, an association dedicated, among other things, to "congeniality and above all inspiring talk." Among the Centurions were Henry Kissinger, Ellsworth Bunker, Sol Linowitz, McGeorge Bundy, David Rockefeller and Cyrus Vance.

New York seemed to be a favorite negotiating place for the Panama Treaties. Previously, Robert Anderson had done a good part of his negotiating for President Johnson in New York also, near the center of the banking world. It is notable that the "highest priority" of President Carter's foreign policy would be negotiated, at least in part, in the city of the banks which ultimately would benefit from favorable Treaties for the repayment of massive loans made to Omar Torrijos's regime.

Negotiations were shifted to Washington. The major points had already been conceded, but detailed negotiations remained for agreement on the size of the economic benefits for Panama, the designation of the land and water areas to be used by the United States in meeting operational and defense responsibilities, possible future expansion and modernization of the Canal and possibly a new canal, and the duration of the new Treaties.[13]

Outside pressure for concessions and quick action included threats of violence and sabotage to the Canal. For example, Panama's chief negotiator Bethancourt delivered a fiery "bomb-at-the-waist" speech to university students against any U.S. military presence after the Treaties took effect, hinting that the Torrijos government would not oppose sabotage, ". . . we can get more, much more, through confrontation. . . . When one wants confrontation, one puts his knapsack on his back, his bomb at the waist, and goes to stage the confrontation."[14]

The first order of business for the negotiators was the matter of sovereignty: Panama would immediately exercise sovereignty and police authority, and the U.S. Canal Zone government would terminate. Such precipitate action, however, posed problems for a smooth transition; and it was decided that the U.S. would continue the basic services relating to schools, hospitals, public utilities and fire protection, subject to regulation by the Panamanians. Next on the agenda was the concept of joint operation of the Canal until the year 2000, and increased Panamanian participation. A joint administration, which later became the Panama Canal Commission, was decided upon, albeit this is an operational concept generally considered contrary to fundamental organization principles wherein responsibility and authority cannot be shared or separated. The third major item was joint defense. Panama demanded total responsibility for the defense of the waterway once the Treaties expired. U.S. representatives claimed permanent defense rights which eventually became part of the Neutrality Treaty as the DeConcini reservation.

Initially in 1977, the negotiators considered two solutions for defense: A joint board of equal numbers of U.S. and Panamanians would consult and plan jointly for the security and neutrality of the Canal. The second proposal would have each country act on its own. The first proposal would create a two-headed command with no commander, and the second would establish two separate commands, each free to go its own way. The eventual solution was the nine-member Panama Canal Commission for operating and maintaining the Canal with defense responsibilities included in the Amendments and Reservations to the Treaties.

The U.S. Canal operators in 1977 had virtually no opportunity for input or suggestions to the negotiators who rushed back and forth settling the details necessary to get ratified Treaties. By one count, Michael G. Kozak, the State Department treaty coordinator, made some two dozen trips from Washington without once contacting the Canal administrators or counselors.

President Carter set June 1 as the target date for the negotiators, just over four months into his term. But the date was not met. Money was the problem. At one point, the Panamanians were demanding one billion dollars as a down payment and an additional 300 million dollars per year during the life of the Treaties—altogether a payment of about $7 billion from the U.S. Treasury. Torrijos had had his young economists draw up this package as a "condition for signing anything."[15]

With time running out on Linowitz's six-months appointment, Carter warned the Panamanians to tone down the money demands or else the U.S. Senate would not approve. Consequently with the important concessions already gained, the Treaties were soon wrapped up. And on August 10, 1977 in Panama, the chief negotiators for both sides held a news conference to announce "agreement in principle" on the basic elements of the Treaties. Only the final language remained to be drafted.[16]

President Carter's goal was in sight. He wanted the blessings of U.S. hemispheric neighbors, and drew up his Declaration of Washington, which resulted, however, in a diplomatic faux pas when he tried to implement it. Latin American heads of state, enroute to Washington for the September 7 signing ceremonies, were handed copies of the Declaration for signature. They balked. Said one angry diplomat, "This action is without precedent in the history of diplomacy." Later, a watered-down version was issued.[17]

Treaties for the transfer of this strategic and economic waterway from the American taxpayers to a debt-ridden dictator constituted a prideful accomplishment for both sets of negotiators. It seemed that the Americans and Panamanians had worked as a team against those opposed to the transfer. Linowitz protested charges that he bowed to pressure from Panama and the banks, saying, "We got a good deal on these Treaties and we ought to recognize that."[18] In turn, Bethancourt told the National Assembly of Panama on August 19, 1977: The United States will have no defense rights after the year 2000, will not decide on the Canal's neutrality, and will not get priority passage for its warships after the year 2000, even in time of war. He added that Panama did not feel obligated to abide by the Neutrality Treaty in cases of foreign attacks or internal disorders and that the United States role would be very limited until the year 2000 and almost nonexistent thereafter.[19]

Professor Donald M. Dozer of the University of California, Santa Barbara was warning about the failure to defend U.S. geopolitical strengths against foreign powers:

As to the policy of the United States, it should be clearly emphasized that when we fail to defend and take advantage of our own geopolitical strengths, of which the Panama Canal is a major one, or, worse, when we allow the national administration to surrender control over them and let them pass out of our possession into the hands of foreign powers, we are contributing to a process of national suicide, and international instability, which serves the interests of these foreign powers. *When a nation fails to defend its own, it is inviting extinction.*[20]

On August 13, 1977, Dr. Dozer repeated his warning: "The State Department's surrender of the Canal Zone, if allowed to be consummated, will be the equivalent of a major military defeat for the United States."[21]

RATIFICATION PROCEDURES ARE QUESTIONED

The long debate over ratifying the 1977 Treaties was in marked contrast to the prompt action by both nations in handling the 1903 Treaty. In 1903 Panama wanted independence and assurances of U.S. support and benefits; the United States wanted a secure route for a trans-Isthmian canal and an end to the bickering. Approval was swift on both sides. By 1977 these pristine motives had changed: An impatient Panama demanded the Canal and more benefits as well. A subdued America was determined to surrender.

When the debates on ratification began, Chairman John J. Sparkman, D.-Ala., of the Senate Foreign Relations Committee had his staff prepare a comprehensive memorandum, titled *The Role of the Senate in Treaty Ratification* (November 1977), for the guidance of his colleagues. This work included procedures and examples on ratifying and abrogating treaties, as furnished by the Congressional Research Service of the Library of Congress. However, in 78 pages of precedents and instructions, there was nothing on perhaps the most relevant treaty of all: the Clayton-Bulwer Treaty (1850) with Great Britain on the subject of an Isthmian canal. What could be more pertinent? This omission may have misled the Committee into believing that the 1903 Treaty could be terminated properly by the 1977 Treaties without further action.

The Clayton-Bulwer example would show that Congress in 1880 responded with a joint resolution authorizing the President to abrogate the Treaty. Such a joint resolution for abrogating treaties is the correct procedure, both under the Constitution (Article VI) as a "Law of the Land" and under *Jefferson's Manual,* the accepted parliamentary guide for Congress. In 1880, proper procedure was observed. In 1900, Great Britain agreed to a "friendly annulment," and the replacement agreement became the Hay-Pauncefote Treaty (1901) which was duly negotiated and ratified, with both nations following their own practices. This latter treaty, stipulating that Canal tolls be non-discriminatory, remains in force even after the 1977 Treaties with Panama.

Why did the analysts of the Congressional Research Service and

Sparkman's Committee *omit,* in their study and consideration, the most obvious treaty relating to the matter at hand: the Clayton-Bulwer Treaty? Was it to avoid a joint resolution that would involve the House of Representatives where opposition to the Treaties was intense?

The President's role in treaty-making stems from Article II of the Constitution which empowers him "by and with the Advice and Consent of the Senate to make treaties, provided two-thirds of the Senators present concur." Therefore, the President *makes and ratifies,* provided he receives a two-thirds vote of approval. U.S. procedures include negotiations, signing, concurrence by two-thirds of the Senators, ratification by the President, exchange of instruments of ratification by the parties, and proclamation, after which the treaties are legally binding. Contrary to popular belief, the Senate does *not* ratify treaties. The President ratifies, but only after the Senate concurs. Nonetheless, the Senate is very influential in concluding treaties.

The procedure in Panama deserves careful attention. The 1972 Panamanian Constitution requires that treaties signed by the Executive covering the Panama Canal must be submitted to a national plebiscite for approval by the people. Whereas, Panamanian Law 33 of September 13, 1977 submitted the two Treaties to the plebiscite of October 23, this law did not provide for future changes to the Treaties.

"Therefore, the law governing the subject (changes) must be interpreted by resorting to sources other than the statutes themselves,"[22] concluded Eduardo Abbot, an Hispanic law expert for the Library of Congress. These "other sources" included Panamanian law professors and distinguished scholars in constitutional and international law, as well as American specialists in this field. Overwhelmingly, the findings called for a second plebiscite for approval of the substantive changes that had been added by the U.S. Senate.

The compelling reason was that an amended treaty is a rejected treaty, requiring reratification as a new treaty by the other party. Both Panamanian and American spokesmen said so at the time, including U.S. Secretary of State Cyrus Vance and Panama's Omar Torrijos, both of whom warned during the early stages of dissent that Senate amendments would require a second plebiscite. But they changed their minds. Mr. Vance reversed himself after Torrijos had "concluded that no new plebiscite will be required." Gambling on a second plebiscite for approval of explicit U.S. rights was not to be chanced.

Among the Panamanians who spoke out for a second plebiscite were Carlos Bolivar Pedreschi, a leading constitutional scholar; Dr. Julio Linares, professor of law; Dr. Cesar Quintero, Dean of the Law and Political Science School of the University of Panama; and Dr. Arnulfo Arias, a former three-times President of Panama.

Among the Americans concerned about a second plebiscite and therefore, about constitutional procedures in Panama were the late Senator Frank Church and former Senator Dick Clark. Moreover, a number of scholars in international law have repeatedly warned that treaties in violation of a nation's constitutional procedures are not legally binding. These experts include Green H. Hackworth, a former legal adviser to the State Department, and Professors L. Oppenheim and J. L. Brierly. But no second plebiscite was held to permit the Panamanian people to vote on the major changes added to the Treaties by the U.S. Senate.

Therefore, the obvious danger to the existing Panama Canal Treaties (1977) is that at any future date, Panama's Supreme Court, empowered with the "guardianship of the integrity of the Constitution" under Article 188 of the 1972 Constitution, could find that the amendments were not officially published and properly presented to the Panamanian people and therefore, unconstitutional and not binding upon Panama. Thus, Panama could legally, under its constitutional procedures, throw out all six U.S. changes to the Treaties, including U.S. rights to defend the Canal unilaterally.

Consequently, the paradox of invalid Treaties haunts both sides: Under its laws, Panama "accepted" Treaties that did not legally contain the U.S. amendments. On the other hand, under its Constitution, the United States "accepted" Treaties that did not legally contain the Panamanian counter reservation that limited U.S. defense rights. Consequently, there are two sets of Treaties.

Question: Did the framers of Panamanian Law 33 foresee possible complications should a second plebiscite ever be needed to approve major changes that the United States might add and therefore, did these framers purposely omit any provision for the people's approval of such changes? If so, they succeeded in avoiding another serious challenge, for the time being, to acceptance of the Treaties while at the same time laying the groundwork for future conflict. And, in effect, this shortcoming of Law 33, whether planned or not, served as another example of deception and ambiguity.

'WOULD YOU PERSUADE, SPEAK OF INTEREST'

While Ambassadors Bunker and Linowitz had done their work in producing treaties that had eluded their predecessors, albeit at a price, the most difficult task lay ahead: ratification. In September 1977, public opinion polls showed 78% opposed to the Treaties, 8% in favor and 14% undecided. Prospects in the Senate were called "dismal." Later, President Carter would write in his memoirs: "If I could have foreseen early in 1977 the terrible battle we would face in Congress, it would have been a great temptation for me to avoid the issue—at least during my first term." He had much persuading to do. "Would you persuade, speak of interest, not of reason" (Benjamin Franklin).

The Senators had interests. Senator Herman Talmadge, D.-Ga., switched in favor of the Treaties after the White House dropped opposition to his pet $2.3 billion farm bill. Senator Dennis DeConcini, D.-Ariz., made up his mind after the Administration dropped its opposition to buying $250 million worth of Arizona copper, causing one official to comment, "I hope the Panamanians get as much out of these Treaties as some United States Senators."[23]

But Senator Paul Hatfield, D.-Mont., paid a price. He cast the deciding vote (the 67th), having been appointed to the Senate a few weeks beforehand by Montana Governor Tom Judge after the death of Senator Les Metcalf, a strong opponent of the Canal Treaties. Hatfield had stepped down as Chief Justice of the Montana Supreme Court. After his unpopular vote, he decided not to run for the Senate in 1978. President Carter then appointed him U.S. District Judge, U.S. District Court, District of Montana, Great Falls Division, still serving in 1985.

Nonetheless, in September 1977 at least a dozen more votes were needed and the assistance of the Senate leadership was important. So, President Carter enlisted the services of former President Jerry Ford, former Secretary of State Henry Kissinger, and the Senate Minority Leader, Howard Baker, R.-Tenn., among others. Then, he requested that none of the Senators speak in opposition to the Treaties until they knew the details. He wrote in his diary for August 9, 1977: "Apparently it worked with most of them except for a few nuts like Strom Thurmond and Jesse Helms."

The President staged an elaborate signing ceremony on September 7, 1977 in Washington, D.C., attended by 18 heads of state, General Torrijos, three foreign ministers, and one vice president, along with ex-President Ford, Lady Bird Johnson and other dignitaries—a great plus for the Treaties and "a vivid demonstration of the international significance of the Treaties," said President Carter.[24]

However, according to Panama's Constitution, Omar Torrijos should *not* have signed the Treaties. Article 163 requires "the President of Panama alone . . . to conduct foreign relations . . . and to enter into international treaties and agreements, . . ." and the President was Demetrio Lakas.

Carter and Torrijos were the principals at the signing ceremony, but Panama's President and Vice President should have done the signing. In regard to President Carter's participation, Alfred J. Schweppe, the veteran attorney from Seattle, Washington, has observed, ". . . the Secretary of State traditionally signs treaties in the first instance, not the President. As I have pointed out, the President does not sign until after the Senate consents to ratification."[25]

A few days later, on September 16, 1977, the President sent the Treaties to the Senate for advice and consent which was given some months later: March 16, 1978 for the Neutrality Treaty and April 18, 1978 for the Panama Canal Treaty. But, in September 1977, Carter had a long way to go. By the end of the year, he had brought to the White House for personal briefings: hundreds of college presidents, editors, party bigwigs, elected officials, campaign contributors and other leaders from across the nation.

Meanwhile, the administrators at the State Department were making over 1,500 appearances throughout the country to explain the Treaties directly to the people in a gigantic public information effort. It appears that no potential supporters were neglected. Other groups receiving special attention were: religious organizations, senior citizens, business leaders, Jaycees, garden clubs, school teachers, Common Cause and labor union officials. These groups and individuals were given the red carpet routine.[26]

Ambassador Sol Linowitz made many appeals to influential groups. One was before a luncheon meeting of civic clubs and trade organizations in Houston, Texas on February 1, 1978. His assertions that sovereignty over the Canal Zone remained with Panama and that the Joint Chiefs of Staff "warmly endorsed" the Treaties were refuted with documentation introduced by the moderator, Mr. Richard M. Miller, a distinguished Houston attorney. Linowitz did not convert this group whose most vocal reaction came from the answer to a question asking if the Treaties gave "head of line" to U.S. warships in emergencies. "It's not in the treaty, but it's understood," answered Linowitz. This answer brought down the house.

PROBLEMS IN SELLING THE TREATIES

While the Carter Administration was selling the Treaties to Americans, the Panamanians were having problems. Some, including the top negotiator, Romulo Escobar Bethancourt, over-eager to prove they had obtained a good deal, were publicly misinterpreting the Treaties, particularly the portions guaranteeing U.S. rights to keep open the Canal and "head of line" priority for U.S. warships in emergency. These points were *not* "understood between the parties," as alleged by Mr. Linowitz.

Panamanian officials were repudiating these "privileges" for the United States. So, on October 14, 1977, President Carter and Torrijos met in Washington and issued their famous Statement of Understanding which was designed to resolve these differences. Even so, General Torrijos did not sign this Understanding and, returning home the next day, charmed a waiting airport crowd, saying, "I hadn't even signed my autograph."[27]

This deception by Torrijos and apparent over-eagerness by Carter bring to mind the emotions displayed incident to the treaty signing a few weeks earlier: President Carter had noted that his respect for Torrijos increased the more "I learned about this man." The Panamanian newspaper quoted his apology to the people of Panama:

The more I read of the history of Panama, the more ashamed I feel. General Torrijos, you and the Panamanian people have been very patient and in my name, I ask forgiveness from your great people.[28]

The next step was the plebiscite in Panama, the constitutional requirement for acceptance or rejection of the Treaties. While the unsigned Carter-Torrijos understanding had no legal standing, it apparently satisfied the Panamanians who approved the Treaties in their October 23, 1977 vote. Next, it was the turn of the U.S. Senate. In due time, both Majority Leader Byrd and Minority Leader Baker announced their support—a great boost since President Carter wanted no amendments to the texts of the Treaties in order to honor his pledge to Torrijos. Nonetheless, additions were made in the form of amendments, reservations, conditions and understandings—all substantive changes that needed approval in Panama by another plebiscite. None was held because of the high risk of disapproval that would mean no Treaties. Senator Griffin predicted, "... there is danger that the dictator Torrijos will accept and ratify these changes himself. Indeed, that's what President Carter expects him to do."[29] Torrijos *did* ratify them by himself, and later voided U.S. defense rights with his counter-reservation.

The big story in October 1977 was the Carter-Torrijos Statement of Understanding that was supposed to clarify three main issues: joint U.S.-Panamanian rights to defend the Canal, unilateral U.S. rights to enter Panama to reopen a closed Canal in emergency, and head of line privileges for warships of both nations. Ultimately, these provisions became the substance of Leadership Amendments 20 and 21 to the Neutrality Treaty and were incorporated in the U.S. instruments of ratification as Amendments (1) and (2) respectively. Two other important additions were attached as Conditions to the Neutrality Treaty: the DeConcini reservation guaranteeing U.S. rights to defend and keep open the Canal, and a proviso for future negotiations for defense sites and for the stationing of U.S. forces in Panama after December 31, 1999. Obviously these are substantive changes, but Panamanians did not vote on them.

In early October 1977, Senator Robert Dole, R.-Kan., released the contents of a confidential State Department cable from Ray Gonzalez, the U.S. Embassy deputy chief of mission in Panama, warning that the Panamanians were placing entirely different interpretations on U.S. rights for priority handling of U.S. warships and rights to reopen a closed Canal. This cable disclosed that a key Treaties adviser to Torrijos, Carlos Lopez Guevara, had taken strong exceptions to statements made by Carter officials before the Senate Foreign Relations Committee. Guevara said, "Panama cannot agree to the right of the U.S. to intervene," and added that Royo and Bethancourt, the Panama negotiators, rejected head-of-line privileges for U.S. warships.

Senators were shocked. But equally shocking was the source of this bombshell: a State Department cable—a cable that revealed another cover up and that confirmed the continuing disparities between the two countries on the most important issues.[30] Moreover, this disclosure specifically contradicted the major arguments for ratification used by Secretary of State Cyrus Vance and the negotiators, Ellsworth Bunker and Sol Linowitz. Further, it demolished the Administration's contention that similar statements by Panama's top negotiator, Romulo Escobar Bethancourt, were only misgivings. Panama's defenders rose to the occasion. Said Linowitz, Bethancourt's remarks were political and merely an attempt to gain support in Panama.

Nonetheless, these were the words of Panama's chief negotiator. He had told the National Assembly of Panama on August 19, 1977, Appendix G, ". . . U.S. warships could not be granted preferential rights" and ". . . the Canal's neutrality was an act relating to Panama's sovereignty."[31] Later, Bethancourt was even more emphatic, telling newsmen in Panama City that the Gringos with their warships would not have special rights under the "famous expeditious passage" amendment. He said, ". . . expeditious passage does not mean privileged passage and the concept of privileged passage was rejected. . . . We cannot go that far."[32]

An important part of selling the Treaties was convincing undecided Senators. Some 45 made the trip to Panama and were briefed by Torrijos and Lt. General Dennis P. "Phil" McAuliffe, Commander of the U.S. Southern Command. President Carter called Torrijos his best salesman, with his calm strength and pledges for democracy, human rights, and cooperation. At one point, when under heaviest criticism, Torrijos offered to resign, but took no action. If he had resigned, he would be relinquishing power seized at gunpoint, and presumably, could have returned the same way.

A number of popular conservatives backed the Treaties, including John Wayne and William F. Buckley, Jr., countering to a degree Ronald Reagan's opposition. Many of Mr. Wayne's arguments were almost verbatim State Department positions, and many "facts" incorrect. For instance, he claimed that Panama's bank debt was only $355 million, whereas the Library of Congress on July 21, 1977 reported "$2.722 billion in claims on Panama by U.S. banks." Wayne's allegations about sovereignty, costs to American taxpayers, and rental of 120,000 acres in the Canal Zone were simply unsupportable.[33] John Wayne had strong personal ties to Panama: He was a friend of President Harmodio Arias and of Arias's sons Tito and Tony, the latter godfather to one of Wayne's daughters.

William Jorden in *Panama Odyssey* defended Wayne and attacked Ronald Reagan for misstatements, inaccuracies, and complete untruths (pp.489-90). He gave as an example Reagan's observation that "once ratified, there's no guarantee our Naval Fleet will have the right of priority passage in time of war," and compounded his error by asserting "that right did not exist under the 1903 Treaty." On the contrary on both counts, Bethancourt rejected many times *guarantees* of priority passage. And under the 1903 Treaty, the United States had sovereign rights "to the entire exclusion" of Panama, and routinely expedited U.S. warships through the Canal. Without question.

John Wayne influenced many people. A Stayskal *Chicago Tribune* cartoon of this period showed a public opinion poll-taker telling his boss: "As for the Panama Canal Treaties, 22% said no, 17% said yes, and 61% said, 'whatever side it was John Wayne said he was on.' "

The Buckley-Reagan television debate on the Public Broadcasting Service network on January 23, 1978 highlighted facts and misconceptions. Buckley ridiculed Reagan's account of Canal Zone history, citing Panamanian pride in providing three-fourths of the Canal work force and urging future cooperation with Panama. By transferring the Canal, said Buckley, the U.S. would be "spiritually better off, economically better off, and militarily better off."

Reagan, in turn, reminded listeners that the other one-fourth of the Canal force comprised U.S. managers and engineers for the most part, that Panama could nationalize the Canal under protection of the UN Charter, and that the United States had paid Panama, Colombia, the French, and the individual land owners and squatters for the Canal Zone—the only time in history where individuals were paid in a territorial transfer nation to nation. Panama had tried, he added, for independence from Colombia 50 times before the U.S. came along to guarantee that independence and construct a canal beneficial to the new nation and to the rest of the world.

This debate was one of many, as both sides sent out their legions to convert the public. Secretary of State Vance had interesting experiences. During the question and answer period in Charleston, W.Va., a Mr. Maloney rose unsteadily to his feet and asked, "What's your name? Lance?" Taken aback at being mistaken for Bert Lance, Carter's former Budget Director, he replied, "No, I'm Vance." A few moments later, Maloney commented, "If this treaty is approved, it will be a bigger scandal than Watergate." Applause.[34]

Audiences at New Orleans, Los Angeles, and Louisville were critical of Vance's assurances of U.S. rights to intervene and keep the Canal open. In New Orleans, Ed Butler, a radio talk show host, received a round of applause in likening the U.S. withdrawal from Panama to the American retreat from Vietnam, "When the United States withdraws, the communists advance." In Louisville, Governor Julian M. Carrol, introducing Secretary Vance, said, "It would have been easy for me to be against the Treaties because . . . only ten percent of the people in Kentucky favor them. But the issue on the Treaties is whether you are willing to send your son or daughter or yourself to Panama to defend our Canal."[35] Strange. If U.S. rights are not to be defended, the United States is finished.

Meanwhile, the "truth squad" was busy: Senators Paul Laxalt and Jake Garn, Representative Larry McDonald, Admiral John C. McCain, Jr., Maj. General John K. Singlaub, among others, were criss-crossing the country with the other side of the story, and, according to reports, winning more applause than the Administration salesmen. The late Larry McDonald drew cheers, "The American people are tired of foreign policy planners who find beauty in retreat and glory in defeat." Admiral McCain, former commander of Naval forces in the Pacific, warned, "The Soviet Union is trying every trick in the trade to take over the Canal. . . . It is absolutely absurd to think of giving it away."

Many members of the Congress who voted to give away the Canal took refuge in the pragmatism of Edmund Burke, the British statesman, who told his Bristol constituency in 1774, "Your representative owes you, not his industry only but his judgment; and he betrays you instead of serving you if he sacrifices it to your opinion." As for judging the outcome of the Treaties debates, Senator Garn was accurate, "There is no doubt in my mind that the Treaties will pass simply because a Democratic President has submitted them to a Democratic Congress."[36]

Many top-level officials worked almost full time in advancing the Treaties through the Senate. On the other hand, Chairman John C. Stennis, D.-Miss., provided a forum for the retired military community and conservatives in general with hearings before the Armed Services Committee. The outspoken condemnation of the Treaties by retired senior officers reinforced public opposition and was a source of frustration for the President, who said, "The active military leaders, with the responsibility for our nation's defense on their shoulders," supported the Treaties. Over 99% of 200 retired senior officers, including Admirals Moorer and McCain, and Lt. General V.H. Krulak, USMC, opposed the Treaties. Mr. Carter wrote in his memoirs:

This was a pattern I was to observe many times while I was President—irresponsibly belligerent statements by older retired officers and carefully considered and reasonable testimony by those still in service.

Active duty officers, however, must support the Commander-in-Chief's policies and those who openly criticize either resign or retire. Retired officers have no such restraints.

THE 'ENTHUSIASM' OF THE JOINT CHIEFS OF STAFF

A persistent argument for ratification was that the Canal could not be defended. In early 1978, Defense Secretary Harold Brown said he preferred a cooperative effort with Panama rather than "an American garrison amid hostile surroundings." General McAuliffe agreed and said he would need 100,000 soldiers for a reasonable defense, a considerable increase from the 7,000 he had estimated in May 1977. Admiral Moorer noted that McAuliffe's 100,000 estimate came from a "worst situation" study based on the assumption that the Cubans could secretly infiltrate 12-15,000 troops into Panama.

General McAuliffe's role in the Carter Administration also involved Nicaragua's fall to the communist Sandinistas who ousted President Somoza on July 17, 1979. Earlier, McAuliffe, on a "human rights" mission for President Carter, reportedly told Somoza, ". . . peace will not come to Nicaragua until you have removed yourself from the presidency and the scene."[37] When asked about this statement on June 7, 1979 during his testimony on the implementation of the Treaties before the House Subcommittee on the Panama Canal, he denied making it: twice to Carroll Hubbard, Jr., D.-Ken., and once to William Carney, R.-N.Y., according to the hearing record (pp.172, 173, 186). When asked if the Canal could be defended, he said, ". . . I have forces enough, and I could call on more forces. . . ." After the Treaties were implemented by Public Law 96-70, Carter appointed McAuliffe the Administrator of the new Panama Canal Commission.

President Carter said on numerous occasions that the Joint Chiefs of Staff enthusiastically supported the Treaties; this became one of his strongest points. Secretary Brown was reported to have said in a speech in Phoenix, Ariz., "If any of the Joint Chiefs of Staff opposed the ratification of the Panama Canal Treaties, they would be 'muzzled.' They would be free to criticize the Treaties, but if they do, they should be prepared to resign."[38]

Opposition to the Treaties by former members of the Joint Chiefs and by retired senior officers was virtually unanimous, one poll showing 321 out of 324 opposed to the Treaties. On June 6, 1977, several months before the intense ratification push began and in time for President Carter to retreat with some grace, four former Chiefs of Naval Operations sent the President a joint letter, saying, in part: ". . . we believe we have an obligation to you and the nation to offer our combined judgment on the strategic value of the Panama Canal to the United States." Appendix H is the text of the two-page letter.

Mr. Carter was reported to have been "taken aback" by this letter from four of the greatest living naval strategists: Admirals Robert B. Carney, Arleigh A. Burke, George W. Anderson, and Thomas H. Moorer, saying:

Mr. President, you have become our leader at a time when the adequacy of our naval capabilities is being seriously challenged. The existing maritime threat to us is compounded by the possibility that the Canal under Panamanian sovereignty could be neutralized or lost, depending on that government's relationship with other nations. We note that the present Panamanian government has close ties with the present Cuban government which in turn is closely tied to the Soviet Union. Loss of the Panama Canal, which would be a serious set-back in war, would contribute to the encirclement of the U.S. by hostile naval forces, and threaten our ability to survive.

The Panama Canal represents a vital portion of our U.S. naval and maritime assets, all of which are absolutely essential for free world security. It is our considered individual and combined judgment that you should instruct our negotiators to retain full sovereign control for the United States over both the Panama Canal and its protective frame, the U.S. Canal Zone as provided in the existing treaty.

This message on behalf of "free world security" had no effect and the President continued. He had the support of the Chairman of the Joint Chiefs of Staff, Air Force General George Brown and all members: Army General Bernard W. Rogers, Navy Admiral James L. Holloway III, Air Force General David C. Jones and Marine Corps General Louis Wilson.

What caused the sharp differences in evaluation between the active duty senior officers and those retired? Colonel Sam Dickens, a former senior member of the U.S. Air Force planning staff, explained that the long-established planning procedures of the armed forces had broken down under political pressure in the case of the Treaties. The shift in position by the Joint Chiefs (JCS), he said, subverted the logical and intensive staff work that had developed a tenable position. This position, among other things, guaranteed an adequate U.S. military access and authorized presence in the Canal Zone for defense and emergency operations once control passed to Panama.[39]

The Treaties contained no such guarantees and this was the worry of the JCS planners, i.e., the senior military officers on the staff of the Joint Chiefs, who have responsibility for planning national defense. Their task was planning the security and defense of the United States and its citizens in the most literal sense of these words, honestly and professionally, and with the highest degree of sincerity and responsibility. To perform this task in any other fashion would be unthinkable for these conscientious planners. As for the Carter-Torrijos Treaties, these JCS planners simply believed them to be flawed and in drastic need of major revisions if United States interests and security were to be protected.

Colonel Dickens described the joint planning procedures in detail where the Armed Service representatives meet with the JCS representatives for the preparation of joint papers on whatever the topic may be. Then, the papers are returned to the Service Chiefs for approval. If there are problems, the papers go to the Joint Chiefs themselves, i.e., to the "JCS Tank." Colonel Dickens continued with frank revelations:

The papers had gone forward and the Joint Chiefs were sticking to their positions and supported what their staffs were doing despite all the pressures that were coming from Dolvin (Lt. General W.G. Dolvin, U.S. Army, (Ret.), called back to active duty to help with the Treaties) and from the State Department.

But the Joint Staff resisted the pressure, and the Service Chiefs and the Joint Chiefs of Staff supported them. Then, without question, there was political pressure on the Joint Chiefs of Staff and also pressure from the Secretary of the Army. This was discussed internally . . . this pressure, we knew the pressure was being exerted, but the Services were holding firm.

And what happened? There was a prayer breakfast—you know, those annual prayer breakfasts that the high officials attend—well, the Joint Chiefs came back from a prayer breakfast and announced they would go along with the Administration's position. They had listened to comments at the prayer breakfast. So, then the Director of the Joint Staff, a three-star admiral, went to the J-5 of the Western Hemisphere Division that had the action for the Treaties and the idea was that the Joint Staff would prepare a position paper to support the decision that had already been made. In other words, the Joint Chiefs of Staff deserted the decision that had been made through the joint process and with the Service participation.

They have authority to do that unilaterally, but now, the three-star officer, Director of the Joint Staff, was looking for supporting paperwork to back this decision. He went to the action officer, a Lt. Colonel on the Joint Staff, and this officer called in the Service representatives of the Army, Navy, Marine Corps and Air Force. They met together. My representative attended and later reported to me that those officers had said, "No"—and all those relatively junior officers, in that they were not the key officials, said "No"—that they'd have nothing to do with development of any paperwork that could substantiate this decision of the Joint Chiefs of Staff and that's the way it ended.

Now, the JCS, of course, have the authority to make decisions on their own, but what I'm saying is that the final decision that paved the way for the final Treaties was based on the JCS themselves making the decision that was not supported by their respective Service Staffs or the Joint Staff. . . .

Without question, it was political pressure on the Joint Chiefs of Staff. It is almost unheard of that the JCS take action that is not supported by their respective planners in the staff process. . . . So, this was very demoralizing when things happen in the military and the Chiefs all cave in . . . also, it shows a lack of appreciation of being out-flanked by the Soviet Union in Central America. . . .

Concern for the Canal nearly always came down to national security. So, if the military doesn't think it (the Canal) is fundamental or vital to national security interests, then that undermines support from Senators and Congressmen who say, "How can we worry about it if the military who are charged with that responsibility are really not concerned?"[39]

THE CONCEPT OF DUAL LOYALTY

The completely opposing views between the active duty military chiefs and their retired counterparts were primarily caused by political pressure: The political leadership did not want advice that conflicted with its goals and preconceptions. Without the support of the Joint Chiefs, the Treaties probably would have failed. The chiefs of the branches of the armed forces are members of the JCS, appointed by the President and serving at his pleasure. Any substantial disagreement with national policy, such as the Panama treaties, would not be tolerated.

The President is not only the Commander-in-Chief. He is also a citizen elected to serve the people—a man desperately in need of the wisest counsel to help him discharge his great responsibilities. He is not an all-wise, omnipotent "emperor chosen by God to head our national family."[40] He needs, and the nation expects, the best professional advice and support available. Hanson W. Baldwin, the author and historian, had written:

The Joint Chiefs, in fact the uniformed officers of all services, owe loyalty and obedience to the Commander-in-Chief but they also have an obligation to the Congress, as well as to the President, to provide frank appraisals of all military matters. The fundamental fidelity is to the nation, not to any single administration, and the founding fathers undoubtedly intended to emphasize the dual loyalties involved.[41]

Some time before the Joint Chiefs faced their dilemma over the Panama Treaties, Mr. Baldwin had written in his review of General Maxwell Taylor's book, *Swords and Plowshares* (Norton, 1972):

The obverse side of the coin is clear: more of our high-ranking military leaders, if faced with the dilemma of supporting military policies which they believe to be dangerous to the nation's future, should resign their posts not as a mutinous gesture but as constructive indication that they cannot carry out the policies of the administration without fatally compromising their duty to the country and their loyalty to the men they command. Resignation, particularly by high-ranking military men, should never be a casual gesture but it can represent the only honorable alternative.[42]

The Joint Chiefs of Staff in 1978, according to Colonel Dickens, experienced reservations about the Canal Treaties. If anyone had resigned to protest the surrender of this strategic asset, it is possible that the Treaties would have failed. Maj. General Thomas A. Lane wrote: "Our military leaders at the highest level cannot dismiss their responsibilities for the safety of the country by saying they obeyed the President." Nonetheless, the President *was* obeyed. This was the new diplomacy, the new politics, the new military. General Lane had said earlier, ". . . that is the 'tradition' which has prevailed in this country since World War II. . . ." The lessons of Nuremberg, in blindly following the leader, had been soon forgotten.

Military subservience to political judgments is a "new tradition" that military leaders must repudiate. Homer Lea, the Virginia-born strategist and author, wrote in his famous book, *The Valor of Ignorance* (Harper and Brothers, 1909), about military officers whose decisions leave demoralized survivors:

The most promiscuous murderer in the world is the ignorant military officer. He slaughters his men by bullets, by disease, by neglect; he starves them, he makes cowards of them and deserters and criminals. The dead are hecatombs of his ignorance; the survivors, melancholy specters of his incompetence.

The Commander-in-Chief expected military subservience to his judgment about the Panama Canal. Maj. General John K. Singlaub was forced into early retirement when he gave adverse opinions of the Treaties, supposedly "off the record" but quoted by the media immediately. Earlier, General Singlaub, as Chief of Staff of the Army Forces Command, had the responsibility of determining the additional funding needed to bring Canal Zone facilities up to the standards prescribed by the Treaties: One billion dollars. Meanwhile, Mr. Carter was telling the people the Treaties would not cost taxpayers a single dime.

The Air Force Chief of Staff, General David Jones, sent out a special message in February 1978 stressing the strategic importance of the Canal and the necessity for "our support of the proposed Treaties." This was, of course, a "muzzling of the Air Force generals." General Jones told his commanders, in part:

The Panama Canal is a major defense asset, the use of which enhances United States capability for timely reinforcement of United States forces.

. . . .

The Air Force actively participated in the development of all defense related aspects of the proposed treaties, and fully supports them. . . . Once the U.S. no longer operates the Canal, the proposed neutrality treaty would provide an adequate basis for safeguarding our interests in the Canal.

It is important that our personnel, particularly our senior people, understand our support for the proposed treaties.[43]

General Jones was evidently rewarded for his support when President Carter later appointed him Chairman of the Joint Chiefs of Staff, the first time in history that successive chairmen had been appointed from the same branch of the armed services.

In the matter of "muzzling" military strategists, perhaps the national leadership, both civilian and military, had given insufficient attention to a basic principle: the traditional bond between the leader and the led (the officer and his men, for example)—the bond that is welded by leadership and trust, beginning at the top. The other basic principle, that appears to have been neglected, was the responsibility of the military leaders to the Congress, as well as to the President, i.e., their "fundamental fidelity to the nation"—not just to the political party that happened to be in power at the moment.[44]

The attrition rate among senior officers who chose to observe this concept of "dual loyalty" has been notable since World War II and particularly during the Korean and Vietnam Wars. During the Panama Canal debate, several senior officers retired early in order to speak freely. Lt. General Gordon Sumner, Jr., U.S. Army and Chairman of the Inter-American Defense Board, was concerned about the economic consequences of Panamanian operation of the Canal with increased tolls and doubtful reliability. He retired.

In another case concerning operation of the Canal, Maj. General Harold Parfitt, U.S. Army and Governor of the Canal Zone, expressed uneasiness about the transfer terms that, in many instances, would give him "responsibility without authority."[45] This apparently was one of President Carter's original premises for "sharing responsibilities," a concept incompatible with command and control.

CHARGES AND COMPLICATIONS BEDEVIL RATIFICATION

The niceties of dual loyalty and free world security were subordinated to the goal of ratified Treaties, but problems remained. On October 17, 1977 an intelligence report from the Drug Enforcement Administration (DEA) linked Torrijos with heavy illegal drug trafficking.[46] Panamanian Ramiro Rivas told DEA's informant, "Panamanian aircraft are being used to transport narcotics from Cuba, Peru and Colombia to Panama" for transshipment to the United States. Senator Dole's efforts to investigate were blocked by Attorney General Griffin Bell who censored about 50% of the documents he was forced to provide under the Freedom of Information Act. He declined to investigate on grounds of hearsay evidence. The Attorney General is the President's lawyer also.

Questions were raised about the President's failure to consult with Congress on matters of mutual concern, such as disposing of U.S. territory, abrogating the 1903 Treaty, and U.S. rights to defend the Canal. President Carter wrote to Senator Ted Stevens, R.-Alas., on November 5, 1977:

Americans say they would support the treaties if . . . ". . . the treaties provided that the United States could always send in troops to keep the Canal open to ships of all nations." As you know, the Treaty of Neutrality and the recent Statement of Understanding provide the United States this right.

The President was dedicated to his cause. In a televised fireside chat, he told Americans that we never owned the Canal Zone, only rented it, and never had sovereign rights, and that the Supreme Court had repeatedly acknowledged Panama's sovereignty—all untrue statements and misleading. He kept a notebook in which to "grade" Senators, and gave special attention to thirteen undecided legislators. Of Georgia's Herman Talmadge and Sam Nunn, he wrote, "I thought theirs might be the deciding votes. . . . Personal friends of theirs; executives from the state banks, the Coca-Cola Company, and the Georgia Power Company; political fund raisers—all joined me in this concerted effort."[47] Of the thirteen undecided Senators, seven voted "aye," and six of the seven were defeated next time at the polls. Of the six who voted against the Treaties, three were reelected and three retired.

The campaign for ratification saw Henry Kissinger, Jerry Ford, Cyrus Vance, and Harold Brown working almost full time on Capitol Hill. Mrs. Carter telephone the wives. The last days were filled with innumerable lunches, dinners, and coffee sessions with the wavering lawmakers. First class White House limousine service up and down Pennsylvania Avenue was routine. Senator Edward Zorinsky, D.-Neb., was a classic example of pampering; but after all the attention, an invitation to a state dinner, and special briefings for Nebraskans invited to the White House, he said, "I think the time has come to make the decision by myself. . . ."[48] On the roll call, his name was last. He voted no.

As the first vote neared, Carter called on Dennis DeConcini, D.-Ariz., for support; but instead of some harmless resolution of understanding, he received "the single biggest threat to the Treaties": the DeConcini reservation, guaranteeing unilateral U.S. defense rights. The President wrote in his diary entry for March 15, 1978, the day before the first vote:

I had to call General Torrijos. He was planning to blast the Senate and reject the Panama Treaties outright because of some amendment language that DeConcini insisted upon. I didn't like the language either, but it doesn't change the text or the meaning of the Treaties themselves. I agreed to send Warren Christopher and Hamilton Jordan down to Panama tomorrow afternoon after the votes are completed to explain the complete action to Torrijos rather than having him overly concerned about one sentence in the resolution.

Thanks to the DeConcini reservation, the Senate approved the Neutrality Treaty on March 16, 1978, 68 to 32, but many Senators disagreed with the President's evaluation that this reservation did not "change the meaning of the Treaties." For the next 33 days, March 16 to April 18, the second treaty was debated, and the hang up, as always, was U.S. defense rights which now were clearly and specifically being guaranteed by the DeConcini reservation.

The clear cut DeConcini reservation was too much for the Panamanians. Ambiguity was needed; specific U.S. rights were unacceptable. Torrijos, under heavy pressure, was demanding in public statements that the reservation be modified and cried, "I ask myself the question: Have we by any chance lost a war? The U.S. didn't demand as much from Japan!" On the evening of April 7, 1978, less than two weeks away from the vote on the second treaty, Carter suggested that Torrijos "issue a reservation about *his* understanding of what the Treaties mean on intervention."[49]

Torrijos quickly accepted Carter's solution, and at the last moment disclosed his reservation that legally voided the DeConcini reservation and guarantees of U.S. unilateral defense rights, and that was not voted on in the U.S. Senate. Said Dr. Breecher, this was the "most substantive change imaginable."

Previously, the Senate had attached a "leadership amendment" to the second treaty (the Panama Canal Treaty) purporting to clarify the DeConcini reservation. It deceived the Panamanians into believing that the

DeConcini "claws" had been removed, and it satisfied 68 Senators into believing that U.S. rights were intact. The Senate's vote for the final treaty was 68 to 32, the same margin as for the first treaty.

Thereafter, with its own final and unchallenged counter-reservation, Panama could feel secure in legally preserving its total sovereignty against any uninvited intervention for any reason. Moreover, the inclusion of the restrictions of the United Nations and OAS Charters against intervention gave added security for Panama. But for the United States, Senator Jesse Helms offered the following scenario, on the day the second treaty was consented to:

Once the transfer takes place, then the United States has no right to assert its interpretation of treaty rights over another sovereign state. The Senator from North Carolina pointed out that our obligations under the United Nations Charter, the Rio Treaty, and the OAS Charter preclude us from using force or the threat of force for any purpose except individual or collective self-defense. Since the Canal will no longer be defended as U.S. territory, it is manifestly absurd to hold that we could defend it as part of collective self-defense with the Republic of Panama.

Once the Canal falls under Panamanian sovereignty, then Panama is the sole judge of any treaty right or of any interpretation of the regime of neutrality. The Treaty proponents are in the position of claiming that the United States has the unilateral right to invade the territory of another nation in order to assert our own interpretation of a treaty right. . . .

In any case, the introduction of U.S. troops into the territory of Panama, without Panama's permission, in order to assert our interpretation of the treaty would be a blatant violation of Panama's territorial integrity and Panama's political process. Whatever political process Panama would use to come to her interpretation of the impact of the treaty on events or situations on her sovereign territory obviously would be violated.[50]

Conversely, if the Canal has not "fall[en] under Panamanian sovereignty," then, legally, constitutionally, and actually, the United States has retained the rights of ownership, defense, and operation of the Canal—and this principle was implicit in the findings of the East Subcommittee on Separation of Powers, June 23, 1983.

Moreover, the transfer has not yet taken place either, contrary to the beliefs of the general public. Specifically, Sections 1503 and 1504 of the Panama Canal Act of 1979 require that the full Congress will have to enact a new law by 1999 in order to transfer the Canal and other U.S. property in the Canal Zone. The Panama Canal is not a dead issue.

President Carter has written that the ratification of the Panama Treaties "will always be one of my proudest moments, and one of the great achievements in the history of the United States Senate." Others have called it a "major military defeat for the United States." Nonetheless, the ratification was a monumental accomplishment in the face of tremendous odds. Some years later, however, five so-called swindles and four smoking guns were discovered along the way—all related to deception and all made possible by the awesome power of the U.S. presidency.

After ratifying the Panama Treaties on June 16, 1978, some nine months ahead of the schedule authorized by the U.S. Senate in its Brooke Reservation, President Carter is welcomed to Fort Clayton in the Canal Zone by Lt. General Dennis P. McAuliffe of the U.S. Southern Command, a strong supporter of the Treaties and later appointed by Carter as the first Administrator of the new Panama Canal Commission. Mrs. Carter applauds. (AP/Wide World Photos)

· 5 ·

'THE WORST FRAUD EVER PERPETRATED'

The French political aspirant and leader of the workingmen's party, Alexandre Ledru-Rollin (1807-1874), won fame of sorts because of an unusual observation attributed to him: "There go many people. I must find out where they are going so I can lead them." [1] In twentieth century America, at the time of choosing up sides on the Panama Canal Treaties, the Senate leadership paused long enough to "find out where they are going."[2] Or, so it seemed.

The Senate leadership, along with several Ambassadors and particularly the President of the United States, were about to become involved in the Panama Canal swindle, called "the worst fraud ever perpetrated on the United States Senate and on the American people" by the late Dr. Charles H. Breecher in his testimony at the 1983 Senate hearing on the constitutionality of the Panama Canal Treaties.

Senator Robert C. Byrd, the Democratic leader, had kept his political distance during the first year of President Carter's Administration. But when the Canal Treaties came along, he soon took up position at the head of the Senators marching toward ratification, though very much out of step with his constituency back in West Virginia. "I told Senator Baker," said Majority Leader Byrd, "if either you or I go against the Treaties, they probably will be defeated. If both you and I go for them, they may be confirmed." [3]

Senator Howard H. Baker, the Republican leader, took his time in testing the political winds before announcing his position. Indeed, Baker, described by a colleague as "a man who has the most chapped forefinger in the Senate," was still trying to decide even as he "negotiated" with Omar Torrijos in Panama in early 1978. A short time later, he came out *for* the Treaties, albeit, like Byrd, out of step with the folks back home. Nonetheless, he was ready to lead; but, as political observer James Boren once said, "It is hard to look up to a leader with his ear to the ground." [4]

Another political observer named "James" had closer ties to Senator Baker: This was James M. Cannon, Baker's Chief of Staff and adviser, who had been Nelson Rockefeller's right hand man for eight years when Rockefeller was Governor of New York. Cannon had served as Special Assistant to the Governor. Soon after Rockefeller was appointed Vice President, Cannon too was given a prominent job in the Ford Administration in Washington. When Rockefeller left, Cannon became Baker's right hand man in the Senate. Thereafter, Baker decided to support the Canal Treaties.

All of this inevitably brings to mind the financial situation of Panama at the time of the Treaties debate, namely, the $2.77 billion debt owed by Panama to international banks and the very evident plan to use some of the Canal revenue to pay off these loans.

Earlier Nelson Rockefeller had "endorsed" Omar Torrijos in a 1969 mission to Panama for President Richard M. Nixon. Just how much was disclosed in Joseph E. Persico's 1982 book, *The Imperial Rockefeller, a Biography of Nelson A. Rockefeller* (Thorndike Press). [5] The following passage suggests the beginning of the relationship between the Rockefellers and the dictator of Panama, Torrijos:

During the Panama visit, he was utterly charmed by the young *caudillo* Omar Torrijos. He liked the Panamanian strongman's energy, his up-from-the-people authenticity. Torrijos wanted one thing from the United States at that moment, helicopters, so that he could get around the country more easily. The U.S. State Department had earlier refused, believing Torrijos would only use them to tighten his grip on the country. Nelson Rockefeller, with a sly grin, disagreed. Panama needed the helicopters for its rural medical programs, he told the State Department people. Omar Torrijos got his helicopters.

"Let me say a word about the gentleman who has been referred to as a tinhorn dictator," he said later. "This is a self-made man, a poor boy who went into the army because that was the only way he could get an education."

The late Mr. Rockefeller may not have done his homework on the young *caudillo's* background because Torrijos's parents were school teachers—but his banking instincts were good. Soon after the helicopters arrived, Panama's banking laws were liberalized, in 1971, facilitating global multi-national operations.

In 1977, however, Panama's primary interest was the Canal—and a sympathetic U.S. Senate leadership was a most important cog in the State Department's machinery for ratification. Moreover, one of State's chief "engineers" for the treaty mechanism was S. Morey Bell, director of Panamanian Affairs and the State Department's top representative on the negotiating team under Ambassador-at-Large Ellsworth Bunker. Mr. Bell's headquarters at one time featured an unusual exhibit.

There on any Spring day in early 1976, a casual visitor to the waiting room outside Bell's office in Foggy Bottom would see a piece of gristle lying on a table with the sign:

THIS IS THE BRAIN OF
P. BUNAU-VARILLA
A CONSTANT INSPIRATION
TO THE U.S. NEGOTIATORS

The scene is described by author Denison Kitchel in his book, *The Truth About the Panama Canal* (Arlington House, 1978): "There in a nutshell was an expression of the *mea culpa* complex, the we-are-on-the-wrong-side approach that has characterized the State Department's negotiating effort and related activities with regard to Panama for the past 25 years." [6]

The often maligned Philippe Bunau-Varilla, however, was anything but gristle-brained. He was the well educated and able French engineer who had been authorized to sign the 1903 Canal Treaty on behalf of the just emerging new provisional government of Panama, headed by Jose Austin Arango. Moreover, Bunau-Varilla's brilliance in treaty-making assured the United States the "rights of sovereignty" needed to construct and operate the Canal, without which there probably would have been no treaty, no Panama Canal, no Panama. [7]

Such a puerile display of pique and bias by a senior negotiator in the State Department was surprising. Had Mr. Bell done his homework? The qualifications of Bunau-Varilla were impressive.

This French diplomat had taken great pains to insert, into Article III of the 1903 Treaty, guarantees of U.S. rights and authority as "if it were sovereign . . . to the entire exclusion" of any Panamanian sovereignty. Which brings to mind an interesting question: If the United States did *not* have sovereignty, as frequently claimed by Messrs. Carter, Bunker, Linowitz and others, and Panama was "entire(ly) excluded" from exercising sovereignty, then, who *did* have sovereignty?

Bunau-Varilla handled sovereignty in this fashion for several reasons: (1) to safeguard the Colombian businessmen who had fomented the Panamanian revolution, (2) to mute criticism by the liberals in the Colombian Senate, and (3) to avoid defining all the attributes of sovereignty which would have encouraged debate in the U.S. Senate by the advocates of the Nicaragua route.

The results were convincing. Indeed, the Panamanian newspaper *Star and Herald* carried the following story in its issue for November 20, 1903:

Washington, D.C., November 18, 1903—The Hay-Bunau-Varilla Isthmian Canal Treaty was signed this evening at the residence of Secretary Hay by Secretary Hay and Minister Bunau-Varilla. . . .

. . .

The treaty is a simpler document than the Hay-Herran treaty though it follows its general lines, *absolute sovereignty is awarded to the United States over the Canal strip*. The convention meets in every way the requirements of the Spooner Act.[8] (Emphasis added.)

There was no question, therefore, in 1903 about who exercised sovereignty in the Panama Canal Zone. Both sides understood and accepted without reservation the terms that had been worked out for the construction of a canal for civilization and for the guarantees of independence and nationhood for the new Republic of Panama.

Nonetheless, in the 1970s outside Morey Bell's office was a piece of evidence indicating history rewritten to conform to the "new politics" of internationalism. Some years earlier, Bell had prepared a position paper stating, for the first time, that "the end objective of future negotiations with Panama would be to surrender U.S. sovereignty over the Canal Zone."

Surprising as this announcement was at the time, at least it identified one State Department official willing to acknowledge, albeit tacitly, U.S. sovereign rights in the Canal Zone. Thereafter, the goal of relinquishing this sovereignty and dismantling Canal operations by the Americans was nurtured and advanced.

SWINDLE NUMBER ONE: THE MISSING DRAFT INSTRUMENT

One of the most bedeviling developments in researching the story of the Panama Canal swindle was the mystery of the missing *draft* Panamanian instrument of ratification (the working paper originally drawn up for the Senate's study and consideration).

However, there is a good reason: Overwhelming evidence established the premise that there never was any working draft instrument, as such, that was *out in the open* for Senators to consider and for the general public to know about. It was concealed until President Carter could get to Panama on June 16, 1978, two months after the Senate had passed the second and final treaty, and take the last and irreversible step of "ratifying" the Treaties.

Only on that date, June 16, did the State Department release the text of Panama's secretive three paragraph counter-reservation that "legally" voided U.S. defense rights over the Canal. That was the bombshell that had been covered up. If it had been made known earlier, the Senate and the public would have resisted and there would have been no Treaties.

There is more. Not only did Carter rush to "ratify" unconstitutionally drawn Treaties without telling the public and the Senate that U.S. rights had been canceled out, but he did so 9 months and 14 days ahead of schedule, i.e., before he had been authorized to do so under the terms of the Brooke resolution of April 17, 1978 that specified that the ratification of the Treaties "shall not be effective earlier than March 31, 1979." How did he get around this? Simply by signing on June 15 and saying it was "effective" on March 31, 1979.

These are facts. They are part of the swindle. Conclusion is that the Treaties were not ratified, legally or constitutionally. The Canal does not belong to Panama. However, 64% of the Canal Zone was transferred to Panama on October 1, 1979 by Public Law 96-70. Separate acts of Congress will be required, as specified by Section 1503 and 1504 of the Panama Canal Act of 1979, if this remaining U.S. territory and property are ever transferred to Panama. Is there sufficient political and moral will in the United States Congress and national leadership to face up to this swindle?

Or, are all these allegations just academic, or conjectural, or are they factual? What is the proof?

To begin with, was there ever a draft, working copy of Panama's instrument of ratification, as such? If so, did it or did it not contain Panama's three paragraphs of unchallenged counter-reservation when it was provided to the Senate leadership and to the members of the Senate Committee on Foreign Relations for their review and all-important advice and consent function required by the Constitution? The answer to this question has become perhaps the paramount single point in the constitutional mandate for advice and consent.

Panama's three paragraphs, of course, had the effect of voiding the DeConcini reservation that guaranteed U.S. rights for unilateral defense and reopening the Canal in an emergency situation. No one has given a clear-cut answer to the simple questions posed above, even after more than 85 letters of inquiry to those involved.

It is unbelievable that not a scintilla of positive and convincing proof has surfaced to confirm State's contention that procedures were constitutional—indeed, inconceivable that not one of the 23 principals queried has offered a definite answer as to whether the Senate leadership and the members of the Foreign Relations Committee saw Panama's three paragraphs *before* the date of the Exchange of Protocols and instruments, i.e., the "ratification" date, June 16, 1978.[9]

In this connection, two dates are important: On April 18, 1978 the Senate consented to the second and final treaty (the Panama Canal Treaty) and on June 16, 1978 the heads of government "ratified" the Treaties by exchanging Protocols and Instruments of Ratification. If the Senate leadership and/or the Foreign Relations Committee *did* see the three paragraphs before the "ratification" date, June 16, 1978, then dereliction of duty has to be considered because of failure to alert the full Senate of a substantive change. On the other hand, if the Senate leaders did *not* see the three paragraphs, then, obviously, malfeasance on the part of the President and the State Department is the question to be examined.

In any event, stonewalling and cover up were the dominant characteristics of our search for the answers to these questions. Indeed, it was like trying to "nail currant jelly to the wall," to borrow a phrase from Teddy Roosevelt when he was trying to get definitive answers from the Colombians during treaty negotiations for canal rights.

The original inquiry by the Harman Committee for Better Panama and U.S. Relations was triggered by the September 20, 1979 letter that Herbert J. Hansell, then Legal Adviser to the Department of State, sent to Representative John M. Murphy, then the Chairman of the House Committee on Merchant Marine and Fisheries. The following portion of Mr. Hansell's letter is pertinent:

... during the preparation of these instruments, the Department provided copies of the draft U.S. and Panamanian Instruments and Protocol of Exchange to the Senate Foreign Relations Committee for review and comment, and incorporated the suggestions of the Committee staff prior to the exchange of instruments. It was our understanding that the Committee was entirely satisfied with the form and content of these documents.[10]

This innocent-sounding report by Hansell would seem to close the case and satisfy the doubters, except for that troublesome question: Exactly *what* was in the copies of the draft instruments and did they contain Panama's three paragraphs of counter-reservation? Moreover, can the State Department produce a copy of the original draft instruments, dated as of the day it was provided to the Senate Foreign Relations Committee for "review and comment," as stated in Hansell's letter to Murphy? The significance of these two questions furnished the impetus for an extensive inquiry.

The Harman Committee instigated a series of some 85 inquiry letters and follow ups. One of the first went to former Senator John Sparkman, the former Chairman of the Foreign Relations Committee at the time of the Treaties. This Democratic leader, who later voted to transfer the Canal, provided no information and suggested contacting the Foreign Relations Committee itself or the University of Alabama, the latter being the depository for the Sparkman papers. [11]

In due time, inquiry letters were sent to the other 14 members of the Foreign Relations Committee at the time of the Treaties, including Senators Baker, Percy, Glenn, Sarbanes, Biden and Pell and former Senators Church, McGovern, Clark, Stone, Case, Javits, Pearson and Griffin. Interestingly, 14 of these 15 voted *for* the Treaties and 9 are no longer in the Senate.

Only Senators Baker and Pell responded to the inquiry letter and both of them advised that the State Department had been asked to assist in finding answers to the questions about the mysterious draft instruments of ratification. Mr. Pell's reply included the information that Panama's draft instrument was not in the files of the Foreign Relations Committee and that the State Department Office of Legal Affairs might help.[12]

So, faithfully, courteous letters of inquiry were sent to six current and former Legal Advisers and Deputy Legal Advisers, including: Davis R. Robinson, Herbert J. Hansell, Arthur W. Rovine, Robert E. Dalton, Michael G. Kozak and Terrence J. Fortune. Not a single one acknowledged the request for a copy of the draft document.[13]

Nonetheless, during the month of November 1983, the author personally interviewed several of these legal advisers with negative results as to solving the mystery of the missing draft documents. For example, Mr. Herbert J. Hansell, State's Legal Adviser at the time of the Treaties and the man in charge of advising the Senate, was asked what the members of the Senate Foreign Relations Committee had to say about Panama's three paragraphs of counter-reservation. He would not discuss this, saying, "I've gone through that issue and I really don't think I want to get into that issue . . . I'm not going to reopen that issue and work that over again. . . ." The date of this brief telephone interview was November 18, 1983.

This was a disappointment. Mr. Hansell had been singled out in the testimony of Robert E. Dalton, Assistant Legal Adviser for Treaty Affairs for the Department of State, at the East Subcommittee hearing on June 23, 1983 as the "Department official responsible for these consultations" with the Senate leadership and members of the Senate Foreign Relations Committee. Moreover, a question, later submitted to the Department of State by Chairman East, asked for copies of the draft instruments of ratification, the identities of the Senators who had been consulted, their responses to Panama's counter-reservation, and just why the State Department had felt it necessary to submit the draft instrument to the Senate.[14]

The State Department's answers to Senator East's questions were incomplete. For example, no Senators' identities or their responses were supplied—only that their staffs had been invited to a briefing and that not all had attended. The remainder of the State Department's answer to East's questions was in general terms about the meeting that "Mr. Hansell had conducted." Omitted were the date of the meeting, the exact location of the meeting, identity of participants (except Hansell), or any letter, memorandum, log or other documentation to authenticate any details of such a conference.[15] There was nothing to substantiate such a briefing except "word of mouth." Such a briefing, that was reported to have been "skipped" by some Senators' staff members, was to have been on the most important single issue of the entire Treaties debate.

In an effort to clarify the reactions of the members of the Foreign Relations Committee, the author interviewed Mr. Dalton and asked about the Department's records for the Hansell briefing or any other meetings concerning Panama's three paragraphs. Our interview took place in the State Department on November 22, 1983. "The nature of these consultations," Mr. Dalton said, "was informal; they were not handled by letter. There were no records, as matters such as this were handled without any written records, or logs, or transmittal memorandums. They are done informally, staff to staff."[16]

Nonetheless, contrary to Dalton's assertions and the official answers to Senator East's questions, there *are* State Department records, according to Powell A. Moore, Assistant Secretary of State for Legislative and Intergovernmental Affairs. Mr. Moore wrote in his July 19, 1983 letter to Senator Alan Cranston:

The Department's records show that the Panamanian draft instruments of ratification and a Protocol of Exchange were made available to the Majority and Minority leaders of the Senate and to the members of the Foreign Relations Committee. The records also indicate that these consultations produced no objection to the Panamanian draft instruments and resulted only in a suggestion for a minor, technical change in the Protocol of Exchange.[17]

At last, perhaps definite proof was available. Mr. Moore said the

Department had records and the records showed that Panama's draft instruments were made available to the Senate leadership and to members of the Foreign Relations Committee—and further, the records showed "these consultations produced no objection."

Mr. Moore's position was virtually identical with Hansell's position in the latter's letter of September 20, 1979 to Congressman John M. Murphy in explaining that the Senate Foreign Relations Committee was satisfied with Panama's draft instruments. Moore went a step further in reporting that the Department had records. This seemed to be a breakthrough. Our letter to Mr. Moore of December 19, 1983 asked the following questions:

What are the "Department's records" that you refer to? Could you please send me an excerpt to authenticate this point, i.e., an excerpt of the "Department's records?"

Did the draft instruments that were made available to the Senators include the three paragraphs that are marked on the enclosure? As you know, these three paragraphs were not in the U.S. instruments.

Please give the names of the Senators whom the Department contacted about the draft instruments. What was the date? Please also send excerpts from the "Department's records" to authenticate the date or dates and the names of the Senators or their representatives who were contacted about the draft instruments?

On such an important matter as ratifying treaties to transfer the Canal, your Department would, of course, have some kind of log or record to indicate all actions taken—or even better, copies of letters which officially transmitted the draft instruments, even though State officials may have hand-carried them to the Senate.

The above answers are so important to recount in my book and I respectfully ask answers as soon as possible.[18]

The State Department's answer to the foregoing letter was another disappointment. It was a form letter dated January 31, 1984, advising that no information could be provided until a fee was paid for researching the records, as authorized by the Freedom of Information Act and that a fee schedule was enclosed. No fee schedule was enclosed, however, and we wrote back asking for one and requesting also that the fee be waived since the information being petitioned was in the public interest, another authorization of the Freedom of Information Act. Consequently, the delays continued and the obstacles mounted. On April 30, 1986 no answer had been received.

A similar case of stonewalling on this same subject was experienced by the Harman Committee in two separate requests to Mr. William Price, Director, Foreign Affairs Information Management Center of the State Department. State's Assistant Legal Adviser for Treaty Affairs had referred

Mr. Harman to Price's office which is the depository for the State Department's records. In his letter of August 13, 1983 to Mr. Price, Harman stated, in part:

The documents that I am seeking are from the Department of State and the Senate Foreign Relations Committee. They are:

1. The draft copies of Panama's 1977 Panama Canal Treaties.
2. The comments of the Foreign Relations Committee staff members regarding Panama's draft instruments.
3. Copies of the consultations that took place between Senate members of the Committee and the Department of State regarding Panama's draft instruments.
4. Any other information that the Center may have regarding Panama's draft instruments.

The draft copies of Panama's instruments and the consultations must have taken place sometime after April 18, 1978 and before June 16, 1978.

No answer was received. According to Messrs. Moore and Hansell, the "Department's records show(ed)" that these documents in question were all available to the Senate leadership and that they had consultations? Where are the records? Interestingly, Mr. Moore's letter of July 19, 1983 assured Senator Cranston that the records showed that everything had been handled properly—but, three weeks later, a request from Harman asking for copies of the records was ignored. Impression is that the State Department cannot authenticate allegations made in the Moore and Hansell letters.

THE STATE DEPARTMENT VERSION OF 'DRAFT INSTRUMENTS'

After nine separate requests made by several Senators and Phillip Harman, the State Department came through in mid-July 1983 with its version of the Panamanian draft instruments of ratification, but the circumstances were unusual. These "draft instruments" contained the elusive three paragraphs but the date was puzzling: *June 16, 1978,* the date that Carter and Torrijos exchanged the Protocols in Panama. How can a draft copy, the working copy, have the same date as the final smooth copy? State did not explain.

Nonetheless, this was State's answer to four separate inquiries made by Senators Howard Baker, Jesse Helms and Alan Cranston and by former Senator Frank Church, as well as five separate requests made by Phillip Harman between July 1982 and April 1983. The cover letter forwarding the "draft instruments" was signed by Assistant Secretary Powell A.

Moore and assured the Senators that the Majority and Minority leaders and the members of the Foreign Relations Committee had had access to the "instruments" and made "no objection."[17]

The concerted effort to obtain copies of the draft instruments prior to the June 23, 1983 hearing before the East Subcommittee in order to discuss them and enter them into the hearing record had failed although the State Department had ample time to furnish them or acknowledge that it could not. Consequently, the Senate investigation into the constitutionality of the Treaties did not have this evidence for consideration "live" at the hearing, June 23, 1983.

After the hearing, the Harman Committee had resumed its efforts to obtain copies of the draft instruments, culminating in release of the State Department's version of "draft instruments." Letters of inquiry had been sent to the Secretary of State, George P. Shultz, and to State's Legal Adviser, Davis R. Robinson, as well as to Mr. Dalton, who had been State's spokesman at the East hearing. The following excerpt from Harman's letter to Shultz reveals some of the difficulties encountered:

Mr. Secretary, I wrote to Mr. Robinson's office as well as Mr. Dalton's office five different times from July 6, 1982 to April 30, 1983 when I realized they were not going to respond to my request. I never at any time ever received a reply from their offices. Altogether there were *nine* requests before the June 23 hearing took place—five from my office and, on my behalf, four requests from Senators Baker, Helms, Cranston and former Senator Church.

After the hearing was over on June 23, I asked Mr. Dalton personally before he left the hearing room to please send me the draft copies of Panama's instruments along with the staff Committee's comments. The next day, June 24, I wrote to him reminding him about my request. I never heard from him until July 15 when I received in the mail an envelope from his office with no letter, only an unreadable copy of the draft Panamanian instrument of the Panama Canal Treaty as well as two unreadable copies of letters from Mr. Powell A. Moore, the Assistant Secretary, to Senators Baker and Cranston about the draft instruments. Not only was the material unreadable but he also failed to send the other draft Neutrality Treaty instrument and the staff Committee's comments on the instruments."[19]

Subsequently, the Harman group *did* receive legible material. Appendix J is the text of a letter to Secretary of State George P. Shultz. The basic question has not been answered: How can the "draft instrument" be dated June 16, 1978 when this is the date of the Protocol of Exchange in Panama?

Attempts to get the answer to this question during our November 1983 interviews in Washington were inconclusive. Mr. Dalton suggested that the date of June 16 was known in advance and therefore, it was typed into the draft instruments much as an attorney might prepare a client's last will and testament, and have the date of signature inserted ahead of time. However, this is one date, we submit, that lawyers leave blank at first typing because of the uncertainty of the date of the client's appearance.

No answers have been received from any of the other State Department officials explaining the unusual date, June 16, 1983, although effort was made to interview Mssrs. Robinson, Hansell, Rovine and Fortune during the Washington trip.

Another prelude to the release of the "draft instruments" by the State Department had been the dead end encountered with the staff of the Foreign Relations Committee. Letters of inquiry and follow up were sent to four current and former staffers of this Committee, including Scott Cohen, Betty Alonzo, Edward Sanders and Robert Dockery. Only Mrs. Alonzo and Mr. Cohen answered, the latter suggesting that the draft instrument might be at the State Department or at the National Archives.

Unfortunately, the Archives spokesman said "no," too soon for the document to be filed there. And, of course, the State Department had long known of our search for the draft instrument. Mrs. Alonzo, a former assistant to Mr. Dockery who had been the staff official in charge of the Treaties for the Foreign Relations Committee, wrote:

I'm afraid I no longer work for the professionals handling Latin America, and Mr. Dockery, who handled the Panama Canal Treaties, is no longer employed by the Committee. Any draft documents which may have been reviewed at that time have in all probability been destroyed.

Former Senator Robert P. Griffin, the only anti-Treaties member of the Foreign Relations Committee at the time of the Treaties debate, advised in his letter of June 14, 1983[20] to Phillip Harman, and in a telephone interview with the author on November 16, 1983, that he had no recollection of seeing the Panamanian draft instruments and the three contested paragraphs prior to the official exchange of Protocols on June 16, 1978.

The attempts of the Harman Committee to locate and identify the working copy of the Panamanian instruments were Gargantuan. A summation of this conscientious struggle is contained in the follow up letter of August 27, 1983 addressed to former Senator Griffin by Mr. Harman. Portions of this letter follow:

The reason I asked you if you remember about the three paragraph statement in Panama's draft instruments is that question is one of the *key points in our hearing* that we had on June 23 in Senator East's Subcommittee on Separation of Powers. I wrote an identical letter on July 29 to the other 14 members of the Committee who were on the Committee in 1978 during the time of the Treaties. You are the only one who voted against the Treaties of the 15 members of the Committee.

I am convinced that the State Department never pointed out to you nor to any other members the significance of the three paragraph statement in Panama's draft instruments. As the statement was clearly a counter-reservation to the DeConcini Reservation *it should have been submitted to the Senate for a two-thirds vote.* No doubt it would have been defeated as it nullifies the DeConcini Reservation; hence, no Treaties.

Your letter mentions about the minutes in the Committee. Ed Sanders, the Staff Director of the Committee, never answered my letters nor did Scott Cohen, the new Staff Director, answer my questions about the minutes. In regards to the Department (of State), I have asked them several times about the draft instruments and the three paragraph statement. They have refused to comment if they pointed out the statement to the members of the Committee. As I would like to put in the public record of the East hearing about the Department's failure to show any of the 15 members of the Committee Panama's draft instruments, so far the only thing I can enter is what you said in your June 14 letter; that is, that you cannot recall if it was submitted or made available to you.[21]

Senator Griffin had closely followed the developments during the 1977-78 debates on the Treaties and was one of the most knowledgeable Senators on the subject. After the vote on the first treaty, in his address of March 20, 1978 before the Economic Club of Detroit, he stated:

As I see it, there is reason for serious concern about the approach pushed upon the Senate last Thursday (the day of the vote). In order to extract a few key votes from reluctant Senators—who were really opposed to the treaty—the Administration "approved" several substantive changes, which were then adopted on the Senate floor. Now, there is danger that the dictator *Torrijos will accept or "ratify" these changes by himself.* Indeed, that's what President Carter really expects him to do. (Emphasis added.)

Mr. Griffin's evaluation was accurate. Two weeks later, as revealed in his memoirs, *Keeping Faith* (Bantam, 1982), Mr. Carter wrote in his diary for April 7, 1978 about his solution for saving the second treaty: ". . . if Torrijos wants to, he can issue a reservation about *his* understanding of what the treaties mean on intervention. . . ."[22] The net result of this suggestion was undoubtedly Torrijos's unilateral three paragraph counter-reservation—the crux of the swindle—indeed, "the most substantive change . . . that can be imagined" (Dr. Breecher) and that the Senate was not permitted to vote on.

As for "ratifying" the second treaty, Senator Griffin told his Detroit audience of his predictions:

The betting is, as the *New York Times* put it on Sunday, that "after some grumbling," the Torrijos government will decide that "getting the Canal is worth the American changes."

Keep in mind that a similar pattern can be expected when the second, or Panama Canal Treaty, comes down to a vote. However, because it is more controversial, even I predict that a greater number of substantive changes will be necessary to win over the requisite number of Senators. It should be obvious that, through such a process, the United States is likely to wind up with a treaty with a dictator—but not a treaty with the people of Panama.

Mr. Griffin's predictions came true and the United States did "wind up" with a treaty with Torrijos, instead of with the people of Panama because of Panama's failure to hold a second plebiscite for voting on the substantive changes that had drastically altered the meanings of the Treaties. Under Panamanian domestic law, therefore, the Treaties are also unconstitutional.

Nonetheless, in the continuing effort to identify and discover who had ever seen the working copy of the instruments of ratification—and, of course, the contents—we checked with former Senator Dick Clark, the Democrat from Iowa who readily admitted that his vote to give away the Canal defeated him at the polls. Mr. Clark's letter of September 8, 1983 suggested asking the Government Printing Office and the Senate Committee. These were dead ends too, as the GPO sent back a routine form marked "out of print" and Senator Pell had previously reported the draft instrument not in the files of the Foreign Relations Committee of which he was a member.

Subsequently, at a personal interview with Senator Clark in his Washington, D.C. office on November 23, 1983, the three paragraphs were discussed in detail. Mr. Clark had no recollection of having seen them during the Treaties debate nor of hearing any explanation of them. He remembered the DeConcini reservation well and, in comparing it with Panama's three paragraphs, observed, "This leads to a lot of misunderstandings, doesn't it?" Senator Clark had been a prominent member of the Foreign Relations Committee and in position to have made the three paragraphs an important part of his business.

A number of other inquiries about the draft instruments were also non-productive: The Senate historian, Richard A. Baker, did not have a copy—nor did the Curator of the University of Alabama locate one among former Senator John Sparkman's papers. The same negative results obtained with the Curators at Princeton University with regard to former Senator George McGovern's documents and at Stanford University regarding the papers of former Senator Frank Church.

The purpose of these inquiries to the members of the Foreign Relations Committee at the time of the Treaties was, of course, to find out if they had copies of the draft instruments and, if so, the contents of the draft, i.e., did it contain Panama's three paragraphs of counter-reservation? All results were negative and every effort virtually a dead end.

Perhaps President Carter's former White House staff might supply information that the State Department and Senate Committee did not have.

BAFFLING EXPLANATIONS OF THE THREE PARAGRAPHS

In a further attempt to solve the mystery of the unilateral three paragraphs that Panama had been able to insert into the Treaties at the last moment without challenge or explanation, appropriate letters of inquiry were sent to former President Carter at both his Plains, Georgia office and Atlanta offices, explaining that an historical accounting of the Panama Canal Treaties was being prepared and that the status of the three paragraphs was an important part. No response or acknowledgment was ever received. The same results obtained with our request for an interview. Neither were answers or acknowledgments received from Henry Kissinger, Cyrus Vance, Warren Christopher or Sol Linowitz.

Our questions to Zbigniew Brzezinski, President Carter's National Security Adviser 1977-81, were referred to Robert Pastor, Brzezinski's former assistant. Dr. Pastor's answer contained a paragraph that seemed to epitomize the official positions of the State Department and staff members of the Senate Foreign Relations Committee, and now, apparently the White House staff as well. In explaining this position, none admit to any substantial differences among the DeConcini reservation, the leadership amendment to the second treaty, and the three paragraphs of Panama's counter-reservation. Pastor wrote in his letter of December 9, 1983:

The DeConcini condition (reservation) to the Permanent Neutrality Treaty for the Panama Canal was modified by the Senate in the second Panama Canal Treaty to make clear that *the U.S. retained the right to use military force to keep the Panama Canal open,* but that we had no intention to use that right to intervene in Panama's internal affairs. This was the clear position of President Carter and of the Senate leadership, Senators Byrd and Baker, and of the 68 Senators who voted to ratify the two Treaties. I view the three paragraphs inserted by the Panamanians in their instrument of ratification as entirely consistent with that position.[23] (Emphasis added.)

When Dr. Pastor states that the DeConcini condition was "modified by the Senate" in the second treaty, he is referring to the so-called leadership amendment. However, the leadership amendment does *not* "make clear that the U.S. retained the right to use military force to keep the Panama Canal open," as Pastor claims. Indeed, that point is exactly what is *not* made clear—because this amendment does not even address the U.S. "right to use military force." It omits this right and merely states ". . . any action . . . shall not have at its purpose . . . a right of intervention. . . ."[24]

Actually, the purpose of this leadership amendment was to make the Panamanians believe that the U.S. "right to use military force" under authority of the DeConcini reservation had been removed. This deception was made clear by William D. Rogers, former Assistant Secretary of State, in his address on April 28, 1979 before the American Society of International Law in Washington, D.C.[25] "All U.S. rights," said Mr. Rogers, "were subject to the nonintervention principles of the U.N. Charter." However, this was *not* the understanding of the "68 Senators who voted to ratify (sic) the two Treaties," as stated by Dr. Pastor.

Consequently, Panama's three paragraph counter-reservation may indeed be "consistent" with the leadership amendment, as Pastor contended, because neither authorizes unilateral U.S. action but, they are *not* "consistent" with the *DeConcini* reservation which specifically permits unilateral U.S. rights. Moreover, Panama's three paragraphs go a step further: Panama must agree to "cooperate" before any U.S. action is taken on Panamanian soil. This requirement circumvents the DeConcini reservation and we return to square one: no agreement.

As a consequence of Pastor's baffling letter, we asked Drs. Brzezinski and Pastor additional questions. No acknowledgment was received from Brzezinski, but Pastor replied with brief notations on our letter.[26] The questions and answers follow:

Q. Was the U.S. right to use military force "understood" and therefore, something that could be omitted in the leadership amendment?
A. Yes.
Q. Since there was uncertainty about various meanings and interpretations, do you think Panama's 3 unilateral paragraphs should have been included in the U.S. instruments also? Would such inclusion not have made things much clearer and beyond dispute?
A. Not necessary.
Q. Since Panama's second paragraph specifies "mutual respect and cooperation" by both parties to reopen a closed Canal, if for any reason Panama decided not to "cooperate," do you feel the U.S. could legally go in? Authority?
A. Yes, the U.S. could enter *legally* by authority of both Treaties.
Q. Could you please tell me what consideration the Carter Administration gave to asking about a Senate two-thirds vote of approval for Panama's three paragraphs that, many contend, change the DeConcini reservation?
A. Don't know. I didn't follow congressional action that closely.
Q. Could you please tell me the date you first saw or knew about these three paragraphs? Also, the date the President first saw them? Could that possibly have been June 16, 1978, the date of the Exchange of Protocols in Panama?
A. Don't recall. Don't know."[26]

Dr. Pastor's answers were clearly in line with the statements of several

Senate staff members and officials of the Department of State. Of particular interest was Pastor's assertion that it was "understood" that the United States had the right to use military force in Panama and that, therefore, this right could be omitted from the leadership amendment.

This matter of issues being "understood" between the two countries, and not written down in the Treaties, drew boos and laughter in Houston on February 1, 1978 when Ambassador Linowitz explained "it's understood between the parties" that the United States has the right to declare an emergency for priority passage of U.S. warships. Mr. Linowitz was trying to convert a group of Texas businessmen gathered at a special luncheon meeting of Houston civic clubs in the Hyatt Regency Hotel to hear the Carter Administration spokesman for the Treaties, Linowitz. Later, Understanding (3) was added to the Neutrality Treaty specifying that the determination of an emergency for a vessel shall be made by the nation operating such vessel.

Of course, the "U.S. right to use military force in Panama" to defend or reopen a closed Canal was one of the most basic issues of the whole debate about the Treaties—and *not* to be specific on this point was more of the same ambiguity that characterized the Treaties. Nonetheless, the leadership amendment to the second treaty contributed to the ambiguity by deceiving the Panamanians and apparently, most of the U.S. Senators. The final "nail in the coffin" was the secretive three paragraphs prohibiting U.S. defense rights unless Panama "cooperates." Dr. Pastor did not admit this.

His answers about not recalling the date he first saw Panama's three paragraphs and not knowing the Administration's position on whether to ask the Senate for advice and consent to this substantive change were essentially the same as those given by officials of the State Department and the Foreign Relations Committee. This circumstance brings to mind Pastor's role in preparing the Carter Administration's 1977 memorandum recommending surrender of the Canal. Had he lost interest in the final outcome? Indeed, these kinds of questions seemed to be the sensitive ones—and in literally hundreds of queries and scores of letters, *no one* remembered any significant details, particularly about the long-lost draft instruments of ratification.

It should be noted, however, that Pastor's "explanation" of the leadership amendment was considerably at variance with that of former Assistant Secretary Rogers. Rogers had contended that U.S. rights were limited by the U.N. Charter while Pastor asserted that the United States "retained the right to use military force," period.

STATE DEPARTMENT EXPLAINS PANAMA'S THREE PARAGRAPHS

Obviously, the way, perhaps the only way, to get answers to the pejorative question about the status of Panama's draft instrument, and the three paragraphs, is for the Senate Committee on the Judiciary or other appropriate investigative body, to hold full-scale hearings with sworn testimony from all principals, using the subpoena power as necessary. In no other manner, it appears, can the full story be dealt with.

In the ratification procedures, Article II, Section 2 of the Constitution was by-passed in the requirement that the Senate give advice and consent to treaties: That is, a substantive portion of the Panama Canal Treaties, Panama's three paragraph counter-reservation, was not given to the Senate for approval of two-thirds of the members present. By this omission, the principle of limitation and separation of powers was violated, i.e., the system of checks and balances, absolutely essential to U.S. constitutional government.

This allegation of by-passing the Senate, and the Constitution, was an important issue before the Senate hearing on June 23, 1983 under Chairman John P. East's Subcommittee on Separation of Powers. Most of the testimony of the State Department witness concerned explanations of Panama's three paragraphs, but not in depth. As a consequence, Senator East and Phillip Harman, Chairman of the Committee for Better Panama and U.S. Relations, submitted some 38 questions to the State Department. Answers were provided some four months later, October 27, 1983, delaying considerably the publication of the hearing record.

The questions were quite specific, as was to be expected, but most answers were couched in generalities and some were evasive. For example, State's answer to the basic question as to any discussion with Panamanians about the three paragraph counter-reservation was: "It is not the Department's practice to disclose the nature of confidential diplomatic consultations with foreign governments."[27] Appendix K contains examples of State's answers.

The State Department answer to the question as to why, under the Vienna Convention on the Law of Treaties, Panama's three paragraphs were not considered to be a reservation was: "This question was discussed *en extenso* in the testimony of Robert E. Dalton in the hearing on June 23, 1983...." To be sure, according to the hearing record of the Subcommittee on Separation of Powers, pages 100-122, the question was indeed discussed but the real answer boiled down to State's assertion that "none of the elements of the three paragraphs purports to modify or exclude the legal effects of any portion of the Treaties."[28] No logical justification was offered.

Among other interesting answers were the following, in paraphrased abbreviated form:

—"Meeting of minds" is not generally applied to treaties.

—Instruments of ratification are not part of treaty texts.

—There is no legal significance to the rejection of the disputed DeConcini reservation by Panama's Foreign Ministry Communique of April 25, 1978, nor to Torrijos's rejection after the Treaties passed the Senate. State did not answer the question about the "practical significance."

—The American public was not made aware of Panama's three paragraphs until June 16, 1978, the day the Protocols were exchanged and the Treaties "ratified" in Panama.

—Panama's three paragraphs were not inserted in the U.S. instruments because such "is not the practice."

—The admission by Ambassador David Popper, the man in charge of getting the Treaties through the Senate, that "ambiguity was essential" was dismissed as Popper's "private view."

Unfortunately, some eight questions were addressed but not answered. Contrary to the State Department's assurance that a "meeting of minds" does not generally apply to treaties, Mr. Herbert J. Hansell, State's Legal Adviser, had pledged to Representative John M. Murphy, Chairman of the House Merchant Marine and Fisheries Committee, in his letter of September 20, 1979 that there had indeed been a "meeting of minds" on the Panama Canal Treaties.[29]

As to the legal and practical significance of Panama's Foreign Ministry Communique, Phillip Harman told Senator East at the Senate hearing:

Whenever Panama's foreign ministry makes a communique, that is an official communique; the foreign ministry is representing the President and the executive branch of the Republic of Panama. That is official. On that day of April 25, 1978, in their communique they listed not once but five times that they do not recognize the DeConcini condition. . . . Five times that was mentioned in their communique; five times.[30]

As to the question of when the public had knowledge of the controversial three paragraphs, Hansell wrote, "Several hundred copies of the documents were made available to the press on June 16, 1978, the day on which the instruments were exchanged."[31]

WILLIAM JORDEN TELLS SECRET OF 3 PARAGRAPHS

The question of secrecy arises. How else to explain the totally negative results in following every known path and uncovering every stone along the way in search of *anyone* who had heard of the three paragraphs before President Carter accepted them on ratification day (R-Day)?

State's Mike Kozak had much to say about the explanations given by Herbert Hansel, Legal Adviser. And Mr. Hansell had written Representative John M. Murphy about "provid[ing] copies of the draft U.S. and Panamanian Instruments and Protocol of Exchange to the Senate Foreign Relations Committee. . . ." But, no one has answered the simple questions: To whom specifically? On what date? And where is the record to prove that the Executive Branch did in fact constitutionally offer Panama's counter-reservation to the Senate for "Advice and Consent?"

These questions were asked many times but they were not answered, even through the efforts of the East Subcommittee on Separation of Powers. But finally, the reasons for the non-answers were discovered in William Jorden's *Panama Odyssey* (University of Texas Press, 1984): They had evidently been "covered up." How? U.S. and Panamanian lawyers worked up the ratification documents in Panama and slipped in Panama's three paragraphs of counter-reservation. Next, the papers were "lost" in Washington and then "found" just in time to be rushed back to Panama in time for the ceremony of ratification—with the three paragraphs in place but without the Senate's knowledge they were there, much less what they said.

Mr. Jorden, in his explicit accounting of virtually every minute detail of the Treaties process, spilled the beans on pages 628 through 631, revealing for the first time many activities not previously known, sketchy but unmistakable and genuine parts of the years-old mystery of the missing draft instruments and the elusive three paragraphs. In his thoroughness, Jorden discloses how the counter-reservation came about and how it was concealed until the last moment. It is a story of intrigue.

Mr. Jorden, the former *New York Times* correspondent and member of the U.S. delegation to the disastrous Vietnam peace talks, was the U.S. Ambassador to Panama (1974-78) during the times of the 1977 Treaties negotiations and ratification. He was a key figure, a full-fledged member of the Carter-Bunker-Linowitz-Kissinger team, and his services seemed indispensable. His book of memoirs, as with the memoirs of President Carter, Senator Howard Baker and Zbigniew Brzezinski, happily told the "secrets" of the "inside story," the narrative no one else knew about. This was a break, for he provided the missing pieces to the puzzle of Panama's unilateral reservation, thereby confirming our own picture which, nonetheless, was a rather complete one on its own.

Shortly before June 16, 1978, R-Day, State Department representatives, Ambassador David Popper, General W.G. "Tom" Dolvin, Mike Kozak and others, according to the Jorden account, had come to Panama to work with Panamanian lawyers, including Carlos Lopez-Guevara, on the texts of the five documents that would be needed for the actual ratification. Each nation required an instrument of ratification for each of the two Treaties, for a total of four documents. The fifth document was the joint Protocol of Exchange. Simple enough.

According to Ambassador Jorden, nine-tenths of the four ratification documents were merely an orderly listing of the various amendments, reservations, conditions and understandings. In effect, this was like a red flag, as Jorden then accounted for the remaining one-tenth. It was a "new feature," he said, "an expression of Panamanian pride and self-protection." It was all that, and much more. It was Panama's unchallenged counter-reservation. It was "tacked on to the Treaties," explained Jorden, after the Panamanians had observed the Senate's debate as one proviso after another had been added. So, the Panamanians decided to add "a couple of their own."

Thus, the famous counter-reservation was born. But it should have been no surprise because Panama's negotiators, Romulo Escobar Bethancourt and Aristides Royo, had told a press conference several weeks earlier that Panama might "present its own reservations when the instruments of ratification are exchanged."

All this is gently explained in the *Odyssey* book (p.630) as just an "understanding" between equal partners where both Panama and the United States were parties to "positive rules of public international law"— meaning the OAS and the U.N. Charters. These rules preclude the use or threat of force between member states or interference in another country's affairs. (Even so, these Charters do not prohibit states from making special treaties with each other for specific purposes, as the Panama Treaties were.)

The second "understanding," continued Jorden, loyal to the negotiating team, simply provided that actions undertaken by either country would be "in a manner consistent with the principles of mutual respect and cooperation . . .," i.e.: "The Treaties are a partnership and partners don't act without consulting each other." (Partners also look at their contracts.) Jorden concluded that these "understandings" did not rule out unilateral action.

On the contrary, if an action requires "cooperation," then non-cooperation prevents the action and does indeed rule out legal unilateral action by the United States. The third "understanding" was not mentioned by Jorden. This one clearly warns that Panama rejects "with decisiveness and firmness" any intervention against its territorial integrity. It reinforces the other two "understandings" and warns of the consequences of non-observance.

These are the three paragraphs that comprise Panama's counter-reservation. They were the "one-tenth" that was added surreptitiously and contained the *only* words not repeated verbatim in both sets of ratification documents. The reason for their omission in the U.S. instruments of ratification was that they nullified the previously approved DeConcini reservation and submission to the Senate would have resulted in rejected Treaties. But Panama included the three paragraphs in its instruments. So, what happened? We are indebted to William Jorden for a story of "lost" documents that may exhaust credibility.

We are asked to believe that the final papers embracing one of the most important diplomatic initiatives in American history, the highest priority of the Carter Administration and the top news story for many months were just misplaced until a few hours before R-Day, first by the Department of State and then by President Carter's National Security Council.

Former Ambassador Jorden reports innumerable small details in his *Odyssey,* e.g., names of secretaries, luncheon menus, favorite drinks, but devotes only one short paragraph to the "lost" documents. He called it a "diplomatic snafu." It had the earmarks, however, of a diplomatic cover up on which readers deserve more than a cursory once-over. Moreover, it was one of the most important single happenings of the whole operation.

The explanation given is that Popper and his colleagues turned in the papers but they got "lost." They went to the "in" boxes, he says, of the appropriate State Department authorities: the Legal Adviser, the Executive Secretariat, Ambassador Bunker and the Panama Desk. The latter two "read and approved them"—but the Secretariat, who was responsible for coordinating major papers with other parts of the government, "just sat on the ratification papers." When pressured, the Secretariat admitted the papers had been "misplaced." He found them and sent the whole package to the White House, where once again they were "lost," this time by the National Security Council.

These papers, of course, represented nearly 14 years of negotiating for "delivery" of the Panama Canal. Are we to believe that the two Executive agencies most involved with carrying the ball for the President on his "highest priority" had "lost" the ball itself?

According to the Jorden account, the papers were discovered a few days before the agreed-to data of ratification, June 16, 1978. How they were "found" is not explained in this inside story. No other dates are offered. And again, Mr. Jorden is vague on specifics after having pin-pointed so many details in his book. Furthermore, the story goes, the papers "were not yet approved" and the question arose: Who should approve the documents first, the Senate or the President? Of course, it is the President who must approve first and then seek the "Advice and Consent" of the Senate, according to Article II of the Constitution.

In his detailed story, Mr. Jorden includes the complete texts of both treaties (in his Appendices C and D), but omits the instruments of ratification and the protocol of exchange (see my Appendix C). These latter documents contain the disputed DeConcini reservation and Panama's counter-reservation, along with five other substantive changes that were added by the U.S. Senate and never voted on by the Panamanian people. Only by examining these additions can one understand the complete provisions of the Treaties and their ramifications.

Among the aberrations that stand out are the following: (1) Panama's unilateral counter-reservation is not included in the U.S. instruments and therefore, was not legally accepted, and (2) the 6 U.S. additions, though repeated by Panama, were not accepted by plebiscite, as required by Panama's Constitution.

In our letter of August 10, 1984, we asked Mr. Jorden about Panama's "understanding" which was really a counter-reservation, no matter what the label was, an addition to the Treaties that had been omitted from the U.S. instruments and that was apparently accepted by him "with the principles of mutual respect and cooperation" (p. 630). His answer was essentially the same as that of the State Department, to the effect that it is "not the usual practice" among nations to repeat each other's reservations or understandings verbatim in instruments of ratification. He wrote, in part:

The really interesting element is not that Panama's "understandings" were not in our instrument of ratification, but that our various reservations and understandings were included in Panama's instrument and—at their suggestion—in the joint protocol.

These assertions are inaccurate and misleading. First, the joint protocol does *not* include the six substantive changes added by the U.S. Senate. However, it does include two of the three paragraphs comprising Panama's counter-reservation—but the U.S. Senate did not give "Advice and Consent" to this major change, only Jimmy Carter and Omar Torrijos Huerrera approved this. Second, the claim that it is "not the usual practice" to repeat reservations and understandings verbatim in instruments, when substantive changes are involved, is not supported by a number of international legal references, including The American Law Institute's Restatement of the Law (Second) of the United States Foreign Relations Law (p.

23), the American Journal of International law, Volume 72 (p. 641) and primarily, the 1969 Vienna Convention on the Law of Treaties.

The hard fact is: There was not a meeting of minds on the Panama Treaties. Articles 2.1(d) and 20.2 of the Vienna Convention could hardly be clearer in this "essential condition." Of course, there was no meeting of minds when the U.S. DeConcini reservation purported to guarantee unilateral U.S. rights for defense and then, the Panamanian counter-reservation (never approved by the U.S. Senate) takes away those U.S. rights in its requirement that Panama's "cooperation" must first be obtained. To argue otherwise is to becloud further the issue of what was supposed to be clear-cut U.S. rights for the future security of the Canal.

FOUR STORY-TELLERS TELL FOUR STORIES

Michael G. Kozak, a State Department legal adviser and for years involved in details of the treaty process, is reported by Jorden to have rushed to the Senate with the ratification documents at the last moment, "showed them to key people in the leadership and on the Foreign Relations Committee, winning unanimous backing." Then, he returned to State and reported that the "ratification instruments had been squared away on the Hill" (p. 631).

But Kozak's account (letter of March 20, 1985 to Phillip Harman) differed considerably from Jorden's: The "key people" were *not* Senators but "members of the staff"—meaning that not a single Senate leader or member of the Foreign Relations Committee was briefed by the State Department on Panama's counter-reservation.

Moreover, Kozak said that Herbert Hansell, Legal Adviser, did the briefing. Jorden said that Kozak did it. Robert Dalton, another legal adviser, said that Hansell and Curtis Cutter did it. Cutter didn't remember (letter of February 4, 1984 to Phillip Harman). Hansell said "the Department provided copies" and the Committee was satisfied.

However, the Committee's chief counsel, Michael J. Glennon, recalled no briefing whatever, particularly no Committee briefing "because that would require a different level of preparation" (letter of May 9, 1985 to Phillip Harman).

Questions: Why so many different stories? Was Panama's counter-reservation discussed? Who did Kozak "square away?" Date? Was it Robert Dockery, a non-lawyer staff man in charge of the Treaties for the Committee? Why did Jorden, usually careful with details, not specify whom Kozak consulted? If any Senator had been personally contacted, would his name not have been disclosed? During our research, answers to such questions were always evasive.

Robert Dalton, State's Assistant Legal Adviser for Treaty Affairs, told the East Subcommittee on June 23, 1983, "In the course of close consultations . . ., the Executive made Panama's proposed instruments available to the Senate leadership and to the Foreign Relations Committee."

Four months later, in written testimony, he stated, "The Department's participants in the consultations were Herbert J. Hansell, Legal Adviser, and Curtis Cutter of the Bureau of Congressional Relations." He added that the Majority and Minority Leaders "had no difficulties with the draft documents. . . ." But, exactly who informed State? No one ever said.[32]

The stories of Messrs. Dalton, Jorden, Hansell and Kozak differ in important particulars: Dalton, in formal testimony, said that Hansell and Cutter participated in "close consultations," implying several sessions. Jorden wrote that his friend, Mike Kozak, did the consultation in one day. Hansell, in his September 20, 1979 letter to Congressman John Murphy, said that copies of the instruments and protocol were provided for "review and comment" to the Committee which agreed "with the form and content."

And Kozak had another variation. In an interview on November 21, 1983, he described a meeting with Senate staff members: "Herbert Hansell distributed material and explained the draft instruments and protocol of exchange. He went through them and explained . . . the three paragraphs. . . ." Of course, Kozak's story was the most nearly "perfect" accounting but he could supply no dates, no names of the attendees, no specific place of the meeting, and no record of the meeting. Neither did Assistant Secretary of State Powell A. Moore after being asked by the author for the "Department's records" that proved prior consultation with the Senate authorities. Powell had written Senator Alan Cranston, D.-Cal., that there *were* such Department records.

Moreover, 85 letters of inquiry to 23 principals of the Foreign Relations Committee, the Senate leadership and their staffs produced not a single person who recalled the briefing alleged to have been given by Mr. Hansell. Nor did any remember the three paragraphs until after R-Day.

Perhaps the believable story, then, may be Jorden's story that Kozak did it all in one quick trip at the last moment. Again however, Jorden, always so specific with details, gave scant coverage to the important days preceding ratification. Certainly, as the U.S. Ambassador and deeply involved at every phase, he must have known what was going on.

Ironically, during the author's inquiries about the elusive three paragraphs, a great concern was expressed about a minor technicality in the Protocol of Exchange. It was called the *only* change that needed both nations' approval. It included transposing the names of the two countries, placing "United States of America" first, apparently one of the few concessions gained by the Americans throughout. The other part of this technicality was insertion of the phrase "in conformity with the resolution of the Senate of the United States of America of April 18, 1978." This was the big deal. Panama had to approve it.

The variations in the four stories of "Advice and Consent" raise questions. Professor Hans Smit, distinguished jurist of Columbia University, expressed concern about the role of the State Department (letter of March 25, 1985 to Phillip Harman):

. . . I believe the State Department did not always provide accurate advice to the senators . . . many senators consulted me about the provisions of the proposed treaties. In fact, I think our treaty ratification procedure is deficient in that it offers little opportunity for those opposed . . . to present their views effectively. The Senate should organize its own legal staff so as to have the benefit of a more neutral and dispassionate consultant than the State Department. . . .

'INSIGNIFICANT REVISIONS' NEED PANAMA'S APPROVAL

Mr. Jorden explained that "those insignificant revisions would have to be explained to and approved by the Panamanian authorities." That is to say, the Executive Branch of the U.S. government, including President Carter, Ambassador Jorden, the State Department and the treaty negotiators, were careful to have Panama understand and approve such trivia as represented by the above noted technicalities while at the same time denying that Panama's unilateral counter-reservation that nullified U.S. rights would have to be "explained to and approved by" the U.S. Senate under its "Advice and Consent" function? Is this believable?

The remainder of Jorden's explanation (p. 631) gave further credibility to the suspicion of cover up. He reported that the final draft of the instruments and Protocol were actually ready only hours "before the final signing occurred." Thus, there was no possible way that any U.S. Senator could have seen the exact wording of the documents which were accepted and ratified unilaterally by the President on June 16, 1978.

It happened this way: When only a few days remained and after the "lost" documents had again surfaced, it became apparent that the final drafting would have to be done in Panama. Perhaps that was the plan all along. Jorden's assertion, that "everyone in Washington who had to approve" the documents had done so, was obviously not correct. Indeed, all evidence indicated that no Senators or staff people had seen the three paragraph counter-reservation. Nonetheless, the scene was to shift to Panama so the Panamanians could approve the final draft first. This move would help guarantee tranquility on the Isthmus, a most important consideration at this last moment. It would also help assure that the secretive three paragraphs would remain under cover.

Plans were made to send Kozak's secretary, Joan Vanderlyke, to work with Political Counselor Elkin Taylor at the American Embassy in Panama to produce the final papers. But Herbert Hansell had second thoughts: he wanted to "do all the instruments here" in Washington. Why did Hansell insist on holding on to the documents? Was it to avoid possible leaks about the three paragraphs which were by then apparently positioned in the instruments of ratification and which had not been made public? Incidentally, the three paragraphs constituted the only item not fully publicized in the whole operation. Did Hansell want to keep the secret locked in the legal adviser's office until the last moment?

Mr. Hansell's job at the State Department was obviously two-fold: (1) make legal rulings for the Department and (2), do whatever is needed to get the Treaties through.

Although author Jorden said "No one understood why," the evidence suggests nervous concerns about possible cover up. Nonetheless, time considerations required that the final draft be done in Panama so the Panamanians could approve it in time for ratification on June 16, 1978. Meeting the President's deadline seemed the primary consideration and all else was subordinated to that goal. Also, the pressure of time could help keep the secret. Consequently, after two more days of delays, "Joan took off for the isthmus less than seventy two hours before the final signing occurred." In our telephone interview of August 31, 1984, Miss Vanderlyke recalled the rush-rush nature of two hectic days of document preparation at the last minute in Panama—"completed just in time," she said.

This last minute maneuver was one of the most appalling manipulations of the entire misadventure. It was also the final piece of the puzzle, the last peg to pin down the how and who of the most important swindle of our story: the withholding of Panama's secret three paragraphs from the U.S. Senate for "Advice and Consent." Too, it was grievous violation of the Constitution.

In summation, then, with the gaps closed and the missing pieces of the puzzle in place, it appears that: Panama's three paragraphs were probably completed in Panama under the tutelage of American representatives, slipped into the instruments, "lost" in Washington two times, "discovered" a few days before R-Day, then rushed back to Panama for final drafting literally at the last moment. So much for "Advice and Consent."

At the three-hour hearing before Senator John East's Subcommittee on June 23, 1983, only four witnesses were heard. Three gave substantial evidence of irregularities in the treaty process and one, Mr. Dalton, supported State's contention that all was well. Of course, State had a vested interest to defend itself. Only the late Dr. Charles H. Breecher's deposition, taken a few months earlier during his illness, was under oath, as he wanted his evidence to be a sworn statement. Senator East decided that the other witnesses would not be sworn.

It seems probable that specifics of the foregoing story of the paragraphs would have been developed had Mr. East called the principals in the treaty-making to testify under oath. Should not the facts be out in the open, if indeed there is a genuine desire for the truth about this important constitutional issue of "Advice and Consent?"

After the hearing, many questions were sent to the Department of State by East and witness Phillip Harman. After a four-month delay, partial answers came back. Many questions were not answered. Typical State Department responses are illustrated in Appendix K where six straightforward questions are asked. Three of them, questions 1, 2 and 6, were not answered at all. Mr. Dalton provided these responses as the official State Department answers to one of the most critical constitutional issues imaginable.

These non-answers and the East hearing record now rest on the shelves of the Archives and the United States Congress. Is this to be the Senate's legacy?

CARTER AND THE TROUBLESOME BROOKE RESERVATION

The issue of secrecy and cover up was further brought into question by the early date of ratification, June 16, 1978, whereas the Brooke resolution of April 17, 1978 called for an effective date of ratification "not earlier than March 31, 1979." President Carter ignored the intent of Senator Edward Brooke's precautionary measure, that had passed the Senate by a vote of 84 to 3, and signed the ratification papers quickly on June 15, specifying that the "effective" date was March 31, 1979. Perhaps there were reasons.

Moreover, does this precipitous move by Mr. Carter suggest additional cover up in order to preclude public examination and Senate knowledge of Panama's counter-reservation until it had become a *fait accompli?* Nonetheless, the net result was "ratified" Treaties before the word was out that Panama had rejected U.S. rights, rights that presumably had been assured by the DeConcini reservation.

President Carter and the State Department knew before June 16, 1978 that Panama would not accept the DeConcini reservation without modification. Carter's diary entry of April 7, 1978 admitted to inviting Torrijos to write *his own* reservation, which ultimately became the secretive three paragraphs. Ambassador David Popper's letter to Mr. Harman dated June 6, 1982 refers to "the basic issue that Sol Linowitz tried to paper over."[33] Mr. Carter's solution apparently was to act swiftly and to keep quiet about the three paragraphs until the day of "ratification." This procedure also avoided nine and a half months of public scrutiny and more congressional argument.

As a consequence, Dr. Breecher pointed out in his testimony, Panama has learned that an American President and his State Department were willing to accept the Treaties without the DeConcini reservation. He added:

It would be in my opinion next to impossible to convince the Panamanian voters that there was not an excellent chance that Panama could eventually get the Canal without the DeConcini reservation.

It's *most important* to note that President Carter himself, in late 1977/early 1978 said again and again that the Treaties had to be accepted "as is," without a significant change, or else under the Panamanian Constitution a new referendum would be required.[34]

The State Department's rationalization for acceptance of the Panamanian counter-reservation, as explained at the East hearing, was that it was an expression of the cooperative spirit "between the two governments." Moreover, this point was perhaps the strongest argument advanced by Mr. Dalton at the hearing:

In essence, the language in Panama's second paragraph simply states Panama's understanding of the spirit in which the rights and duties under the Treaties, including the DeConcini condition, will be effected. The principles of mutual respect and cooperation referred to in this paragraph form the foundation of the Treaties themselves. They are reflected throughout those documents and they continue to govern the relationship between the two governments.[35]

Nonetheless, Panama had nullified the DeConcini reservation. Dr. Breecher compared this situation to a marriage ceremony where the priest asks the man, "Do you accept this woman for your lawful wedded wife, to have and to hold and to cherish, forsaking all others," and the man replies, "Yes, I do so on the understanding that I may keep my mistress." In regard to the Canal Treaties, Panama accepted everything the Senate put in, including the DeConcini reservation, and then turned aside and said, "on the understanding that I may keep my mistress."[36]

On the record, the United States did not constitutionally accept Panama's three paragraph counter-reservation which is in Panama's instruments of ratification *only—not* in the U.S. instruments. President Carter signed the Protocol of Exchange containing two of the three paragraphs but this was a presidential act—not done with the advice and consent of the Senate in that what he signed was a substantive change in the meaning of the Treaties. The President ignored the fact that there was no meeting of minds expressed in writing.[37]

GENUINE DRAFT INSTRUMENT NEVER FOUND

Another interesting revelation about the mysterious draft instrument of ratification came from the former Panamanian Ambassador, as excerpted from the testimony of Phillip Harman before the East Subcommittee:

In a May 1, 1983 meeting I had in Miami with Gabriel Lewis Galindo, the former Panamanian Ambassador to Washington at the time of the Canal Treaties in 1978, I showed him a copy of Panama's three paragraphs long counter-reservation. He said this is the first time he had ever seen these three paragraphs nor did he know anything about the draft Panamanian instrument that was sent to the Committee.[38]

If there ever existed a genuine Panamanian draft instrument that contained the three paragraphs, common sense cries out that it would have been discovered from the avalanche of letters and other inquiries to all major sources of potential information: the Department of State, the Senate Committee on Foreign Relations, former President Carter and former members of the White House staff, as well as some two dozen other government officials.

Moreover, it should be noted that nine members of the Foreign Relations Committee were attorneys and that their legal training would undoubtedly have alerted them to the inconsistency between the DeConcini reservation and the three paragraphs, i.e., if they had had a chance to compare them. Furthermore, if the Panamanian draft instrument with its contested three paragraphs *did* exist and was out in the open, there was still sufficient time after the vote on the second treaty (April 18, 1978) and before the Exchange of Protocols (June 16, 1978) for President Carter to submit Panama's counter-reservation to the Senate for a two-thirds vote. He did not do this.

Senator Jesse Helms warned the Senate of this danger on June 15,

1978, the day before the Protocols were to be exchanged. In reference to Panama's three paragraphs of counter-reservation, Mr. Helms said, in part:

It has been reported to me that the language (of the counter-reservation) has been held in the Foreign Relations Committee for a week, but no attempt was made to transmit the text to all Senators, nor even to those who were particularly active in the treaty debates.

Appendix L contains the full statement. It was ignored by the Senate leadership and by the Carter Administration, just as were other warnings and requests.

The performance of the Department of State in handling the last minute, secretive Panamanian counter-reservation and in responding to legitimate requests for a copy of the draft instrument of ratification left much to be desired. The same is true of State's responses to important questions asked by Senator East and Mr. Harman as a consequence of the Senate's official inquiry into the constitutionality of the Treaties. Specific answers to these specific questions could have gone far to restore confidence in the State Department's handling of the Treaties.

As to the informal and casual handling of the instruments of ratification between the State Department and the Senate Committee on Foreign Relations, as well as with the Senate Majority and Minority leaders, as contended by Mr. Hansell and others, an elementary question is inescapable: Would not logic and rudimentary business practices demand accurate accounting for interdepartmental and interoffice transactions, most especially on such an important matter as ratifying treaties to transfer American territory and $10 billion worth of taxpayers' property? And on a matter so important to national security? Even though the draft copy of the proposed instrument may have been hand-carried to the Senators and their staffs, certainly letters of transmittal and/or Department logs or journals of some kind would have been used to record such an important transaction. Where are they?

On the other hand, where are the records or journals from the Foreign Relations Committee or from the Majority and Minority leaders to authenticate that such transactions took place, and the details?

Neither the State Department nor the Senate authorities have explained the lack of authentication to prove the close consultations concerning the instruments of ratification. In many respects, this anomaly seems a fitting capstone to this story of stonewalling and cover up. To be sure, if the full Senate had known, or had taken the time to heed Senator Helms's last minute warning (Appendix L) about Panama's counter-reservation that nullified U.S. rights under the DeConcini reservation, there would have been no approved Treaties.

Furthermore, not permitting the Senate to vote on this new reservation by Panama undermined the Senate's constitutional duty for concurrence in treaties and, in effect, constituted gross violations of oaths of office by those who condoned or perpetrated this fraud. Indeed, this deception was the major part of the five part Panama Canal swindle—labeled Swindle Number One.

Great credit is given to the Harman Committee for exhaustive and penetrating efforts to locate an authentic copy of the draft instruments of ratification, and some proof that Panama's three paragraphs were constitutionally handled between the Executive and Legislative Branches. This task was *not* non-productive. It was productive in establishing grounds for conclusions of cover up and stonewalling. At best, if there ever *was* a working draft copy, its implications were glossed over or not explained.

A concise summation of the non-ratification status of the Panama Canal Treaties was included in the sworn testimony of Dr. Charles Breecher before the East hearing. The late Dr. Breecher stated:

. . . the Panama Canal Treaties have not, I repeat "not," been ratified in international law, and . . . they, therefore, did not go into effect on October 1, 1979. The reason is very simple: in their instruments of ratification the United States and Panama did not agree to the same text of the Treaties. Instead Panama added in both its instruments of ratification unilaterally an "understanding" on which it made its agreement to the Treaties contingent. This Panamanian "understanding," three paragraphs long, would, had it been accepted by the United States, have nullified the DeConcini reservation under which the United States has permanently the right to use independently, without Panamanian consent or even against Panamanian opposition, military force in Panama to keep the Canal open and operating. Since the United States has not accepted this Panamanian "understanding," which is a further amendment to the text of the Treaties as amended by the President in the U.S. ratification documents, pursuant to Senate advice and consent, there are no Canal Treaties in international law. This documented fact is beyond any dispute.[39]

·6·

'COULD ALWAYS SEND IN TROOPS'

When Socrates dared speak on behalf of eight generals of the Athenian navy on trial in 406 B.C. for dereliction of duty after the great battle against the Spartans at Arginusea, the people were clamoring for blood. The state obliged and so intimidated the assembly that was trying the generals that they were condemned to death. Socrates identified the defendants as "victims of an insecure government and abuse of law." Indeed, he told his fellow Athenians, "The true teacher must offer himself as a model of what he preaches."

An analogy may be the Carter Administration's surrender of the Panama Canal under threats of intimidation and a clamoring for justice. We recall that Candidate Carter had promised the voters never to give up control of the Canal.[1] Why did he change his position? Possibly he thought he could surrender U.S. rights of sovereignty without "giving up control."

When President Carter was campaigning for ratified Treaties in November 1977, he had long since abandoned his promise of "control" and was assuring Senator Ted Stevens of Alaska and other fellow Americans, that at least "the Treaties provided that the United States could always send in troops to keep the Canal open to ships of all nations."[2]

Unfortunately, this promise was abandoned too when Panama used its secretive counter-reservation to nullify U.S. rights to "send in troops," and President Carter, without the advice and consent of the Senate, unilaterally accepted it on the day the Treaties were ratified, June 16, 1978.

Mr. Carter and his State Department had contended from the first that the United States "could always send in troops;" they preached it— but, in the end, abandoned this clear-cut right in order to get ratified Treaties. Alas, the American people were the "victims of an insecure government and abuse of law," just as were the Athenian naval generals some 24 centuries ago.

The finale of the Canal swindle was Panama's secretive three paragraph counter-reservation, contained in the missing draft instrument of ratification, that was unveiled only at the ratification ceremony between the two Heads of Government. This was Swindle Number One. Nonetheless, there were four other swindles in varying degrees of culpability, each one serious and each one essential for the progression of the Treaties toward success.

SWINDLE NUMBER TWO: THE CLEMENTS CLAUSE IS DELETED

The quiet omission of the Clements Clause from the 1977 draft treaties was the beginning of the end for U.S. rights to "send in troops," as promised by the new President. This unilateral right to enter Panama to protect the Canal had been won through hard negotiations with the Panamanians in 1975; but it was excluded without explanation when the negotiations began in 1977.

Deputy Secretary of Defense William P. Clements, Jr. had made a special trip to Panama in 1975 to negotiate this critical point with Omar Torrijos. Accompanying Clements were General George Brown, the Chairman of the Joint Chiefs of Staff, and William D. Rogers, the Assistant Secretary of State for Inter-American Affairs.[3]

The argument for U.S. rights to "send in troops" began in earnest in 1975 and it never ended. Previously, the Defense Department had wanted a definite slice of the Canal Zone for defense purposes, i.e., specific real estate under U.S. jurisdiction to stand on. Impossible, said State, Panama would never agree. So, the "stacked deck" concept in negotiations continued in the effort to satisfy Panama.

As a consequence, the State Department, the Pentagon and the National Security Council negotiated among themselves and decided on a cooperative arrangement in which the United States and Panama would work closely together to develop a "combined defense" of the Canal.

The mission of the Clements delegation in 1975 was to discuss this concept of "combined defense" with dictator Torrijos and Panamanian President Demetrio Lakas, both of whom agreed with the plan. Subsequently, a security clause later known as the Clements Clause was formulated and cleared through the Pentagon, the National Security Council and the State Department. Thus, the Clements Clause was born. It became an important tenet of the then-agreed draft treaty and a part of national policy.

Specifically, this Clause guaranteed U.S. rights to "take such . . . military measures it deems necessary" against any threats to the Canal:

In the event of any threat to the neutrality of the Canal, the Parties shall consult concerning joint and individual efforts to secure respect for the Canal's security and neutrality, through diplomacy, conciliation, mediation, arbitration, the International Court of Justice, or other peaceful means. If such efforts would be inadequate or have proved to be inadequate, *each Party shall take such other diplomatic, economic or military measures as it deems necessary* in accordance with its constitutional procedures. (Emphasis added.)

This firm statement of U.S. rights was discarded by Mr. Carter and his negotiators. Indeed, when the Treaties were finally presented at the public signing ceremony on September 7, 1977, the ground that previous negotiators had worked for so diligently had been cut away. And, in its place was a co-equal, parallel rights statement implying that both countries would work concurrently and in cooperation in all cases. It was a vague and watered-down paragraph that became Article IV of the Neutrality Treaty:

ARTICLE IV

The United States of America and the Republic of Panama agree to maintain the regime of neutrality established in this Treaty, which shall be maintained in order that the Canal shall remain permanently neutral notwithstanding the termination of any other treaties entered into by the Contracting Parties.[4]

A comparison of Article IV and the rejected Clements Clause reveals distinct differences. For example, what happened to the right of each Party to use "military measures . . . it deems necessary?" Why would Panama accept ambiguity? Perhaps, because in later years, if the United States tried to "send in troops" to defend or reopen the Canal, Panama could rely on world opinion for assertion of its supreme sovereignty over the Canal and all its territory, the Treaties notwithstanding. Moreover, to Panama, the threat of ambiguity and future confrontation was mostly a technicality at this phase—after all, she wanted the Canal.

In testifying before the Senate Armed Services Committee on February 1, 1978, Mr. Clements was asked if the Clements Clause would have given the United States the unilateral right to intervene to protect the Canal. "Yes," said Clements, according to legal counsel of the Departments of State and Defense.[5]

Why was this Clause omitted from the Neutrality Treaty? Did Torrijos oppose its inclusion, fearing that the Panamanian people would reject the Treaties in the plebiscite of October 23, 1977 if the Clause remained? If so, what was the justification for the State Department and the U.S. negotiators to abandon the United States defense position by taking away the most basic right for the security of the Canal?

The Carter Administration was responsible, of course, for deletion of the Clements Clause. This action is also apparent from the letter of July 14, 1983 that Mr. Clements sent to Phillip Harman, the Chairman of the Committee for Better Panama and U.S. Relations, quoted in part:

You asked me a question, ". . . why President Carter and the treaty negotiators deleted your Clause in the 1977 Panama Canal Treaties when the Clements Clause gave the United States the unilateral right to intervene in Panama to protect the Canal?" I cannot answer your question.

President Carter certainly did not consult me nor did the State Department or the individuals who negotiated the treaty. This of course was a major change from the conditions that I had previously negotiated with Omar Torrijos. I can't say for sure that Torrijos did not try to change his mind, but he agreed and signed my conditions. It is inconceivable to me that the State Department would not have held him to the original treaty.

I am sorry I cannot answer your question. You will have to ask someone who served in the Carter Administration.[6]

The weakness and ambiguity of the proposed Article IV, the substitute for the Clements Clause, stirred up dissension in the public and congressional debates that followed. The Treaties were threatened and President Carter asked General Torrijos to come to Washington for emergency consultation on October 14, 1977. There, in order to save the Treaties, they issued their *unsigned* Joint Statement of Understanding regarding "head of line" privileges for warships in time of emergency and unilateral defense rights.[7] This was the agreement about which Torrijos told a waiting airport crowd, "I hadn't even signed my autograph."

Senator James B. Allen, D.-Ala., called the statement an "unsigned, meaningless, nonbinding and confusing document" and added, "Unsigned documents clarifying nothing, understandings of no binding legal effect, reservations not agreed to by the other party, are not going to be sufficient. Fanfare and hoopla in the press are not going to be sufficient. The only course of action is extensive . . . consideration and amendment of each and every provision in both Treaties. . . ."[8] Thus, abandoning the clear-cut

Clements Clause was a problem; also, this was a major reason that there was no meeting of minds for the Treaties.

Unfortunately, the media misinterpreted the Carter-Torrijos Statement as reaffirming U.S. rights. The Majority Leader, Senator Robert Byrd, still uncommitted on the Treaties, hailed the document as "a very important diplomatic achievement," and as allaying many fears. Not so, declared Senator Paul Laxalt, R.-Nev., who disagreed saying the agreement "doesn't reach the basic issue. . . ."[9]

From the beginning, the debate and disagreement over the Treaties usually centered on the subject matter of the Carter-Torrijos Statement: the right of U.S. warships to priority passage in emergency and the right of the United States to "send in troops" to assure the neutrality and defense of the canal. Consequently, many Senators demanded that the Statement be incorporated into the treaty itself (the Neutrality Treaty).

At one point, the Foreign Relations Committee voted to include it as an amendment to the treaty. Since this would have added a new article, proposed as Article IX, the State Department objected on the grounds that it would be a major change requiring a second plebiscite in Panama, a contingency that Carter had promised Torrijos to avoid.

Accordingly, the Foreign Relations Committee obliged and agreed to include the same material in two parts which became amendments to Articles IV and VI of the Neutrality Treaty. In the Senate they were called Leadership Amendments 20 and 21. Earlier U.S. negotiator Sol Linowitz had said, "It is what a statement does, not what it is called, that is important."[10]

This move for political expediency by the Foreign Relations Committee, seconded by Linowitz, was a sort of self-indictment for what transpired later: The late Senator Dewey F. Bartlett, R.-Okla., was rebuffed for trying to ascertain that Panama had observed legal and constitutional requirements for ratification in that substantive changes called for another plebiscite. Initially, the substance of the added-on amendments to Articles IV and VI were judged to be major changes requiring a new Article IX to the treaty itself; but to honor a commitment by Mr. Carter to avoid a second plebiscite, the Senate bent the rules to accommodate the President. But the subject matter did not change and the necessity for a second plebiscite, under Panamanian law, was not removed.

Moreover, these leadership amendments to the Neutrality Treaty, although judged as major additions by the Foreign Relations Committee, continued the uncertainties. They also helped compound the uncertainties about constitutional ratification procedures in Panama. Said Alphonse Karr (1877), "Uncertainty is the worst of all evils, until the moment when reality makes us regret uncertainty."

LEADERSHIP AMENDMENTS FAIL TO DISPEL
AMBIGUITY

The amendment to Article IV of the Neutrality Treaty omits the unilateral U.S. defense rights; and the vague co-equal, parallel rights theory is enhanced. Cutting through the verbiage, this amendment simply says that *both* nations "have the responsibility" to keep the Canal open and secure "in accordance with their respective constitutional processes."[11] It says nothing about guaranteeing U.S. rights, whether Panama agrees or not.

Moreover, this amendment goes beyond the co-equal, parallel theory. In a separate paragraph, it warns against interference in the internal affairs of Panama and emphasizes territorial integrity and political independence—a clear reference to Panama's firm and undiluted sovereignty over its soon-to-be-acquired territory, the Canal Zone.

In like manner, the amendment to Article VI appears at first glance[12] to provide expeditious passage for the warships and auxiliaries of both nations, including "head of line" in case of need or emergency. However, it does not define need or emergency, nor specify who will define them. Later, however, this matter was corrected by Understanding (2) to the Neutrality Treaty, providing: that either party may take "unilateral action to defend the Panama Canal" and that determination of the "need or emergency" shall be made by the nation operating the warship or auxiliary vessel. Original planning had been flawed.

These additions to the Treaties in the form of amendments, reservations, conditions and understandings, particularly Panama's uncontested three paragraphs of counter-reservation, all ensure future misunderstandings and possible confrontations. Senators Griffin, Allen and others wanted renegotiated Treaties as the only way for a meeting of minds. Unfortunately, ambiguity was condoned, even promoted in order to satisfy the Panamanians. For example, one result was the harsh rhetoric of Panama's senior negotiator, Romulo Escobar Bethancourt, who avowed, even before the Treaties went into force, that the Gringoes with their warships would not have priority and that "the concept of privileged passage was rejected."[13]

The meeting of minds was not achieved during the negotiations phase, nor in the final Treaties. Moreover, during the years-long debates and compromises, a total of five U.S. statements regarding defense rights were considered. Of these five, only the Clements Clause (junked by the Carter negotiators) and the DeConcini reservation (the temporary savior of the Neutrality Treaty, later killed by Panama's unchallenged three paragraphs)—only these two U.S. statements explicitly defined each nation's authority to act independently, i.e., as it saw fit. And both were lost. The other three statements lacked definition and were based on the non-specific co-equal, parallel theory. They were not solutions.

Incidentally, the idea for the DeConcini reservation may have originated from the testimony of Colonel John P. Sheffey, U.S. Army (Ret.), before the Senate Foreign Relations Committee on January 25, 1978. This former member of the treaty team spoke against the ambiguous Article IV and recommended advice and consent to the Treaties only with the reservation that Panama agree that

in the event of any failure to keep the Canal in operation . . ., unilateral U.S. action on Panamanian territory, aimed solely at restoring the Canal to operation, would not be considered an act of war or intervention in Panama in violation of the Rio Pact and the UN Charter.

The DeConcini reservation followed this pattern, adding the stronger words, "independently" and "use of military force," words that were avoided in the leadership amendments.

Obviously, the DeConcini reservation was a substitute for the abandoned Clements Clause, the latter having been quietly buried by the State Department during the period between September 1975 and September 1977, apparently because it was offensive to the Panamanians. To be sure, if the Treaties had contained the Clements Clause, they would very probably have been soundly rejected in the Panamanian plebiscite of October 23, 1977—hence, no Treaties.

On the other hand, the Americans were offended too, particularly after seeing the diluted Article IV in the Neutrality Treaty. As a result, the DeConcini reservation became an absolute must if the Treaties were to survive. Indeed, this was the purpose of the DeConcini reservation—the survival of the Neutrality Treaty. Mr. Carter made this clear in his memoirs four years later when he admitted having to accept the DeConcini "language" in order to "save the Treaty."[14]

In reference to the DeConcini "language" which Mr. Carter found objectionable, herewith is a portion of Senator DeConcini's statement to the Senate on March 16, 1978, the day of the vote on the first Treaty:

The purpose of this amendment is quite simple, Mr. President. It is designed to establish a precondition to American acceptance of the Neutrality Treaty. That precondition states that regardless of the reason and regardless of what any other provision of the Neutrality Treaty might say or what interpretation it might be subject to, if the Panama Canal is closed, the United States has the right to enter Panama, using whatever means are necessary, to reopen the Canal. There are no conditions, no exceptions, and no limitations on this right. By the terms of the amendment, the United States interprets when such a need exists, and exercises its own judgment as to the means necessary to insure that the Canal remains open and accessible.

A good deal of the discussion involving the Panama Canal Treaties has centered upon threats to the Canal which might come from third parties—more specifically—the Communist countries. While this concern is certainly justified, I have been equally bothered by the possibility that internal Panamanian activities might also be a threat to the waterway, should we give it up. Labor unrest and strikes; the action of an unfriendly government; political riots or upheavals—each of these alone or in combination might cause a closure of the Canal. . . .

The amendment contains a very specific reference to the use of military force in Panama. I believe these words are absolutely crucial because they establish the American right—which I am not convinced is adequately provided for either in the body of the Treaty or the leadership amendment—to take military action if the case so warrants. It further makes it clear that the United States can take military action on Panamanian soil without the consent of the Panamanian Government.

Appendix M is Senator DeConcini's entire statement, including his "language" and intentions in attempting to assure essential rights to the United States for the security and defense of this strategic waterway. It was well received by the Senate which on the same day adopted the DeConcini reservation by a vote of 75 to 23 despite opposition by Senator Edward M. Kennedy, D.-Mass., and other proponents of more liberal Treaties.

The other three amendments out of the five that were considered by the United States were based on the parallel, co-equal theory: (1) the ambiguous leadership amendment to Article IV of the Neutrality Treaty; (2) Article IV itself, the weak substitute for the firm rights in the discarded Clements Clause; and (3) the so-called leadership amendment to the second treaty (the Panama Canal Treaty), the eleventh hour amendment that had been authored on an early Sunday morning by Senators Byrd, Church and Sarbanes with the help of Deputy Secretary of State Warren Christopher, Panamanian Ambassador Gabriel Lewis Galindo and William D. Rogers, a former Assistant Secretary of State.

Unfortunately, none of these three provisos address unilateral U.S. defense rights—a primary requirement for the security of the canal—nor do they provide for any resolution of potential disagreements between the United States and Panama. Fortunately for Panama, however, they do accentuate non-interference and supreme sovereignty.

The reaction to the DeConcini guarantees of U.S. rights in unequivocal "language" was revealing on both sides. The clear-cut objectives were not acceptable to the Panamanians, who had found out since the Clements negotiations of 1975 that they could get more from the new United States negotiators. They also found out they had allies in the U.S. Senate, many of whose members opposed DeConcini's "language" as well.

KENNEDY AND ILLUECA ATTACK RIGHT TO 'SEND IN TROOPS'

One of the most vocal opponents to the DeConcini "language" was Senator Kennedy who spoke against offending the Panamanians with an amendment "which starkly insists on our rights to use military force in Panama" against a "small, proud, sovereign state." In his March 16, 1978 speech, the date the Senate consented to the Neutrality Treaty, Kennedy also said, "It stirs up what is already an emotional issue in Panama, without adding to the rights of the United States already recognized by the treaty."

Mr. Kennedy was mistaken, however, because the Treaties did *not* recognize the specific rights outlined in the DeConcini reservation. Obviously, the Panamanians disagreed with Kennedy too, because it took a surreptitious three paragraphs long secretive reservation to satisfy them. Mr. Kennedy's address to the Senate, just before the critical vote, contended, among other things, that Panama had waited 75 years for the resolution of the "unfairness" that had characterized Panamanian-U.S. relations since 1903, the date of the original treaty. Kennedy called for an "end (to) American occupation of Panama's heartland." Senator Kennedy's assessment had little to do with the real situation in 1903, however.

Shortly after the DeConcini-Kennedy debate, the Panamanian Ambassador to the United Nations, Jorge E. Illueca, presented his country's objections to the DeConcini reservation to the UN General Assembly. He included the statements of both Kennedy and DeConcini in his address to the delegates. Illueca's report included the regrets of Senator Kennedy that Panama "must wait 22 years before it achieves full control over its national territory" and was being asked to accept "an amendment which has the ring of military interventionism—not just during this century, but for all time."

Illueca closed his statement with the following plea for "solidarity" among the members of the international community:

Since the Treaty provides for accession by all States to the Protocol whereby the signatories would adhere to the objectives of the Neutrality Treaty and agree to respect the regime of neutrality, the Panamanian Head of Government has considered it his duty to address this letter to the Heads of State or Heads of Government of States members of the international community that have in so many instances offered their solidarity and support to the Panamanian nation in its long struggle to reach a peaceful solution to the Panama Canal question based on the recognition of her sovereignty over the totality of its national sovereignty.

Also a part of Dr. Illueca's inflammatory declaration was a March 27, 1978 Communique from the Ministry of Foreign Affairs of Panama, succinctly reminding the members of the United Nations of Panama's "decolonization programme" and that the UN Security Council had met in Panama in March 1973 and, in effect, had "vetoed the United States for not removing the cause of conflict engendered by the presence of a foreign government within the Panamanian territory." Illueca and the UN Security Council, however, were incorrect. The Canal Zone was *not* Panamanian territory, of course, and Dr. Illueca, the trained attorney, no doubt knew this. His inflammatory rhetoric, nonetheless, served to exacerbate an already tense situation.

This performance was in character though for Jorge Illueca who, on January 9, 1964, had urged Panama's President Roberto Chiari to break diplomatic relations with the United States after the three-day "flag war" that erupted because of efforts by Panamanian students to fly their flag at Balboa High School. As editor of the newspaper, *El Panama America,* Illueca had written on January 2:

We are confident that an intelligent and timely representation of our foreign ministry, and a spirit of understanding and foresightedness on the part of the representatives of the U.S. government, will make it possible that a harmonious solution to the problem will be found.[15]

The situation worsened and Jules Dubois described what next happened in his book, *Danger Over Panama:*

That harmonious solution was not to be found, and Illueca's emotions were to explode as violently as some of the most responsible people of the government, from President Chiari down, and he was to be among the first to demand that Panama charge the United States with aggression and to urge Chiari to break diplomatic relations. This he did on the night of January 9. The fire and brimstone of his days in the *Frente Patriotico de la Juventud* had been revived. . . ."[16]

Subsequently, diplomatic relations were suspended until April 4, 1964; then, mutual recognition was reestablished through the offices of the Organization of American States.[17]

As for Jorge E. Illueca, the pro-communist firebrand, his rise in the Panamanian hierarchy took him to the presidency on February 13, 1984 upon the sudden and unexplained resignation of President Ricardo de la Espriella.[18] Thus, Illueca, the defender of Cuba's Fidel Castro and Granada's Maurice Bishop, assumed an office he had long sought just three months before Panama's first presidential election since 1968 when Arnulfo Arias was ousted by a military coup just a few days after taking office on October 1. Ever since, the military had run the country directly or indirectly. Military control was especially dominant up to the 1981 death of Torrijos in an aircraft crash.

The issue of sovereignty over the Canal Zone had always been contentious, some Panamanians claiming that the International Court of Justice had been involved. So, a direct inquiry was made by Phillip Harman, then Director of Information of the Canal Zone Non-Profit Public Information Corporation. Harman's letter of January 28, 1977 to the Hague-based Court of Justice follows:

Through the years I have been told by various citizens of the Republic of Panama that the matter of sovereignty and ownership of the Panama Canal Zone has been brought up for discussion at the International Court of Justice.

Would you be kind enough to let me know if this matter has ever been brought up for discussion at the International Court of Justice?[19]

The answer from A. Pillepich, First Secretary of the International Court of Justice, dated 9 February 1977, was conclusive:

In answer to your letter of 28 January 1977 I wish to inform you that the questions of the ownership of the Panama Canal Zone, and of the sovereignty thereover, have never been brought up before the International Court of Justice for discussion.[20]

In making his anti-American declaration before the United Nations condemning the DeConcini reservation, Ambassador Jorge Illueca may or may not have done his homework—or, perhaps it did not matter. The historic American role in the disease-infested jungles of the former Colombian Province had long faded from relevance. Perhaps William Hazlitt (1778-1830), the British critic, had just the words for this situation: "Though familiarity may not breed contempt, it takes off the edge of admiration."

There was apparently no lack of admiration in the early 1900s when the U.S. action in the Isthmus of Panama assured the independence and solvency of the new nation, the Republic of Panama. An editorial writer of that day in recounting the excitement of the Panamanian revolution wrote in the newspaper *Star and Herald* for November 25, 1903:

Well might the Isthmian thank Divine Providence that the telegraph was not in working order during the 6th to the 10th of November (when Colombia was trying to scuttle the Hay-Bunau-Varilla Treaty of 1903).

Their gratitude to the United States Government should certainly have no bounds for the moral support given after they struck for liberty and autonomy.[21]

Illueca's condemnation of the DeConcini reservation, as delivered to kindred souls in the United Nations, was a kind of call to arms, a sounding of the tocsin for Third World nations and world opinion against United States defense rights in the Canal Zone. The Panamanian, of course, knew the Canal Zone was not his country's "national territory" but this was all part of the continuing misinformation to influence the uninformed.

It is unfortunate that the U.S. media did not challenge such blatant misstatements. It would have been easy, for example, to set the record straight with a few lines simply stating that the U.S. Supreme Court in 1907 had found the Canal Zone to be U.S. territory in the historic *Wilson v. Shaw* case[22] and that as late as 1972 the U.S. Circuit Court of Appeals for the Fifth District had found the same thing.[23] Nonetheless, the allegations of Panamanian sovereignty caught the headlines and indeed, were always important arguments for the Kennedys, the Carters and others who either failed to understand or else, chose the most convenient "answer."

The mysteries of the elusive draft instrument of ratification and the deleted Clements Clause (Swindles One and Two respectively) may forever remain locked in the depths of Foggy Bottom—or in the consciences of those who know—unless the Senate Committee on the Judiciary, or other jurisdictional body, decides that the Canal swindle and its constitutional ramifications deserve full-scale examination. Even then, such an inquiry will succeed only if there is determination to find the truth. Is there political and moral will in the Congress for this kind of probe? Meanwhile, an aroused public may demand the truth with such fervor that the national leadership will *find* the will power to face the unconstitutional practices used in surrendering the Panama Canal.

· 7 ·

'CLASH-TRACK RAILROAD JOB'

An unexpected anticlimax to the elaborate treaty-signing ceremony of September 7, 1977 was the laudatory radio message sent to Fidel Castro by Omar Torrijos on his return to Panama—as he flew over Cuba: "In Latin America your name is linked to sentiments of dignity which have been directed toward the ending of all vestige of a shameful colonial system."[1] This comrade-in-arms greeting, sent after Torrijos's embrace of Carter at the Washington extravaganza, would be no help in easing the Treaties through the U.S. Senate.[2]

A major concern of many Senators, then called upon to approve the Panama Canal Treaties, was the communist influence in the Panamanian government and its impact on the future security of the Canal. Many high-level officials were known to be communist or pro-communist: for example, the Vice President, the treasury minister, the minister of labor and the minister of education. It was a zig-zag arrangement with approximately half of the senior positions occupied by communists or pro-communists. Moreover, the personal adviser to Torrijos was the highly active and outspoken communist, Romulo Escobar Bethancourt, who became Panama's chief negotiator for the Treaties. Dr. Bethancourt's influence also extended to the educational field where he had served as chancellor of the University of Panama, reputedly the center of communist activities in Panama.[3]

Incidently, it was the University of Panama that hosted a meeting of the Anti-Imperialist Tribune of Our America (TANA) on November 26, 1983. One objective of this gathering of delegates of some 30 leftist organizations from nine Third World countries was to condemn President

Ronald Reagan "as the representative of U.S. imperialism" and to demand "total restitution and compensation for the aggression, exploitation, looting and damage."[4] Thus, the promotion of anti-Americanism from Panamanian institutions had continued from the days of the debates on the Treaties.

The mood of the Carter Administration and the leadership in the Senate in 1977 was that, once the negotiators had delivered proposed Treaties, nothing must stand in the way of a two-thirds vote of approval by the Senate and official ratification by the President. Of course, the Senate did not *have* to consent to the Treaties—nor did the President *have* to ratify them. Either party could have stopped at any point up to the day of the ratification, June 16, 1978.

A sufficient reason to stop procedures would have been the official Panamanian Foreign Ministry Communique of April 25, 1978 which was publicized a full seven weeks prior to President Carter's "ratification." Mr. Carter had time and cause to halt the process. The cause? Panama's Communique repudiated the five U.S. reservations and one understanding that had been added to guarantee basic U.S. rights for the future defense and neutrality of the Canal. Some were rejected outright and others included elaborate "understandings" diametrically opposite to U.S. positions. Panama was telling the world, after the U.S. Senate had completed its final action, that she accepted the Treaties only on her conditions and according to her own interpretations.

The Senate-approved changes to the Treaties not only guaranteed U.S. rights but had also won over the five or six additional supporters needed for a two-thirds vote of concurrence. Senator Helms warned on June 5, 1978:

The differences between the Senate's intent, as expressed in the treaty debates, and the Panamanian interpretation is so great that the potential for disputes, acrimony and dissension will be vastly increased by the ratification of the Treaties. Once Panama assumes sovereignty over the Canal, the United States will either have to acquiesce to Panama's demands, or withdraw early. We will be mousetrapped.[5]

At that time, the Congress could only hope to influence the President about a dangerous development and to urge clarification, even renegotiation of the Treaties. But the State Department and the President were not receptive to further delays. Victory was at hand. Representative George V. Hansen, R.-Ida., called the Treaties procedures a "clash-track railroad job" during our interview of November 18, 1983 in Washington, D.C. Mr. Hansen had strongly opposed the Treaties and had traveled the country speaking out against them. He Said:

There was such a clash-track railroad job going on among the parties who were attempting to turn over the Panama Canal: The big banks were putting the pressure on the U.S. government because of the involvement they had in trying to find a way to retrieve their bad loans; and the only way they apparently felt they could do it was to have the taxpayers and consumers of the United States underwrite it. Then, there was the effort by the Senate to make the Senate treaty considerations the only authority. They attempted to deny the House of Representatives, under the constitutional authority they had, the responsibility of passing on any transfer of property—and what we got was tokenism.[6]

Representative Hansen was referring to the constitutional requirement that *both* Houses of the Congress dispose of U.S. territory and property—not just the Senate alone.[7] He had made legislative history in 1978 as the first national lawmaker to walk from the House of Representatives to the Senate demanding that the prerogatives of the House of Representatives be honored. It was a "parliamentary" move that failed, however.

Three other parliamentary moves failed also. They involved former Senator Robert P. Griffin and the late Senator Dewey F. Bartlett—and they comprised the other three swindles. They included stonewalling and tabling of important resolutions.

SWINDLE NUMBER THREE: STONEWALLING SENATOR GRIFFIN

On the afternoon of March 16, 1978 the Senate leadership decided that the "crossing of the Rubicon" was at hand for the decision on the Treaties.[8] It was time to vote and further delay was unacceptable. The withholding of essential information from the Senators before their crucial vote approving the DeConcini reservation and the first treaty (the Neutrality Treaty) constituted this swindle.

Republican Robert P. Griffin of Michigan, who had taken on the job of managing the opposition to the Treaties in the Senate, had followed developments closely and a few weeks earlier had denounced the Treaties as "pregnant with the seeds of acrimony and strife . . . fatally flawed and riddled with ambiguity."[9]

Nonetheless, the Administration and the Senate leadership had pressed on. The reaction of the Panamanians to the DeConcini reservation was feature news on the CBS radio and television stations on the morning of the first vote, March 16,1978. The *New York Times* headlined the vote on the Neutrality Treaty the following day. This was the big story, of course, but it also reported that "General Torrijos and the Panamanian negotiating team were particularly depressed by the [DeConcini] reservation."

The headline for the *New York Times* story on March 17, 1978 was

"Panamanians Reluctantly Indicate They Accept Pact's Reservation," but the fine print said otherwise. Torrijos was emphatic in letting newsmen know that any reservation that impeded "the exercise of Panamanian sovereignty" or that allowed "interference in our internal affairs disguised as neutrality" was unacceptable. Another *Times* headline that day was more ominous: "Storm of Protest Expected." A *Washington Post* headline for March 17, 1978 read "Panama Hails Vote: Senate Reservation May Cause Trouble."[10]

Of course, the "reservation" that worried the Panamanians and the media was the DeConcini reservation, guaranteeing U.S. rights to defend and keep open the Canal, with or without Panama's consent. This was the "ghost" that persisted in spoiling the celebrations. Indeed, earlier *New York Times* headlines said "U.S. Worried Over Panamanian Reaction," and another, "Panamanians, Assured by Torrijos, Confident on Pacts" went on in the fine print, asserting that the "use of troops" by the U.S. to reopen a closed Canal (as guaranteed by the DeConcini reservation) would be "rejected if put to a vote."

These were the concerns and circumstances that prompted Senator Griffin's request to the Senate leadership and the White House for clarifying information for himself and his colleagues about the reported outburst in Panama.

When the information was not forthcoming, and shortly before the vote was taken, Senator Griffin made a motion to send the Treaties back to the President with instructions to negotiate new Treaties that would better serve the interests of both nations. Senator Frank Church, D.-Ida., warned that adoption of the Griffin motion would end with no further negotiations being held and with the U.S. forces in Panama "behind pointed bayonets." The motion was tabled by a vote of 67 to 33.

The information was not provided when it was needed, and the DeConcini reservation together with the first treaty were consented to. This was Swindle Number Three.

March 16, 1978, therefore, may have been the most crucial day in the 22 days and 152 hours of the Senate debate and the 1,000 pages of the *Congressional Record* that was consumed in handling the Neutrality Treaty.[11] Senator Griffin had taken the floor early that morning and told his colleagues about an alarming news report to the effect that Panamanian Ambassador Gabriel Lewis Galindo had called at the White House the day before to tell President Carter and Secretary of State Vance that the Panamanians were extremely upset by the Senate additions to the Treaty. Mr. Griffin asked for confirmation from the White House and from the Senate leadership "so that we can intelligently decide our responsibility." He made the following statement before the vote:

Mr. President, I was interested to learn of a report this morning by CBS radio—and television, I take it, about the fact that the Ambassador of Panama called at the White House on yesterday and let the President and Secretary Vance know that General Torrijos is extremely upset over Senate additions to the Treaties, as I understand the report.

I also understand on the basis of the report that the President called General Torrijos on yesterday and attempted to calm him down and to assure him that, really, what the Senate was doing here was not making any significant changes in the treaty.

I can only read between the lines, Mr. President, but I suspect that the concern is not only about what the Senate already has done but also what the Senate may be about to do this afternoon. I refer, in particular, to an amendment to be offered by the Senator from Arizona [Mr. DeConcini].

. . . .

This, of course, would fly in the face of the Panamanian interpretation of the Neutrality Treaty, which is that the United States cannot come in with military force to defend the neutrality of the Canal unless it is with the permission of the Republic of Panama.

The public press reports now are that President Carter—I do not know if it is true or not—has agreed to go along with this amendment by the Senator from Arizona, which obviously would be a significant change in the Treaty as it has been interpreted and understood in Panama.

. . . .

I would think that, in light of the situation in the Senate, it would not be unreasonable to ask the White House to inform the Senate if it is true, as reported by CBS, that General Torrijos and top Panamanian officials have expressed their outrage about the action taken in the Senate and about to be taken today, and whether such an exchange of views took place on yesterday. Also, how about informing the Senate, so that we can intelligently decide our responsibility?[12]

Again, Senator Griffin had explained in explicit language the continuing disagreement between the United States and Panama that had not been resolved. Neither the White House nor the State Department replied that day to Griffin or to the Majority or Minority leaders. The "Rubicon was crossed," and both the DeConcini reservation and the Neutrality Treaty were agreed to. Unfortunately, the Senate had received no information from Mr. Carter that Senator Griffin was correct in assessing that the DeConcini reservation was indeed "a significant change in the Treaty as it had been interpreted and understood in Panama."

It is ironic to compare the attitudes prevalent on March 16, 1978 about U.S. unilateral rights with the State Department testimony at the East Subcommittee hearing on June 23, 1983 to the effect that Panama's three paragraphs of uncontested counter-reservation were only a part of the "mutual respect and cooperation" that underlaid the Treaties. Had the "cooperation" that was missing in 1978 suddenly materialized in 1983?

Undoubtedly, on March 16, 1978, if the Senate had known that Panama rejected U.S. rights in the DeConcini reservation, as was later confirmed by Ambassador David H. Popper's letter of June 5, 1982,[13] there would have been no consent to the Neutrality Treaty that day. Although President Carter and the State Department have offered no explanations for withholding essential information from the Senate, i.e., no known explanations, the reason is obvious.

On the following day, March 17, more details of this swindle were revealed by the following colloquy between Senator Griffin and the late Democratic Senator from Alabama, James B. Allen:

Mr. GRIFFIN. However, a matter that disturbs this Senator very much relates to an exchange, within the last 48 hours, of telephone calls and an exchange of letters between the President and General Torrijos relating to the reservations that were being considered in the Senate. I find now by reading the morning papers—not from any information provided by the White House—that a letter was received at the White House yesterday from General Torrijos, apparently sent in response to a letter sent by President Carter to General Torrijos on Wednesday, and that these letters pertain directly to the matters under discussion in the Senate. Despite the fact that this Senator, early in the debate on yesterday, following a CBS report by Phil Jones, called upon the White House to provide us with a report as to previous telephone conversations and the letter sent by President Carter, no information was provided to the Senate.

Mr. ALLEN. Is the Senator talking about the amendments to the resolution of ratification?

Mr. GRIFFIN. And certain reservations, particularly the one offered by Senator DeConcini.

Mr. ALLEN. In other words, [President Carter was] agreeing to something here that he was assuring Torrijos did not mean anything, is that right?

Mr. GRIFFIN. Obviously, until we can see the letters, it is difficult to say what is in them. . . . But there is every reason to be concerned that while Senators were being assured, on the one hand, that their amendments were meaningful in order to get their vote, there were assurances being given to the Panamanians or to General Torrijos that the same amendments would not change anything.[14]

Later developments proved Mr. Griffin to have been correct: President Carter had been assuring Senators that their amendments were needed to provide U.S. rights while telling Torrijos that the same amendments would not change anything. The discussion between Senators Griffin and Allen had been on the day (March 17) after the Neutrality Treaty and the DeConcini reservation had been approved with a one vote margin.

More and more Senators including Minority Leader Baker, were joining in the call for the letters. Within an hour, they were handed to Senator Byrd on the Senate floor.

President Carter's letter to Torrijos was dated March 15 (the day *before* the vote) and stated, in part:

In the Senate debate, we have fortunately been able to prevent any amendments to the Treaty other than the so-called "Leadership" amendments to Articles IV and VI. These incorporate exactly the terms of the Statement of Understanding published after our conversation of October 14.

In considering its Resolution of Ratification of the Treaty, the Senate will almost certainly attach a number of reservations, conditions or understandings reflecting certain of its concerns. We have made every effort and have been successful to date in ensuring that these will be consistent with the general purposes of our two countries as parties to the Treaty. I hope you will examine them in this light. [15]

In this letter, President Carter was implying to another head of state that he controlled the actions of the U.S. Senate which he expected to conform to the presidential will, thereby degrading the constitutional requirement for separation of powers between the Executive and Legislative Branches. North Carolina's Jesse Helms observed in this connection, ". . . the President's letter to Torrijos is a demeaning instrument expressing contempt for the constitutional obligations of the Senate." [16]

Mr. Carter *was* controlling the actions of the Senate when the contents of his telephone conversations and letters to Torrijos were not made available before the March 16 vote. In answer to Carter's March 15 letter, Torrijos wrote on the same day to Carter, in part:

In your letter and conversation, you informed me that the Senate will introduce some reservations, but that they will not alter nor detract from the content of what was agreed upon in the Neutrality Treaty and in our Declaration of October 14, 1977. In this respect, I wish to inform you that the Government of Panama will proceed to study carefully these reservations and *will take its position once the Senate has voted on both Treaties*. The situation is thus because in the plebiscite held in Panama the Panamanian people voted for the Treaties together and not in separate form.

I do wish, nonetheless, to point out that such a study will be based on the following concepts: For Panama any reservation would be unacceptable which blemished our national dignity, which altered or changed the objectives of the Treaty or which were directed at hindering the effective exercise of Panamanian sovereignty over all of its territory, the transfer of the Canal, and military withdrawal on December 31, 1999. For that reason, I received with great gratitude your words that these objectives will absolutely not be changed by means of amendments or reservations. This reaffirms my estimate concerning the great morality and honesty which characterize you as a political leader and as a person.

The Panamanian people would not accept words, misplaced commas, or ambiguous sentences which had as their objective, or which might signify, occupation in perpetuity disguised as neutrality or intervention in their internal affairs.[17] (Emphasis added)

Thus, even before the DeConcini reservation was voted on, Torrijos had rejected it in this letter to Mr. Carter, who chose not to notify the Senate. Moreover, Torrijos stated that the Government of Panama would "proceed to study carefully these reservations [DeConcini] and will take its position once the Senate has voted on both Treaties." Panama did "take its position" after the U.S. Senate had approved the Treaties—in the form of the three paragraph counter-reservation that cancelled out the rights provided by the DeConcini reservation. Furthermore, Panama's negotiators, Romulo Escobar Bethancourt and Aristides Royo, said the same thing at a press conference the day after the Senate vote, warning that Panama would "present its own reservations when the instruments of ratification are exchanged." So, the Senate was forewarned on many occasions.

In a later development, Torrijos sent a letter to the heads of state of all UN members, denouncing U.S. plans for interventionism under the DeConcini reservation. Panama's UN Ambassador Jorge E. Illueca then explained Torrijos's action in his letter of March 28, 1978 to the UN Secretary General, saying in part:

... the DeConcini Amendment is intended to give the United States of America the unilateral and perpetual right to "take military action on Panamanian soil without the consent of the Panamanian Government," pretending that said Amendment must be construed to permit the United States to intervene in Panama in the event of labour unrest, strikes, a slowdown, or any pretext labeled as interference in Canal operations....[18]

This letter to the United Nations, and to the world, was another "official" denouncement of the DeConcini reservation and it led to further U.S. efforts to satisfy: The immediate result was the vague leadership amendment to the second treaty (the Panama Canal Treaty). The Panamanians believed this leadership amendment had voided the DeConcini reservation. But to make sure, they added their secretive three paragraph counter-reservation which President Carter accepted without the consent of the Senate.

Panama went further to "take its position" in a sweeping 25 page Foreign Ministry Communique dated April 25, 1978. This official document repudiated the DeConcini reservation in no uncertain terms, saying explicitly that the "national government firmly expressed its rejection of that amendment [DeConcini]" and that the new leadership amendment to the second treaty impacted retroactively to the Neutrality Treaty so there was not the slightest doubt that the Deconcini reservation "has been eliminated."[19]

Panama's understanding was diametrically opposite to that of the United States. Moreover, the stonewalling of Senator Griffin's request for information, the third swindle, had exacerbated an already touchy situation: the acceptance of clear-cut U.S. rights. All this could have been avoided if the White House had leveled with the Senate, or for that matter, if the Senate leadership had acted responsibly, with all cards on the table.

In a belated effort to get an opinion about the propriety or legality of withholding important information affecting the business of the Senate, the Harman Committee sent a letter of inquiry on July 3, 1983 to Senator Ted Stevens, Chairman of the Select Committee on Ethics, asking the question: Can the Executive Branch withhold vital information from the Senate, information that the Senate had requested, knowing that this information would prevent passage of a reservation as well as a treaty?

Similar letters were sent to former Senator Griffin and to Representative Donald J. Albosta, D.-Mich., regarding the House of Representatives policies.

SWINDLES FOUR AND FIVE: BARTLETT TABLED TWICE

On the same day that Senator Griffin was stonewalled, March 16, 1978, on his request for information about Panama's rejection of the DeConcini reservation, another important Senate parliamentary action took place: It was the vote to table Bartlett Reservation Number 4 to the Neutrality Treaty, a move designed by the late Senator Dewey F. Bartlett, R.-Okla., to require President Carter to determine "that the Republic of Panama has ratified the Treaty, as amended, in accordance with its constitutional processes."[20]

We call this Swindle Number Four because it involved ratification procedures in Panama that were contrary to the Panamanian Constitution and that conceivably could cause later rejection of the Treaties by a future regime.

Basic to Senator Bartlett's Reservation was the fact that six changes to the Treaties (five reservations and one understanding) that had been approved by the U.S. Senate had *not* been approved by a second plebiscite in Panama as required by Article 274 of Panama's 1972 Constitution, an article specially crafted to protect the people of Panama, saying, in part, "Treaties . . . with respect to the Panama Canal . . . shall be submitted to a national plebiscite."

Panamanian law, therefore, required a new plebiscite because all six changes were considered to be substantial modifications to the Treaties, particularly the DeConcini reservation whose guarantees of U.S. unilateral rights had always been contested. Indeed, any rejection of the DeConcini reservation was rejection of the foundation upon which the Treaties structure had been built.

The six U.S. changes that altered the Treaties and that the Panamanians did not vote on were:

1. The Nunn Reservation to the Neutrality Treaty, modifying Article V so as to permit future negotiations for the stationing of U.S. troops in Panama after the year 2000.

2. The DeConcini Reservation to the Neutrality Treaty, authorizing U.S. troops unilaterally to enter Panama to put down a threat to the neutrality of the Canal.

3. The Hollings-Heinz-Bellmon Reservation to the Panama Canal Treaty, providing that the U.S. is not obligated to pay any outstanding balance under the annual $10 million contingency payment (Article XIII, 4, c) when the Canal is turned over in the year 2000. The contingent payment would not be included in the estimated toll base, would never be earned, and never paid.

4. The Brooke Reservation, providing that the instruments of ratification be exchanged effective not earlier than March 31, 1979, and the Treaties not enter into force prior to October 31, 1979, unless the implementing legislation was passed earlier.

5. The Cannon Reservation that the Panama Canal Commission reimburse the U.S. Treasury for interest on investment and amortization of assets.

6. The Danforth Understanding that toll rates need not be set to cover payment of the contingency payment.[21]

Senator Bartlett's Reservation Number 4 to the Neutrality Treaty was for the purpose of protecting the interests of both the United States and Panama by assuring that constitutional procedures and the standards of the 1969 Vienna Convention on the Law of Treaties were complied with. His Reservation follows:

Reservation No. 4 (Bartlett), March 16, 1978—Tabled 60—37.

Summary. Provided that prior to the exchange of the instruments of ratification, the President of the United States would have to determine that Panama had ratified the Treaty, as amended, in accordance with its constitutional processes, including the process prescribed in Article 274 of the Panamanian Constitution. The specified article of Panama's Constitution requires that treaties regarding the Panama Canal, the Canal Zone, the construction of a sea-level canal, or a third set of locks be submitted to a national plebiscite.

Text. Before the period at the end of the resolution of ratification insert a comma and the following: "subject to the reservation that before the date of the exchange of the instruments of ratification the President shall have determined that that Republic of Panama has ratified the Treaty, as amended, in accordance with its constitutional processes, including the process required by the provisions of Article 274 of the Constitution of the Republic of Panama.[22]

The Senate voted 60 to 37 to table this Reservation to the first treaty. The same treatment was later accorded Senator Bartlett's Reservation Number 3 to the second treaty (the Panama Canal Treaty), a similar reservation designed to call upon President Carter to assure the Legislative Branch that Panama's processes of ratification had been proper, i.e., by national plebiscite. This reservation was tabled also, this time by a vote of 63 to 36.

The tabling of Senator Bartlett's second reservation has been labeled Swindle Number Five, as it too had far-reaching effects.

Why? Seven days after the Senate had passed the second treaty, completing its advice and consent function for the President's Treaties, Panama issued its detailed analyses of the Treaties in its April 25, 1978 Foreign Ministry Communique, rejecting all five U.S. reservations and one understanding to the Treaties. Obviously, this Communique had been under preparation for some time. It was a part of Torrijos's answer to President Carter, promised in his letter of March 15, 1978 (the day before the first treaty was approved) that Panama would "take its position once the Senate has voted on both Treaties."

As to why the President and the Senate leadership permitted the Bartlett Reservations to be defeated can best be answered by them and by the State Department. Even so, of interest is the observation of Zbigniew Brzezinski, Carter's National Security Adviser, in his memoirs, *Power and Principles* (Farrar-Strauss-Giroux, 1983), regarding the vote on the first treaty: "If we had lost, there is no doubt that our policy on SALT and most importantly the Middle East would have been dead ducks."[23]

The importance of "linkage of objectives" is obviously what Brzezinski meant, i.e., did Mr. Carter *not* want to determine if Panama had constitutionally ratified the Treaties, knowing that a new plebiscite would reject them—hence, no Treaties, and very probably no SALT agreement and no Mid East accords?

Earlier, Senator Bartlett had developed his position on these two reservations through the testimony of former Deputy Secretary of Defense William P. Clements, Jr. before the Senate Armed Services Committee on January 31, 1978 in the following exchange:

Senator BARTLETT. You raised an interesting point. You believe that a signed statement by President Torrijos and the President of the United States, or a resolution or amendment to the treaty adopted by the Senate, or a unilateral statement by the Senate, wouldn't suffice. There needs to be a plebiscite in Panama so that they are following their legal processes of supporting the treaty from their point of view as we would be supporting it from our point of view if there were amendments made to it, and it was ratified by the Senate.

Could you expand on that a little bit?

Mr. CLEMENTS. Yes, sir. The legal counsel that I have consulted with, and not one but several, have told me that in the eyes of the world, in their judgment, the constitutional process which apparently calls for this plebiscite or referendum in Panama must be observed and obviously Mr. Torrijos thought so with respect to the treaty as originally drafted. Therefore, you would have to go back and do the same thing with any amendments that might be made.

I am satisfied that this is correct. I certainly know that in the business world, in a contractual sense, a side letter, so to speak, to a verbal understanding has no basis in law at all with respect to a basic contract.

If you want something in that contract it must be in the signed, legitimate, on-record instrument; otherwise, it is tainted.

I am satisfied that that is correct on the basis of the advice I have received. Any kind of amendments, and I want to make clear that I do not agree with the amendments as submitted, need to be refined. The treaty needs to be refined; it needs to be restructured.

I hope I have made that clear to you.

Senator BARTLETT. Yes, sir.

Mr. CLEMENTS. Whatever changes might be made that might include a clause reflecting the sense of the Senate must be resubmitted to the people of Panama through exactly the same process as the original proposed treaty.[24]

Perhaps many Senators simply did not understand that substantive changes to the Treaties were not binding on the Republic of Panama without a second plebiscite. Senator Bartlett tried to explain this important point to his colleagues on the Senate floor on the day the second treaty was approved, April 18, 1978. He said:

In recent years, Panama has mounted a major diplomatic effort to secure a treaty with the United States which would grant sovereign rights and operational control of the Canal to Panama. Anticipating such a treaty, and remembering the dissatisfaction with the manner in which the 1903 treaty was negotiated, the new Panamanian Constitution of 1972 provided that treaties relating to the Panama Canal must be approved by a plebiscite of the people of Panama. On the 23d of October last year, the people of Panama gave their approval in a plebiscite to the versions of the two Panama Canal Treaties originally negotiated. At the time of that plebiscite, the people of Panama were not voting on future amendments, reservations or other changes which might be made by the U.S. Senate.[25]

As for the reluctance and refusal of the Carter Administration and the Torrijos government to call for a second plebiscite, Mr. Bartlett said this:

Fear of a second plebiscite in Panama grows out of apprehension that the people of Panama might reject the changes made to the Treaties or that they might even reject their own government for having inadequately represented their interests.

Nevertheless, there are many of us who feel that good relations with Panama will be possible only when there is agreement and satisfaction as to the terms of the new Treaties. . . . Furthermore, we feel that changes in the Panama Canal Treaties should be dealt with in a straightforward and honest manner, by both nations.

International law also supported Senator Bartlett, according to Professor L. Oppenheim's *International Law* (paragraph 517) and Professor J.L. Brierly's *The Law of Nations,* which provide that if a treaty is modified, as were the Panama Canal Treaties, the other State has to approve or reject the modification. Further, a former legal adviser to the State Department, Mr. Green M. Hackworth, in his *Digest of International Law* stated, "If the Senate attempts to alter it [the treaty], consent of the other nations must be obtained to the alteration."[26]

As a matter of interest, the following 36 Senators in the 1984 Senate, including Howard H. Baker, Jr., voted on April 18, 1978 to table Bartlett Reservation Number 3 which had been devised solely to assure proper ratification procedures in Panama and for the protection of future U.S. rights, as well as Panama's:

Howard Baker	Gary Hart	Howard Metzenbaum
Lloyd Bentsen	Mark Hatfield	Daniel Moynihan
Joseph R. Biden	John Heinz	Bob Packwood
Dale Bumpers	Ernest Hollings	Claiborne Pell
Robert C. Byrd	Walter Huddleston	Charles Percy
John Chafee	Daniel Inouye	William Proxmire
Lawton Chiles	J. Bennett Johnson	Donald Riegle
Alan Cranston	Edward M. Kennedy	Paul Sarbanes
John Danforth	Patrick Leahy	Jim Sasser
Dennis DeConcini	Russell Long	Robert Stafford
Thomas Eagleton	Charles M. Mathias	Lowell Weicker
John Glenn	Spark M. Matsunaga	Edward Zorinsky

Three of the four members of the Senate leadership (Byrd, Baker, and Cranston) voted to table. The Minority Whip, Senator Ted Stevens, voted not to table. Of the 63 Senators who voted to table, 27 have since been defeated at the polls or retired. Of the 36 remaining in the 1984 Senate, and who voted to table, 34 also voted to approve the Treaties.

In November 1983, individual letters were sent to Senator Baker, the

Majority Leader, and to the other 35 Senators who voted to table Bartlett Reservation Number 3 on April 18, 1978, stating, in part:

The reservation required the President prior to the exchange of the instruments of ratification to determine that Panama had ratified the Treaties, as amended, in accordance with its constitutional provisions.

The reservation was tabled 63 to 36. What I would like to know . . . for my study is why the reservation was tabled.[27]

Senator Lloyd Bentsen, D.-Tex., answered, "It was beyond the jurisdiction of the Senate to require Panama to hold another plebiscite. . . ."[28] At issue, however, was compliance with the 1969 Vienna Convention specifying that treaty changes be accepted by all parties. Moreover, the Senate should refuse "Advice and Consent" for *any* sufficient reason.

Two other rejected treaty changes could be labeled Swindles 6 and 7. Amendment No. 13, tabled by 50 to 37 and introduced by Senator Malcolm Wallop, R.-Wyo., on March 20, 1978, provided that if Panama abrogated any part of the Treaties both Treaties would terminate and the 1903 Treaty "shall reenter into force."

The 7th Swindle was Amendment No. 34, tabled 58 to 40 and introduced by Senator Thurmond on April 18, 1978, also would have protected against Panama's counter-reservation and would require that President Carter not ratify the Treaties unless the Senate "has given its advice and consent" to any Panamanian reservation "binding on the United States." Thurmond said, "In this manner the Senate can evaluate the reservation and decide if it . . . require[s] further Senate action."

In order to give "Advice and Consent" the Senate itself must decide what additions are substantive, not the President. In rejecting the Wallop and Thurmond Amendments, the Senate leadership acted contrary to a later Library of Congress report, dated December 14, 1978, stating in part:

The Senate is formally involved in this process at the "Advice and Consent" to ratification stage; the President is responsible for all other stages, including ratification.

Therefore, the Senate is solely responsible for "Advice and Consent" to the contents of Treaties—and did in fact consider nearly 90 proposed amendments from February 8 to April 19, 1978. Why then was Panama's counter-reservation withheld from the Senate's evaluation?

Wallop and Thurmond were psychic in foreseeing the Carter-Torrijos secret counter-reservation. Obviously a hard core majority of Senators were devoted to saving the Treaties for President Carter and nothing, not even security for the United States, would dissuade them.

In future years, all this will be tested, particularly treaty changes never voted on by the Panamanian people. The failure to hold a second plebiscite portends future confrontation when Americans will be forced to use military power to uphold rights. At that time, the alleged misdeeds of Teddy Roosevelt and Bunau-Varilla will be dwarfed by denouncements of the Carter-Torrijos deceptions.[29]

THE BROOKE RESERVATION IS IGNORED

Another questionable circumstance was Mr. Carter's handling of the Brooke reservation which stated, in part:

Exchange of the instruments of ratification shall not be effective earlier than March 31, 1979, and the Treaties shall not enter into force prior to October 1, 1979, unless legislation necessary to implement the provisions of the Panama Canal Treaty shall have been enacted by the Congress of the United States of America before March 31, 1979.[30]

Carter ignored it. This reservation to the second and final treaty had passed the Senate 84 to 3 on April 17, 1978. Its author, Senator Edward W. Brooke, R.-Mass., intended to guarantee sufficient time for preparation of implementing legislation to create the Panama Canal Commission, establish rate-making procedures, transfer of property, defense arrangements and installations, and the myriad of administrative and other details that eventually became the Panama Canal Act of 1979.

The idea was that the heads of state would *not* exchange instruments *before* March 31, 1979—and that they should be exchanged *later* in order to provide the Congress ample time to plan an orderly transfer. For the same reason, the Treaties would not enter into force before October 1, 1979, preferably later in order that implementing legislation could be drawn with prudence and moderation.

But this was not to be. President Carter moved quickly to exchange the instruments of ratification, the final act of ratifying, on June 16, 1978 and made the "effective date" March 31, 1979, calling this an exchange "in escrow." It was also devious—and such use of the "effective date" suggests that the State Department had a hand in the drafting of Senator Brooke's reservation. This surprise action helped prevent discovery of Panama's secretive counter-reservation that killed U.S. defense rights and that was unveiled at the last minute in Panama on June 16, 1978,—the first time it had been publicized.[31]

In their precipitate move, both Carter and Torrijos had also ignored a specific provision of the Neutrality Treaty. Article VIII provides that "This Treaty shall enter into force . . . six months from the date of the exchange of the instruments of ratification." Both men knew about the scheme for an "effective date"—but, of course, a sure "victory" was more important than Treaty requirements. Predictably, Panamanians later complained bitterly that the Treaties should be effective six months after the actual ratification date and that the United States had already violated them—all in all, just one more instance of unpleasantness and rough-riding.

Presumably, if Mr. Carter had waited nine and a half months to exchange ratification documents, i.e., until at least March 31, 1979, the objectionable three paragraphs of Panama's counter-reservation would have been discovered and there would have been embarrassment for the Administration and upheaval in the Congress. Consequently, the Treaties were quietly "ratified" but in a manner hardly fair to the Senate and to the American people, and destroying Carter's pledge of an "open Administration."

Undoubtedly another reason to hurry up the "ratification" was to avoid another plebiscite in Panama where opponents of the Treaties could very well have rejected them.

By ignoring the time frames of the Brooke reservation, Carter had placed the Congress under the gun with a deadline date of October 1, 1979 for the implementing legislation—a date that could not be guaranteed in June 1978. Indeed, the Panama Canal Treaty entailed a wholesale reorganization of the entire Canal enterprise. And, the use of the word, "effective," had brought on this problem: It gave license to ratify at any time and say: "effective" March 31, 1979.

Senator Brooke made clear that he did not expect ratification until the President had had time to review the situation in Panama and the Congress had time to act. Action *after* March 31, 1979 was indicated. Mr. Brooke recognized the difficulties in producing the necessary legislation, including the constitutional crisis that could ensue if the President acted too hastily. He said, in part:

If the Treaties come into effect before the United States has passed the legislation, we would find ourselves in the rather untenable positon of being bound by a legitimate international obligation but unable to carry out our responsibilities under it. Such a situation would, at a minimum, be damaging to our international image. Moreover, it could precipitate a constitutional crisis if the Executive acted to implement the Treaties by Executive Order rather than wait for the needed action by Congress.[32]

The Brooke reservation of April 17, 1978 was an effort to cooperate with the Executive Branch and at the same time to protect the nation's interests. On the following day, April 18, an exchange of letters between Brooke and Carter became known. These letters seemed to suggest a deal, at least an implied understanding: if Brooke would vote for the Treaty,

Carter would not oppose his Reservation. Excerpts of the two letters follow:

Brooke: Under the so-called DeConcini condition, does the United States reserve itself the option to take whatever actions are necessary, including the unilateral decision to use military force on the territory of Panama, if necessary, to ensure the Canal will be available for the passage of U.S. vessels, regardless of whether the threat to the Canal comes from any source external to Panama or from some source within Panama?[33]

Carter: The answer to that question is affirmative. Thus, the provisions of the Neutrality Treaty are clearly consistent with our existing international obligations concerning non-intervention.[33]

In his letter, Mr. Carter had told Senator Brooke unequivocally that the United States could "send in troops" to ensure the Canal's neutrality and defense—but only eleven days before, on April 7, he had, according to his diary entry for that day and as disclosed in his memoirs four years later, assured Omar Torrijos of the U.S. "non-intervention commitment," as repeated in the OAS and UN Charters. What did he mean? How could he have it both ways? Obviously, he wanted Brooke's vote and Torrijos's tranquility.[34]

Senator Brooke *did* vote for the Treaty and was subsequently defeated in his bid for reelection several months later. Why did President Carter not honor the intent of the Brooke reservation? His answer to this question has not been heard. Obviously, much pressure came from the Panamanians to consummate the deal so they could get at the Canal. But probably the most urgent reasons for a quick "ratification" were (1) to avoid discovery of the hidden three paragraph counter-reservation that killed the U.S. rights under the DeConcini reservation, and (2) to pre-empt the Treaties opponents who were demanding a second plebiscite in Panama for a vote on the substantive changes to the Treaties.

At that moment in history, each head of government possessed the power, the unilateral power, to achieve one of his greatest ambitions: Carter, the humanitarian, to "correct an injustice" and Torrijos, the dictator, to get the Canal for his people. Both acted quickly and unilaterally, leaving constitutional and legal debates behind.

What did Senator Brooke think of having his Reservation completely circumvented? "The early ratification was improper in my opinion . . . and not . . . compatible with the understanding between the Congress and the Administration . . . ," said Mr. Brooke in a February 15, 1985 answer sent by his Executive Assistant, Elaine Richardson. Moreover, he added, Panama's counter-reservation made the "DeConcini reservation subject to differing and probably conflicting interpretations under international law" with "legal aspects quite complex."

Senator Brooke had wanted time for the orderly preparation of legislation to implement the Treaties. This procedure was ignored by the President. Another debilitating move against the Senate was the delay by the State Department in providing "the essential components" for implementing the Treaties, such as costs, tolls, employment practices and the myriad of details involved in the transfer of the Canal Zone. In his testimony of September 29, 1977, Herbert J. Hansell, the State Department Legal Adviser, had promised:

Finally, Mr. Chairman, I am pleased to have this opportunity to report to this committee on the proposed legislation to implement these Treaties that is being prepared for submission to Congress in the near future. That legislation, of course, will be the essential component of the overall program of implementation of the Treaties.

We hope to have a complete draft available for submission to both Houses of Congress within several weeks. We have been at work on it for some period of time. Certainly well before the end of October we expect to have it to you.[35]

Unfortunately, however this pledge to the Foreign Relations Committee was not honored. And on February 2, 1978, Senator Harry F. Byrd, IND.-Vir., told his colleagues:

But October has come and gone, November has come and gone, December has come and gone, January has come and gone—and still the implementing legislation is not available to the Congress.

Under the questioning Tuesday, Mr. Hansell could not tell the committee when such legislation might be available.
. . . .

The fact that the legislation was promised to the Congress in October but is not yet available in February suggests to me that it is, indeed, "an essential component" and must, indeed, have wide ramifications and much complexity. Perhaps as a matter of strategy the *Administration wishes to withhold* this "essential" component *for fear of weakening support for the Treaties.*[36] (Emphasis added)

Moreover, it was March before the Administration offered even a rough draft of the implementing legislation containing the "essential components." The final draft did not appear until long after both Treaties had been approved. Was this another instance of stonewalling? With this lack of cooperation, the Brooke Reservation was becoming academic.

In their Foreign Ministry Communique of April 25, 1978, the Panamanians sought the earliest possible date for the entry into force of the Treaties. First, they alleged that the Treaties should become effective six months after the Senate's approval, whereas both Treaties specified that the effective date would be six months after ratification. So, by actually ratifying on June 16, 1978 and saying that the *effective* date of ratification was March 31, 1979, Mr. Carter not only confused the issue, he also probably saved the Treaties and certainly, he put pressure on the Congress for legislation to implement the Treaties.

In their Communique, the Panamanians set October 1, 1979 as a deadline. But it was not a deadline because under the Brooke Reservation, October 1, 1979 was the earliest possible date, not the latest. In this manner, Panama repudiated the Brooke Reservation and eventually so did President Carter and the Congress in hastily pushing through implementing legislation to meet Panama's incorrect interpretation.[37]

Obviously President Carter was anxious to ratify, to complete his victory. He could have used the Brooke Reservation as a trump card to play at any time he felt the Congress was delaying the implementing legislation. Instead, he gave in to Panama's pressure and more important: He had avoided the problems of a possible second plebiscite in Panama as well as the danger that the secretive Panamanian counter-reservation would be discovered. Either of these events would surely have disrupted everything. Prompt action was needed.

Whether in a railroad marshalling yard or in the Halls of Congress, one might well think of a "clash-track railroad job" in reflecting on the handling of the Panama Canal Treaties and the five swindles and the perpetrators who made them all possible. Indeed, without each swindle skillfully executed, there probably would have been no Treaties.

Some years later, as often happens with cover up and stonewalling, smoking guns were discovered, adding more substance to the extensive evidence that had already been gathered.

*Senate Minority Leader Howard Baker, R-Tenn.,
center, holds up the hand of Panama's strongman
Omar Torrijos in a championship gesture after
being introduced at a rally in Colon, Panama on
January 4, 1978. Baker along with Senator John
Chafee, R-R.I., right, and Senator Jake Garn, R-
Utah, had traveled to Panama to negotiate sticky
points in the Treaties in apparent contravention of
the President's obligation to negotiate treaties
under Article II, Section 2 of the Constitution. A
number of Senators "negotiated" on their own,
circumventing both the Constitution and the
Logan Act which restricts foreign policy to the
President alone. (AP/Wide World Photos)*

·8·

THE SMOKING GUNS OF
FOGGY BOTTOM

The spirit of the Spanish-Americans who were to inhabit the Isthmus of Panama was perhaps epitomized by the dashing young explorer, Vasco Nunez Balboa. This Spanish adventurer discovered the Pacific Ocean on September 25, 1513 after he and his helmeted band of *conquistadores* had slashed their way through the dense Panamanian jungle, seeking gold and conquest.[1]

French historian Jean Descola described the excitement: "On the morning of the twentieth day, the detachment reached the foot of a hill. A keen breath suddenly succeeded to the suffocating smell of the jungle. Balboa inhaled deeply . . . . At the foot of the further slope, something immensely blue mirrored the blaze of the tropic sun: It was the sea."

Three days later, Balboa took formal possession of the "Southern Sea" in the names of the King and Queen of Castile:

At low tide, he strode forward towards the sea. His armor, his helmet and his naked sword flashed in the sunlight. He held aloft the banner of Castile and Aragon. He entered the sea until it was half-way up his body and took possession, in the names of Ferdinand and Isabella, sovereigns of Castile, of Leon and Aragon, of this southern ocean with all its ports, islands and coasts. And he took care to specify possession "royal, corporeal, present and eternal."[2]

Balboa had taken "possession" of the Pacific Ocean "with all its ports, islands and coasts," and although his countrymen did not hold Central America "eternally," they ruled and exploited the area for three centuries, leaving their character and temperament in the civilization that succeeded them.[3] This Spanish-American temperament included a fierce national pride and quick sensitivity to any infringement on sovereignty or other rights.

Former Panamanian President Harmodio Arias had this attitude in mind when he spoke of his people's reaction to the Panama Canal. He said, ". . . they cannot but regard with anxious care a measure that not only would curtail the national jurisdiction, but supplant it as the necessary result of the coexistence of two public powers in a given territory, the one national, the other foreign."[4]

It was the Panamanian temperament that rejected the idea of any future U.S. "intervention" for the defense and security of the Canal after it was transfered to Panama, no matter what the Treaties said. The U.S. Ambassador to Panama, William J. Jorden, told the Senate Foreign Relations Committee in 1978 about the Panamanian concept of intervention:

Now, intervention in Panama and in the minds of the Latin Americans has a very special meaning. When Latin Americans think about intervention they think of foreign troops coming, killing their people, removing their government or replacing their government, taking over and running the show, and that is the context of intervention for the past 50 years in Latin America. They remember the Spanish, they remember the French in Mexico, they remember Haiti and Nicaragua and all the rest of it. When they talk about intervention that hits a very sensitive nerve and it is bloody difficult for any Panamanian to say, "Yes, we have given the United States the right to intervene."[5]

Of course, the United States concepts and intentions were entirely different, solely to fulfill obligations under the Treaties to protect the Canal, not to harm the people or threaten the government. Moreover, Mr. Jorden told the Committee that the other Latin American countries, such as Peru and Ecuador, for example, want the Canal protected and safe and "would be quite happy if the United States did protect it."

Even so, the Panamanians objected and such protection was not agreed to in the final treaty—as their last minute counter-reservation cancelled the U.S. rights under the DeConcini reservation. Except for this secretive counter-reservation that had been initiated at President Carter's suggestion, all the other Panamanian positions were out in the open, and there were apparently no "smoking guns."

For example, within seven days of final approval of the Treaties by the U.S. Senate, Panama had publicized its contentious Foreign Ministry Communique of April 25, 1978, denouncing all six changes that the United States had attached to the Treaties.[6] These were vital measures for the U.S. Senate, without which there would have been no two-thirds vote of consent.

In a similar manner, three months after the U.S. Congress had enacted implementing legislation (the Panama Canal Act of 1979), Panama was ready with a long strident letter of complaint. In his letter of January 8, 1980 to President Carter, Panamanian President Aristides Royo alleged that the United States had violated the Treaties in many instances and had provided insufficient funding for the Canal transfer and operations.[7] Thus, Royo was accepting a $10 billion gift from American taxpayers with demands for more. Ironically, Mr. Royo was criticizing specific actions of the internal affairs of the U.S. government in detail, whereas, a few months earlier, certain U.S. Senators were severely reprimanded for asking President Carter to ascertain that Panama had legally ratified the Treaties, the most basic principle imaginable, because, the critics said, this would be interference into Panama's internal affairs.

Royo closed his unusual letter to Carter stressing the tenacious struggle and "sacrifice of blood" for the important achievements of the recent Treaties, including the struggle to "raise the banner of justice to achieve the genuine sovereignty which certain U.S. sectors . . . still seek to disregard."[8] But this is misleading, even presumptuous. Far more American blood was sacrificed through disease and accidents in building the Canal than Panamanian blood that, the record shows, was spilled mainly through acts of looting, arson, and other law-breaking violence against the Canal operators. Moreover, without the Canal, Panama would still be a jungle province of Colombia.

Nonetheless, the Panamanians, except for their secretive three paragraphs of counter-reservation, took their positions openly and firmly, much as their predecessors might have done—Balboa and his *conquistadores*. On the other hand, the American treaty-handlers in reaching their goals of ratified Treaties and "correcting an injustice" found it necessary to use indirection and cover up.

The evidence was discovered several years after the fact, much of it from the books and speeches of the treaty-makers, apparently proud of their accomplishments against heavy odds and finally feeling free to tell how it was done. These, then, are the "smoking guns" of Foggy Bottom:

1. The admission by former Ambassador David Henry Popper that "ambiguity was essential" in negotiations and was deliberately injected into the Treaties in order to gain approval of all concerned.

2. President Carter's invitation to Omar Torrijos to write *his own* reservation as to what intervention meant, causing a secretive insertion into the Treaties, unchallenged.

3. The disclosure by former Assistant Secretary of State William D. Rogers that the purpose of the leadership amendment was to eliminate U.S. rights in the DeConcini reservation.

4. The ex officio and unconstitutional treaty-making of Senators Howard Baker, John Chafee and Jake Garn in traveling to Panama to negotiate directly with Omar Torrijos on the Neutrality Treaty.

SMOKING GUN NUMBER ONE: 'AMBIGUITY WAS ESSENTIAL'

A simple inquiry and a belated answer produced one of the most surprising smoking guns of the campaign. The query to former Ambassador Popper was innocent-sounding and cordial: "Dear David: . . . I was wondering why President Carter didn't make Panama withdraw its 'understanding' that was contrary to the DeConcini Condition. I would appreciate your comments on this."⁹

Mr. Popper had been the State Department's top representative for easing the Treaties through the Senate; in fact, that was his full time assignment.¹⁰ After a three months delay, Mr. Popper answered with his letter of June 5, 1982, saying, in part: ". . . a certain degree of *ambiguity was essential* if we were not to let disputation about a distant and unlikely contingency torpedo the whole treaty enterprise." (Emphasis added)

The substance of Popper's letter to Phillip Harman of the Committee for Better Panama and U.S. Relations follows:

You recall of course that the DeConcini Condition, and certain other Senate reservations, embodied a concept of *unilateralism* in defense of the Canal that was *never acceptable to the Panamanians*. It was the same basic issue that Sol Linowitz attempted to paper over through the October 1977 formula, which was incorporated in the Treaty. In the end we concluded that the Panamanians had as much right to interpret the Treaty as we did, and that a *certain degree of ambiguity was essential* if we were not to let a disputation about a distant and unlikely contingency torpedo the whole Treaty enterprise. We thought the fudgy language the Panamanians inserted in their instruments of ratification committed us to no more than motherhood; any action we took would of course have to be justified on international legal grounds. If we should ever be required to intervene unilaterally, we will have a first-class problem, no matter what the Instruments say.

The foregoing is a rough statement, not for public attribution to me. But it explains why we did what we did. (Emphasis added)¹¹

Mr. Popper's assessment, four years after the fact, is a concise summation of circumstances and corroborates in every detail the evidence that has been assimilated. "Ambiguity was essential" in order to move the Treaties through the Senate and in order to make the Panamanians believe that the "imperialistic claws" of the DeConcini reservation had been removed and that any U.S. defense rights were subject to Panama's consent. As "for public attribution" to Popper, legal counsel advised that to withold the letter would be to participate in the cover up.

It was the issue of unilateral rights that Sol Linowitz had been trying to "paper over." And unilateral rights were never agreed to. There had been no meeting of minds on this funamental issue, the "concept of unilateralism." For this reason, a number of Senators declared the Treaties to be "fatally flawed."

Senator Jesse Helms spoke to this fault on the Senate floor on the day the second Treaty was approved, April 18, 1978:

For sovereignty is the ultimate power. It answers the question: Who has the right to decide what actions may take place within a defined territory? As long as the United States is free to exercise all the rights of a sovereign within the territory of the Canal Zone, there was no doubt that we could do whatever was necessary to defend it. There was no question of intervention in the internal affairs of Panama. There was no question of violating the territorial integrity of Panama.

But the moment that the United States surrenders its sovereign rights, then everything that we do now, every action, is subject to the will of Panama. It is as simple as that. When Panama is sovereign, Panama decides.

At the root of the problem is a fundamental unresolved contradiction that our negotiators failed to solve. The Treaties are an attempt to paper over that contradiction.

The ultimate issue in sovereignty, of course, is the right to use force. That is what sovereignty is all about. There may be disputes about actions of a lesser level, but in the end, they come down to the issue of who has the right to use force.

The Treaties attempt to pretend that there will never be any division of opinion between the United States and Panama on how the ultimate right to use force will be exercised. But that is an absurd supposition. It is an insult to the people of Panama. It assumes that they will be forever subservient to the desires of the United States.[12]

Obviously, such an assumption was never acceptable to the people of Panama and subsequently, their final three paragraphs of counter-reservation cancelled out the rights that the United States assumed were guaranteed. The U.S. had pretended to hand back sovereignty to Panama but to retain the ultimate right to use force, even against the people of Panama, if necessary.[13]

President Carter stated in his letter of April 17, 1978 to Senator Brooke, in effect, that the United States intended to use force against any threat to the Canal. He wrote:

It is abundantly clear, therefore, that the United States can, under the Neutrality Treaty, *take whatever actions are necessary* to defend the Canal from *any threat regardless of its source*.[14] (Emphasis added)

Therefore, in defending against any threat to the Canal, the President included the Panamanian people who may, at some future time, be the threat to the Canal's security. The DeConcini reservation attempted to bring this point out into the open; but the Senate leadership and other treaty-handlers preferred to obscure the true meaning; i.e., "ambiguity was essential."

In speaking of the cynical attitude adopted by some of his colleagues, Senator Helms noted that their problem was "not in the concept of the Treaties, but in stating it openly." He added:

In other words, they say that it is all right for the dictator of Panama and the President of the United States to have a private understanding that the United States has the right to exercise the ultimate sovereign power of force, but that it is wrong to state it in writing.[15]

OAS AND UN CHARTERS: 'NOT PREVENT . . . A LATER TREATY'

This deception was not accepted in the official Foreign Ministry Communique of April 25, 1978 in which Panama's interpretation was explained in detail, citing a number of authorities for repudiating U.S. rights under the DeConcini reservation. For example, Article 8 of the Seventh Pan American Conference: "No state has the right to intervene in the internal and external affairs of another."[16] The Communique called Article 8 "a clear Latin American contribution to the development of international law."

The Foreign Ministry also cited the declaration made by the U.S. commission to the Convention on the Rights and Duties of States in Montevideo, Uruguay in 1933:

Any observing person must clearly understand now that under the Roosevelt Administration the U.S. government is as opposed as any other government to the interference with the liberty, sovereignty or other domestic affairs or processes of the governments of other nations.[17]

The Panamanian Communique also cited articles from the United Nations and OAS Charters on the principle of nonintervention, as well as portions of the U.S. Senate debate by Senators Frank Church, Mike Gravel, George McGovern, Jacob Javits, Paul Sarbanes, Edward Kennedy and others stating that "the interventionist policy of the United States is a thing of the past."[18]

Nonetheless, the Panama Canal Treaties were devised for special purposes and took into account the provisions of other treaties and international agreements. The late Dr. Charles H. Breecher, the former State Department treaty specialist, told the East Subcommittee on Separation of Powers on June 23, 1983:

The fact that the United States and Panama have both adhered to the Charter of the United Nations and the OAS, multinational treaties, does not prevent the U.S. and Panama to make a later treaty among themselves in partial derogation of the provisions of the OAS Charter only. And that is exactly what the DeConcini reservation is—a very limited exception, applicable to the U.S. and Panama only under special circumstances . . .[19]

The Panama Canal Treaties *were* designed for "special circumstances," the UN and OAS Charters notwithstanding, but unfortunately there was never a meeting of minds. The basic disagreement on U.S. residual rights was always "papered over"—and David Popper's letter of June 5, 1982 was an important "smoking gun" of further confirmation.

Consequently, in July 1982, approximately 150 copies of the Popper letter were sent to key officials in the White House, the Department of Defense, the Department of Justice, the Senate and the House of Representatives.[20] There was no groundswell of enthusiasm for this new development, but it was tolerated. Even so, the Popper letter along with numerous and persistent requests by conservative groups undoubtedly helped precipitate the hearing before Senator John P. East's Subcommittee, although more than a full year passed between the discovery of the Popper "smoking gun" and the hearing date, June 23, 1983. Much additional evidence, of course, was also available.

Just why former Ambassador Popper made the disclosures in his letter is not clear. Perhaps he considered the matter of no further consequence. Nonetheless, it was a succinct validation of the "whole Treaty enterprise," as he called it, from a man in a position to know.

Mr. Popper had retired from the State Department in 1980 after long service, including duty as U.S. Ambassador to Chile and many years as a Foreign Service Officer. Other affiliations included the left-leaning Institute of Pacific Relations and the Foreign Policy Association, as well as membership on the editorial board of the *Amerasia* magazine, reputed to be a communist espionage conduit.[21] This background is on the public record. Even so, he was State's man to replace Linowitz in June 1977 at the time Linowitz's six-months appointment as treaty negotiator expired. Popper's assignment then included "the task of preparing the Treaties for approval for the Senate, and the task of obtaining that approval."[22]

In a brief telephone conversation between Mr. Popper and the author on November 13, 1983, our attempt to gain further information about the meanings of his letter was not fruitful. Unfortunately, Popper was not a witness before the East Subcommittee either.

A number of questions for Popper come to mind:

1. What was the basic issue that Sol Linowitz attempted to paper over? Why was it necessary to paper over?

2. What was the "fudgy language" that the Panamanians inserted in their instruments of ratification?

3. If President Carter and the State Department did not think that Panama's three paragraphs of counter-reservation modified the DeConcini reservation, why were they not included in the U.S. instruments of ratification?

4. Explain why "ambiguity was essential."

The answers to these questions are obvious from the evidence that has been assembled, but Mr. Popper's answers should be on the record. He was the State Department's top official for "preparing the Treaties for approval [and for] obtaining that approval." Moreover, he has been the only high official, or former high official, to admit, in effect, that the DeConcini reservation was never accepted by Panama, although that fact was always clearly apparent.

The DeConcini reservation was all-important for approval of the Treaties by the U.S. Senate. Indeed, President Carter stated, shortly before the vote on the first Treaty (the Neutrality Treaty), "Two or three Senators informed me their votes, too, were contingent on this language [the DeConcini reservation] being adopted. We finally yielded to save the Treaty."[23] Once again, the Panamanians knew the United States President was willing to ratify the Treaties without the clear-cut DeConcini language and that, in the long run, they could get the Canal without it.

The significance of the DeConcini reservation was proved by a 1982 survey of 37 Senators who had voted for the Treaties. The Committee for Better Panama and U.S. Relations asked what, if any, effect the DeConcini reservation had on their votes. Of the 13 who responded, 6 admitted that it had influenced them to favor the Treaties.

Primarily at issue at the time of the Senate vote on the first Treaty were the words, "in Panama," in the DeConcini reservation—a guarantee for U.S. troops in Panama if the Canal were threatened internally or externally. Carter had promised Torrijos to avoid the "in Panama" part and accordingly, tried to persuade DeConcini to delete those two words. He was unsuccessful.[24] Just how military force might defend the Canal *outside* Panama was not explained.

Other questions about Mr. Popper's "smoking gun" involve the State Department: (1) Why did not Mr. Popper or Secretary of State Vance advise the Senate leaders that "ambiguity was essential" if Treaties were to be obtained? (2) And that, in order not to "torpedo the whole Treaty enterprise," a certain degree of flexibility would have to be tolerated? The answers to these questions, evidently, is that ratified Treaties took priority over any meeting of minds. Nonetheless, Popper had disclosed that ambiguity was the plan, something that no other treaty-handler had admitted—although it was always apparent to most.

SMOKING GUN TWO: 'WRITE HIS OWN RESERVATION'

Another smoking gun was President Carter's admission in his book, *Keeping Faith* (1982), that he told Panama's Head of Government, Omar Torrijos, on April 7, 1978, to write his own "reservation about *his* understanding of what the Treaties mean on intervention into the internal affairs of Panama."[25]

This confession by former President Carter, four years after the fact, may have shocked many readers of the presidential memoirs, but it also helped explain the secretive Panamanian counter-reservation, which was apparently the direct result of Carter's suggestion and which was attached to Panama's version of the treaties at the last moment. Panama's unilateral action was *not* a part of the U.S. Treaties. Mr. Carter accepted it, however, without the "Advice and Consent" of the Senate when he ratified the Treaties on June 15, 1978, thereby allowing U.S. defense rights to be subject to Panama's "cooperation."

Just two months earlier, on April 7, Torrijos was threatening to renounce both Treaties because of the language of the DeConcini reservation, i.e., the plain terms that assured U.S. rights. The language was too explicit for Torrijos. This was a critical moment for the survival of the Treaties.

Mr. Carter used the word, "reservation," in his suggestion to Torrijos who responded with a "reservation" that altered one of the most basic issues of the Treaties: unilateral U.S. rights for defending the Canal. However, Torrijos labeled his "reservation" an "understanding" in attempting to avoid the requirement for a second plebiscite in Panama and resubmission to the U.S. Senate for another round of "Advice and Consent." Of course, a contrary position was taken by the State Department witness at the East inquiry on June 23, 1983 in contending that Panama's three paragraphs did not constitute a "reservation," merely an "understanding" of how Panama interpreted the basic issue.[26]

A main portion of the argument by State's witness, Robert E. Dalton, the Assistant Legal Adviser for Treaty Affairs, was the following:

In essence, the language in Panama's second paragraph simply states Panama's understanding of the spirit in which the rights and duties under the Treaties, including the DeConcini condition, will be effected. The principles of mutual respect and cooperation referred to in this paragraph form the foundation of the

Treaties themselves. They are reflected throughout these documents and they continue to govern the relationship between the two governments.[27]

Mr. Dalton was saying, in effect, that Panama's words do not mean a thing, just good will and cooperation. If so, why did the United States not return the compliment by repeating this good will in its own instruments? Carter did not suggest to Torrijos that he write an "understanding"—he asked for a "reservation about his understanding of what the Treaties mean." Moreover, the Senate Foreign Relations Committee Staff Memorandum, titled "The Role of the Senate in Treaty Ratification" (November 1977), states that what is important in changes to treaties is what they do, i.e., the content and effect, whether they be labeled amendment, reservation, understanding, interpretation, declaration, or statement.[28]

Furthermore, the State Department Legal Advisor, John R. Stevenson, wrote on March 22, 1971:

A statement made in accompanying the ratification of a treaty constitutes a reservation when it would exclude or vary the legal effect of one or more of the provisions of the treaty in their application to the reserving State.[29]

This State Department legal opinion written in 1971 almost exactly fits the situation with the Panama Canal Treaties in 1978. Panama's counter-reservation did "vary the legal effect of one or more of the provisions of the treaty" by requiring Panamanian "cooperation" before any U.S. action to defend the Canal in Panama, such unilateral action having been explicitly authorized by the DeConcini reservation. Indeed, Dr. Breecher told Senator East's Subcommittee that Panama's counter-reservation (incorrectly labeled an "understanding") was the "most substantive change in the text of the treaty that can be imagined."[30] Breecher added:

. . . if the patently false argument should be made that any nonsubstantive unilateral "understandings" in instruments of ratification need not be accepted by the other party, the decisive reply is first that every such "understanding," or whatever it is called, must be verbatim and formally accepted by the other party, without inquiry whether it is substantive or not, or else there is no ratification. The correct procedure can be seen from the ratification documents themselves, the Panamanians accepting some clearly nonsubstantive amendments like the requirement that the President shall include in the U.S. instruments of ratification what the Senate said in the ratification resolutions. Since the President had already done this, that's nonsubstantive.[31]

Moreover, Whiteman's *Digest of International Law* states that "the text of the treaty is usually set forth 'word for word' in the instruments of ratification."[32]

The issue of reservation versus understanding was further addressed in the March 22, 1971 memorandum from the Office of the Legal Adviser of the Department of State in these words:

A statement intended by a ratifying State to exclude or modify the legal effect of one or more provisions of a treaty as applied to that State should be designated by that State as a "reservation." Where a State wishes to set forth its interpretation of the provisions of a treaty without intending to change the legal effect as understood by it, the statement should be designated as an "understanding."

The designation by the ratifying State is not controlling. Whether the statement modifies the legal effect or merely expresses its true intent depends on the substance of the statement and is not solely within the judgment of the State making the statement.[33]

Therefore, Panama's designation of its controversial three paragraphs as an "understanding" was not controlling. What was controlling, of course, was the meaning and impact on the Treaties.

On that Thursday evening of April 7, 1978 when President Carter invited Torrijos to write his own reservation, the Treaties were in trouble, both in the U.S. Senate and in Panama. Mr. Carter needed help. He called on the Senate leadership, Robert Byrd, Frank Church and Paul Sarbanes "to see if we could clarify our position and assuage the concerns of the Panamanians and the Senators at the same time." He also decided to call in Panama's Ambassador Gabriel Lewis Galindo, Deputy Secretary of State Warren Christopher, and former Assistant Secretary of State William D. Rogers to work with the Senate leaders and to deal with Senator DeConcini who had become a problem for Carter.[34]

SMOKING GUN THREE: 'ELIMINATE U.S. RIGHTS'

The third revelation was the collusion of the Senate leadership with treaty handlers in a plan to eliminate the clear-cut U.S. rights of the DeConcini reservation without making it too apparent. The scheme involved State Department officials and Senators whose mission was to come up with something to "make clear that nothing controverted the nonintervention language in the treaty texts,"[35] and at the same time to allude to the elimination of unilateral U.S. rights in the DeConcini reservation without actually saying so. It was a delicate assignment in semantics. One year later, Mr. Rogers would tell the Washington Society of International Law about "the search for a solution . . . on an early Sunday morning in Senator Church's hideaway office on the Hill. . . ."[36]

The "solution" was the leadership amendment to the second treaty (the Panama Canal Treaty) and the purpose was to assure passage of the final treaty by satisfying both the doubtful Senators and the Panamanians. It succeeded. To be sure, it deceived the Panamanians into believing that the unilateral U.S. rights under the DeConcini reservation had been eliminated, whereas the U.S. position was that the rights remained but the language was smoother. The leadership amendment was readily adopted by the Senate and became a reservation to the Panama Canal Treaty:

(a) RESERVATIONS:

(1) Pursuant to its adherence to the principle of nonintervention, any action taken by the United States of America in the exercise of its rights to assure that the Panama Canal shall remain open, secure, and accessible, pursuant to the provisions of the Panama Canal Treaty, the Treaty concerning the Permanent Neutrality and Operation of the Panama Canal, and the resolutions of ratification thereto, shall be only for the purpose of assuring that the Canal shall remain open, secure, neutral, and accessible, and shall not have as its purpose or be interpreted as a right of intervention in the internal affairs of the Republic of Panama or interference with its political independence or sovereign integrity.[37]

This reservation restates principles that presumably had been settled before: the principle of nonintervention and noninteference in Panama's affairs in the event of any U.S. action to keep the Canal open and operating, and the principle of noninterference in Panama's "sovereign integrity." However, nothing is said in this reservation about the U.S. right to send in troops, when necessary to guarantee an open and neutral Canal. Apparently, this kind of language was to be avoided; it was too explicit.

The meeting on that Sunday morning in Senator Church's office assured success for the following Tuesday's vote. Indeed, Panama's ambassador was there and he too was satisfied with the new arrangement. The next day, April 17, the Senate leadership drew up the leadership amendment to the second treaty.

Senator DeConcini agreed with the results, telling the press, as reported in the *Congressional Quarterly,* that he was "very satisfied" that the compromise did no violence to his reservation.[38] He was basically right, except that nothing had been said about U.S. rights. It was an ambiguous amendment that had not really changed anything; it was a smoke screen to help insure ratified Treaties. But it did the job for the U.S. Senate which agreed to the Panama Canal Treaty on April 18, 1978 by a vote of 68 to 32, the identical margin of victory a month earlier with the Neutrality Treaty.

Interestingly, it took a special leadership amendment to pass the second treaty and a special amendment (the DeConcini reservation) to pass the first, both amendments on the same subject: U.S. rights to keep the Canal open, using troops in Panama if necessary. This had always been the major U.S. requirement and the major Panamanian objection, unfortunately never legally or constitutionally resolved.

In his speech to the international lawyers in 1979, Mr. Rogers asserted that Senator DeConcini "had tried to inject into the treaty package the principle that the United States could intervene with military force in Panama" to restore operation of the Canal. Senator DeConcini did indeed inject this principle—that was the purpose of his reservation, which specifically states that each nation shall independently have the right to reopen the Canal or restore operations, "including the use of military force in the Republic of Panama."[39] 75 Senators supported DeConcini.

A pertinent excerpt from Mr. Rogers' speech before the Society of International Law follows:

I speak of Panama and the strains it has induced in international lawmaking not as a disinterested observer. A year ago, again almost to the day, the Senate had given its advice and consent to the first of the two treaties in a resolution which you will recall contained the celebrated DeConcini reservation. You will also recall that Senator DeConcini had tried to inject into the treaty package the principle that the United States could intervene with military force in Panama forever to restore, as he put it, the operations of the Canal, a notion scarcely consistent with the treaty design of transferring the Canal to the sovereign state of Panama. Panama seriously considered, and in fact came within an ace of rejecting the Treaties then and there.

I was asked by the United States and Panama to lend my private good offices to the search for a solution. I did so for some frenzied period during the debate on the second treaty. At the last minute we were able to come up with language acceptable to Panama in the Senate's second resolution of advice and consent which made it clear that *all U.S. rights, including that expressed in the DeConcini reservation were subject to the nonintervention principles of the U.N. Charter.*

But it was notable that the final compromise was negotiated directly with the Senate leadership itself on an early Sunday morning in Senator Church's hideaway office on the Hill on an issue the President had called the most important foreign policy initiative of his Administration, with Senators Church, Byrd and Sarbanes. It was this which finally avoided the constitutional crisis.[40] (Emphasis added)

Mr. Rogers' contention that U.S. rights under the DeConcini reservation were "scarcely consistent with the treaty design of transferring the Canal to the sovereign nation of Panama" places Panama's sovereignty ahead of the agreed-to U.S. rights for the future security of the Canal—and it means that the leadership amendment was designed to eliminate those U.S. rights. As for the "treaty design," it is proper, of course, to alter treaties during the advice and consent phase, as may be desired.

In the post-treaty inquiries to various Senators who had supported the Treaties, the question was asked as to what influence the DeConcini reservation had had on their votes. Senator Howard Baker, the Minority Leader in 1978, gave a confusing answer in his January 4, 1983 letter:

I would answer your question by saying that the DeConcini reservation had no effect on my decision on the Treaties. I felt then and still believe that the leadership amendment was completely sufficient for the need and couched in much less inflammatory language.[41]

Nonetheless, the leadership amendment does *not* give the United States the right to go in and reopen the Canal if it is closed. Indeed, this right is not mentioned. Only the DeConcini reservation grants this right and, to be sure, that was the reason for the DeConcini reservation that had been so decisively approved for the first treaty.

Comparisons are in order: On January 4, 1983, Senator Baker was saying that the DeConcini reservation had no effect on his support for the Treaties since the leadership amendment protected U.S. rights sufficiently for him. On November 5, 1977, President Carter was assuring Senator Ted Stevens (R.-Alas.), that the Treaties always provided U.S. rights to "send in troops."[42] And on April 28, 1979, Mr. Rogers was sure that the leadership amendment eliminated U.S. rights to "send in troops," as we read his address. Each man was in disagreement with the other two.

These are confusing statements coming from principals in the Treaties episode. What did they mean? Or, was it semantics, as a way to get ratified Treaties and to deliver the Canal to Panama? Obviously, U.S. officials had no "meeting of minds" among themselves—or with the Panamanians.

Nonetheless, Mr. Rogers' speech, apparently delivered with a degree of pride, was beneficial in understanding better the history and purpose of the leadership amendment that so completely fooled the Panamanians into believing that the "imperialistic claws" of the DeConcini reservation had been removed. At the same time, this amendment convinced certain U.S. Senators that the U.S. rights under the DeConcini reservation remained intact, thereby assuring enough votes for a two-thirds approval.

SMOKING GUN FOUR: 'WON'T PASS UNLESS WE CAN AMEND IT'

Howard Baker, the Senate Minority Leader in 1978, went to Panama in January of that year and told Omar Torrijos, "I came here to tell you that the treaty won't pass unless we can amend it."[43] Baker, along with Senators Jake Garn and John Chafee, had gone to negotiate directly with the Head of Government, Torrijos, notwithstanding the U.S. constitutional requirement that only the President shall "make Treaties," including negotiations and ratification, and that the only Senate function is to give "Advice and Consent."[44]

A short time later, Senate Majority Leader Robert Byrd, would tell Baker, " . . . if either you or I go against the Treaties, they probably will be defeated."[45] This proved to be an accurate prediction. Both Byrd and Baker were effective supporters of the Treaties which barely passed with a one vote margin. Unquestionably, if Baker had opposed them, his influence would have carried other Republicans with him and the Treaties would have been defeated. So, in many respects, Senator Baker was the key to successful Treaties, both as legislator and as negotiator.

Not content with the normal constitutional role of "Advice and Consent," and not observing the separation of powers between the Legislative and Executive Branches, Mr. Baker went to Panama as a negotiator.

Some years earlier, Teddy Roosevelt had gone to Panama on a different kind of mission: to view with pride and satisfaction the Canal under construction. He landed at Colon on November 14, 1906 for a three-day visit,[46] the first U.S. President to visit a foreign country while in office. T.R. had opponents too. He was criticized for his role in helping Panama's revolutionists gain independence from Colombia, so the way would be cleared for the construction of the Canal. Some time after the Canal opened, Roosevelt answered his critics: "People say that I fomented insurrection in Panama prior to the time I became President. While I was President, I kept my foot down on those revolutions so that when the revolution referred to did occur, I did not have to foment it; I simply lifted my foot."[47]

Again, comparisons are in order: In 1903 the revolutionists wanted to help the Canal builders while in 1978, the roles were reversed as the Canal builders wanted to help the revolutionists take the Canal, even under duress. One should remember, an unelected and revolutionary government put Torrijos in power when his "friend" and fellow officer, Major Boris Martinez with the backing of the Panamanian National Guard ousted the legal regime of the Harvard educated Dr. Arnulfo Aris from the presidency with a *coup d'etat* on October 11, 1968. Shortly afterward, on February 24, 1969, Torrijos handcuffed Martinez and shipped him off to Miami.

This, then, was the Torrijos who became the unelected Head of State, in every respect illegal under the laws of Panama. Nonetheless, he was the object of the visit during January 3-7, 1978 by Senators Baker, Chafee and Garn whose mission was to negotiate directly with Torrijos for U.S. rights to keep the Canal open against any threats and to guarantee the rights of American ships to go to the head of the line in time of war. The authority for U.S. Senators to negotiate with foreign governments is not known. Baker does not mention authorization in his book, *No Margin for Error* (Time Books, 1980), nor that anyone asked him to negotiate for the Executive Branch, although he does say on page 186, "I talked with Jimmy Carter about it and I talked with Majority Leader Bob Byrd."

Neither does Mr. Carter mention the Baker mission in his book of memoirs, *Keeping Faith* (Bantam, 1982), nor that he asked the Legislative Branch to negotiate for him. As a matter of fact, however, there were some

39 other Senators who appeared to be negotiating the Treaties at one time or another. What had happened to the constitutional processes?

In considering these unusual treaty procedures and their great importance to national security, one might question the meanings of the titles of Carter's and Baker's books: Was Mr. Carter "keeping faith" with the spirit and words of the U.S. Constitution? Was there really "no margin for error" in Baker's usurpation of authority for treaty-making in his direct negotiations with Panama's Head of Government? How else can the following colloquy with Torrijos be classified?

Torrijos: Will the Senate pass this treaty?

Baker: Not without a couple of changes they won't.

Torrijos (upset): What can I do to pass it? What can I do to make it happen?

Baker: I'm not sure you can do anything other than agree to these amendments.

Torrijos: You're being tough.

Baker: No. I'm being realistic, and I came here to tell you that treaty won't pass unless we can amend it.[48]

Whereupon, according to Baker's account, Torrijos carefully examined the two proposed amendments (the two leadership amendments to the Neutrality Treaty) for some time, then exclaimed, "You're trying to negotiate a new treaty." After the Panamanian understood that President Carter knew about the amendments, he decided to go along. Mr. Baker concluded his chapter with these words of assurance: "The amendments were accepted. Panama got what was necessary to her dignity and we got what was essential to our security."[49] Unfortunately, the latter half of Senator Baker's statement is subject to question, as these amendments did *not* provide explicitly for U.S. rights to defend the Canal.

Moreover, what is the authority for U.S. Senators to negotiate international agreements on their own? Does not the Logan Act specifically prohibit American citizens without authority from attempting to influence or negotiate matters pending between the United States and foreign countries?

One of the most frightening episodes in William Jorden's book, *Panama Odyssey,* is the amazing scene described on pages 602-605 where the Majority Leader of the United States Senate is kneeling before a coffee table on Sunday morning, April 16, 1978, negotiating the leadership amendment to the Panama Canal Treaty with Panama's Ambassador Gabriel Lewis Galindo. Watching Senator Robert Byrd were the late Senator Frank Church, in whose hide-away office (Room S-208) the bargaining was taking place, Senator Paul Sarbanes, Deputy Secretary of State Warren Christopher and the former Assistant Secretary of State for Inter-American Affairs, William D. Rogers, who was apparently a consultant for Panama that day. Also present was Lewis Galindo's deputy, Ricardo Bilonick, Legal Adviser to the Panamanian Embassy. The purpose of the "secret" meeting was to help the Executive Branch get Treaties that would pass the Senate.

Mr. Jorden was impressed with this scenario too, as he wrote:

It was the only time in history a majority leader of the Senate and a foreign ambassador had negotiated wording that would become part of an international treaty. But it was done for a very simple reason, which everyone in S-208 understood: there was no other way to save the treaties (p.603).

Totally disregarded, and apparently never considered by anyone, was the constitutional principle for the separation of powers between the Legislative and Executive Branches of government. How can Senators negotiate a treaty on Sunday and vote objectively on that treaty on Tuesday? How was it possible for the Senate to exert any check on the Executive when one of the most controversial parts of the Treaties had been negotiated by the Majority Leader, Robert Byrd, in Washington with Panama's Ambassador Lewis Galindo, and by the Minority Leader, Howard Baker, in Panama with Omar Torrijos?

What consideration had been given by Messrs. Byrd, Baker, Church and Sarbanes to their oaths of office to preserve the Constitution, one of whose most basic features was the separation and limitation of powers? Not only did these Senators disregard the Constitution and their oaths to protect it, they also ignored the Logan Act which makes it against the law to usurp the Executive's function in negotiating with foreign powers.

Nor did former Ambassador Jorden understand apparently, as he wrote, "there was no other way to save the treaties." What about saving the Constitution? The Treaties did not have to be saved; they should rise or fall on their own merits, developed in accordance with Article II of the Constitution—not in the all-out, anything goes procedures that were actually used. The American public deserves better.

The camaraderie and headiness of high power had produced a success for the second and last treaty, the inconveniences of the Constitution notwithstanding. Vice President Walter Mondale joined in the upbeat mood in welcoming the Panamanian Ambassador, Rogers and Christopher in his official residence that afternoon, telling the Ambassador that President Carter "doesn't want to preside over a reinstitution of a colonial foreign policy." But this seemed like groveling because the United States never has had a colonial foreign policy, much less any intention of reinstituting one. Mondale added that he thought the U.S. Senate would produce workable Treaties. But, the Senate does not produce treaties under the Constitution, of course. Nonetheless, here was another classic example of the Carter-Mondale thinking—anything for the Treaties. Incidentally, Mr. Mondale was involved in advising the U.S. negotiators about the economic package that would accrue to Panama by the Treaties.

INTO NEGOTIATIONS: 'THE SENATE CANNOT INTRUDE'

In sensing an urgency for clarification in treaty matters in 1977, Senator John J. Sparkman, D.-Ala., Chairman of the Senate Committee on Foreign Relations, had his staff prepare the comprehensive report, *"The Role of the Senate in Treaty Ratification."* Nowhere in its 78 pages does this monograph indicate or imply authorization for Senators to strike out on their own to negotiate treaties. On the contrary, much evidence prohibits it.[50]

Moreover, the onus is on the President to negotiate, using his designated representatives within the Executive Branch, as prescribed by the Constitution. In a 1936 ruling by the U.S. Supreme Court, Associate Justice George Sutherland wrote that "the Senate cannot intrude" into the field of negotiations. Indeed, Senate Document No.92-82 of the 92d Congress, *"The Constitution of the United States of America: Analysis and Interpretation,"* explains:

Actually, the negotiation of treaties has long since been taken over by the President; the Senate's role in relation to treaties is today essentially legislative in character. "He [the President] alone negotiates. *Into the field of negotiations, the Senate cannot intrude;* the Congress itself is powerless to invade it," declared Justice Sutherland for the Court in 1936. The Senate must, moreover, content itself with such information as the President chooses to furnish it.[51] (Emphasis added)

This document is emphatic about the "presidential monopoly" in matters dealing with other nations, quoting Thomas Jefferson in 1790:

The transaction of business with foreign nations is executive altogether. It belongs, then, to the head of that department, except to such portions of it as are specifically submitted to the Senate. Exceptions are to be construed strictly.[52]

The Logan Act is particularly designed to prevent unauthorized negotiations with foreign nations. Indeed, its title is "An Act to Prevent Usurpation of Executive Functions" and has been a fundamental law since 1798 when a Phildelphia Quaker named Logan travelled to Paris on his own to negotiate with the French government in an effort to prevent war between

France and the United States.[53] Obviously the United States must have only one official voice with foreign powers, that of the Chief Executive. We recall that President Carter's brother, Billy, was investigated for having dealings with Libya's Muammar Khadafy for possible infractions of the Logan Act.

Senator Sparkman's report on the treaty responsibilities of the U.S. Senate primarily focused on the advice and consent function, the handling of reservations and amendments, and the degree of consultation with the President—all in the interest of having "the Senate to share fully with the President in the power to make treaties."[54] The only reference to actual negotiating is a short passage on pages 26 and 27:

If the treaty is very important, such as the United Nations Charter, members of the Senate and of the House of Representatives as well may be put on a negotiating delegation or accompany the delegation in an advisory capacity.[55]

Another important reference delineating authority for making treaties is the *Jefferson's Manual of Parliamentary Practice*.[56] This Manual was Thomas Jefferson's guide and it has been applicable since 1801 except when "inconsistent with the standing rules and orders." In paragraph 594, among other things, the *Manual* provides:

The Constitution thought it wise to restrain the Executive and Senate from entangling and embroiling our affairs with those of Europe. Besides, as the *negotiations are carried on by the Executive alone,* the subjecting to the ratification of the Representatives such articles as are within their participation is no more inconvenient than to the Senate.[57] (Emphasis added)

George Washington not only participated in preparing the Constitution but wrote extensively about its meanings and interpretations as long as he lived:

Having been a member of the General Convention, and knowing the principles on which the Constitution was formed, I have ever entertained but one opinion on this subject; and from the first establishment of the Government to this moment, my conduct has exemplified that opinion, that *the power of making treaties is exclusively vested in the President,* by and with the advice and consent of the Senate, provided two-thirds of the Senators present concur, and that every treaty so made, and promulgated, thenceforth became the Law of the land.[58] (Emphasis added)

No authorization has been found to justify the kind of negotiating that Senator Baker conducted with Omar Torrijos on January 4, 1978 on the Panama Canal Treaties. However, Logan Act violations carry minimal penalties and considering the individuals involved, their conduct would be considered as ex officio "good will"—a part of the new diplomacy, the new society, the new world. Evidently, the urgency for ratified Treaties was the first consideration, constitutional niceties notwithstanding. The word, "anachronistic," was heard so frequently during the debates about the original 1903 Treaty. Is it possible that some of the 40 ex officio Senator negotiators could have felt that way, even subconsciously, about the Constitution? Washington warned in 1786 about suffering the Constitution to be "trampled upon whilst it has an existence."[59]

In traveling to Panama to negotiate with Torrijos, Senator Baker apparently usurped prerogatives of the Executive Branch and in so doing, he neglected his oath of office to "preserve, protect and defend the Constitution of the United States," including its unique system of separation of powers. Even if President Carter had designated Mr. Baker to proceed with his Senate negotiating team, the propriety of such action is questioned. Without an official designation, it was an unconstitutional act.

Such a procedure, in many respects, is tantamount to placing the powers of prosecutor, judge and jury into the hands of one person. That is, as negotiator, Baker acted as a sort of prosecutor to win his case. Then later, as a Senator, he sat in judgment of his handiwork. In essence, he was indeed prosecutor, judge, and jury. The Constitution, of course, separates power into the three Branches of government (Legislative, Executive, and Judicial) for the express purpose of establishing a system of checks and balances in order that too much power would never be vested in one Branch or person. Of course, this is elementary civics but it is also basic to the American system—and seems to have been disregarded in handling the ratification of the Treaties.

Historically, the separation of powers has been observed. So, Senator Baker's dilemma, even if he recognized it, was not without precedent. Others, however, handled it differently. For example, after the War of 1812 with England, President James Madison appointed Henry Clay, the Speaker of the House, and Senator James A. Bayard of Delaware to attend the peace conference at Ghent, as negotiators. Clay and Bayard resigned from the Congress, believing they could not constitutionally serve in two capacities.[60]

In another case, this one after the Spanish-American War, President William McKinley sent three Senators to Paris for the peace conference, as negotiators. A resolution of disapproval was introduced in the Senate, though it did not pass. The objection was that the President might have too much influence over the Senate because, as negotiators, Senators might be "less inclined to independent judgment when the treaty should come up in the Senate for ratification [sic]."[61]

In many respects, old-fashioned principles and absolute truths seem to have lost out to situational ethics. This danger was not acceptable in the beginnings of the republic. Alexander Hamilton, for one, saw to that with his *Federalist* papers. His advice about unwarranted assumption of authority constitutes an absolute truth:

There is no position which depends on clearer principles than that every act of a delegated authority contrary to the tenor of the commission under which it is exercised is void. No legislative act, therefore, contrary to the Constitution can be valid. To deny this would be to affirm that the deputy is greater than his principal; that the servant is above his master; that the representatives of the people are superior to the people themselves; that men acting by virtue of powers may do not only what their powers so authorize, but what they forbid.[62]

What was the authority for Senator Baker to deal directly with the head of a foreign government in a matter reserved by the Constitution exclusively to the Chief Executive? Even if he had been authorized by the President, what is the justification for violating the principle of separation of powers as established by the Constitution? Was a guaranteed Panama Canal for Omar Torrijos worth a constitutional crisis?

In the Foreward to his book, *No Margin for Error*, Senator Baker wrote, "In recent years, although most of the American people . . . are fully aware that we are lucky to live in a republic where freedom is the rule and not its exception, we have grown uneasy about the manner, the methods, and the failures of those we elect to lead us."[63]

Senator Baker was a key figure in the loss of the Canal. Without his talents and leadership in the Senate, the transfer would have very probably failed. Americans are not forgetting the Panama Canal—and this fact was unmistakable in the many contacts made in the research for this book. As Senator Baker indicated, the people do indeed speak of "those we elect to represent and to lead us," and as for "no margin for error," this would not fit the mood.

Moreover, when the people learn about the smoking guns that saved the Canal Treaties, old wounds are reopened—and the crisis in Central America becomes real and more ominous. Indeed, many feel that the margin for error was well known and that the error itself was not acceptable.

·9·

THE NEW DIPLOMACY: DOUBLE-SPEAK IS ESSENTIAL

When diplomats and negotiators feel free to articulate at will about meeting of minds, interpretations and procedures in treaty-making, they often reveal unusual motives and techniques. A case in point was former Secretary of State Henry A. Kissinger's testimony before the Senate Foreign Relations Committee on October 14, 1977. He was explaining U.S. rights to defend the Canal and the "ambiguous statements of Panamanian officials understandably concerned with their own ratification process. . . ." He said:

Ambiguity, of course, is the essence of diplomacy; it often permits each side to maintain its domestic position while safeguarding essential international interests. *I have resorted to it* in negotiations on several occasions.[1] (Emphasis added)

Dr. Kissinger was echoing the new diplomacy of the State Department—in essence, it appears, a kind of savoir-faire style of diplomatic elegance in which double-speak is essential and gentlemen of good will do not mind. Several years later, Ambassador David H. Popper, one of the treaty negotiators and State's man assigned to steer the Treaties through the Senate, was relaxed too. Indeed, he said much the same thing as Kissinger in explaining why the Panamanians had not been asked to withdraw their three paragraphs of counter-reservation which were contrary to the DeConcini reservation: ". . . *ambiguity was essential* if we were not to let a disputation about a distant and unlikely contingency torpedo the whole

Treaty enterprise. We thought the fudgy language the Panamanians inserted in their instrument of ratification committed us to no more than motherhood. . . ."² (Emphasis added)

However, any logical consideration of Panama's unchallenged counter-offer, and particularly the history behind it, indicates otherwise. For example, Panama at no time was "fudgy" about its intentions to prevent any U.S. intervention to defend or reopen the Canal except on Panama's terms, i.e., "*cooperation.*" All this was part of the pattern for quick ratification and confusion to obscure the true meaning.

'COULD SOW THE SEEDS OF FUTURE CRISIS'

Amplifying his concept of essential ambiguity in foreign affairs, Kissinger continued his statement to the Foreign Relations Committee on that October day in 1977:

I have never considered ambiguity of language acceptable, however, if it masked a true difference of interpretation. Whatever the words of an international agreement may say, it is vital in my experience that both sides share the same understanding of the intent of that instrument. In this particular case, ambiguity or lack of public understanding could sow the seeds of future crisis if in fact the parties are not of a single view as to the central provisions of the treaties."³

Taken together, this seemed to be a kind of double-talk that, many contend, has characterized the Kissinger brand of compromise and negotiations. This approach was brought to an apogee by Kissinger who devised a method of finding a semantic expression to paper over basic disagreements. We noted this negotiating symbiosis in Vietnam, with SALT I and even in the Shanghai Communique.

Kissinger simply laid opposing positions down side by side, pontificated at length, and then announced, "Now we have agreement;" whereas, in truth, there *was* no agreement. Nonetheless, with suave temporizing and Procrustean finality, he was able to dust over many conflicts and incongruities—only to reap a later harvest of reality: withered "agreements" with no roots, terrorized fleeing refugees, and unchallenged Soviet arms build up. This was certainly true, unfortunately, with his solutions for Vietnam, Lebanon, SALT I and the Helsinki Accords, as the record shows.

In his testimony that day before Senator Sparkman's Committee, Kissinger made a number of imprecise and unfortuante assertions, sufficient to mislead and confuse the Senators listening, as well as the public:⁴

—He incorrectly stated that Article IV of the Neutrality Treaty "gives the United States the continuing right, unilaterally if necessary, to defend the Canal and its operations against threats to the neutrality of the Canal. . . ." The fact is, Article IV does *not* authorize *unilateral* action, merely that both States "agree to maintain the regime of neutrality. . . ."

—He was concerned that Panama might abrogate the 1903 Treaty. The fact is, the United States on that day exercised sovereignty in the Canal Zone to the entire exclusion of Panamanian sovereignty. Did it matter, except academically, what Panama did?

—Once again, Kissinger stated erroneously that the Canal was "located in Panamanian territory." This was untrue. And once again, did Kissinger not know, or not believe, that the 1907 Supreme Court decision, *Wilson v. Shaw,* and the 1972 Fifth Circuit Court of Appeals decision, *U.S. v. Husband R. (Roach),* found the Canal Zone to be U.S. territory?

In concluding his testimony, Dr. Kissinger called for harmony and cooperation, including the plea that "The Senate interpretation [of U.S. rights] should be reduced to formal and *explicit* language . . . which would ensure that it becomes the authoritative and mutually acceptable explanations."[5] (Emphasis added)

This was a switch. Kissinger was vacillating; he was being all things to all people. Indeed, it was hardly consistent with his previous advocacy of ambiguity "in safeguarding international interests," i.e., the "essence of diplomacy." Even so, it *was* consistent with his longtime policy of laying opposing positions side by side and semantically assuring all concerned that agreement had been reached. In truth, of course, precision and a meeting of minds are the basic ingredients for successful contracts, and certainly for international agreements, Kissinger notwithstanding.

Another former Secretary of State testified that day. He was Dean Rusk. Dr. Rusk apparently agreed with the need for precise terms:

Treaties are the primary source of international law partly because they are drafted in relatively *precise terms* of legal obligation and more importantly, because they represent the consent of the sovereign parties who agree to them.[6] (Emphasis added)

In his brief statement, however, Rusk was also misleading and sadly inaccurate on several basic points:

—In one sentence, Dr. Rusk misstated two important principles: "Even if we had acquired *absolute title,* which we did not, the general international policy and practice of *decolonization* would have rendered the *status quo* in Panama untenable." (Emphasis added) First, the United States *never* had a colony in its history; and the Canal Zone was U.S. *territory,* legally purchased and Court tested. Second, the term "absolute title" is a smoke screen: The distinguished attorney, Alfred J. Schweppe, rather conclusively eviscerated arguments that the U.S. did not have title. He simply quoted Article III of the 1903 Treaty, the two court decisions noted above, and the definition of "title" given many years ago by one of the most respected property law professors in the country, Dean Everett Frazer of the University of Minnesota. Frazer defined "title" as "a right to possession which no one can effectively deny," or put differently, "a right to possession in perpetuity, good against all the world."[7] Obviously Dean Frazer and Dean Rusk disagreed.

—Rusk told Sparkman, "I would suggest to you that, in the modern world, one nation cannot maintain a presence within another nation without the consent of the second nation." In an unreal comparison, Rusk cited the U.S. withdrawal from bases in France, Libya, Ethiopia, Pakistan and Turkey.[8] This was like a *non sequitur*, situations totally different. In the Canal Zone, the U.S. had sovereign rights and owned the land "in perpetuity."

—In a third misstatement, which is enough for our purposes, Rusk relied on the application of Article IV of the Neutrality Treaty for U.S. rights to defend and keep open the Canal. In truth, of course, Article IV provides *no guarantee* and has always been a weak straw.

Throughout Rusk's presentation, the thread of defeatist diplomacy was weaving an unbelievable pattern of negativism: afraid of what the International Court of Justice might do to the 1903 Treaty; apologetic for the U.S. veto of the 1973 U.N. resolution condemning the United States for holding onto the Canal; and fearful that the "anachronistic Treaty of 1903" was too weak to "keep the Canal functioning and safe."[9] Rusk preferred the new 1977 Treaties with which the U.S. would defend the Canal from afar, i.e., with no military bases on Panama's soil.

With this kind of testimony, both Rusk and Kissinger made a substantial contribution to the surrender of the Canal, indeed to the great swindle itself. Both were emphatic about transferring the Canal, albeit their arguments were incomplete and flawed in many respects. Even so, some three weeks earlier, these former Secretaries of State told Representative Andy Ireland, D.-Fla., of the importance of Article IV of the Neutrality Treaty in their decisions to support the Treaties. Unfortunately, Article IV is the parallel and co-equal authorization which has absolutely no assurance of unilateral action.

Mr. Ireland's question, in his dialogue with Messrs. Rusk and Kissinger, was straight to the point on perhaps the most basic issue of the Treaties:

My real concern is that should the Congress approve such a treaty based on Article IV, based on the interpretation that we do have these rights, and the Panamanians approve the treaty based on the fact that we don't have the rights, what good is the treaty with such a very basic difference of opinion in it?[10]

Congressman Ireland had asked a question that negotiators and ratifiers preferred to duck; it was embarrassing and besides, as Dr. Robert Pastor indicated in answer to the author's questions of December 15, 1983, it was best to have things such as this "understood." But, of course, such things should be clearly stated without equivocation; but, sadly, never were. Rusk's answer was accomodating:

Now, if at the time of the exchange of ratifications there is a fundamental difference publicly expressed by the two sides on this point, then we may have to go back to the drawing board. . . .[11]

Kissinger's response, unfortunately, seemed to be a carry over from his philosophy of essential ambiguity. He said, still clinging to the mistaken idea that Article IV somehow gave the U.S. *unilateral* rights:

I must say my own support of the agreement hinges importantly on the neutrality clause and it is my understanding that it gives us the possibility to defend the neutrality of the Canal *unilaterally*. . . .[12] (Emphasis added)

With Rusk calling for "precise terms" and Kissinger advocating ambiguity at times and a "single view" at other times—with these contradictions in mind, Kissinger's statement to Ireland that Article IV of the Neutrality Treaty "gives us the *possibility* to defend the neutrality of the Canal *unilaterally* . . ." (emphasis added) was a classic in the "new diplomacy." The question is: Just what do you mean?

Harold G. Maier, Professor of Law and Director of Transnational Legal Studies of Vanderbilt University, gave his understanding of just what was meant, seven years later, in his article about "Studied Ambiguity" in the Winter 1984 issue of the *Virginia Journal of International Law*. In many respects, this was a near perfect follow-up to the smoking gun of David Popper: Ambiguity was essential.

Dr. Maier, former consultant to the Secretary of the Army (1976) and, in 1984, Counselor to the Department of State, followed the principles of the "new diplomacy" in his essay, contending that the issue of defense rights over the Canal "was never effectively resolved" because ambiguity was necessary "to create the appearance of agreement" for the purpose of home consumption. Thereby, each nation could claim that it "won" the negotiations.[13]

"The political importance of defense rights . . . was much greater than practical importance," wrote Maier, and "the legal right to defend the Panama Canal . . . is relatively unimportant." He concluded that the United States would use military force to defend the Canal regardless of the legal basis for such an act.[14] With this kind of counseling in the State Department, why have treaties? Use the Army, Navy and Air Force. Certainly, a secure legal foundation is the best place to begin.

Professor Maier's contention that an attack on the Canal would be answered by U.S. military force with the "*full cooperation of the Republic of Panama*" (emphasis added) is conjectural: Panama's counter-reservation to the Treaties requires Panama's *cooperation* before the U.S. can act. Moreover, Maier's article totally fails to mention this important three-paragraph last minute counter-reservation. In such a lengthy and thorough treatment of "Studied Ambiguity" why was nothing said about the most contentious provision of all: Panama's three-paragraph counter-reservation that was in fact hidden from the U.S. Senate and from the American people until the very day of ratification, June 16, 1978?

Another serious misconception contends that Senator Dennis DeConcini accepted the leadership amendment to the Panama Canal Treaty in
order to avoid a second plebiscite in Panama.[15] But this was incidental. Of
primary importance was the fact that Panama's Constitution requires a
plebiscite for Canal treaties and the DeConcini reservation was one of the
most substantive changes that can be imagined.

Correctly, Maier's analysis points out that the Neutrality Treaty does
not prevent Panama's alliance with other powers, even one with interests
inimical to those of the United States. As a sovereign nation, Panama
would indeed have such rights, and interviews in August 1984 in Panama
with President-elect Nicolas Ardito Barletta[16] and Deputy Canal Administrator Fernando Manfredo confirmed this understanding.[17] Therefore,
Panama under this Treaty could call in the Soviets or Cubans or Nicara-
guans for assistance in managing, operating and securing the Canal.

A number of misstatements are contained in the Maier essay: the
"annuity" was to recompense Panama for revenues lost by reductions in
the operation of the Panama Railroad, it was never a rental fee; Torrijos
did *not* do the 1968 coup, it was Boris Martinez; Panama was *not* "territorial sovereign" over the Canal Zone in 1974, it had been "excluded" from
the exercise of sovereignty by Article III of the 1903 Treaty; the transfer of
the waterway is *not* "an accomplished fact" because separate legislation
(not yet enacted) is required for this (Sec. 1503, Public Law 96-70)—not to
mention substantial evidence that the 1977 Treaties themselves are invalid.

In conclusion, Dr. Maier recommends that the United States and Panama attempt to resolve the legal aspects of defense rights in the 1984 atmosphere of cooperation—without the emotionalism that characterized the
negotiations and ratification of the Treaties in 1977 and 1978, looking
toward the need to preserve and protect the Canal as partners. More
important, however, is the constitutional requirement that the U.S. Senate
give "Advice and Consent" to Panama's three paragraph counter-reservation, i.e., vote on it. Then, the Senate should examine other constitutional
aspects of these Treaties, viz., how the 1903 Treaty was handled and how
United States territory was purportedly disposed of without participation
by the House of Representatives.

THE KISSINGER ROLE: PAST AND PRESENT

Henry Kissinger's role in the loss of the Panama Canal was perhaps
exceeded by no one, not even by President Carter. A letter of caution about
his power and procedures appeared in the September 9, 1983 edition of

The Washington Times, a letter that was sent also to the *New York Times* and the *Washington Post* but not used by the latter two papers. The following portions of Phillip Harman's letter bespeak an insecure and uncertain Latin America because of the Kissinger approach:

Much has been written about Henry Kissinger's appointment as the chairman of the new commission on Central America, but I have not seen one word mentioned where Kissinger was directly responsible for the first domino in Latin America—the Panama Canal Treaties.

. . . .

Certainly Kissinger someday must be held accountable for his 1974 loss of America's most precious asset—the Panama Canal—which became the first domino.

The story of the Canal swindle would not be complete without explaining the Kissinger role. He was, in many respects, the key to swindling the American people out of perhaps their most precious jewel. His background and record are pertinent.

Henry Kissinger's most telling part in the loss of the Canal occurred on February 7, 1974, when as Secretary of State he signed, together with Panama's Foreign Minister Juan Tack, an 8-point Statement of Principles which eventually became the framework of the 1977 Treaties. Points 3, 4 and 5 stipulated, incorrectly, that the Canal Zone was Panamanian territory.[18]

This was an inexcusable error and became a precedent for future mischief and misunderstanding. To be sure, it laid the foundation for surrendering the Canal. Dr. James McClellan, the former Chief Counsel and Staff Director of the Senate Subcommittee on Separation of Powers, commented on Kissinger's unwarranted assumption and tragic irresponsibility. During our interview November 15, 1983, he said:

What Kissinger did was legally incorrect. To accomplish his objective, Kissinger simply tried to undermine the well-known fact that the United States owned that land. . . . This was a part of the game plan that was pursued right up to the final vote in the Senate . . . in order to undermine our moral and ethical claim to the territory. Kissinger was part of the orchestrated movement to condition the American people that the United States did not own that land.[19]

Nor were the members of the Harman Committee satisfied with Kissinger's assertions that the Canal Zone was Panamanian territory. Particularly, they were concerned that a U.S. Secretary of State had pretended to overturn the ruling of the U.S. Supreme Court in *Wilson v. Shaw* (1907) that the Canal Zone *was* U.S. territory. After the usual long series of letters to gain attention, the following came through from Michael Rodak, Jr., the Clerk of the Supreme Court:

In response to your letter of June 2, 1975, please be advised that the Court has not overruled its ruling in *Wilson v. Shaw,* 204 U.S. 24 (1907).

Through another lengthy series of letters, which was the norm for touchy subjects of course, the Harman Committee attempted to determine if Kissinger violated U.S. law by his presumptuous action in proclaiming the Canal Zone to be on Panamanian soil. This time, the Court answered, in its August 4, 1975 letter, that it would not advise if "any individual is in violation of the law" and suggested contacting the Office of General Counsel of the State Department.

This was done with a September 30, 1975 letter to Monroe Leigh, the Legal Adviser to the Department of State. The following paragraph is pertinent:

As you are the Legal Adviser to the State Department, I would appreciate your legal opinion, as suggested by the U.S. Supreme Court, whether or not Secretary Kissinger is in violation of the law concerning this matter. If he is not in violation of the law when he signed the document last year with the *de facto* government of Panama, could you inform me on what legal grounds can the Secretary of State overrule a ruling of the U.S. Supreme Court?[20]

This was an unwelcome question to the Legal Adviser to Dr. Kissinger, of course. It was ignored until Senator Adlai E. Stevenson, D.-Ill., interceded. Then, the Assistant Secretary of State for Congressional Relations, Robert J. McCloskey, replied to Senator Stevenson by letter dated December 3, 1975, saying, in part:

For many years, U.S. government officers have responded to Mr. Harman's numerous requests for information and views. However, because of his continued advocacy of a particular point of view and the repetitive nature of his inquiries, this Department has determined to discontinue correspondence with him. In short, it has become an unreasonable burden to occupy a number of the Department's personnel in responding to Mr. Harman. That is the reason Mr. Leigh has not answered Mr. Harman's letter of September 30.[21]

It is easy to relate to the frustrations of the Harman Committee in efforts to obtain information that might reflect unfavorably on the State Department, or impugn motives and character. Delays and deceptive answers always seem to characterize these exchanges.

Subsequently, in his December 10, 1975 letter to McCloskey, Harman repeated his original requests, including the following observations:

As I speak in the United States on behalf of the gagged people of Panama who have been denied freedom of speech, they have deplored the treaty negotiations with the treasonous regime in their country who do not speak for nor do they represent the people of Panama. Their legal Constitution, like our own, clearly states that only a constitutional government can negotiate a treaty with a foreign country.

. . . .

Concerning my question to Mr. Monroe Leigh, the Legal Adviser to the State Department, as to whether or not Secretary Kissinger is in violation of the law when he overruled a ruling of the Supreme Court, you state that Mr. Leigh has not answered my letter of September 30 inasmuch as "it has become an unreasonable burden to occupy a number of the Department's personnel in responding to Mr. Harman." However, I feel that Mr. Leigh as a Federal employee has an obligation to respond to my question regarding the Secretary of State and his possible violation of the law. I also would like to know from Mr. Leigh if, in his legal opinion, the Secretary of State is in violation of the law, just what is the penalty for this violation of the law.[22]

Of course, these questions were never satisfactorily answered.

To be sure, another star was added to Kissinger's crown when President Reagan appointed him to head his Commision on Central America in 1983. This was also an attempt to win the public support needed to run the communists out of the Western Hemisphere, perhaps a nod toward the Monroe Doctrine. Was Kissinger the man for this job? Cuban and Soviet adventurism dominated the Caribbean.

Even so, a Machiavellian-minded Congress and a sensation-seeking media became debilitating complications to a danger even greater than the 1962 Cuban missile crisis. In 1962, however, the media, the Congress and the people closed ranks behind President Kennedy. Unfortunately, this was not so in 1983 when the media generally minimized communist encroachments into Central America and the attendant threat to national security, including the safety of the Panama Canal. Meanwhile, vote-conscious legislators were cutting President Reagan's plans for economic and military aid to the beleagured Salvadorans and Nicaraguan patriots fighting for freedom and self-government.

In this context, Dr. Kissinger entered the arena, ostensibly to save Central America for democracy—specifically, to reverse U.S. public opinion and "lay the foundation for a long-term unified national approach to the freedom and independence of the countries of Central America" (Reagan's words).

MAN OF DESTINY OR MASTER OF DOUBLE-SPEAK?

Dr. Kissinger assumed the kind of mission in Central America that he apparently revels in: shuttle diplomacy, media worship, quixotic benevolence—all in a laid-back atmosphere of "mutual respect and cooperation," the details of which are always salvageable with semantics. Even so, he assumed no responsibility for the outcome of his recommendations. Nonetheless, his brilliance cannot be denied. But, what purpose? Who is this man who would steer the ship of state? His philosophy? Indeed, where is he coming from?

His was a rocket-like rise to national pre-eminence: from a 20-year old naturalized citizen in 1943 through three Harvard degrees to PhD;

protege of the Rockefeller brothers, David and Nelson; trusted adviser and confidant of presidents; and ultimately, Secretary of State where he starred as negotiator *extraordinaire* and, some say, giveaway specialist supreme. Throughout, Kissinger honored his membership in, and the objectives of, the Council on Foreign Relations and the Trilateral Commission—those international organizations dominated by the Rockefeller influence. All this, of course, is on the public record.

Also, on the public record, are the Kissinger deals that failed U.S. interests, chief of which is probably his role in the loss of the American-owned Panama Canal. For example, in the Kissinger-Tack agreement of 1974, Kissinger not only incorrectly stated three times that the Canal Zone was Panamanian territory, but by doing so, he also threw away all the U.S. bargaining chips for future negotiations.[23]

Indeed, Panama was able to negotiate with a stacked deck all in its favor because the American Secretary of State had already surrendered the five principal negotiating chips: U.S. rights of sovereignty; the right of unilateral operations; the concept of perpetuity; the value of U.S. (taxpayers') property; and the sharing of future economic benefits. Consequently, there was not the usual give-and-take of bilateral negotiations: merely, U.S. offers to *give* and Panama's demands to *take*. It was an unusual circus and Kissinger was ring master *in absentia*.

Another example of this philosophy of defeatism was the Vietnam debacle whose "solution" by Kissinger won him the Nobel Peace Prize. Some peace. As U.S. forces withdrew, the communist hordes overran the countryside, pillaging, raping and murdering—and Kissinger, the U.S.A. and the Peace Accords be damned.

Alas, Kissinger was the foreign policy expert who presided over a detente policy that gave the Soviets grain and high technology; the Helsinki Accords that doomed European captive nations to enslavement; a SALT treaty allowing Soviet military superiority; and "peace" negotiations that lost Vietnam, Laos, Cambodia and Angola. In addition, he has toadied up to Castro on many occasions, pursuing a policy of normalization.

Ergo, in 1983 Kissinger was in Central America "solving" problems orchestrated by the same Castro. He has been called the apostle of appeasement. In 1976 Ronald Reagan questioned Kissinger about his "stewardship of a U.S. foreign policy that coincided precisely with the loss of U.S. military supremacy." Nonetheless, in 1983 Kissinger was Reagan's steward in Central America.

President Reagan repeatedly charged the Soviets, Cubans and Sandinistas with the turmoil in Central America. The evidence was overwhelming and irrefutable. Even so, one of Kissinger's first acts after being appointed was to challenge Reagan on this. Indeed, did the Kissinger panel see the urgency for a communist *military defeat*, followed by development programs and social justice? The editor of *Human Events* wrote on July 30, 1983, "Kissinger revels in ambiguous statements and uncertain trumpet calls."[24]

Another point: In 1976 the *San Francisco Chronicle* reported discordance between Dr. Kissinger and retired Navy Admiral Elmo Zumwalt, former Chief of Naval Operations: Zumwalt: "Kissinger feels the U.S. has passed its historic high point . . . is on the downhill. . . . He states his job is to persuade the Russians to give us the best deal we can get . . . but that the American people have only themselves to blame because they lack the stamina to stay the course. . . ." Kissinger's response: "Contemptible falsehoods." Zumwalt: "Kissinger's answer is just one more indication that liars lie."[25]

Nonetheless, this view of the Kissinger diplomacy has become rather commonplace in conservative journals. For example, columnist M. Stanton Evans wrote about Kissinger shortly after his appointment to the Central American Commission:

It is difficult to think of a policy area—South East Asia, strategic arms, the Panama Canal—where the net effect of Kissinger's policy was not a further drastic weakening of our position. Such outcomes were of course in keeping with his pessimistic world view which perceived the West in case after case as *historically fated for defeat*, and the task of our diplomacy the *graceful negotiation of the obvious*.[26] (Emphasis added)

Nonetheless, this was the man President Reagan selected to stabilize Central America—to preside over "the graceful negotiation" of surrender? Many members of the Congress have cooperated in the "graceful negotiation of the obvious" by their votes to deny U.S. aid to the freedom fighters in Nicaragua and El Salvador, seeking to protect their country from the communists. Nonetheless, the voters keep returning these people to Congress—in many cases, the same ones who agreed to surrender the Canal. They keep coming back.

Also, Dr. Henry Kissinger keeps coming back. Why? Kissinger has written and spoken many times about "the way to a new international order" and in his book, *The Troubled Partnership* (Greenwood Press, 1965), he chided "institutions based on present concepts of national sovereignty." Now, twenty years later, Kissinger and his philosophy seem ensconced at the highest levels of government—still making policy and still steering America toward internationalism. Unfortunately, the same can be said for many others who controlled the Panama Canal tragedy, some wittingly, some out of a sense of just doing good. Nonetheless, the Canal Treaties opened the door to the Central American turmoil that followed.

HOW TREATY-MAKERS VIEW
MEETING OF MINDS

Ambiguity was indeed essential for the Panama Canal Treaties, but not a meeting of minds. These circumstances were consistently manifest in a number of interviews with the treaty-makers during a visit to Washington, D.C. in mid-November 1983, just before the 98th Congress adjourned.

As to the relevance of unilateral declarations and meeting of minds in treaties, William D. Rogers, the former Assistant Secretary of State for Inter-American Affairs, said on November 14, 1983 in regard to the DeConcini reservation versus Panama's three paragraph counter-reservation:

On both sides it is a unilateral declaration. The language of the treaty itself, of course, is what counts. That's the only thing [the Treaties] that really constitutes a meeting of the minds of the two countries. So, what we said [in the declaration] doesn't amend the treaty language. It expresses our understanding of the treaty language or reservation with which we accept it, but it doesn't bind the other side.[27]

This is a surprising statement. Moreover, why make a substantive declaration, reservation, or understanding if "it doesn't bind the other side?" These additions are parts of the treaty and if not accepted by all parties, there has been no agreement. As to the alleged insignificance of a "unilateral declaration," according to Mr. Rogers, the 1969 Vienna Convention on the Law of Treaties says virtually the exact opposite in cases that modify the legal effect of the treaty, which is the case with Panama's counter-offer. Article 2.1(d) states, ". . . a 'reservation' means a unilateral statement, *however phrased or named,* . . . modify[ing] the legal effect of certain portions of the treaty in their application to that State." (Emphasis added) Article 20.2 goes even further, ". . . when it appears . . . that the application of the treaty in its entirety between all the parties is an essential condition of the consent of each one to be bound by the treaty, a reservation requires acceptance by all the parties."

How does this apply to the Panama Canal Treaties? It is the central and controlling principle: The DeConcini reservation authorized *unilateral* rights for U.S. defense and reopening of the Canal, with or without Panama's consent. Then, Panama's last minute counter-reservation simply said, in effect, NO—only if we decide to *cooperate.* To argue that this is not a central, controlling and substantive change to the Treaties is to repudiate logic and the English language.

In addition, the Vienna Convention clearly provides that the *label* of a unilateral statement—whether "phrased or named" a reservation, understanding, or condition, for example—is *not important,* but that the "legal effect" of the statement *is.* Who can argue that Panama's three paragraphs have no legal effect?

Another example of the Kissinger philosophy of double-speak and essential ambiguity was apparent in an observation by Dr. Robert O. Pastor, former assistant to Dr. Zbigniew Brzezinski, the National Security Adviser to President Carter during the period 1977-81. Incidentally, Pastor was the architect of the 1977 National Security Council memorandum that advocated surrendering sovereignty in the Canal Zone, thereby initiating the 1977 negotiations.

Pastor said, in a telephone interview on November 13, 1983, that Panama's three paragraphs merely reaffirmed Panamanian sovereignty and were not in conflict at all with the DeConcini reservation, but merely eliminated "the harsh, objectionable language." Any objective reading of the DeConcini reservation, however, reveals clear-cut statements of U.S. rights, perhaps the plainest language in the Treaties, all designed to lift the fogs of ambiguity. This, then, was not acceptable to Omar Torrijos.

Nonetheless, without that "language" there would have been no Senate approval—nor would there have been any Senate approval, many have contended, if the "language" of Panama's counter-reservation had reached the Senate floor. Even so, Pastor, in our interview, saw "no problem" should the U.S. ever need to reopen a closed Canal. Indeed, he said, the United States could act with Panama's "cooperation."[28] And if Panama decides not to "cooperate"?

A man who agreed with Dr. Pastor's line of reasoning was the Deputy Legal Adviser to the Department of State, Michael G. Kozak, who was the Assistant Legal Adviser assigned to the Treaties during the period 1971-78. His views on declarations and understandings coincided with the Kissinger philosophy, as we discovered during our interview on November 21, 1983. Mr. Kozak declared:

The Senate went to some length to be specific about what the Treaties meant [in their reservations and conditions]. I don't think there's anything in the Panamanian understandings and declaration [in the three paragraphs] *that alters this one iota.. . .* An understanding is a term that means interpretation or clarification. It's not a change. A declaration is usually a statement of policy.[29]

Kozak's assertion, however, is not in accord with Article 2.1(d) of the 1969 Vienna Convention on the Law of Treaties which covers the importance of unilateral statements *"however phrased or named"* when such statements "modify the legal effect of certain provisions of the treaty in their application to that State." (Emphasis added)

Pursuing the conflict between Panama's three paragraphs and the DeConcini reservation, we interviewed Robert E. Dalton, the State Department Assistant Legal Adviser for Treaty Affairs, on November 22, 1983. Our questions produced essentially the same answers that Dalton had given on June 23, 1983 before the Senate Subcommittee on Separation of Powers. He reiterated that there was no conflict at all, and that a meeting of minds applied to domestic law, contract law, but not to international agreements such as treaties.[30]

Moreover, he contended, international consultations simply did not require the accuracy, for example, that banking transactions might require, i.e., no meeting of minds was necessary. In essence, these were the same answers that the State Department had provided to a series of questions asked after the East hearing had concluded live testimony.

In soliciting other ideas, we moved on to Sherman Hinson, the political officer on the Panama Desk at the State Department, asking simply if Panama's three paragraphs of counter-reservation might defuse the DeConcini reservation that authorized certain unilateral U.S. defense actions regarding the Canal. Mr. Hinson's answer was a surprise: "As far as I'm concerned, the question that you're asking is so hypothetical and speculative that it is meaningless . . . it's not a real question."[31]

In a follow up question, we asked about U.S. treaty rights to reopen a closed Canal should, for example Marxists take over the Panamanian government, call a strike and, for any reason, close the Canal. Mr. Hinson continued: ". . . I think your question is as totally unrealistic as asking whether a Marxist government of the United States would cooperate to walk into Panama. . . . The likelihood of a Marxist government in Panama is probably somewhat less than that of a double eclipse. It simply is not a realistic proposition."

Clearly Mr. Hinson deserves an answer. The questions that he calls meaningless, speculative and unrealistic address the most basic issues regarding the future security of the Canal. Indeed, they were the issues debated so intensely in the Senate and the House. Moreover, the future cooperative "partnership" between the United States and Panama is at stake. More germane questions would be hard to imagine.

Furthermore, a number of reports have indicated the strong communist influence in the Panamanian government[32]—and, of course, the powerful communist push into Central America is a real threat to every nation in that area. When one considers that communist adventurism in the Western Hemisphere is another threat to the stability of Panama and that Panama has long been "the land of endemic revolution and political turmoil," how does Mr. Hinson justify such expletives of confidence? His answers may be dogmatic, but hardly convincing.

Obviously the pursuit was getting more interesting. These views of State's representatives were in line with the Department's official position, as presented to the East Subcommittee[33]—to the effect that there were no inconsistencies between the two sets of Treaties, the Vienna Convention and the U.S. Constitution notwithstanding.

SENATORS AND STAFF 'DON'T RECALL' THREE PARAGRAPHS

In attempting to obtain definite answers from Senators and their staff members, the Harman Committee sent some 85 letters of inquiry and follow ups to 23 principals in the Treaties episode. None of those who answered could specifically recall the three paragraphs or any explanations as to their meanings. Twelve Senators and some half dozen staff members acknowledged. Response from the State Department was almost nil. Undoubtedly, that was an unpopular subject.

Nonetheless, our personal visit to Washington, D.C. during November 1983 was more productive. Former Senator Dick Clark, D.-Iowa and former member of the Foreign Relations Committee, stated, during our interview of November 23, 1983, that he simply could recall nothing about the three paragraphs nor, of course, any explanations of them. However, he did have a vivid recollection of the DeConcini reservation.[34]

Former Senator Robert P. Griffin, R.-Mich., stated on November 15, 1983 that he did not recall the three paragraphs either, or anyone explaining them to the members of the Foreign Relations Committee.[35] Senator Griffin, an experienced attorney, had been one of the most active opponents of the Treaties and the only one of the fifteen members of the Foreign Relations Committee to vote against them. With his keen interest and legal training and experience, it seems extremely unlikely that he would not have recalled three paragraphs that, in effect, gutted all previous efforts to obtain guaranteed U.S. treaty rights.

Senator Steven Symms, R.-Ida., who defeated Frank Church in the senatorial elections in 1980, had no enthusiasm for the three paragraphs during out interview of November 18, 1983. He had followed the Treaties closely and recalled the warnings given to the fence-straddling Senators that Panama would be coming back with something like the three paragraphs to take care of the DeConcini restrictions on Panama's resistance to U.S. rights to defend the Canal.[36] He was right.

While in Washington, our repeated attempts to interview Senators Byrd, Baker, DeConcini, Sarbanes, Biden, Hatch, Stevens, Percy, Pell, Cranston and Glenn regarding their parts in the Panama Canal Treaties were not successful. Even so, a brief hand-written questionnaire on the impact of the three Panamanian paragraphs was left for each Senator named above, answers to which have not been forthcoming at this writing in April, 1986.

Subsequently, interviews with many key staff members were more productive and very interesting. The gist of their answers was that they simply did not remember the three paragraphs or any explanations about their meanings. Some of the specifics may be helpful:

For example, Robert Dockery, the former staff member of the Senate Foreign Relations Committee in charge of the Treaties, in response to a direct question as to whether State Department representatives ever called his attention to the three paragraphs, said, during our interview on November 15, 1983, "I don't recall. I don't recall."

Dockery's position at the time of the Treaties was perhaps one of the most sensitive for detecting all details concerning the much discussed Treaties. He was the Chairman's right hand man for the Treaties.

A follow up question was used in attempting to learn anything about State's contention that the staff members of Senators and of the Committee had been briefed as to the meanings of those Panamanian paragraphs that were not placed in the U.S. Treaties. Dockery, after some delay and explanation of ratification details and other procedures, answered, "I have to tell you, I honestly don't recall . . . I honestly don't recall" the State Department's explanations to the Foreign Relations Committee.[37]

Mr. Dockery continued, "But I can also tell you that I would be terribly surprised if there was something done by Panama, subsequent to the Senate approval, and then incorporated into the documents that we signed without some notification to the Senate."[38]

But, of course, "there *was* something done . . . without some notification to the Senate" (emphasis added)—it was Panama's three paragraphs surreptitiously slipped into Panama's version of the Treaties. And President Carter, without any "notification to the Senate," signed the Protocols of Exchange which included Panama's counter-reservation objecting to and nullifying unilateral U.S. defense rights over the Canal.

Another high staff official who did not remember Panama's three paragraphs either was Norvill Jones, the former Chief of Staff of the Foreign Relations Committee during the debate and ratification of the Treaties. He said, "I couldn't say whether I did or not. . . ." In answer to our question about a reported meeting of staff members with Herbert Hansell, the State Department Legal Adviser, for the purpose of explaining the three paragraphs, Mr. Jones replied, "I can't recall meeting with Hansell specifically. . . ."[39]

An interview on the same day with Richard McCall, the former Deputy Director of the Foreign Relations Committee, was also inconclusive about whether he had seen them or had them explained. Our question about the legal rights of the United States to go into Panama to reopen a closed Canal brought an interesting rejoinder, "I think it would have to be done in conjunction with the Panamanians. . . ."[40] McCall apparently had no illusions that the United States had *unilateral* rights to enter Panama to defend the Canal or keep it operating; it would have to be done with Panama's cooperation.

A number of other interviews with staff members of the Senate Foreign Relations Committee, both present and past, failed to turn up *anyone* who remembered the three paragraphs before June 16, 1978 (the day the Protocols were exchanged). Nor did anyone remember any explanation of them by Mr. Hansell or any other State Department representative.

This is an interesting anomaly, particularly so in view of the statement on November 21, 1983 by Michael Kozak, State's Deputy Legal Adviser, the man who had worked on the Treaties since 1971. Mr. Kozak was quite positive, in our interview that day, in his answer to the question: "Were the three paragraphs shown to the Senate leadership?" He said:

Yes, well, let me state that more precisely. They were shown to . . . what we did was we invited the staff of the Senate Foreign Relations Committee, the staff of both the Majority and Minority Leaders and, I think, also the personal staffs of the Senators who had been particularly interested. . . . Representatives of all these people were invited and a number of them showed up and Herbert Hansell who was the Legal Adviser at the time distributed material to the group assembled and explained at that time the draft instruments of the United States and Panama and the Protocols of Exchange. He [Mr. Hansell] went through them and explained what was in each of them, including these three paragraphs and the paragraphs in the U.S. instruments . . . and asked if they would provide comments or state any problems they saw with them. What I can't vouch for is what each staff man did in communicating with his own Senator. . . ."[41]

If these three hotly disputed paragraphs were indeed properly presented to the staff members of the Senate leaders—after all, the Senate's work is really done by the staffs—how is it possible that *not a single one* remembered them until after the Protocols were exchanged? Were they actually explained and then discussed, or were they glossed over? Unfortunately, Mr. Hansell declined to discuss anything about the three paragraphs or the Treaties when we tried to arrange an interview with him on November 11, 1983 in Washington, D.C. He was certainly a principal figure.

Our question to Hansell seemed fair enough: "When you were the Legal Adviser to the State Department, I'm sure you recall Panama's three paragraphs that were not in the U.S. instruments of ratification. Your Department is reported to have explained them to the Foreign Relations Committee. Could you please tell me what Committee members had to say about them?" This was the end of the "interview," as Mr. Hansell said, "I've gone through that issue and I don't think I want to get into that. . . ."[42]

Of course, free men may refuse questions with impunity. Even so, the American people, who bought the Panama Canal and depend upon their elected government for ethical transactions in public affairs, deserve straightforward answers, in depth answers, to such basic questions as: (1) Were the three paragraphs explained to the Senators? (2) If so, what did they say? The American people will not get these answers—unless the appropriate Senate committee or other investigative body holds full scale hearings with all principals required to testify, examined and cross-examined under oath, i.e., unless the peace and tranquility of the principals involved supercede the need for the truth about the Canal swindle.

In regard to the very interesting interview with Mr. Kozak, we asked him about feedback from the staff regarding the instruments of ratification: No one, he said, had any problems with the language in the instruments. Asked if the Senators' staffs raised any questions about the three paragraphs, Kozak's answer was:

The fact that these three paragraphs were there was called to the staffs' attention in this meeting that we had [the one where Hansell passed out the material] and it was explained why they [the Panamanians] had put those paragraphs in there, at least to the best of our understanding, and why we thought them as being consistent with the Treaties—and apparently they [the staff] agreed with that because the response after they had had a day or two to review them with their members [Senators] was that just no one saw any problems with it and the rationale for that is: If you look at these understandings, then the first one simply seems to be saying there are obligations both the U.S. and Panama have under the UN Charter and the OAS Charter. . . .[43]

The rest of Mr. Kozak's long discourse had to do with the spirit of cooperation and partnership, mutual respect in all treaty actions, the various leadership amendments, the conditions, the reservations, the declarations, the understandings—which, he said, "All taken together define the rights of the United States and Panama with respect to the Treaties."

On the other hand, these things "all taken together" were also in line with the "new diplomacy" as well as the Kissinger manner of negotiating:

ambiguity to save face in "essential international interests" and *precision* to save face in "domestic positions." For example, Torrijos used his secretive three paragraphs to preserve his "domestic position" with the Panamanians by excluding the United States from intervening legally while, unfortunately, the Americans never knew what was going on.

Kozak's recollection of so many details concerning the consultations with staff members of the Senate leadership and the Foreign Relations Committee was in marked contrast to the total lack of recollection by some six staff members who had been involved with the Treaties in 1978 and who were personally interviewed by the author in November 1983. Without exception, the staff officials interviewed could "not recall" the briefings.

Nonetheless, Mr. Kozak's answers were almost exactly the same as the official State Department replies to the questions from the East Subcommittee.[44] They also coincided with the contents of the September 20, 1979 letter from State's Legal Adviser, Herbert J. Hansell, to Representative John M. Murphy, Chairman of the House Committee on Merchant Marine and Fisheries.

In reference to the positive statements made by both Hansell and Kozak that the Senate representatives had been briefed, why is it that no one remembers except the State Department officials? Moreover, where is the record to validate the dates and place of the briefings, and the participants? In State's concern and rush to deliver Treaties to President Carter, were the potential inconsistencies of the three paragraphs glossed over with assurances that all was well, everything in order?

Where is the record that even one U.S. Senator saw the three paragraphs before final action on June 16, 1978, the day of ratification? Or, had them explained to him? Why did the State Department wait until the day of ratification to release the three paragraphs to the public?[45]

The fact that Panama's unexamined three paragraph counter-reservation was withheld from the American people until President Carter could get to Panama to sign the final act of ratification suggests that (1) Carter was afraid of public denouncement because of the loss of U.S. rights for unilateral defense of the Canal and (2) both Carter and Torrijos feared an outcry for a second plebescite so the Panamanian people could vote on the Treaties that had been substantially changed by six U.S. additions.

Moreover, both of these concerns help explain Carter's action in ratifying the Treaties nine and a half months ahead of schedule. The Brooke Reservation called for an effective ratification not earlier than March 31, 1979, but Carter acted on June 16, 1978 and said it was "effective" on March 31, 1979, thereby sealing off any substantial opposition. After all,

Carter's political party controlled the Congress. The membership had acted to preserve the "prestige of the presidency," one of the main arguments for passing the Treaties—and, once the Treaties were "ratified," the President's party was not likely to take adverse action. And, of course, it did not.

The State Department's contentions that Panama's counter-reservation was merely a statement of good will and a continuing cooperative attitude were discredited also by the four smoking guns that were discovered long after the "ratification." The fact that the Department of State offered no concrete evidence to support its opinion is a part of its new diplomacy: double-speak to "solve" issues that have not really been solved.

At the East hearing on June 23, 1983, two former State Department treaty handlers took exception to the fudgy language and smoke screen of the first paragraphs of Panama's counter-reservation. The late Dr. Charles H. Breecher called it "clever lawyers' obfuscation at its worst,"[46] and Dr. Herbert W. Dodge labelled it a device of "petty fogging" lawyers.[47] Then, they explained how Panama's other two paragraphs constituted a clever counter-reservation that totally nullified the U.S. rights under the DeConcini reservation—therefore, there had been no meeting of minds and no legally and constitutionally ratified Treaties.

The perseverance and patience of the Harman Committee in attempting to collect and correlate the many pieces of the puzzle of the Panama Canal Treaties operations have been truly remarkable, also courteous in every respect. The rebuff by Assistant Secretary of State McCloskey to the effect that the State Department was tired of the repetitive questions of the Harman Committee was unusual. It suggests that if forthright answers had been provided the first time there would have been no repetition of the questions. With patience and perseverance, the members of the Harman Committee had been able to assemble important evidence.

*Influential Senators troop across one of the gates
at Miraflores Locks on January 6, 1978 while in
Panama to "negotiate" on their own with Omar
Torrijos. Senatorial "negotiations" were common
practice at this time in order to help the President
with Treaties that the Senators could later officially give "Advice and Consent" to. Separation of
powers was momentarily forgotten. The Minority
leader, Howard Baker, R-Tenn., center, and Jake
Garn, R-Utah, right, are escorted by the Canal
Zone Governor, Harold Parfitt.
(AP/Wide World Photos)*

· 10 ·

'PRESERVE, PROTECT AND DEFEND THE CONSTITUTION'

Some two hundred years ago the Framers of the U.S. Constitution were meeting in Philadelphia to structure "the edifice of constitutional American liberty." It was a difficult time in the life of the new nation: the Articles of Confederation had become a farce, the Executive had no means to enforce the laws of the new Congress, and the Judiciary was largely ineffective.[1]

The euphoria of freedom from British tyranny and the flush of victory in the Revolutionary War had driven the patriots to extremes in loose and uncontrollable government. Indeed, they understood that revolutions, whether democratic or republican, had usually produced despotism—and they were determined to avoid this trap. The ancient Greek city-states had, for example, deteriorated from democracies to dictatorships; and the Roman Empire had evolved from a republic into the absolute rule of emperors. The new America was not to follow this route, but the Articles of Confederation was not the way either.

The 55 members of the Constitutional Convention, under the leadership of George Washington, Benjamin Franklin, James Madison and Alexander Hamilton debated through the hot summer of 1787. On September 17 they unveiled the unique U.S. Constitution—not a "bundle of compromises," as many historians contend—but solid agreement on the fundamentals of a form of government never before tried in human history: Besides laying constraints on state governments, the new Congress was to legislate on all matters of national concern and all matters with which the states could not deal adequately, including the power to regulate commerce, to tax and to spend money for common defense and general welfare.[2]

The system of checks and balances was the cornerstone, designed to prevent any one of the Legislative, Executive or Judicial Branches from seizing power, unless the others deliberately allowed it. For example, the Senate and the House of Representatives were checks against each other in legislation, and the President had the veto power over both. The federal Judiciary with life tenure for its judges could check the other two Branches while being subject to the impeachment check against its own members. Finally, the President, also subject to impeachment, was to exercise a high degree of initiative; but he was also checked by the Congress which voted money for his programs. Moreover, in treaty ratification, the President was required to obtain the advice and consent of the Senate, another check.

Nonetheless, the ultimate source of power was to be the people. Accordingly, another check against despotic power was that no political party could ever gain total possession of the government at a single election because of the manner of selecting officials: Senators every six years, Representatives every two years, the President each four years and federal judges for life tenures. The voters controlled this check against tyranny.

In order to have a governing document suitable for the ages, the Framers provided for Amendments to the Constitution and authorizations for the Congress "to make all laws necessary and proper" for carrying into effect the specific powers "and all other powers vested by this Constitution in the government of the United States. . . ."[3] Thus, reason triumphed over violence and bloodshed, and Americans had once again rededicated themselves—this time, to their own faith in the power to govern by a peaceful and constitutional process.

Abraham Lincoln revered the Constitution, saying:

. . . let it be taught in schools, in seminaries, and in colleges, let it be written in primers, in spelling books and in almanacs, let it be preached from the pulpit, proclaimed in legislative halls, and enforced in courts of justice. And, in short, let it become the political religion of the nation, and, in particular, a reverence for the Constitution.[4]

In his eulogy on George Washington in 1832, Daniel Webster, the great statesman and orator, said:

Other misfortunes may be borne, or their effects overcome. If disastrous wars should sweep our commerce from the oceans, another generation may renew it; if it exhaust our treasury, future industry may replenish it; if it desolate and lay waste our fields, still, under a new cultivation, they will grow green again, and ripen to full harvest.

But who will reconstruct the fabric of demolished government?

No, if these columns fall, they will be raised not again. Like the Coliseum and the Parthenon, they will be destined to a mournful and melancholy immortality. Bitterer tears, however, will flow over them than were ever shed over the monuments of Roman or Grecian art; for they will be monuments of a more glorious edifice than Greece or Rome ever saw, the edifice of constitutional American liberty.[5]

Questions about "a reverence for the Constitution" have been raised in a number of areas in the handling of the Panama Canal Treaties, for example: the advice and consent function of the Senate; the method used to abrogate the 1903 Canal Treaty; the Carter plan for transferring U.S. territory; and the assignment of non-resident aliens to the Panama Canal Commission. Other questions concern international and domestic law, including: the failure of both nations to ratify the same set of Treaties; Panama's acceptance of Treaties judged invalid under her Constitution; and Panama's official repudiation of six major U.S. changes to the Treaties.

Moreover, any unchallenged violations of the U.S. Constitution overshadow the loss of U.S. territory and property. For, as Daniel Webster said, ". . . who will reconstruct the fabric of demolished government?"

'ADVICE AND CONSENT' FUNCTION GLOSSED OVER

One of the witnesses before the Senate Subcommittee on Separation of Powers hearing on June 23, 1983 was Dr. Herbert W. Dodge, a retired State Department Foreign Service Officer of some 30 years experience. He summed up his view of invalid Treaties, as follows:

The issues we are bringing today before this committee are very simple and you do not need a long lawyer's argumentation about them. First, the Panama Canal Treaties are not valid because the parties have not agreed to the same texts. In other words, there is no meeting of the minds.[6]

Earlier, he had written to the Chairman, Senator East, ". . . the issues related to the Treaties . . . are so simple and basic that any concerned American citizen of average education could deal with them."[7]

The Carter Administration chose not to observe fully the requirement under Article II of the Constitution for the "Advice and Consent" of the Senate to the Treaties. Whereas, the Treaties themselves and all six U.S. changes (reservations, conditions and understanding) had received the necessary two-thirds vote of approval from the Senate, nonetheless, when Panama submitted its last minute counter-reservation nullifying U.S. rights, President Carter and his State Department failed to ask for "Advice and Consent" on the "most substantive change in the text of the treaty that can be imagined."[8] This was not constitutional.

Briefly, here is the situation: The text of the U.S. instruments of ratification to the Neutrality Treaty gives the United States the unilateral right to keep open the Canal, with or without Panama's consent or cooperation and without any restriction on the use of U.S. troops in Panama. This is the DeConcini reservation and it is clear-cut.[9] President Carter never accepted it at face value and neither did a number of Senators.

The text of Panama's instruments of ratification first repeats the DeConcini reservation, then unilaterally adds its three paragraph long counter-reservation. This counter-reservation, which was kept from the Senate and from the American people until after ratification was completed, states in unequivocal language that the U.S. can use military force in Panama only under the terms of Article 18 of the OAS Charter, i.e., only in self-defense—and further, only in the spirit of "mutual respect and cooperation," leaving Panama the option not to "cooperate."

The U.S. rights under the DeConcini reservation, therefore, were cancelled by Panama's counter-reservation. The fact that President Carter, State Department officials and certain Senators, who were privy to the information, failed to ask for the constitutionally-required "Advice and Consent" from the Senate for Panama's counter-reservation raises questions about violations of their oaths of office taken to "preserve, protect and defend the Constitution." Were the treaty-makers so anxious to succeed that they would by-pass constitutional obligations?

America's forefathers had cherished the Constitution. George Washington, who had held together the Constitutional Convention during that turbulent summer in Philadelphia, called it "the guide I shall never abandon" and "the choice of an enlightened people." He told his friend, Henry Lee:

. . . let the reins of government then be braced and held with a steady hand, and every violation of the Constitution be reprehended; if defective, let it be amended, but not suffered to be trampled upon whilst it has an existence.[10]

As much as at any time in history, perhaps the reins of constitutional government needed to be "held with a steady hand" during the emotional transfer of the Panama Canal.

In the matter of treaty ratification under international law, the two nations must agree to the same texts in bilateral treaties in order to ratify. They cannot "interpret" in their instruments of ratification unless the other state accepts such "interpretation" verbatim. The United States did not accept Panama's counter-reservation. Therefore, there was no ratification under international law and hence, no Treaties, according to Drs. Dodge and Breecher at the East hearing.[11]

The fundamental difference between the Treaty "ratified" by the United States and the one "ratified" by Panama is illustrated by the following scenario, related by Dr. Dodge:

Let us assume a strike by Panamanian workers that closes the Canal. This strike, say for U.S. wage rates, is supported by the Panamanian government. Picket lines cannot be crossed, except by giving strike-breakers military protection.

Now under the DeConcini reservation, the U.S. could enter independently, without agreement or cooperation by Panama, use military force so picket lines can be crossed and the Canal operated. But under the Panamanian unilateral understanding, the cooperation of Panama would be necesary which Panama could of course deny. So the U.S. would be helpless.

It would make all the difference in the world with the U.S. public whether the U.S. has really the right to go ahead with military force against Panama's will and undoubted resistance, or whether Panama can maintain that the Treaties give the U.S. no such right, unless Panama agrees to its exercise. And it would equally make a great deal of difference say with our European allies. [12]

ILLEGALITY UNDER THE VIENNA CONVENTION

In addition to the question of valid Treaties under the U.S. Constitution because of failure to obtain advice and consent for a substantive change, there is also the fundamental question of legality under the 1969 Vienna Convention on the Law of Treaties for the same reason: failure to accept the other state's reservation. This principle was not accepted in the State Department's position paper entitled "State Department Position on Ratification of the Panama Canal Treaties" which states, in part:

The Department's view, in sum, remains that the three paragraph statement in Panama's instruments of ratification does not purport to modify the legal effect of any portion of the Treaties, and therefore is not a reservation requiring Senate approval. This conclusion becomes particularly clear when it is understood that the Panamanian statement was added to the same instruments of ratification in which Panama expressly accepted and repeated all the United States reservations, including the DeConcini Conditon. [13]

Although the State Department contends that Panama's three paragraphs do not modify the Treaties and therefore, do not require Senate concurrence, nonetheless, the *meaning* constitutes a fundamental modification. And although Panama did repeat the DeConcini reservation in its instruments, as well as in the Protocol of Exchange, its unilateral counter-reservation was not accepted by the United States. It could not be accepted because the Senate had not approved it. Moreover, if Panama's three paragraph statement is not a reservation requiring Senate approval, why wasn't it in the U.S. instruments of ratification?

It should be noted that after accepting all the U.S. Senate changes, Panama stated in its three paragraph counter-reservation:

The Republic of Panama *agrees* to the exchange of the instruments of ratification of the aforementioned Neutrality Treaty *on the understanding*. . . .[14] (Emphasis added)

Under international law Panama "agrees to the exchange of the instruments" with the "understanding" that is contained in its three paragraphs which modified the Treaty, particularly the DeConcini reservation.

Dr. Breecher stated that since the United States did *not* accept Panama's counter-reservation (misnamed "understanding") which was a last minute amendment to the Treaties, as amended by the President in the U.S. instruments of ratification, pursuant to the Senate "Advice and Consent," there are no Treaties under international law. Said Breecher, "This documented fact is beyond any dispute."[15]

He added that "to ratify a bilateral treaty, the parties must agree in their instruments of ratification to the same written text. Otherwise, there is no meeting of minds as required for ratification. There is no ratification if one party makes its agreement to the Treaties contingent on any amendment, condition, or whatever it wants to call it, that is not formally and verbatim accepted by the other party."[16]

The 1969 Vienna Convention on the Law of Treaties is the authority. This Convention has been signed by the United States, though not ratified because of an esoteric point in classification. Even so, it is almost exclusively a codification of existing international law and its provisions have been the guide for U.S. policy.[17] Article 2.1(d) of the Convention states:

. . . 'reservation' means a unilateral statement, however phrased or named, made by a state, when signing, ratifying, accepting, approving, or acceding to a treaty, whereby it purports to exclude or to modify the legal effect of certain provisions of the treaty in their application to that State.

In the case of the Panama Canal Treaties, being bilateral, such a "reservation" in the instruments of ratification of one state must be approved specifically by the other state. In addition, Article 20.2 reiterates the requirement for acceptance by all parties:

When it appears . . . that the application of the treaty in its entirety between all parties is an essential condition of the content of each one to be found in the treaty, a reservation requires acceptance by all parties.

The Panamanians picked up this point in their Foreign Ministry Communique of April 25, 1978:

We can assert that, regardless of the term used, what matters is if the condition, reservation, amendment, or declaration made by one party to the other modifies or changes what has been agreed to by the plenipotentiaries. If that change has been made, it is unquestionable that the treaty has not been ratified but, rather, that a counter-offer has been made which the other is at liberty to reject, modify, or approve. Only if it approves the counter-offer is the consent or perfecting [perfeccionamiento] of the wish of both parties to obligate themselves realized.

Senator Paul Sarbanes, D.-Md., one of the floor managers of the Treaties, also understood this point about counter-offers not being accepted, during the Senate debate of March 15, 1978, saying:

I am now quoting Charles G. Fenwick, *International Law*: "Since the signature of a treaty represents a meeting of minds of the several parties upon specific provisions involving reciprocal obligations, any changes or amendments inserted by one party as a condition of ratification must be accepted by the other party if the treaty is to come into legal effect.

"I ought to point out that ever since 1922 the technique which the Senate has used to alter the legal effect of provisions contained in a treaty, in exercising its advice-and-consent function, or the primary technique, has been through amendments to the articles of ratification as reflected in reservations. These, of course, then have to be agreed to, or accepted by the other party to the treaty if, in fact, there is to be a treaty."[18]

A number of other authorities contend that Senate concurrence is required for variation in the text of bilateral treaties if it modifies "the legal effect." In the instant case, Panama's three paragraphs modified the DeConcini reservation. One such authority is the American Law Institute in the *Restatement of the Law (Second): Foreign Relation Law of the United States*. On page 423 we find the circumstances facing Mr. Carter and the State Department: The Senate had already given concurrence to the Treaties before Panama made its counter-reservation public in its instruments of ratification. Therefore, Senate consent to the new reservation was required, but was neither asked for nor given. The applicable portion follows:

The situation may arise . . . in which the Senate has given its consent to the treaty before the other state makes its reservation. In such a case, the Senate consent to the acceptance of the reservation is required.[19]

Another authority who says much the same thing is Covey T. Oliver, president of the American Society of International Law and coauthor of *The Restatment of the Law*. Dr. Oliver, in his statement before the Senate Committee on Foreign Relations on January 19, 1978, warned against the use of reservations and understandings, especially in bilateral agreements such as the Panama Canal Treaties. He said, "It is fundamental learning with respect to reservations and understandings, that any variation in the text of a bilateral treaty is in effect a counter-offer. *The Restatement of Foreign Relations Law* states that quite flatly and I think correctly."[20]

Oliver's testimony had been given almost five months before Panama's counter-reservation and could have alerted Senators to the pitfalls of last minute reservations and understandings. But, of course, the Senate had no chance to vote on Panama's last words.

Some years later, Dr. Oliver expounded further on the principle that understandings are to be identified and formally accepted by the other treaty partner. On March 23, 1982, he wrote:

The Restatement is still the word on U.S. practice as to understandings. They are to be identified and formal acceptance requested of the other treaty partner. In the Panamanian case the U.S. chose to depart from this principle, in contrast to the U.S. insistence in the Niagara Power case in referring a strictly internal "condition" to the Canadians for approval.[21]

Why should President Carter and the State Department ignore this principle of "formal acceptance . . . of the other treaty partner" in Panama's case but not with the Canadians? Torrijos, of course, knew exactly what his "understanding" meant but could not ask Carter to get the U.S. Senate's advice and consent. He knew the Senate would reject it. Hence, no Treaties.

Why did Mr. Carter not object to Torrijos's last word "understanding" which voided the DeConcini reservation? Why did he not seek Senate approval for this substantive change, as constitutionally required? Perhaps the answer may be found between the lines of his diary entry for April 7, 1978, as published in his memoirs, *Keeping Faith* (Bantam, 1982):[22] He did not want to fail.

OTHER VIEWS ON PANAMA'S 'UNDERSTANDING'

Questions about constitutionality and reservations were asked of Harold G. Maier of the Vanderbilt Law School, a former legal consultant to the Department of Defense. Dr. Maier replied that "the international legal issue seems to me to be completely resolved by the fact that the two nations have, thus far, apparently treated the Treaties as if they are legally binding and thus, have consented to be bound by them."[23]

But this raises further questions. Panama did not consent to be bound by Treaties that permit U.S. rights to reopen the Canal. Of course, both nations have "treated the Treaties as if they are legally binding" because each wishes to believe that it has what it bargained for: Panama just wants the Canal and does not wish to rock the boat while the U.S. State Department has vested interests in protecting its past performance. The Senate remains somnambulant.

The American Bar Association was asked the same questions. After a delay of eleven months, the answer came from Gerald Aksen, Chairman of ABA's Section of International Law and Practices, saying, in essence, that Panama's "understanding" did not modify or alter the treaty text:

It seems logical to infer that President Carter did not submit the Panamanian

Instrument "understanding" language to the Senate because he was advised that the language thereof *did not purport to modify* or alter the text of the treaty....[24] (Emphasis added)

This is almost identical language to that in the State Department position paper, a copy of which was sent to Mr. Aksen. Did the ABA research this matter on its own, or rely on State's opinion? Did it consider Articles 2.1(d) and 20.2 of the 1969 Vienna Convention which require "acceptance by all parties" for any substantive change? Was the ABA aware that Panama's Foreign Ministry Communique of April 25, 1978 rejected U.S. treaty rights for defending the Canal? If so, no indication of any research was indicated in its brief answer.

Dean Rusk, former Secretary of State in the Kennedy and Johnson Administrations and co-architect of the American retreats in the Korean and Vietnam Wars, was also asked about Panama's "understanding." He supported the State Department's position, saying:

The statement by the Republic of Panama of its "understanding" is not, in my judgment, a reservation to the texts of the Treaties. The actual texts of the Treaties remain unchanged and the "understandings" are simply a statement by Panama as to how they would look upon such problems in the future. A formal reservation, on the other hand, would *pro tanto* amend the formal text of the treaty.[25]

Of course, international treaty law emphasizes that unilateral statements, "however phrased or named," that modify the legal effect of the treaty must be accepted by the other side. This was simply not done in the case of Panama's counter-reservation, labelled an "understanding."

A determined effort was made by the Committee for Better Panama and U.S. Relations to get an answer to the question: Why didn't President Carter make Panama withdraw its last minute "understanding" which totally voided the DeConcini reservation? Letters were sent to the following principals involved with the Treaties:

Jimmy Carter, former President

Cyrus R. Vance, former Secretary of State

Warren M. Christopher, former Deputy Secretary of State

Sol M. Linowitz, former Ambassador and treaty negotiator

Herbert J. Hansell, former Legal Adviser, Department of State

David H. Popper, former Ambassador assigned to Treaties

William D. Rogers, former Assistant Secretary of State

Michael G. Kozak, Deputy Legal Adviser, Department of State

Arthur W. Rovine, former Assistant Legal Adviser, Department of State

Senator Robert C. Byrd, D.-W.Va.

Senator Paul S. Sarbanes, D.-Md.

Former Senator Frank Church, D.-Ida.

Former Senator Edward W. Brooke, R.-Mass.

Of these thirteen officials, only two responded. A follow up letter to Mr. Hansell, the State Department's Legal Adviser at the time of the Treaties, produced the answer from his administrative assistant that he was no longer in an official position and believed it not appropriate to answer such questions.[26] The other answer was from Mr. Popper and this became Smoking Gun Number One, the belated confession that ambiguity had been essential all along in order to assure ratified Treaties.

'TREATIES ABROGATED BY LAW'

One of the most presumptuous abuses of the 1977 Panama Canal Treaty (the basic treaty) is found in the very first Article: After purporting to terminate all previous Canal treaties by means of this new treaty, the Article then states, among other things, ". . . the Republic of Panama, as territorial sovereign. . . .," giving readers the impression that Panama always had sovereignty. Nowhere does the new Treaty acknowledge that U.S. sovereign rights were being returned to Panama by the terms of the new agreement.

And the United States *had* been vested with sovereign rights: Article III of the 1903 Hay-Bunau-Varilla Treaty contained the specific contract provision that the Republic of Panama vested in the United States "all the rights, power and authority within the zone . . . [as] if it were the sovereign of the territory . . . to the entire exclusion of the exercise by the Republic of Panama of any such sovereign rights, power and authority." For the benefit of the theoreticians and academics in general, who may be formulating their challenges about who had sovereignty, one might ask: If the United States had the rights of sovereignty, and Panama was entirely excluded, who had the sovereign power?

Article III of the old treaty was the contract for U.S. rights of sovereignty; it had been ratified and accepted in 1904 by both countries in good faith. Basic law, propriety and common sense demand that when a contract is done, it must be undone by another contract when its basic provisions are changed.

Henry A. Kissinger had long compounded the misinformation about alleged Panamanian sovereignty over the Canal Zone, the most notable being his assertions in the 1974 Kissinger-Tack Statement of Principles, which was the basis of the 1977 Treaties, of course. Such deception about sovereignty had for many years been practiced by the State Department in confusing and softening up the opposition.

Even if the old 1903 Treaty could have been abrogated by the new 1977 Treaty, which cannot be done constitutionally, such a basic and honorable principle as sovereign rights should be addressed formally, fully and decently. Apparently the State Department, and its disciples of the Kissinger "new diplomacy," could not bring themselves to include the simple acknowledgment that the United States was hereby relinquishing the sovereign rights vested in it by the old 1903 Treaty and was returning the said sovereign rights to the Republic of Panama. However, such a straightforward expression of American self-respect may not have been acceptable to the Panamanians.

A second abuse in this very first Article of the basic treaty is the presumption that treaties may be terminated by later treaties. The fact is, "treaties [are] abrogated by law," not by other treaties, and many sources document this requirement.

"Treaties being declared, equally with the laws of the United States, to be the supreme law of the land, it is understood that an act of the legislature alone can declare them infringed and rescinded."[27] Nonetheless, this dictum from *Jefferson's Manual,* advertised in Parliamentarian William Holmes Brown's *House Rules and Manual* (1979), was not observed in the cases of abrogating the Hay-Bunau-Varilla Treaty of 1903 and its ancillary treaties of 1936 and 1955.

These three treaties and all other agreements and conventions pertaining to the Panama Canal were purported to have been abrogated by Article I of the Panama Canal Treaty in the regular treaty-making procedure. No "act of the legislature," i.e., an act agreed to by both Houses of the Congress, was involved because the House of Representatives did not participate. Thus, the abrogation was done by the President and the Senate in contravention of *Jefferson's Manual* and the Constitution itself—past practices and the rule of consensus notwithstanding.

What is the authority of *Jefferson's Manual?* Thomas Jefferson prepared his *Manual of Parliamentary Practices* for guidance when he was President of the Senate (1797-1801) and later, its provisions were adopted for application to both Houses of the Congress "in which they are not inconsistent with the standing rules and orders of the House." The *Manual* was "compiled as it was for the use of the Senate exclusively."[28] Consequently, on the record, *Jefferson's Manual* is the authoritative guide for both Houses of the Congress to the degree stipulated—which includes the handling of treaties as "legislative acts."

Indeed, the *Manual* states in paragraph 593: "Treaties are legislative acts. A treaty is the law of the land. It differs from other laws only as it must have the consent of a foreign nation, being but a contract with respect to that nation."[29] *Jefferson's Manual* contains 178 pages in the thousands of copies printed for the 96th Congress in 1979. If its rules are not to be observed, why was the Manual published? What is the explanation for ignoring its explicit provisions?

Unquestionably, Jefferson's understanding of the Supremacy Clause of the Constitution (Article VI) included the handling of treaty abrogation in the same manner that federal laws are terminated: by an "act of the legislature," (both Houses). This interpretation was accepted and used for generations until it was supplanted by political expediency and modern "efficiency."

The late Professor Donald Morquand Dozer, an acknowledged authority on Latin America and recipient of the Alberdi-Sarmiento award for distinguished contributions to inter-American friendships,[30] addressed this question of treaty abrogation in his Memorandum, "The United States Constitution and the Panama Canal Treaties," which appears as Appendix N. He wrote, in part:

A law of the land, including treaties, can be set aside constitutionally only by the procedure which requires the consent of both Houses of Congress as well as the signed concurrence of the President. At no time from the beginning of the negotiations to the signing of the Treaties was this requirement met. If the President wants a new treaty with Panama superseding the treaty of 1903 he can point to no power that exempts him from this explicit and prescribed constitutional procedure.

The Dozer Memorandum of September 17, 1979 goes on to note the violations of the "principles of separation of powers and limitation of powers which are fundamental to our frame of government." In our unique system of checks and balances among the Legislative, Executive and Judicial Branches, Dr. Dozer reminds, none has exclusive power within itself.

In the matter of treaties, for example, the President is not all-powerful—nor can he cite any authority that permits the abrogation of a treaty except by an act of the legislature (both Houses). He cannot rule by decree, nor can the Senate acting alone. Because of the failure to abrogate properly, Dozer wrote, "The treaty of 1903 between the United States and Panama therefore remains unabrogated and continues to be entitled as the law of the land for the United States governing our relations with Panama."

Charles E. Rice, Professor of Law at Notre Dame University, disagreed with Dozer's assessment, stating: "A treaty is automatically superseded by an inconsistent later treaty, just as a statute would be superseded by a later inconsistent statute."[31] But Dr. Rice offers no back up authorization. Is he accurate?

Is not this an anomalous comparison? Statutes require action by both Houses of the Congress—and so do treaties, according to *Jefferson's Manual* (paragraph 599), a treaty being a law of the land on a par with other federal laws, according to the Constitution (Article VI). Therefore, even if a treaty could indeed be "superseded by an inconsistent later treaty," then it would have to be acted upon by both Houses of the Congress, just as with statutes. In the case of the Panama Canal Treaties, of course, the House of Representatives was excluded from its role in the abrogation of the 1903 Treaty. Moreover, it is not agreed that authorization exists for superseding one treaty by use of another treaty. If it does, where is it? "An act of the legislature alone can declare them infringed or rescinded."[32]

Moreover, the historical record of the Constitutional Convention (1787) reveals the careful attention given to the processes of making and ratifying treaties. Several plans were debated until Alexander Hamilton's idea prevailed. He wrote in one of his *Federalist* papers:

that treaty-making is neither legislative nor executive, but that it appeared that the executive is "the more fit agent in these transactions, while the vast importance of the trust and the *operation of the treaties as laws* plead strongly for the participation of the whole or a portion of the legislative body in the making of them."[33] (Emphasis added.)

Consequently, it was decided, the President would make and ratify treaties provided two-thirds of the Senators present gave advice and consent. The matter of abrogation was evidently not debated at all as treaties were placed in the same category as federal laws (Article VI) and could therefore be terminated just as laws were.

Considering the historical background and the clear mandates of the Constitution and *Jefferson's Manual,* why did the Executive Branch and the Senate purport to abrogate the 1903 Canal Treaty by means of another treaty, the Panama Canal Treaty of 1977? What is the authority? Was the Constitution circumvented in order to avoid another tough vote on surrendering the Canal, this time a vote in both Houses of the Congress?

To take Dr. Rice's point to the Constitution, Article VI proclaims as the "supreme Law of the Land": (1) laws made pursuant to the Constitution and (2) all treaties made under authority of the United States.[34] Therefore, treaties are laws and laws are rescinded by both Houses of the Congress: it follows prima facie then, that treaties must also be rescinded by both Houses of the Congress, e.g., by a joint resolution. Moreover, the joint resolution is a part of the system of checks and balances.

Attorney Paul Douglas Kamenar of the Washington Legal Foundation took much the same position as Dr. Rice, stating that a new treaty "automatically" supersedes an old one on the same subject. In his letter of July 20, 1979 to Attorney Jerry N. Jordan of Dallas, Texas, he wrote, in part:

Your theory that both Houses of Congress have to disapprove the old Panama treaty before a new one can take effect has not been the normal method of treaty formation. Under both international and domestic law, a new treaty with a country supersedes automatically the prior one on the same subject. There is no necessity for a separate action to first terminate the old one before the new one is ratified.

Again, as with Dr. Rice's argument, broad generalizations are made without specific authorizations or dicta to support them. For example, what *specific* authority is there "under both international and domestic law" for superseding an old treaty with a new one, as contended by Mr. Kamenar? And further, what citations or dicta uphold Kamenar's assertion that this is "the normal method of treaty formation"? Many citations and dicta do not support Kamenar's views.

Presumably, he is talking about "settled diplomatic practice" which, the record shows, in recent years has been inconsistent with earlier practices, the Constitution and *Jefferson's Manual of Parliamentary Practice.* Again, to be specific, Article VI of the Constitution makes treaties, federal laws and the Constitution "the supreme Law of the Land." It follows, therefore, that all three are to be handled as laws are handled—by the Congress (both Houses). Moreover, *Jefferson's Manual,* in paragraph 599, equates treaties with laws, and specifies that an act of the legislature (both Houses) is required to abrogate them.

Additionally, Louis Henkin in his authoritative work, *Foreign Affairs and the Constitution,* writes that "the Federal Government has the constitutional power to terminate treaties on behalf of the United States. . . ." and, further, that *Jefferson's Manual* "is still recognized as authoritative and underlies the current rules of both Houses of Congress."

The distinguished jurist and well-known constitutional lawyer, Charles Maechling, in his March 29, 1985 letter to Phillip Harman, apparently agreed that "out-of-date treaties . . . are declared to be no longer valid by statute."

Moreover, an important note is appended to paragraph 600 of the *Manual:* "The Senate now has rules governing its procedures on treaties." These rules are explicit and the guidebook for almost two centuries has been *Jefferson's Manual.*

Earlier, President Theodore Roosevelt had cautioned:

As for existing treaties—I do not admit the "dead hand" of the treaty-making power in the past. A treaty can always be honorably abrogated—though it must never be abrogated in dishonest fashion.[35]

While the President and the Senate act under the Constitution to make a treaty, they cannot undo the treaty by themselves as with a regular statute. A majority approval of both Houses on the Congress is required to abrogate a treaty, unless the President vetoes their action, in which case the veto may be overridden by a two-thirds vote of each House.

Associate Justice of the Supreme Court Hugo L. Black in the *Reid v. Covert* (1957) case wrote on the parity between treaties and statutes:

This Court has repeatedly taken the position that an Act of Congress, which must comply with the Constitution, is on a full parity with a treaty, and that when a statute which is subsequent in time is inconsistent with a treaty, the statute to the extent of conflict renders the treaty null. It would be completely anomalous to say that a treaty need not comply with the Constitution when such an agreement can be overridden by a statute that must conform to that instrument.[36]

IS 'SETTLED DIPLOMATIC PRACTICE' CONSTITUTIONAL?

In his classic discourse on the U.S. Constitution, Thomas James Norton wrote unequivocally in 1940, "Once a treaty is made, it requires both branches of Congress to abrogate it; that is, the President and the Senate cannot undo their work." For example, on July 7, 1798, the Congress (both Houses) set the precedent by abrogating a treaty with France that had been made by the President and approved by the Senate. Congress thereby established an important historical and constitutional precedent. It was done with a joint resolution declaring the treaty "no longer Obligatory on the United States." Norton added, "As a law of Congress may supersede a treaty, so a treaty may supplant an act of Congress, the latest expression of the National will controlling."[37]

The precedent begun in 1798 was broadened by the joint resolution of April 27, 1846, in which the Congress authorized President James K. Polk to notify Great Britain of the abrogation of the Convention of August 6, 1827, relating to the joint occupation of the Oregon Territory. This was another important precedent in establishing the constitutional procedure that international conventions (treaties) "to which the United States is a party, even those terminable on notice, are terminable only by act of Congress."[37] Article VI of the Constitution is the guide, making treaties and federal statutes "the supreme Law of the Land"—both terminable by an

act of the Congress, but with the *special* enactment (ratification) procedures of Article II for treaties. Thus, treaties are brought into force in a
special way (Article II), but both treaties and laws are terminated in the
same way (Article VI).

Two historic treaties relating to the Isthmus of Panama focus on the
constitutional procedures for making and terminating treaties: the Clayton-Bulwer Treaty (1850) and the Hay-Pauncefote Treaty (1901), both
between the United States and Great Britain, and both relating to construction of a ship canal across the Isthmus. The Clayton-Bulwer Treaty, which
admitted Great Britain to a joint protectorate with the United States over
any Isthmian canal, was addressed by a joint resolution of both Houses of
the Congress, initiated by House Resolution 250 on March 22, 1880,
thereby complying with the procedure of Article VI of the Constitution.
Appendix O is the text of this resolution and illustrates the constitutional
way to terminate treaties.

The Hay-Pauncefote Treaty (1901) came 21 years later and provided,
among other things, for the general principle of neutralization and for entire
equality of tools for all users of any canal that might be constructs.
Although Article I of the Hay-Pauncefote Treaty stipulated that the Clayton-
Bulwer Treaty was being superseded, this had not relieved the U.S. Congress
and the McKinley Administration of the constitutional obligation to abrogate the old treaty with an act of the legislature (joint resolution in this
case).

For the convenience of the reader, and as a matter of historical reference, the texts of the Clayton-Bulwer Treaty (1850) and the Hay-Pauncefote Treaty (1901) are also provided, Appendices P and Q respectively.

We should particularly note that Article I of the Hay-Pauncefote
Treaty purported to "supersede" the Clayton-Bulwer Treaty. However,
according to both the Constitution and *Jefferson's Manual,* an act of the
legislature (joint resolution) is the proper way.[38]

The fact is, abrogating an existing treaty by making a new treaty on
the same subject is not possible under the Constitution. The rules of *Jefferson's Manual* and the system of checks and balances on this point are based
on Article VI of the Constitution which, to repeat, equates treaties with
federal statutes as the law of the land. Using this rule, the Hay-Bunau-
Varilla Treaty (1903) with Panama has not been abrogated constitutionally.

In 1880 President Rutherford B. Hayes intended to use a legislative
act to "supersede" the old treaty (Clayton-Bulwer), but by 1901 the desire
for a "friendly annulment" apparently superseded the constitutional procedure. This evidently was the point made in William Roscoe Thayer's
books, *The Life and Letters of John Hay,* a two volume biography of Presi-

dent William McKinley's Secretary of State. Thayer wrote of Hay's concern for procedures and propriety:

To his mind the great fact to be striven for was the friendly annulment by England of the Clayton-Bulwer Treaty. He had succeeded in persuading England to do this:[39]

Another interesting example of careful observance of constitutional procedures, as well as conscientious compliance with treaty provisions, was President Woodrow Wilson's "Panama Canal Tolls Message" to the 63rd Congress on March 5, 1914. Appendix R contains the text of this short message. Wilson asked for and received Congress's approval for the repeal of that portion of the Panama Canal Act of August 24, 1912 which exempted "vessels engaged in the coastwise trade of the United States from payment of tolls."

This change brought the United States into compliance with Article III, section 1 of the Hay-Pauncefote Treaty (1901) which specified "entire equality" in toll charges for all nations. Since treaty provisions were involved, some Presidents might have claimed the right to make this change under their treaty-making power of Article II of the Constitution. But not Mr. Wilson, who went to the whole Constitution, including Article VI.

Woodrow Wilson probably knew the Constitution as well as any President since Thomas Jefferson, having taught constitutional history at Princeton University before he became President. He provided another historic example of a President's dedication to constitutional practices. He did the proper thing in order to correct non-compliance with an existing treaty: He went to the Congress and obtained a joint resolution.[40]

In other cases, the Congress used similar joint resolutions, usually carried out by the President, though not invariably. For instance, Presidents Wilson, Harding and Coolidge balked on grounds of propriety. Even so, both Houses of Congress had participated in terminating treaties, as prescribed by *Jefferson's Manual* and the Constitution, and as explained by constitutionalist Thomas James Norton.[41]

Other examples of abrogating treaties by legislative acts, or by joint resolutions, are documented in the Library of Congress publication, *The Constitution of the United States of America, Analysis and Interpretation* (1973), including the following: A joint resolution was prepared during the Administration of William Howard Taft (1909-1913) to abrogate the 1832 treaty with Russia.[42] Joint resolutions were also used by President Ulysses S. Grant to alter the treaty of 1842 with Great Britain; by President Rutherford B. Hayes to modify the treaty of 1868 with China; and by President Wilson in the La Follette-Furuseth Seaman's Act of March 4, 1915, designed to modify certain treaties which the Congress believed "terminable on notice."[43]

Throughout the section titled "Treaty-Making Power" of this authoritative Library of Congress publication, many references are made to the abrogation of treaties by legislative acts (both Houses of the Congress), e.g., "legislative repeal of a treaty as a law of the land." On page 502 are these words:

All in all, it would seem that the vast weight both of legislative practice and of executive opinion supports the proposition that the power of terminating outright international compacts to which the United States is party belongs, as a prerogative of sovereignty, to Congress alone. . . .[44]

Contrary viewpoints have been expressed by Charles E. Rice, J. Terry Emerson and Herbert J. Hansell, among others—though none of them quoted, in the essays and correspondence seen by this author, any constitutional or legal citations, merely precedents and practices. Indeed, Mr. Emerson states in his 1978 essay in the Notre Dame "Journal of Legislation" that "it is well settled diplomatic practice that the later treaty supersedes or revises the earlier one on the same subject."[45] This was the same thing that Dr. Rice, also of Notre Dame, had said. However, neither offered any documentation for his conclusions.

When Mr. Hansell was Legal Adviser to the State Department in 1978, he tabulated in a 45 page memorandum to the Secretary of State some dozen examples of unilateral actions by previous presidents in terminating treaties without any congressional action. Even so, these were on trivial matters, for the most part, some obviously inconsequential.[46] Nonetheless, constitutional requirements had been by-passed. Incidentally, of the twelve treaties cited, five had been cancelled by President Franklin Delano Roosevelt, one of the most activist presidents.

Hansell in his memorandum noted that "the Constitution does not specifically address the question of treaty termination" and that the Constitutional Convention (1787) did not discuss it. The fact is, treaty termination was covered in Article VI (the Supremacy Clause) of the Constitution by stating in plain words that treaties rank equally with federal laws as the "supreme Law of the Land."

It follows that if laws are laws, they are handled as laws. When a law is terminated, the legislature does it. When a treaty is terminated, only the legislature has the authority because treaties have co-equal status with federal laws under Article VI. Obviously this is why the Constitutional Convention did *not* discuss termination of treaties, as noted by Mr. Hansell. But, the Convention *did* take great pains to prescribe exactly how treaties were to be made, as set down in Article II, Section 2.

Further enlightenment on the intentions of the Constitutional Convention may be found in Jefferson's draft of the Kentucky Resolution (1798), stating in part: "General government was constituted for special purposes . . . wherever the general government assumes undelegated powers, its acts are unauthoritative, void, and of no force." For example, the Constitution does not delegate to the President and the Senate the power to abrogate treaties acting alone any more than it delegates to them alone the power to annul any other law of the land.

Further, James Madison's report on the Virginia Resolution (1798) states, in part, "that if a power is not expressed in the Constitution, the next inquiry must be whether it is properly an incident to an express power and necessary to execution. If it be, it may be exercised by Congress."[47] Again, the action "may be exercised by Congress" (both Houses) if doubt exists about the proper method to abrogate treaties, it seems clear from Madison's reasoning.

In the instances of treaty abrogation without legislative acts, it has been noticeable that no authorizations were ever quoted. Numerous examples were cited as precedents or as "historical practices" or as "settled diplomatic practice." But does such rationalization supersede constitutional and parliamentary standards and requirements? Do many things done wrong finally make it right? Or, is it unchallenged erosion of the Constitution? A breakdown in the separation and limitation of powers, i.e., in the system of checks and balances? Is government to be by the rule of consensus? Or, by the Constitution?

Moreover, what is the authority for President Carter and the United States Senate of the 95th Congress to abrogate the Hay-Bunau-Varilla Treaty (1903) by means of the Panama Canal Treaties of 1977? What is the authority for not using a legislative act for this purpose? Was a separate act of Congress, or a joint resolution, considered too inefficient, too tedious? Did political expediency or long-sought diplomatic goals of the Executive Branch justify arbitrary power based on the rationalization that "settled diplomatic practice" justified circumventing the Constitution?

Associate Supreme Court Justice Louis Dembitz Brandeis (1916-1939) addressed similar questions on the dangers of autocracy some 60 years ago:

The doctrine of separation of powers was adopted by the Convention of 1787, not to promote efficiency but to preclude the exercise of arbitrary power. The purpose was not to avoid friction, but, by means of the inevitable friction incident to the distribution of governmental powers among the three departments, to save the people from autocracy.[48]

Moreover, in a 1983 Supreme Court decision against the "legislative veto," Chief Justice Warren Burger seemed to be echoing Brandeis's warning against legislative "efficiency":

... it is crystal clear ... that the Framers ranked other values higher than efficiency. ... With all its obvious flaws ... we have not yet found a better way to preserve freedom than by making the exercise of power subject to the carefully crafted restraints spelled out in the Constitution.[49]

Perhaps only a decision at the Supreme Court level will ever resolve the constitutional issue of the proper method of treaty abrogation. It is an important part of the system of checks and balances and the separation of powers—and should not be glossed over just because the Executive had the Congress under control at the time of the 1977 Treaties.

Incidentally, it should be noted, the proposed 1967 treaties worked up by Robert Anderson, President Johnson and Panama's Marco Robles and his negotiators were almost the exact prototype for the 1977 Treaties. The 1967 treaties would also have abrogated the 1903 Treaty by means of the new treaty. Indeed, the phraseology was almost verbatim. The thinking was the same, i.e., it was another proposal to by-pass Article VI of the Constitution.

The arguments of Messrs. Rice, Hansell, Emerson, Schweppe, Jordan, Oliver, Maier, Dozer, Kamenar, Henkin, Black, Norton, Polk, Wilson, Hayes, both Roosevelts, Jefferson, Madison, Burger, Brandeis, the Library of Congress and many others should all be heard in court—in the U.S. Supreme Court and the correct constitutional practice established.

A similar concern was expressed in the hearing record of the Senate Subcommittee on Separation of Powers, February 1978, in the inquiry into the disposal of United States property and territory in connection with the Panama Canal Treaties (1977):

The manner in which the Executive Branch, contrary to statute and often to the Constitution, has taken over much of the substance of governance has always been a matter of grave concern to the Subcommittee. The development of overwhelming executive power cannot be accepted with equanimity; issues of fundamental constitutional importance are raised by it, not the least of which is the decline of the traditional doctrine of separation of powers and the intrusion of the executive and judiciary into the responsibilities of Congress. But the Congress has not been without fault in permitting this to occur. For far too long, both Houses have somnolently acquiesced in a massive transfer of the legislative power of government from the Congress, where constitutionally it should reside, to the Executive Branch and to the Judiciary, neither of which has the constitutional authority to exercise it.[50]

The American people have not been apprised of the infringements against the Constitution brought on by overzealous officials seeking ratified Panma Canal Treaties as their first priority. It is a precedent that is not acceptable. "All bad precedents began as justifiable measures" (Julius Caesar, c. 1st century B.C.). "The people should fight for their law as for their city wall" (Heraclitus, c. 500 B.C.).

DISPOSAL OF U.S. PROPERTY: ANOTHER 'BAD PRECEDENT'

President Carter mounted a powerful effort to transfer the territory of the Panama Canal Zone and U.S. property within the Zone to Panama without observing the requirements of Article IV, Section 3, Clause 2 of the Constitution which reads:

The Congress shall have Power to dispose of and make all needful Rules and Regulations respecting the Territory or other Property belonging to the United States. . . .

Ordinarily, this Article would be seen as granting exclusive power to both Houses of the Congress to dispose of taxpayers' property and territory, should the need arise, without any hint of sharing power with the Executive Branch (the President). The Carter Administration did not agree. Its goal was to use the Canal Treaties as self-executing documents without the concurrence of the Congress (both Houses).

Moreover, the Administration argued, the President's treaty-making power (Article II, Section 2) included disposal of property too. Consequently, the Panama Canal Treaties, which were designed 100% for the transfer of U.S. property and territory, were ratified without the participation of the House of Representatives.

Thus, President Carter and the Senate avoided another obstacle in the path of successful Treaties by excluding the House from any part in the treaty-making. Approval of the Treaties was going to be difficult and this was one less worry. A second worry, of course, was the threat of having to abrogate the 1903 Treaty by a legislative act involving both Houses of the Congress. Again, the House of Representatives was excluded from this constitutional duty, inasmuch as no act of Congress was used. The 1903 Treaty was purportedly terminated by Article I of the Panama Canal Treaty of 1977, another action for which there is no authority, only precedent. Consequently, two constitutional provisions were by-passed—and thus, two more obstacles were removed from the path of the Treaties.

Immediately after the negotiators had completed their work in draft form on August 10, 1977, Attorney General Griffin B. Bell was ready with his affirmative answer to the question: May a treaty dispose of territory or property belonging to the United States without statutory authorization? To be sure, his letter of August 11 to the Secretary of State was a weak affirmative, later demolished by constitutional experts before congressio-

220 • THE PANAMA CANAL TREATIES SWINDLE

nal committees, but it was an important part of the Carter offensive for the Treaties, and was in hand, ready and waiting, five weeks before the Treaties were sent to the Senate for advice and consent.[51]

Attorney General Bell cited some twelve court cases in attempting to support his conclusion that "territory and property of the United States may be disposed of by action of the President and the Senate under the treaty clause,"Article II, Section 2 of the Constitution. However, the "paucity of each argument" was exposed by Professor Raoul Berger, a Fellow of Harvard Law School, during his testimony before the Senate Subcommittee on Separation of Powers in February 1978. Dr. Berger concluded that the Attorney General "failed to make out a case for 'concurrent jurisdiction' with Congress in the disposition of United States property."[52] Moreover, Berger found most of Bell's citations irrelevant.

Berger cited numerous court rulings that destroyed "the new theory of concurrent jurisdiction over property disposal." One was an 1899 opinion of the Attorney General:

The power to dispose permanently of the public lands and public property in Puerto Rico rests in Congress, and in the absence of a statute conferring such power, cannot be exercised by the executive department for the government.[53]

Among the arguments advanced to support Carter's plan to exclude the House of Representatives was that "the property clause [Article IV] contains no language excluding concurrent jurisdiction of the treaty power."[54] But, of course, the Constitution cannot *exclude* all possible agencies that might wish to dispose of public property. The list would be endless. The Senate Subcommittee report included two cardinal rules of constitutional construction. One is the rule that express mention signifies implied exclusion:

When a statute limits a thing to be done to a particular mode, it includes the negative of any other mode.[55]

The second rule is that the specific governs the general:

Where there is in an act a specific provision relating to a particular subject, that provision must govern in respect to that subject as against general provisions. . . .[56]

Moreover, Chief Justice John Marshall (1755-1835) wrote in 1819 in *McCulloch v. Maryland,* 17 U.S. (4 Wheat.) 316, 405, on the constitutional doctrine of enumerated powers:

This government is acknowledged by all to be one of enumerated powers. The principle, that it can exercise only the powers granted to it, would seem too apparent to have required to be enforced by all those arguments which its enlightened friends . . . found it necessary to urge. That principle is now universally admitted.[56]

These cardinal rules of constitutional construction also dispel the contentions of Herbert J. Hansell, State Department Legal Adviser, that "there is no restraint *expressed* in respect to disposition."[57] A further refutation of Hansell is a 1942 Supreme Court decision that "the Constitution places the authority to dispose of public lands *exclusively* in Congress [both Houses]"[58] (Emphasis in originals).

The incisive inquiry into the disposal of U.S. territory and property, as conducted by the late Senator James B. Allen and his Subcommittee on Separation of Powers, in February 1978, wrecked the Administration's case as well as that of the Foreign Relations Committee, most of whose members had favored the Treaties from the beginning. Indeed, every citation of previous treaties alleged to have transferred territory and property without a legislative act was discredited; many had "no bearing whatsoever."[59] The Subcommittee's research had produced devastating evidence—to be buried in the record.

The by-passing of the Constitution in favor of the political expediency of the moment brought this rejoinder from Professor Berger:

This disregard to constitutional requirements in the proposed Panama Canal Treaties will haunt those who are closing their eyes to it down the years because it will be brought up by the people who will succeed Hansell and Erickson. They will say that they have a precedent. The Senate retreated and in the future they will insist on it as a matter of executive right.[60]

The official finding of Senator Allen's Subcommittee in February 1978 was publicized several weeks before the Senate votes of approval on the Treaties, in time for corrective action if such had been intended by the Senate leadership. The finding was straightforward:

The Subcommittee on Separation of Powers of the Committee on the Judiciary, having studied the issue of the authority of Congress to dispose of territory or property belonging to the United States as set forth in Article IV, Section 3, Clause 2 of the Constitution, finds that the constitutional prerogatives of Congress require that Congress authorize, by the enactment of appropriate legislation, any disposition of the property of the United States in the Isthmus of Panama.[61]

Even so, the House of Representatives did not participate in the treaty-making involving the transfer of U.S. taxpayers' property. If any "pound of flesh" was to be had in this episode, it may be the House role in preparation of the treaty-implementing legislation, known as the Panama Canal Act of 1979. This House-sponsored law (Public Law 96-70) assured that the United States property and Canal in the Isthmus of Panama would *not* be so easily disposed of after all:

Sec. 1503. No property of the United States located in Panama may be disposed of except by law enacted by the Congress.

Sec. 1504. . . . (c) the Panama Canal, . . . shall not be transferred to the Republic of Panama prior to December 31, 1999.[62]

Therefore, the people of the United States still own the Canal—and if ultimately, it is to be lost, the people's representatives in both Houses of the

Congress will have to make a new law by 1999 in order to surrender it finally to Panama, if at that time the Congress accepts the Panama Canal Treaties (1977) as legal.

The Treaties that President Carter had presented for "Advice and Consent" required something else before they could become the "Law of the Land." They needed specific implementing legislation. Two long-standing Supreme Court decisions establish this principle: *Foster v. Nielson* (2 Pet. 253, 1829) and *Taylor v. Morton* (2 Curt. 454—1855 and U.S. 481—1862). Simply stated, these decisions provide that where a treaty is not self-executing, it lacks force and effect without "affirmative action of the Congress."

Although many arguments were advanced at the time to go along with the Senate and support "national policy," the House of Representatives had the chance several times in 1979 to heed the desires of the majority of the people and refuse to transfer the Canal by rejecting the implementing legislation—if its members had been so inclined. The events leading up to the final vote on September 26th were significant; and the system of checks and balances was on trial.

CHECKS AND BALANCES WORK—TEMPORARILY

On September 20, 1979 the House of Representatives rejected the implementing legislation by a vote of 203 to 192 and many Americans believed the Canal had been saved because this was the *compromise bill* between the House and Senate and it had been turned down. They also believed that the system of checks and balances had worked. However, they failed to take into account the "rules" that permitted Speaker Thomas P. "Tip" O'Neill, Jr., D.-Mass., and Majority Leader Jim Wright, D.-Tex., to commit and recommit compromise bills back to conference until they had what they wanted. And if this should be insufficient, there were other ways: unanimous consent and suspension of the rules.

A few days later the final compromise bill, the Panama Canal Act of 1979 (H.R. 111), was agreed to by the Senate, 63 to 32, on September 25—and by the House, 232 to 188, on September 26. At this point, many asked if the country had been forced from a nation of laws to a nation of men. They also asked what the House Minority Leader, John J. Rhodes, R.-Ariz., had done to protect the rights of the minority. And had the rules "operated as a check and control on the actions of the majority . . . and [as] a shelter and protection to the minority, against the attempts of power."[63]

What rules? The rules are contained in *Jefferson's Manual and Rules of the House of Representatives,* adopted in 1837 and amended from time

to time.[64] Some of the applicable rules are as follows: Paragraph 545: "...
where a report is disagreed to in either House, another conference is usually asked." Paragraph 449: "A conference report being made up but not
acted on at the expiration of a Congress, the bill is lost." Paragraph 551:
"When either House disagrees to a conference report the matter is left in
the same position it was in before the conference was asked. . . . Motions
for disposition are again in order."

As to revenue treaties (paragraph 597), the House in a number of
cases has asserted its prerogatives in the negotiation of these pacts. Paragraph 912: "When managers [of conference bills] report they have been
unable to agree, the report is not acted on by the House." The House has
"constitutional power" to make its rules (paragraph 388), but not rules
that contravene the intent of the Constitution. Therefore, what about rules
that circumvent the system of checks and balances?

Conference reports are explained in the House booklet, "How Our
Laws Are Made," presented by Peter W. Rodino, D.-N.J.[55] For example,
"the report is not subject to amendment in either body and must be
accepted or rejected as an entirety" (p.42). Further, "if the House does not
agree to a conference report that the Senate has already agreed to, the
report may not be recommitted to conference because the Senate conferees
are discharged when the Senate agrees to the report" (p.43). But, of course,
the majority may then appoint a new conference because it has the votes to
override any objection. Nonetheless, "if the House does not accept the
amendments insisted upon by the Senate, the entire conference process
begins again with respect to them" (p.44). In this latter circumstance, some
would add "in the next session of the Congress." Not necessarily.

The rules for unanimous consent (Rule XIII) and for suspension of
rules (Rule XXVII) provide additional power for the majority to prevail.

The application of these rules of parliamentary practice is evident
from the legislative chronology of H.R. 111:[66] On May 17, 1979 the
House accepted the rules for floor debate by the narrow margin of 200 to
198, portending future problems with House members nervous about constituent reactions and about their own constitutional power under Property Clause (Article IV) for transfer of the Canal. Nonetheless, on June 21,
the House passed the committee bill, 224 to 202, agreeing to the transfer,
but with stringent controls disliked by the Carter Administration. On July
26, the Senate passsed an amended bill, 64 to 30, close to Mr. Carter's
desires.

Next, the conference compromise bill was worked up on H.R. 111
and was reported out of conference on September 17. Three days later, on
September 20, the Senate approved it, 60 to 35, but the House voted disap-

proval, 203 to 192. The system had presumably gone full cycle and the system of checks and balances had worked. Not quite. The power of the presidency and of House Speaker O'Neill and the majority next came into play.

The White House was alarmed and alerted Henry Kissinger and other influential leaders to warn House members of the consequences if the bill were rejected. Another conference was quickly called and a second compromise bill was prepared and submitted. Meanwhile, several conservative Democrats and liberal Republicans had been converted to the President's side and thus, the second compromise bill was approved, 63 to 32, by the Senate on September 25 and accepted, 232 to 188, by the House on the following day, September 26. Under the rules and with majority control, the bill could have been recycled indefinitely.

Nonetheless, the people's representatives in the Congress had, contrary to the will of their constituents, paved the way for Vice President Walter F. Mondale to assist in raising the huge Panamanian flag on Ancon Hill on October 1, 1979, signifying Panama's sovereignty over the former American Canal Zone.

Are there no limitations to the number of times a compromise bill can be recommitted? Could it be done indefinitely until the Administration and the Speaker had what they wanted? Under the existing rules, there is no limit; such a situation suggests tyranny.

These questions and others were answered by the Congressman who had shepherded H.R. 111 through the House, the former Chairman of the Committee on Merchant Marine and Fisheries, John M. Murphy, D.-N.Y., who stated in an interview on October 25, 1984: "With unanimous consent, you can do most anything in a legislative body. So, as long as you get unanimous consent to recommit, that's all it would take and no rules would be violated."[67] Are we to understand that not one Senator, not one Representative, was willing to object, i.e., to oppose the leadership's plan for unanimous consent in order to recycle H.R. 111 until it passed?

But, how about the system of checks and balances? Could not the House have simply refused to implement the transfer of U.S. property under Article IV of the Constitution? "Sure it could have," answered Mr. Murphy, "but if Congress did not issue implementing legislation, that would be the worst of all worlds." He explained that Panama could then apply its own interpretations to the Treaties and that the U.S. State Department would have the lion's share of control and could cave in to every demand Panama made.

With H.R. 111, he continued, the role of the Defense Department was strengthened and the United States would control the Panama Canal Commission in operating the Canal until the year 2000—a "solid wall that could not be breached by Panama's whims and demands." Moreover, the Commission was made a federal agency subject to annual congressional funding and control.

President Carter lobbied hard for the implementing legislation, having invited over a hundred Congressmen to the White House in solicitation of their votes. He won again. Nonetheless, he repudiated Sections 1503 and 1504, which postponed actual transfer of the Canal and certain other U.S. properties until the year 2000 and which also required separate legislation to do so.

Relying on his split-decision victory in the 1978 *Edwards v. Carter* case (U.S. Court of Appeals, District of Columbia Circuit) that found the Treaties to be self-executing, Mr. Carter declared at the signing ceremony for H.R. 111 on September 27, 1979:

It remains the position of the Administration that the Treaty is self-executing with respect to the transfer of property, and thus no additional legislative authority is required.[68]

Thereby, the President was warning the Congress that these sections of H.R. 111 (Public Law 96-70) were not acceptable. This was a surprising statement and together with the court decision prompted one prominent jurist to write, "Making the Zone-Canal treaty self-executing was a near-to-irresponsible act. . . ." It also meant that the President might act on his own, conceivably making an early transfer and setting an "effective date" in a manner similar to his circumventing the Brooke Reservation in ratifying the Treaties nine and one-half months before the prescribed date and saying it was "effective" March 31, 1979.

This possibility of unilateral action by the Executive Branch had been a major concern of the House Committee on Merchant Marine and Fisheries in preparing legislation to implement the basic treaty (the Panama Canal Treaty). Former Chairman Murphy stated on October 25, 1984:

The intent of the House was to protect America's interests because if we didn't, the Treaty would have legislative effect—and it was so ambiguous that the Administration could have done most anything it wanted to do with it. Many House members said, "If we vote for your bill, many of our constituents would perceive this a vote for the Treaties." So, we fought the Administration and the leftists, trying to bring some rationality in putting together the strongest possible language to protect America's interests. I think we did it.[69]

HOUSE SWAPS ARTICLE IV FOR EXPEDIENCY

The implementing legislation became law (Public Law 96-70), albeit denounced in part by President Carter and almost *in toto* by the Panamanians who continued their demands for more concessions, including agitation for an early turnover of the Canal. While the Treaties were designed to be ambiguous,the House did not have to be. Nonetheless, it reneged on its foursquare opportunity to clarify and set a precedent for its constitutional role (Article IV) in the transfer of U.S. property.

The majority decided to go along with H.R. 111 in order to avoid what Mr. Murphy had called the "worst of all worlds." The House then had been faced with dilemmas: (1) the threat of a self-executing ambiguous treaty without any real controls which might be implemented by Executive order at any time; (2) a straightforward execution of Article IV in refusing to transfer this U.S. property on constitutional grounds; or (3), passing whatever implementing legislation that could be agreed to, using its fail-safe rules of procedure.

Did the House use the rule of expediency in order to avoid complicated after effects and international charges that the United States failed to honor commitments—charges, incidently, made by those who failed to understand the U.S. constitutional system of checks and balances? As for honoring commitments, it should have been explained from the beginning that the Treaties were subject to House approval of funds for implementation and agreement to the disposal of the U.S. property under the Constitution.

The House was under no constitutional obligation to pass this legislation and could have legally and properly refused to transfer the remaining portions of the Canal Zone then and there under authority of Article IV. Emergency legislation could have been used to continue operation of the Canal and its supporting systems.

A persistent argument for the implementing legislation was that the Treaty was the "Law of the Land." Not quite. The fact is, even had the Treaty been constitutionally ratified and otherwise valid in international law, it could not have become the "Law of the Land" under Article VI of the Constitution, and a rule for the courts, "without the passage of implementing legislation which the Congress was free to enact or not to enact." Why? Because a treaty is a "Law of the Land" *only* when it is self-executing.[70]

The basic decision on this point has stood up since 1829 when Chief Justice John Marshall, speaking for the Supreme Court, said in *Foster v. Nielson:*

Our Constitution declares a treaty to be the law of the land. It is consequently to be regarded in courts of justice as equivalent to an act of the legislature whenever it operates of itself without the aid of any legislative provisions. But when the terms of the stipulation import a contract, when either of the parties engages to perform a particular act, the treaty addresses itself to the political not the judicial department and the legislature must execute the contract before it can become a rule for the court.[71]

In the case of the treaty in question, the Panama Canal Treaty of 1977, the contract could not be executed under the Constitution without the enabling legislation that would spell out the "particular act[s]" that each party would perform—and there were many particulars to be spelled out.

Chairman Murphy had a similar view on August 17, 1977, at the time the Treaties were first unveiled. He reminded his Committee in reference to the disposal of U.S. property that Thomas Jefferson interpreted the Constitution to mean "that while the President and Senate can make treaties, whenever they include matters confided by the Constitution to the legislature, an act of legislation will be required to confirm the treaty, and that the House is 'perfectly free to pass the act or refuse it, governing themselves by their own judgment, whether it is for the good of their constituents to let the treaty go into effect or not.'"[72]

This was the initial stages of the House battle to participate in the treaty-making procedure. Two years later, Mr. Murphy led the way to Public Law 96-70, obviously believing there was no satisfactory alternative.

There *was* an alternative: Invoke the right of the House under the Property Clause of the Constitution (Article IV) to agree or disagree to the disposal of the Canal and other U.S. properties in the Canal Zone. In the process, respect the constitutional procedures and the rights of the minority party as outlined in *Jefferson's Manual,* a main provision of which is "uniformity in proceeding in business not subject to the caprice of the Speaker or captiousness of the members."[73]

In the closing minutes of the debate on September 26, the Speaker, Mr. O'Neill, entered the well of the House to support H.R. 111.

The substance of his reasoning was a conversation a few years earlier with golf professional Chi Chi Rodriguez when the "little fellow from the Caribbean" told him at the 18th hole, "Don't you appreciate the shabby and shady manner in which you acquired the Panama Canal? When are you people going to do anything about it?"

Mr. O'Neill then told his colleagues that he had never before given any thought to the Canal and that now we should think about the "rights of the people from whom we acquired the Canal." Then, he concluded, "I think you are going to witness a friendlier Western Hemisphere."[74] This was the rationale of the Speaker of the House of Representatives for surrendering the strategic waterway. It was an amazing performance and it astonished his listeners.

The final vote agreed to the second compromise conference report and a motion to reconsider was laid on the table. At that point, H.R. 111 was ready to be enrolled for the President's signature.

But did the system of checks and balances work? It could not be effective if votes and revotes were permitted until the majority party won. The purpose of checks and balances is to prevent tyranny. Is it tyrannical for the majority to recommit bills, for example, on the constitutional issue of disposal of U.S. territory until such bills are accepted? Rejection is not permitted? Of course, the converse is never heard of: where accepted bills are revoted until they are rejected? At what point is the line of propriety drawn?

After the House rejected the Senate's revised H.R. 111 on September 20, the bill was lost—except that the rules and unanimous consent permitted recycling indefinitely until success was achieved or until patience and the legislative calendar demanded otherwise.

The argument may be made that H.R. 111 was not a normal bill. It was a revenue bill, an implementing bill, for a treaty and was initiated by the House under the authority of Article I, Section 7 of the Constitution. When the House-Senate compromise bill was defeated on September 20, the system of checks and balances had worked—but only up to that point. The House had decided on that day to keep the Canal. Perhaps some Congressmen momentarily remembered the threats of Soviet troops in Cuba, communists in Nicaragua and Panama's role in supplying them.

As for the confusion on October 1st that would have resulted from defeat of H.R. 111, should not a more serious concern be for the oath of office to protect the Constitution, in this case Articles I, IV and VI? These constitutional concerns include the House function in disposing of revenue bills and for transferring U.S. territory and property. Equally important was the Supreme Court ruling in *Foster v. Nielson* on the requirement for implementing legislation for treaties that require actions by the treaty partners.

On the strictly constitutional issue of checks and balances and the prerogatives of the Property Clause (Article IV, Section 3, Clause 2), the House could have refused implementing legislation. Had the House refused to enact implementing legislation, this action in itself could have become a "rule for the court," as explained by Chief Justice Marshall in *Foster v. Nielson,* and another historic and needed Supreme Court decision would have been in the making. Meanwhile, it is conceivable that President Carter, claiming self-executing Treaties under authority of the *Edwards v. Carter* court decision, could have used Executive Orders for various actions under the Treaties, handling them much as legislative acts.

Editorial writers at the time, including William F. Buckley, Jr., failed to recognize the Constitution's built-in protection for the limitation of powers (checks and balances). Article IV specifically requires the approval of both Houses of the Congress for the disposal of "Territory or other Property belonging to the United States." To argue, as Buckley did, in his July 6, 1979 issue of *National Review* (pp.878-9) that the House of Representatives was naughty to interfere with the "transfer" of the Canal Zone and other U.S. property and that the "one discipline indispensable to self-government . . . is acquiescence in a political *fait accompli*" is an argument that ignores the basic provisions of checks and balances planned by the Framers of the Constitution.

The Senate had refused House participation in the treaty-making procedures—and President Carter had usurped the power to dispose of the Canal by his treaty-making authority of Article II, whereas Article IV is the specific guide for the "transfer" of the Canal Zone and all appurtenances. To be sure, the system of checks and balances comes into play when the time comes for the actual "transfer" of U.S. property. The House had the constitutional right to balk at the "transfer," Buckley and other editorialists and politicians notwithstanding.

Mr. Buckley made much to do about the threat to the 1977 Treaties, writing, "Under the circumstances, the treaty scheduled to go into effect on October 1, 1979 would be *frozen for lack of funds required for implementation*" (emphasis added). Certainly, they'd be frozen; that's what checks and balances are for and that's what Article IV of the Constitution is for. In politics, aren't "frozen funds" the common denominator of the opposition? What "stopper" stops better than "frozen funds"?

Mr. Buckley went on with his lamentation: "This would leave us with what? Not with the treaty of 1903? That treaty was formally repealed by the Senate when the fresh treaties were enacted. There is no way [to] bring back the old treaty."

The old 1903 treaty does not have to be brought back; it is still in force because it was never constitutionally terminated. Article VI and *Jefferson's Manual of Parliamentary Practice* prescribe that treaties are the "supreme Law of the Land." Consequently, "an act of the legislature," meaning both Houses of the Congress, is required to terminate them. This was not done with the 1903 Treaty. Instead, the President and the Senate purported to terminate it via Article I of the 1977 Treaties. Therefore, the Hay-Bunau-Varilla Treaty (1903) remains in force and quite legal under the U.S. Constitution.

Even if Mr. Buckley had been accurate in asserting that the 1903 treaty had been "formally repealed," would this have precluded a conscientious discharge of duty by members of the House of Representatives in observing Article IV of the Constitution for the disposal of U.S. property and territory? Either way, a "legal mess" would have been created, but it was a "mess" spawned by refusing House participation in the treaty-making procedure regarding property disposition.

Therefore, William Buckley was not correct on these two counts. He called his 1979 piece "The Panama Quagmire" but it was quagmire only because people like Buckley made it a quagmire by hasty conclusions slanted toward possible bias and inadequate research and fundamental understanding.

As for the underlying reason for restricting the treaty-making to the President and the Senate and for excluding the House of Representatives, pure politics undoubtedly controlled everything: With congressional elections coming up, the House would not have agreed to the Treaties—or, if they had, a great many would have been defeated.

In the *Mickey Edwards v. James Earl Carter* case (decided April 6, 1978) in the U.S. Court of Appeals for the District of Columbia, Circuit Judges Charles Fahy and Carl McGowan found for the majority opinion that the Canal Zone and it related properties could be transferred without the consent of both Houses of the Congress, i.e., such action was "consonant with the Constitution." Primarily, they cited a number of Indian treaties as dicta.

In 22 pages of their Court document No. 78-116, they concluded that the "decision to cast some but not all of the articles of conveyance in non-self-executing form was a *policy choice;* it was not required by the Constitution" (emphasis added). In fact, it was ten billion dollars worth of "policy choice." The Fahy-McGowan opinion stated in concluding:

In deciding that Article IV, Section 3, clause 2 [of the Constitution] is not the exclusive method contemplated by the Constitution for disposing of federal property, we hold that the United States is not prohibited from employing an alternative means constitutionally authorized.

But where is there any "alternative means constitutionally authorized?" Does not the above amazing statement imply that the Constitution does not mean what it says and therefore, may be loosely applied? Moreover, ambivalence and superficiality seemed to characterize this brief rationalization to get Mr. Carter off the hook.

The dissenting opinion in the *Edwards-Carter* lawsuit comprised an in-depth 128 pages of analysis by Judge George E. MacKinnon who cited many precedents where both Houses of the Congress acted to dispose of U.S. property. As for the Indian treaties, MacKinnon pointed out, the Act of March 3, 1871 (16 Stat. 566) "recognized that the Indian treaties were something different than the treaties referred to in the Constitution."

Among Judge MacKinnon's incisive conclusions were the following: There is no instance in the entire history of the United States that has been brought to our attention where any disposition of United States property even approaching the character and magnitude here involved was ever handled by a self-executing treaty.

. . . .

If any reasonably general statement were to be formulated for drawing the line where the President's treaty power terminates, it would be at that point where the Constitution indicates that a legislative power was to be exercised.

. . . .

Art. IV, Sec. 3, cl. 2, however, is very specific and limited. It refers only to territory and property. . . . Thus, the specific nature and limited scope of the paragraph are reasons why the ratification procedure thus required should not be taken from Congress and obviated by self-executing treaties.

. . . .

However, regardless of disputes on other issues, one conclusion is certain. That is that if the present attempt successfully usurps the constitutional right and duty of the House of Representatives to vote on the disposition of United States' property of the tremendous magnitude and value of our Panama holdings a precedent of such enormity will be created that the constitutional right of the House of Representatives to vote on transfers of property to foreign nations *need never again be seriously recognized* (emphasis added).

Judge MacKinnon has written far-reaching and frightening words— words which warn that, if the Fahy-McGowan decision is allowed to stand, the constitutional rights of the House of Representatives ever to transfer U.S. territory or property have been scuttled by a two-man ruling in the Court of Appeals. The crux of MacKinnon's dissent is contained in the following paragraph:

To the extent that the President may have discretion to choose between proceeding by treaty or other forms of international agreement, he cannot avoid the constitutional requirement that the entire Congress pass on all attempts to dispose of United States' territory and property to other nations. All past practices in this field indicate that prior Presidents have recognized that obligation even when property of much less value and significance was involved.

Why did Judges Fahy and McGowan not specify "alternative means" that were authorized by the Constitution? Dr. Covey T. Oliver, one of the foremost professors of law in the country and co-author of *The Restatement of United States Foreign Relations Law,* suggested an "alternative means"—but it would require the consent of both Houses of the Congress. Professor Oliver, as a former Assistant Secretary for Inter-American Affairs and a man who worked to settle things after the 1964 "Flag Riots," apparently believed that the settlement of territorial jurisdiction in the Canal Zone was a political necessity, though disagreeing with Carter's method.[75]

He said that Carter should have sought approval and implementation of a "single joint resolution" by simple majority in both Houses. Such procedure would not only have been legal under Article IV of the Constitution, but would have met the full requirements for disposal of U.S. territory or property by the Congress (both Houses).

Why did Mr. Carter not go that route? Did he fear the wrath of certain Senators who opposed any House participation? Was he afraid, based on his political estimates, that he could not get even a majority in the House for the transfer of the Canal Zone? Certainly a simple majority in both Houses would have been easier than a two-step route, i.e., a two-thirds approval in the Senate and simple majority in the House. Consequently, if the Administration had lost the *Edwards v. Carter* case, Mr. Carter would have had a much tougher problem on his hands.

Moreover, another important point should be taken into account in the matter of spending taxpayers' money for certain properties and then disposing of those properties that had been purchased with tax money. Should the same general route be followed? The Constitution says yes.

Article I, Section 7 of the Constitution specifically authorizes the House of Representatives and only the House of Representatives to originate "all Bills for raising Revenue"—which then must pass the Senate. That is, all money bills must begin in the House, the body closest to the people. Article IV, Section 3, Clause 2 requires the Congress (both Houses) to dispose of U.S. "Territory or other Property." So, in the case of the Canal Zone (and its purchase from four different "owners"), the House originated funding for payment by U.S. taxpayers for their new property in Panama, as the Framers of the Constitution intended. The Framers then provided that the taxpayers' property would only be disposed of by both Houses of the Congress, basically the same principle as used in the original purchase. Thus, Article I requires action by both Houses to provide tax money to buy U.S. property—and Article IV requires action by both Houses to dispose of taxpayers' property—that is, one House acting alone shall not do it.

This principle was apparently not considered in the Fahy-McGowan decision that saved the day for President Carter. And, thus, these Circuit Court Judges made their own significant contributions to the "surrender" of the Panama Canal because, if either had voted with MacKinnon, chances are that the people's representatives in the House would have refused to "surrender" the Canal. Thereby, another obstacle to the Treaties was surmounted.

Nonetheless, in a few lines in his *Panama Odyssey,* former U.S. Ambassador William J. Jorden, a strong promoter of the Treaties, dismissed consideration of the House's constitutional duties to dispose of U.S. territory or property as "vitriolic" as "House members argued ad nauseam," even "extremist" and "beyond their competence" (pp.664-5). Jorden's argument of "two hundred years of history . . . and the long-standing legal view that there was another equally valid way . . ." to dispose of U.S. property offered no proof or documentation whatever and, as with certain other major assertions in his book of the story of the Treaties, no cited evidence backs him up.

Contrary to Mr. Jorden's view, the constitutional role of the House of Representatives in the disposition of taxpayers' property is firmly established by precedent and documentation. Our preceding analysis highlights this point.

The fact that the U.S. Court of Appeals for the District of Columbia found otherwise—and that the Supreme Court refused to review—does indeed validate the dismissal of the *Edwards v. Carter* case. But not necessarily forever or justly. Didn't the Supreme Court once find that a black man was not a person (Dred Scott) "in American law"?

While many House members objected strongly to being prohibited from participating in the disposal of "property" during the treaty-making in 1977-78, nonetheless, the majority was willing to give in by 1979 when they had their constitutional chance to check the Senate. So, truly, perhaps the majority of the people's representatives wanted Panama to have the Canal—or else, failed to understand their constitutional prerogatives.

Appendix A-1 lists the 232 *Representatives* who made possible the "final act" for the Canal Treaties by approving the implementing legislation. Appendix A lists the 68 *Senators* who gave "Advice and Consent" to the Treaties. Of the 196 Democrat Representatives named in Appendix A-1, 31.6 percent no longer serve and are indicated by an asterisk (*). 50 percent of the 30 Republicans are no longer in the Congress, also marked with an asterisk, suggesting that the Republican voters came down harder on their Representatives, all other things being equal.

NON-RESIDENT ALIENS AS U.S. OFFICIALS

Another important constitutional issue is the provision in Article III of the Panama Canal Treaty of 1977 for the appointment by the President

234 • THE PANAMA CANAL TREATIES SWINDLE

of the United States of four Panamanian (non-resident aliens) to serve as "directors" on the nine-member Panama Canal Commission, the U.S. government agency charged with operating the Canal through December 31, 1999. All such "directors" are U.S. civil officers, as defined by the Supreme Court ruling in *Buckley v. Valeo*, 424 U.S. 1 (1976).

These Panamanians, therefore, hold federal offices in a U.S. government agency, as stipulated in the Panama Canal Act itself: "Each member of the Board shall hold office at the pleasure of the President, and . . . shall take an oath to discharge faithfully the duties of his office."[76]

The late Dr. Breecher, in his testimony before Senator East's Subcommittee on Separation of Powers on June 23, 1983, gave a summation of the situation:

But the U.S. Constitution unequivocally bars non-resident aliens, owing allegiance to their government and not the United States, from becoming U.S. civil officers, without violating the Constitution. This unsurmountable bar is expressed by the Constitution in the same way as, e.g., for infants, by requiring that all executive officers shall bind themselves by oath or affirmation to support the Constitution, Article VI, Section 3.

A non-resident alien owing allegiance to Panama can obviously not swear that oath. Further, the Constitution provides that all executive officers can be removed from office on impeachement for, and conviction of, treason, Article II, Section 4.[77]

However, the Department of Justice did not agree and in the February 28, 1979 statement made by H. Miles Foy, an attorney-adviser, attempted to justify, before the House Subcommittee on the Panama Canal, President Carter's appointments of Panamanians as officers of the Panama Canal Commission, as provided in the Panama Canal Treaty of 1977.[78] Foy's argument was, in the main, that the Panamanians were not "officers of the U.S. in the constitutional sense," and therefore, not subject to the provisions of the U.S. Constitution.

However, this interpretation was not supported by any documentation or citation. And Foy's argument was, in effect, rejected by the Subcommittee—and later, by the full Congress in the Panama Canal Act of 1979. Moreover, the Section by Section Analysis of this act states on page 41:

The nine members of the Board of the Canal Commission, on the other hand, are clearly officers of the Executive Branch.[79]

Article II, Section 2 of the Constitution requires Senate confirmation of "Officers of the United States." Therefore, constitutionally, these four Panamanians cannot be excluded from Senate confirmation. Moreover, the provisions of the Panama Canal Act of 1979 requiring that only U.S. "directors" be subject to the Senate's confirmation are without precedent and cannot be carried out without violating the Constitution.

Of course, non-resident aliens cannot qualify as "Officers of the United States" because they cannot swear to support the U.S. Constitution nor be tried for treason as the Constitution stipulates for all executive officers.

In a further development, the Chairman of the House Subcommittee on the Panama Canal, Democrat Carroll Hubbard, Jr. of Kentucky, asked President Reagan on April 7, 1981 if it were constitutional to use appropriated funds to pay expenses of the Panamanians on the Panama Canal Commission. Thirteen months later, on May 17, 1982, the answer came from the Justice Department stating that such payments were justified for "aliens who perform services deemed worthwhile" as in the "employment of aliens in the Departments of Defense and State."[80]

Again, an important principle was by-passed. The "employment of aliens" in the Departments of Defense and State is entirely different from presidential appointments as "Officers of the United States." No precedent or authority was cited for the appointment of non-resident aliens as federal officers.

Chief Justice Burger said in a 1978 case: "The right to govern is reserved to citizens," thus excluding even resident aliens.[81]

And once again—as with the failure to get the Senate's approval of a major change in the Treaties, the failure to abrogate properly the 1903 Treaty, and the exclusion of the House of Representatives from its role in disposing of U.S. property—once again, the Constitution was trampled upon: this time with the appointment of non-resident aliens as U.S. officials.

James Madison said, "Wherever the real power in a government lies, there is the danger of oppression." And Associate Justice Hugo L. Black: "Ours is a government of divided authority based on the assumption that in division there is not only strength but freedom from tyranny."[82]

Obviously, the "real power" in American government lies in the Executive Branch, particularly in the Office of the President in claiming authority it does not possess. The Congress itself allowed this to happen. Professor Berger told the Senators, i.e., those who would listen, "If Congress slumbers in the face of such claims, it will awaken like Samson shorn of his locks."

The President, the Senators and Representatives, and all executive and judicial officers of the United States and all military officers, as well as state officers and legislators, under Article VI of the Constitution, are "bound by Oath or Affirmation to support this Constitution," and to execute faithfully the duties of office.

The President's oath is prescribed under Article II, Section 1, Clause 8:

I do solemnly swear (or affirm) that I will faithfully execute the Office of President of the United States, and will to the best of my Ability, preserve, protect and defend the Constitution of the United States.

Were these oaths of office observed by the President and by the leaders in the Senate, as well as by certain Ambassadors and other U.S. officers in the Department of State, in their individual and collective handling of the Panama Canal Treaties of 1977 and in the abrogation of the 1903 Canal Treaty?

1. In the advice and consent function of Article II, Section 2?

2. In the disposal of U.S. territory or other property under Article IV, Section 3?

3. In the abrogation of the 1903 Treaty as a "supreme Law of the Land" under Article VI, Clause 2?

Much evidence supports negative answers to these questions—indeed, sustains the conclusion that political expediency and legislative "efficiency" won out over old-fashioned "anachronistic" constitutional government.

One other question. Where were the Parliamentarians, Murray Zweben for the Senate and William Holmes Brown for the House of Representatives, when the established parliamentary procedures of *Jefferson's Manual* and Articles II, IV and VI of the Constitution were being by-passed in the processing of the Treaties through the Congress? Both the Senate and the House use Parliamentarians, appointed by the leadership of each body, to assist not only in correct parliamentary decisions but also to keep the practices and precedents uniform.[83]

Perhaps we have just asked an academic question when it is perfectly obvious that the leadership in both Houses can use, or prescribe, whatever rules or procedures are necessary in order to get the desired result—if the stakes are high enough.

· 11 ·

THE KEY TO THE WESTERN HEMISPHERE

When Horatio Bunch reached the end of the furrow he was plowing that summer day in 1828, Davy Crockett was waiting for him. Colonel Crockett needed votes for reelection to the House of Representatives. Mr. Bunch gave him a sockdolager instead, "I'll not vote for you again." The problem was Crockett's vote to give $20,000 to victims of a fire in George-town. Bunch asked, "Where do you find in the Constitution any authority to give away public money in charity? . . . The power of collecting and distributing money at pleasure is the most dangerous power that can be intrusted to man."[1] Crockett confessed the error and his Tennessee constit-uents returned him to Congress—and by 1986 $300 billion of public money went to federal charity programs.

In 1828, however, the nation was young and demanded honesty and accountability. Only a few years earlier, in 1823, the Monroe Doctrine had proclaimed to the world that future colonization in the Americas would be a "manifestation of an unfriendly disposition towards the United States."[2] President James Monroe announced his famous doctrine on December 2, 1823, after consulting with Thomas Jefferson and James Madison about the advances of Russia's Tsar Alexander I, whose forces had pressed almost to San Francisco Bay. Alexander's ukase had declared the Northern Pacific closed to navigation. The Spanish empire, with title to California, was disintegrating and the Cossacks were moving into the vacuum.[3]

Monroe's Secretary of State, John Quincy Adams, warned Russia's

Baron Tuyll on July 17, 1823, that the U.S. would contest *any* territorial establishment on the American continent. Tuyll responded that the Emperor would guarantee "the tranquillity of all States of which the civilized world is composed," a 19th century progenitor to the 20th century Soviet objective to dominate the world. Adams promptly advised Tuyll that such guarantees had better "be limited to the affairs of Europe" and could not "embrace the United States of America, nor any portion of the American Hemisphere."

'NOT ... SUBJECTS FOR FUTURE COLONIZATION'

Adams's declaration became the theme of the Monroe Doctrine which soon followed and which stated in part:

... the occasion has been judged proper for asserting, as a principle in which the rights and interests of the United States are involved, that the American continents, by the free and independent condition which they have assumed and maintain, are henceforth not to be considered as subjects for future colonization by any European power.

We owe it, therefore, to candor and to the amicable relations existing between the United States and those Powers, to declare, that we should consider any attempt on their part to extend their system to any portion of this hemisphere, as dangerous to our peace and safety. With the existing colonies or dependencies of any European Power, we have not interfered, and shall not interfere. But, with the Governments who have declared their independence, and maintained it, and whose independence we have, on great consideration, and on just principles, acknowledged, we could not view any interposition for the purpose of oppressing them, or controlling, in any other manner, their destiny, by any European Power in any other light than as the manifestation of an unfriendly disposition towards the United States.[4]

Sounding much like a Soviet Gorbachev of 1986, Alexander denounced the Monroe Doctrine as exaggerating "principles so contrary to the rights of European powers that it merits only the most profound contempt." Even so, the Doctrine prevailed and at the April 5-17, 1824 convention, the Tsar withdrew his claim to the North Pacific and made other concessions.

Twenty-two years later, President James K. Polk, the doughty North Carolinian, "cut quite a figure when contrasted with modern makers of American policy" by invoking the Doctrine three times (1845-1849): in 1845 against British and French designs on Texas; in 1847 against British plans for Oregon and California; and in 1848 in protecting the inhabitants of Yucatan from Indian warriors and blocking any European take over. Polk had added a Corollary to the Doctrine: The U.S. would oppose even the *voluntary* transfer of territory to any European power.[5]

President Ulysses S. Grant strengthened the "No Transfer" Corollary in two instances during the Civil War: The first was France's installation of Archduke Maximilian as Emperor of Mexico and the second was Spain's attempt to re-annex Santo Domingo. Astute diplomacy by President Lincoln and the persuasive power of General Philip Sheridan's 50,000 troops convinced both powers to abandon their adventures.

In 1895 President Grover Cleveland added his Corollary when settling by arbitration the boundary dispute between British Guiana and Venezuela: No advance of frontiers by European *systems* in the Americas.[6] The Monroe Doctrine became the foundation of American foreign policy for the Western Hemisphere. Alfred Thayer Mahan, the naval strategist, wrote, "The Monroe Doctrine centers around the Ishtmus of Panama."[7] Charles Evans Hughes said, "The Monroe Doctrine is not a policy of aggression: it is a policy of self-defense...."[8]

The Monroe Doctrine was a shield against aggression until the Bay of Pigs debacle in April 1961 when President John Kennedy reneged on his promise of air cover for the Cubans trying to retake their homeland. Thereafter, Castro remained entrenched and Kennedy became the first President to allow a major crack in the Monroe Doctrine.

Alarmed at communist successes in the Caribbean, the Congress on October 3, 1962 adopted a Resolution (P.L. 87-733), based on the Monroe Doctrine and vowing to prevent Marxist "subversive activities" in this hemisphere. It was on time for the October 22-28, 1962 Cuban missile crisis; it was also a grand piece of rhetoric. After the missiles had supposedly been removed, Castro continued exporting his revolution unmolested.

The following examples illustrate activities that helped the communists. On March 20, 1984, the House of Representatives Majority Leader, Jim Wright, along with nine other Congressmen, in disregard of the Logan Act, sent a joint letter to the communist leader of Nicaragua, undercutting President Reagan and pledging their support for Commandante Daniel Ortega's plans for democracy, and asserting opposition to U.S. "action directed against . . . Nicaragua." The other Democrats were Michael Barnes (Md.), Bill Alexander (Ark.), Matthew McHugh (N.Y.), Robert Torricelli (N.J.), Edward Boland (Mass.), Stephen Solarz (N.Y.), David Obey (Wis.), Robert Garcia (N.Y.), and Lee Hamilton (Ind.). In another 1984 activity, the Rev. Jesse Jackson visited Nicaragua, Cuba, and El Salvador, praising communist programs for those countries and criticizing the U.S., another violation of the Logan Act (18 U.S.C. 953).

The Attorney General, William French Smith, was silent. His assistant, Mr. John L. Martin, advised the author that he could not prove that anyone "communicated with a foreign government . . . with intent to influence the measures of the U.S. . . . and no investigation will be conducted." This answer was produced after some 15 letters back and forth, 75 days, and intervention by two Senators and one Congressman. Mr. Martin also said he had "no judicial precedents."[9]

Two recent Presidents used the Monroe Doctrine: Lyndon Johnson sent in the Marines in April 1965 to prevent a communist take over in the Dominican Republic. And in October 1983, Ronald Reagan routed the communists from Grenada to the cheers of the conservative world and to the jeers of the Soviets and the U.S. media, the latter livid because they were not invited along. In both cases the Presidents stood their ground and the general public gave them high marks.

President Carter set his own record, with two cracks in the Monroe Doctrine: (1) aid to the communist Sandinistas in their conquest of Nicaragua, and (2) surrender of the Panama Canal (the Key to the Western Hemisphere) to the pro-communist regime of Omar Torrijos. While James Polk, with scant military power, stood his ground three times before superior European might, John Kennedy and Jimmy Carter, with military supremacy, blinked. Mr. Carter's legacy will likely be the Panama Canal Treaties.

Soviet satellites (colonies) in the Western Hemisphere violate the letter and spirit of the Monroe Doctrine. Nonetheless, on September 15, 1983, the Senate by a vote of 60 to 36 tabled Senator Helms's motion to ask the President to "re-emphasize the inconsistency of the Soviet military presence in the Western Hemisphere with the Monroe Doctrine."[10] Many of the Senators who tabled this mention of the Monroe Doctrine also had voted to surrender the Canal a few years earlier.

The face down between President Monroe and the Russian Tsar took place during the lifetime of Commodore Matthew C. Perry (1794-1856), the great U.S. naval leader, who said shortly before his death:

It requires no sage to predict events so strongly foreshadowed . . . the Saxon and the Cossack will meet once more, in strife or in friendship, on another field. . . . The antagonistic exponents of freedom and absolutism must thus meet at last, and then will be fought that mighty battle on which the world will look with breathless interest; for on its issue will depend the freedom or slavery of the world. . . . I think I see in the distance the giants that are growing up for that fierce and final encounter; . . . that battle must sooner or later be fought.[11]

WHAT THE NEW TREATIES PURPORT TO DO

The Panama Canal ranks among the greatest engineering feats of all time. Its heroes include John F. Stevens, chief engineer and basic architect of the Canal (1905-1907); Army Colonel George W. Goethals, chief engineer (1907-1914); Dr. William C. Gorgas whose medical team cleared the

Isthmus of yellow fever, cholera, and malaria; and President Teddy Roosevelt whose leadership launched the project.[12]

Future archaeologists will marvel at a civilization that could construct such a wonder of the world. Thirty-four years in building, the Canal and Zone cost $561.5 million in 1914, and was valued at $10 billion in 1977.[13] Its six sets of 1000-foot "paired" locks lift ships 85 feet to cross the Continental Divide, then down to sea level in the 51 mile transit of the Isthmus. Two man made lakes, Gatun and Miraflores, store the water for the locks. Much of the original equipment is still in service, although maintenance standards are reported deteriorating since implementing the new Treaties.[14]

The Canal system became the responsibility of the Panama Canal Commission on October 1, 1979 when its Board of five Americans and four Panamanians took over. On that date Panama assumed sovereignty over the Canal and Canal Zone, taking over police and court authority. Upon termination of the Panama Canal Treaty on December 31, 1999, Panama will assume full responsibility for the Canal system, and all U.S. military forces must have departed. Defense of the Canal remains primarily the responsibility of the U.S. through 1999 with the Panama-based Southern Command, comprising some 10,000 personnel: the 193rd Infantry Brigade and supporting Air Force and Navy units. Under the Neutrality Treaty, both nations shall continue indefinitely to have the right to defend the Canal.

The Treaties are monuments to deception and confrontation. Panama's Foreign Ministry Communique of April 25, 1978 (Appendix S) denounced all U.S. changes, and repudiated the DeConcini reservation five times, as explained by Phillip Harman in testifying before the East Subcommittee:

... believing that the leadership amendment (to the second treaty) eliminated U.S. unilateral rights in the DeConcini Condition, Panama then inserted the DeConcini Condition in their instrument of ratification of the Neutrality Treaty. Furthermore, not once, but several times, Panama's belief that the unilateral language in the DeConcini Condition was eliminated by the leadership amendment is publicized in their Communique:

1. Via diplomatic channels the national government firmly expressed its *rejection* of that amendment . . . (the DeConcini Condition).

2. . . . . there would not be the slightest doubt that the DeConcini amendment added to the Neutrality Treaty would *not continue in force*.

3. The specter of new interventions at the end of the 20th century, which rightly

caused concern to all Panamanians, has been *eliminated* (the DeConcini Condition).

4. Therefore our citizens expressed with righteous firmness their *repudiation* of Senator DeConcini's words used in explaining his amendment.

5. With it the DeConcini reservation *has been rid of* its imperialistic and interventionist claws. . . .[15] (Emphasis added)

Mr. Douglas Bennett, Assistant Secretary of State, in his letter of June 14, 1978 told Senator Helms that Panama's Communique had "no legal effect."[16] Communiques, however, are comparable with U.S. State Department Bulletins; and the term "via diplomatic channels" is used in official notifications, in this case rejection of the DeConcini reservation, as explained in detail at the East hearing. Did State prefer to keep the point ambiguous in order not to complicate the ratification schedule since the Senate had already approved the Treaties?

Omar Torrijos also repudiated U.S. rights under the DeConcini reservation (Appendix T), telling a *La Prensa* reporter in 1980:

In order to have intervention, there has to be a reason to intervene. If some day this intervention does arise, it will find a country that does not want to be intervened. And if the intervention is to defend the Canal, what they may get is the impossibility of traffic through it.[17]

Earlier Torrijos had said, "Panama in no way intends to allow the United States to unilaterally use armed forces on Panamanian territory for the purpose of defending the Canal's neutrality." Panama's chief negotiator, Romulo Escobar Bethancourt, agreed, "Those are the facts of the matter and we are not giving the United States the right of intervention."[18]

PANAMA CRITICIZES U.S. TREATY CHANGES

In addition to rejecting the DeConcini reservation, the Panamanian Communique also discredited the other five U.S. changes—changes constitutionally approved by the U.S. Senate, but not voted on in Panama by plebiscite as required by its Constitution for substantive changes. The Communique rejected the Hollings-Heinz-Bellmon Reservation that clarified the fact that Panama would receive *no* roll over payment when the Canal is turned over in the year 2000 for the reason that none would have been earned under Article XI of the Panama Canal Treaty. Panama anticipated $10 million per year, but since the toll base planned no surplus money, there would be none.

The Communique also found fault with the Brooke Reservation for delaying ratification in order to allow time for orderly transition; with the

Nunn Reservation for proposing future negotiations for stationing U.S. troops in Panama after the year 2000; with the Cannon Reservation for reimbursing the U.S. Treasury for interest on investment and amortization of assets; and with the Dansforth Understanding that Canal tolls would not be raised for contingency payments to Panama.[19] In reiterating its grievances, Panama casts serious doubt about good faith and cooperation in accepting the Treaties. Erroneously claiming rights to payment of $10 million annually under Article XIII, paragraph (4)(b) and to another $10 million under paragraph (4)(c), the Communique fairly bursts into threats:

By virtue of the principle of good faith which prevails in the observance of the Treaties, Panama expects the United States to accomodate its policy on expenditures so that this article (Article XIII (4) (b) and (c)) can be the means by which Panama receives a fairer retribution for its contribution to the Canal work. To the extent that the Panamanian people are satisfied with the Canal administration due to the products they derive from it, they will continue protecting their Canal. But if a stingy spirit prevails, aggravating the injustice suffered by Panama since 1903, then a circle of friendship will not have been built around the Canal but rather one of hatred, with possible grave consequences if a crisis occurs which the national government would be the first to deplore.[20]

The Senate deserves credit for protecting taxpayers from the ambiguous language of Article XIII, which was a ploy by the negotiators apparently to get the Panamanians to sign. The Senate's changes, however, removed uncertainties: There would be no payments because there would be no profits. Panama's Communique is hypocritical. First, it incites the people to react if America's "stingy spirit" withholds payments of $20 million annually. Next, it expresses unwillingness to protect the Canal, even "grave consequences" if the people are not paid a "fairer retribution." Finally, the Communique says, if a crisis does occur, "the national government would be the first to deplore it." Thus, Panama would create the crisis, then deplore it.

Perhaps the Senate's concern over $20 million was only academic; there are other ways to milk the treasury. Panama received grants of $30 million in 1984 and $22 million in 1985 after changing its official position on tax cases involving U.S. employees of the Canal Commission. The switch benefitted the Internal Revenue Service and the State Department which arranged the $52 million direct grants.

In his analysis of the Communique on June 5, 1978, ten days before President Carter ratified the Treaties, Senator Helms warned the Senate: "It says to the American people that the treaty does not represent a true agreement, a true meeting of minds, but is a transparent device for a rapid and total take over of the Canal. For the President to ratify the Treaties under such circumstances would be to break faith with the Senate and the American people."[21] It is clear, he said, that Panama purports to accept the Treaties only as a short term tactical maneuver, as evidenced by the following paragraph:

The achievements obtained in the negotiations are conquests which belong to the Panamanian people. They cannot be destroyed or renounced but can be taken to their ultimate culmination by future generations. Let us strengthen these conquests, the most feasible now, and when better circumstances for struggle exist, we will again undertake the task to improve the terms of the relationship.

'GREATEST LEGAL MESS IN HISTORY'

The late Dr. Charles H. Breecher called the invalid Panama Treaties "the greatest legal mess in history, carefully covered up to date." Much of the "mess" resulted from differing forms of government in the two countries. In Panama, in effect, the dictator approved the Treaties. In the U.S. the President accepted provisional treaties subject to change by the Senate. Panama held a plebiscite, but Torrijos ran it, prompting Senator Barry Goldwater, R.-Ariz., to observe during the testimony of Herbert J. Hansell before the Senate Armed Services Committee on February 1, 1978:

Now you discussed the [Panamanian] Constitution. Isn't it true that General Torrijos in an election prints the ballots and supervises the voting of the ballots by the National Guard? . . . I think it is about as crooked a way to hold an election as I can think of, and I would not put any stock at all in the statement that the Panamanian people approved this treaty.[22]

The specter of the double standard comes to mind: In the right wing government of El Salvador, for example, Senators and Congressmen had no compunctions about going into that country on March 25, 1984 in order to certify the fairness of the national election. But, for the left wing regime of Panama, such intrusion to observe a plebiscite for transferring one of America's greatest assets would have been unheard of.

The legality of the Treaties was the theme of the East Subcommittee hearing in 1983. In the U.S., invalid Treaties resulted from errors in the advice and consent function, in abrogating the old treaty, and in disposing of U.S. territory. In Panama, invalid Treaties were caused by failure to hold a second plebiscite for approval of the U.S. changes and because President Lakas did not sign the Treaties; both were violations of Panama's 1972 Constitution. Based on documented legal opinions from the top Panamanian and U.S. authorities on Panamanian law, in evidence before the East hearing, the conclusion was "overwhelming that the 1977 Panama Canal Treaties have not been ratified properly by the government of Panama under their domestic law [constitutional law]."[23]

Dr. Julio Linares, professor of law, said on Panama National Television on January 25, 1978:

If the treaty is approved by the U.S. Senate with reservations and those reservations require an amendment to the . . . treaty, it is undeniable that it will have to be submitted to a plebiscite in order for Panama to be able to accept it.[24]

Dr. Cesar Quintero, Dean of the Law and Political Science School of the University of Panama, noted that the plebiscite should include the Carter-Torrijos Statement of Understanding (the leadership amendment).[25] Similar views were expressed by Carlos Bolivar Pedreschi, a leading constitutional scholar; by Eduardo Abbot, Hispanic law expert for the Library of Congress; and by Dr. Arnulfo Arias, a former three-time President of Panama.

Dr. L. Oppenheim in his *International Law* (para. 517) wrote that treaties violating constitutional procedures are not legally binding:

That occasionally a State tries to modify a treaty while ratifying it cannot be denied; but conditional ratification is not ratification at all, but is equivalent to refusal of ratification coupled with a fresh offer which may or may not be accepted.

Panama's Head of Government, Omar Torrijos, signed the Treaties, whereas, Article 163 of the Constitution of Panama states that the "president of the Republic alone" is authorized to "conduct foreign affairs . . . and to enter into international treaties and agreements."[26] Mr. Alfred J. Schweppe, international treaty expert, observed: "Certainly anyone reading the Constitution of Panama has to conclude that the signature [on the Treaties] is void unless supplemented by the signature of the qualified constitutional officer [in this case, Demetrio Lakas]."[27] The issue was sidestepped. The State Department applied Article 277 which gave Torrijos power "to direct foreign relations." "A weak left-handed answer," said Mr. Schweppe, "it requires a good deal of liberty to construe 'to direct foreign relations' as including the power to sign treaties."[28] In Panama, contending that Torrijos illegally signed the Treaties, the Independent Lawyers Movement sued to suspend the 1977 plebiscite. Panama's Supreme Court ruled the suit "inadmissible."[29]

The Canal Administrator, Lt. General Dennis P. McAuliffe, U.S. Army (Ret.), reported the Canal "alive and well" in his article in *The Retired Officer Magazine* of October 1982, with near-perfect services, improved traffic control, and binational cooperation to "help ensure that the waterway will continue to operate effectively at no cost to the U.S. taxpayer."[30] Contrary findings were reported by William Wright in his articles in *The Washington Times* in late summer 1982. Wright, a bilingualist and long on Canal experience, interviewed over 25 employees during two transits of the Canal, including senior pilots and key operators. He described maintenance and operational problems: a three-weeks out of commission status of backup gates for Miraflores Locks; inadequate mosquito control; and deteriorating morale. Veteran pilot Joe Christian said, "I reckon that on about 75% of my trips something goes wrong either with a piece of machinery or because somebody is not doing his job."[31] Periodic reports from Captain John Wallace, another senior pilot, indicated problems in operations and morale, particularly, he said, a new policy of retiring U.S. pilots "if not 100% physically fit" in order to make way for the Panamanian pilots.

THE VALUE OF A 'VITAL MARITIME GATEWAY'

The Panama Canal is one of the world's four vital maritime gateways. The others are the Suez Canal, the Gibraltar Straits, and the Malacca Straits; whoever controls them has major strategic and economic leverage. The United States lost its leverage at Panama. Admiral Thomas H. Moorer, former Chairman of the Joint Chiefs of Staff (1970-1974), testified before the Congress as an experienced naval strategist concerned with loss of the Canal, "I have yet to hear any convincing justification. . . . In military affairs, there is no substitute for the ownership of the territory and the ability to control or deny the waters and air space." An earlier Chairman of the JCS (1962-1964) disagreed. General Maxwell D. Taylor, U.S. Army (Ret.), observed, during his testimony before the Senate Foreign Relations Committee on October 10, 1977, "Under the terms of these Treaties, the U.S. and Panama would be bound in partnership based on self-interest. . . ."[32]

In his testimony, Admiral Moorer feared loss of priority use of the Canal by the U.S. Fleet, saying, "We don't have any contingency plans of note that don't assume [our] priority passage through a secure Canal." As Pacific Fleet Commander, Admiral Moorer depended on the Atlantic side for rapid logistic support through the Canal. The Canal was essential for the Korean and Vietnam operations, and during the Cuban missile crisis; and, he noted, without question the availability of the Canal shortened World War II by many months.[33] As for the aircraft carriers that cannot transit the Canal, these ships, said Moorer, must be prepositioned at times of international tensions and other routes "are safer than the Soviet-infested waters of the Caribbean."[34]

In January 1978, the Chief of Naval Operations, Admiral James L. Holloway III defended the down-grading of the Canal from "vital" to "major" asset. This switch helped the Treaties through the Senate. Admiral Holloway added, ". . . without access to the Canal, the U.S. could still accomplish its defense mission although it would be extremely difficult."

Four former CNOs did not agree, and sent President Carter a joint letter dated June 8, 1977 (Appendix H), two months before negotiations ended. Admirals Moorer, Arleigh A. Burke, Robert B. Carney, and George Anderson advised the Commander-in-Chief:

The Panama Canal represents a vital portion of our U.S. naval and maritime assets, all of which are absolutely essential for free world security. It is our considered individual and combined judgment that you should instruct our negotiators to retain full sovereign control for the United States over both the Panama Canal and its protective frame, the U.S. Canal Zone as provided in the existing treaty.

The admirals' advice to Mr. Carter, virtually ignored by the media, was in stark contrast to the State Department's allegations down-grading the importance of the Canal. Said the admirals, "Contrary to what we read about the declining strategic and economic value of the Canal, the truth is that this inter-oceanic waterway is as important, if not more so, to the United States than ever."

The strategic and economic value of the Isthmus of Panama remains undiminished. Alaskan oil is transshiped via the Panama Pipeline; and critical materials and manufactured goods pass through the Canal and the Caribbean as always. The Treaties grant to the U.S. the right to improve the Canal, hardly an inspiring option, however, for property under Panamanian sovereign ownership. At a 1982 conference on trans-Isthmian transportation, Japan, Panama, and the U.S. discussed the sea level option. Panama's conferee preferred modernization of the existing canal, but the matter of who pays was left on the table.[35] On September 5, 1985 a four-year trilateral feasibility study of both options, costing $20 million, was announced. Meanwhile in Nicaragua, said the Intelligence Digest of England, the Soviets are doing their own unilateral feasibility study for a trans-oceanic canal along the San Juan River.

THE TERMINAL LAKE—THIRD LOCKS PLAN

A realistic Canal modernization plan was presented on May 20, 1943 to high Canal officials by the Navy Captain of the Port of Balboa, Commander Miles P. DuVal, Jr. His plan won immediate support from experienced operators and engineers, and later, from two Canal Zone Governors and President Franklin D. Roosevelt. Called the Terminal Lake—Third Locks Plan, it was based on ease and safety of operations—best for engineering and best for navigation.[36] Operational problems included the bottleneck at Pedro Miguel, double handling of ships on the Pacific side, and surges in water level caused by operating the Pedro Miguel Locks. Night fogs were also troublesome.

Basically, DuVal's plan would remove the Pedro Miguel Locks and elevate Miraflores Lake and Gatun Lake from 87 to 92 feet, thereby providing uninterrupted transit between the Atlantic locks and the Pacific locks. For larger vessels, widening of Gaillard Cut and expanded locks would be required. By 1970 widening of the Cut and partial excavations for a third locks had been completed at a cost of $171 million.[37]

Captain DuVal testified many times before Congress about his plan which, if executed, would make him the "architect of the future Canal." He had based his proposal on the design of the Frenchman, Adolphe Godin de Lepinay, who warned Ferdinand de Lesseps, the hero of the Suez Canal, that a sea level canal in Panama would be a "great disaster." He was correct, as the de Lesseps sea level project later went bankrupt. On that day in 1879 in Paris, de Lepinay said:

Build a dam at Gatun and another at Miraflores. . . . Let the waters rise to form two lakes about 80 feet high, join the lakes with a channel cut through the Continental Divide, and connect the lakes with the oceans by locks.

Although the Treaties provide for U.S. rights to improve the Canal and for joint studies, practical considerations of ownership and sovereignty demand prudence. Experienced authorities stress that major modernization "be undertaken at no risk to the U.S. taxpayers and investors, and only under the undiluted sovereign control of the United States over both the Canal and its indispensable protective territorial frame."[39] This is impossible with the 1977 Treaties.

THE 1983 SENATE INQUIRY INTO TREATY RATIFICATION

Five years after the Treaties were ratified and after irregularities had surfaced, the Senate Subcommittee on Separation of Powers conducted a three-hour hearing under Chairman John P. East, R.-N.C., who deserves credit for his willingness. The theme of the June 23, 1983 inquiry was the President's failure to obtain Senate approval of Panama's counter-reservation. Senator East said, "I don't think we got what we thought we were getting" on the fundamental question of separation of powers where the Executive Branch can "diminish what power we were sharing" and declare a *fait accompli*.[39]

The record of the East hearing is 404 pages of documentation and testimony (Senate Document 98-452). The following conclusions can be drawn although none are formally stated:

—U.S. rights to defend and keep open the Canal with troops were not agreed to by Panama.

—The Executive Branch failed to observe the constitutional requirement for Senate advice and consent to Panama's counter-reservation, thereby violating the separation of powers.

—The assignment of non-resident aliens as U.S. officers on the Panama Canal Commission was unconstitutional.

Four of five Subcommittee members were absent: Jeremiah Denton, R.-Ala.; Alan Simpson, R.-Wy.; Max Baucus, D.-Mont.; and Howard Metzenbaum, D.-Ohio—because, said East, "business in the Senate." Senators Helms and Paul Laxalt, R.-Nev., testified briefly. At one point, when East left to vote in the Senate chamber, it seemed weird to see witnesses testifying to bare walls for a record that was to be placed on the shelf—a record of incriminating evidence on what has been called the "worst fraud."

The deposition of Dr. Charles H. Breecher was under oath, at his request. Senator East did not require sworn testimony, he said, because this was not "an inquiry into facts" but only "opinions and interpretations of facts." Strange. Must not facts be established first, then interpreted? Other witnesses were Robert Dalton, a State legal adviser, Dr. Herbert Dodge, a retired Foreign Service Officer, and Phillip Harman, all of whom testified elegantly and freely.

The hearing appeared primarily to be an exercise in appeasement to placate the complaining witnesses. Mr. Dalton, however, was defending the State Department; he read a long statement that asserted, in effect, "We are right, you are wrong." A special counsel with subpoena power could have summoned the treaty-makers and *established facts* under oath with questions such as the following: Did State show Panama's counter-reservation to the Senate leadership? To Senator Byrd? To Baker? To Sparkman? When and where exactly? Who were the State officials? What did the Senate leaders say? Provide a copy of the State Department records to prove that this consultation took place. When did President Carter first see Panama's counter-reservation? What did he do? What did he mean by telling Torrijos to write his own reservation? What did Mr. Popper mean by saying that "ambiguity was essential?" (However, like medicine, politics is an art, not a science.)

MEDIA NOT INTERESTED IN UNCONSTITUTIONAL TREATIES

The national media virtually ignored the East hearing although 26 of their Washington representatives had been notified well in advance and informed of the subject matter. Word of mouth and routine legal

announcements in *The Washington Times* and *Washington Post* were sufficient, however, to fill the committee room.

Television officials were asked why they belittled an issue so disturbing to 80% of the public a few years ago. Emerson Stone of CBS said he
had other stories "deemed of greater interest."[40] ABC's George Watson was
covering the budget and besides, he wrote, all major media "reached
approximately the same judgment" about the East inquiry.[41] William Placek of NBC "could cover only so many stories" and East was out.[42]

The major print media were also advised, including the Associated
Press, United Press International, *New York Times, Washington Post, U.S.
News & World Report,* and *Wall Street Journal,* but none were interested.
The conservative media responded with stories by the Copley News Service, Knight-Ridder newspapers, *The Spotlight,* and *The Washington
Inquirer.* Consequently, Americans received minimum coverage on an
inquiry that left grave questions unanswered about constitutional procedures and fraudulent international agreements that purported to surrender a priceless military and economic asset to an unstable Latin dictator
against the people's will just five years before.

In contrast, in 1977-78 the Canal was front page almost daily with the
media promoting ratification and "justice for Panama." For example,
ABC's Geraldo Rivera admitted in a *Playboy* magazine interview that he
slanted his stories to fit his bias, particularly when the Senate was about to
vote on the Neutrality Treaty and Panama threatened rioting. "That was
the day," said Rivera, "that I had to be careful . . . because I could defeat . . .
what I wanted to achieve [passage of the treaty]."[43] Later he was ebullient
at having helped develop American foreign policy. The Panama Treaties
were one of the most discussed foreign affairs subjects in history. In 1983-
84, as in 1977-78, evidence of impropriety concerning them was minimized by the media or omitted entirely.[44]

In the mid-1970s, when it appeared the Canal was in danger, many
citizens organized into groups. Among these bodies were the following:
Save the Panama Canal Club, James H. Townsend, Chairman, with
165,000 members; Canal Zone Public Information Non-Profit Organization, Phillip Harman, Director; Emergency Committee to Save the U.S.
Canal Zone, Donald M. Dozer, Chairman; Not One Square Inch, Ralph
Winkler, Chairman. There were others, one in the Canal Zone.

Among other individuals particularly active were Charles H. Breecher, Carl R. Hoffmann, Jr., Frank B. Turberville, Jr., Alfred J. Schweppe,
John C. Webb, Jr., Ann Lenick, Arthur L. Denchfield, Jr., Deming Hobart,
Dorothy Bursey, Herbert W. Dodge, and Spruille Braden. Two active and
well-informed groups still keeping alive the specter of invalid Treaties in

1986 are Harman's Committee for Better Panama and U.S. Relations, and Turberville's Canal Watchers' Educational Association.

Many respected national organizations opposed loss of the Canal: American Legion, Propeller Clubs, Veterans of Foreign Wars, American Conservative Union, Heritage Foundation, American Security Council, and Military Order of the World Wars. There were many others.

On the other side were the mainline churches, supporting the Treaties as "justice for Panama," including the U.S. Catholic Conference, National Council of Churches, United Methodist Church, United Presbyterian Church, Episcopal Church, and many others. The bishops and other church leaders were prolific, undoubtedly influencing parishioners who in turn contacted their Senators.[45] Many resolutions and statements, however, were deceptive. For example, Methodist Bishop William Cannon told his flock, "All we did was rent the territory" and let's "do unto others as we would have others do unto us."[46] He was mistaken. The U.S., of course, did *not* rent the Canal Zone, but bought it four times with taxpayers' money from the U.S. Treasury. And the Golden Rule (Matt. 7:12, KJV), it appears, would be Panama's problem in coveting property it did not own. Perhaps the Eighth Commandment, "Thou shalt not steal" (Ex. 20:15, KJV), would be a more appropriate moral lesson.

In another case, the Rev. L. M. McCoy of the United Methodist Church called the 1903 Treaties "immoral" and "usurpation of the national sovereignty of Panama," obviously without real knowledge of the facts and circumstances. The issue goes far beyond prideful Latin sovereignty; it involves the strategic Key to the Western Hemisphere, guarded for generations by the North Americans. Should not church leaders speak for their country as well as for their denominations? It is inexcusable for the church in the United States to misrepresent the issue when correct information is plentifully available in the *Congressional Record* and in the libraries of the land.[47]

President Carter reflects a somber mood as he
views the operation of the Canal at Miraflores
Locks on June 17, 1978, the day after he had rati-
fied the Panama Treaties, the "final act" in the
planned surrender of this strategic asset.
Implementing legislation remained to be enacted;
and questions of constitutionality of the
Treaties have not been resolved.
(AP/Wide World Photos)

· 12 ·

THE FUTURE OF 'SHARED CONSTITUTIONAL POWER'

While President Carter was savoring one of his "proudest moments," i.e., the ratification of the Panama Canal Treaties in 1978, he was also leaving behind a legacy of what has been characterized as swindles and smoking guns, together with a plethora of unanswered questions about the procedures he used to get the Treaties through. Virtually every effort to get answers has been stonewalled or covered up. This was officially and abundantly clear from the testimony at the East Subcommittee hearing.

Every swindle and smoking gun was related to the one single issue that was never agreed to: U.S. rights to defend or open the Canal. The treaty-makers succeeded in obscuring these rights to the very end. Perhaps the worst swindle was Mr. Carter's failure to get the Senate's "Advice and Consent" to Panama's last minute reservation that killed U.S. rights. And the hottest smoking gun was Ambassador Popper's admission that "ambiguity was essential" in order to get ratification. The surprise, of course, was the admission of ambiguity—not the ambiguity itself.

Our story has documented each transgression and woven a pattern of deception and cover up at the highest levels of government. The story includes substantial evidence that the Treaties unquestionably are suspect, portending future embarrassments and confrontation. National security is very much involved.

Was there a meeting of minds on these Treaties? No. Mr. Carter said, the United States "could always send in troops." Torrijos said, try it and you will get the "impossibility of traffic" through the Canal. The Treaties said, "head of line" for U.S. warships. Panama's Bethancourt said, "If the Gringos with their warships say, 'I want to go first,' then, that is their problem. We cannot go that far."

Americans deserve to know why the Panama Canal, that precious jewel in the crown of America, was lost almost totally against their will and how the national government, Executive and Legislative, can by-pass constitutional procedures with impunity. The apparent disregard, in several particulars, for the Constitution, oaths of office and international treaty law is even more threatening than the loss of the Canal. Indeed, the focus of the East Subcommittee was on diminished constitutional power for the U.S. Senate. Even so, the Senate allowed it to happen. In summing up the constitutional aspects, Mr. East said:

I am convinced as much as I can be that if the U.S. Senate by that one vote margin, had known then what we know now about Mr. Torrijos's paragraphs [the three paragraphs of counter-reservation] and his extra comments outside the instrument, I doubt if it would have passed because they would say, "The Government of Panama is not agreeing to the same thing we are consenting to, and the Executive Branch has compromised us at the same time they compromised their own position. They are in the same boat with us, but they did the compromising; we did not. And some way or other, they have *diminished our constitutional power.*"[1] (Emphasis added)

In other comments, East observed, concerning the separation and limitation of powers as required by the Constitution, that "our shared power is compromised" which, in turn, "compromised the constitutional process."[2]

Senator East's views and conclusions were derived, of course, from his study of the issue and from the testimony and documentation presented at the hearing. Additional documentation and background are contained within this book. The following is a tabulation of the main points and issues of the Panama Canal swindle. Taken together, they have "compromised the constitutional process," perpetrated fraud against the American people and violated the principles of the international law on treaties:

—The text of the U.S. instrument of ratification of the Neutrality Treaty gives the United States the right *independently* to use military force in Panama for the defense and operation of the Canal, if necessary (the DeConcini reservation). Then, Panama's two instruments of ratification first accept this, but then add *unilaterally* a three paragraph long counter-reservation (misleadingly called an understanding, though nomenclature makes no difference in international law).

—Panama's counter-reservation was kept from the Senate and from the American people until after the Treaties were ratified. It said in unequivocal language that the United States can use military force in Panama *only* in self-defense pursuant to Article 18 of the OAS Charter (the very thing the DeConcini reservation amended in a very limited way) and *only* in the spirit of cooperation with Panama (the very thing the DeConcini reservation does not require).

—Since the United States did not accept Panama's counter-reservation and since international law (the Vienna Convention) requires that the two parties in a bilateral treaty accept the same text when ratifying, there has been no ratification and hence, no treaties.

—Since Panama's counter-reservation was not offered to the U.S. Senate for advice and consent, as a substantive part of the Treaties, Article II of the U.S. Constitution was violated and hence, there are no Treaties under constitutional law.

—Since the House of Representatives did not participate during the treaty-making phase in the disposal of the U.S. territory and property in the Canal Zone, as required by Article IV of the U.S. Constitution, the said territory and property have not been disposed of constitutionally and continue under the ownership of the American people. The ownership continues also because legally the 1903 Treaty remains in force.

—Since the 1903 Treaty was not abrogated by an act of the legislature as a "supreme Law of the Land," as required by Article VI of the U.S. Constitution, the 1903 Treaty remains in force constitutionally and has not been terminated.

—The assignment of non-resident aliens (Panamanians) as "directors," i.e., as U.S. civil officers, on the Panama Canal Commission under the provisions of Article IV of the Panama Canal Treaty of 1977 is unconstitutional, a violation of Article VI, clause 3 of the U.S. Constitution that requires an oath of office to "support this Constitution."

The five so-called swindles and four smoking guns that have been identified and described in detail all contributed to the formulation of the Canal swindle, indeed are the main parts of the fraud:

—*Swindle One:* The failure of the Carter Administration to explain adequately to the Senate leaders the counter-reservation of Panama's that voided U.S. defense rights.

—*Swindle Two:* The failure of the Carter Administration to retain the Clements Clause, guaranteeing U.S. rights, in the 1977 Treaties.

—*Swindle Three:* The stonewalling of Senator Griffin's request for information about Panama's rejection of U.S. rights.

—*Swindle Four:* The tabling of Senator Bartlett's motion, just before the vote on the Neutrality Treaty, asking about a second plebiscite in Panama for constitutional approval of the substantive changes made in the Treaties.

—*Swindle Five:* The tabling of Senator Bartlett's motion just before the vote on the second treaty (the Panama Canal Treaty), again asking about a plebiscite in Panama for approval of the changes added to the Treaties.

—*Smoking Gun One:* The Popper letter confessing that "ambiguity was essential" in order to get ratified Treaties.

—*Smoking Gun Two:* The Carter confession in his memoirs that Torrijos was told to write his own reservation (a reservation that was not consented to by the Senate).

—*Smoking Gun Three:* The Rogers speech admitting that the purpose of the leadership amendment to the second treaty was to remove U.S. rights under the DeConcini reservation.

—*Smoking Gun Four:* The unauthorized Baker negotiations with Torrijos, as disclosed in his 1980 book titled *No Margin for Error.*

These, then, are the main issues and facts relating to unconstitutional Treaties, as well as to the cover up and stonewalling. Defenders of the Treaties have produced no supportable evidence to the contrary. Dr. Breecher observed in his testimony:

Mr. Chairman, I recognize that it is most unusual that there should be a case in international law or in constitutional law, in which the Executive Branch can present precisely nothing. My explanation is that this is what one can get if busy Presidents negotiate their own Treaties, and if passions run so high, and if so many careers appear at stake that the most basic arguments are just not listened to at the time.[3]

WHAT CAN AND CANNOT BE DONE

The question of unconstitutional Treaties remains. Panama has been quiet on this subject, of course, not wishing to hazard its "gains." In this connection, Senate Minority Leader Robert Byrd reminded his colleagues on March 19, 1984 that the Panama Canal Treaties were "paying off for the United States" in Central America in our "close and mutually cooperative relationship" with Panama.[4] He complimented President Reagan for accepting the treaties; and based a good part of his optimism on a two-year old letter from then Secretary of State Alexander M. Haig, Jr.

Of course, there is a good reason for this situation: Panama has what it considers to be favorable Treaties and every reason to cooperate. But the important question for Senator Byrd and his associates, and for the President, is the cloud of uncertainty that hangs over the Treaties. Panama knows about this. If not cleared up, a future crisis will test the Treaties severely. It is one thing for the President and 68 Senators to consent to the transfer of the Canal, but quite another to violate constitutional procedures and their oaths of office to defend the Constitution. Will the President and the members of the Senate just close their eyes in the face of the evidence and accept the "worst fraud ever perpetrated on the . . . American people"?

Senator Byrd's euphoria about the "remarkable success story" with Panama is a somewhat myopic view of the situation in Central America.

U.S. capitulation was the signal to the Soviets of unwillingness to defend U.S. interests and rights in the region. Consequently, their encroachments increased into Nicaragua, El Salvador, Honduras, Guatemala and Grenada—all of which became "success stories" for the communists except for the U.S. rescue mission into Grenada.

In failing to hold a second plebiscite for approval of the six changes to the Treaties, the Panamanian Government did not honor the requirements of its own Constitution. Consequently, many scholars of Panama law have stated that Panama never ratified any treaties with the United States.

Moreover, the evidence shows that the United States never ratified any treaties with Panama either. Senator East stated that the June 23, 1983 hearing was "valuable in terms of building this record, and we can continue to build upon it."[5]

A substantial record *has* been built. The time has come for full scale hearings and testimony under oath before the Senate Committee on the Judiciary in order to examine the constitutional and other legal aspects of the ratification procedures. Two other Senate committees may also be involved: Foreign Relations and Armed Services, both of which held extensive hearings in 1977-78.

The following witnesses and their staff members who handled the Treaties are indicated: former President Carter and Vice President Walter Mondale; former National Security Adviser Zbigniew Brzezinski and his associate, Robert Pastor; former Secretaries of State Cyrus Vance, Henry Kissinger and Dean Rusk; former Deputy Secretary of State Warren Christopher; former Ambassadors Sol Linowitz, David Popper and William Jorden; former Assistant Secretary of State William D. Rogers; Senators Robert Byrd, Dennis DeConcini, Joseph Biden and Paul Sarbanes; former Senators Howard Baker and Edward W. Brooke; and State Department Legal Advisers Herbert Hansell and Michael Kozak. Substantial evidence is also available from Senators Orrin Hatch, Jesse Helms and Paul Laxalt; and from Representatives Philip Crane and Carroll Hubbard, Jr., as well as from former Representative George Hansen. High level Senate committee staff members, past and present, may provide valuable detailed testimony. The important questions about the 1977 Panama Treaties should be answered and the main points laid to rest.

The Panama Canal has *not* been transferred to Panama. The United States still owns it—and Section 1504 of the Panama Canal Act of 1979 (Public Law 96-70) states, in part, "The Panama Canal . . . shall not be transferred to the Republic of Panama prior to December 31, 1999." The June 23, 1983 hearing before Senator East's subcommittee produced evidence to prove that the 1977 Panama Canal Treaties had not been ratified under international law nor under the U.S. Constitution. When this documented fact becomes known to the American people, will the Congress still move to enact the legislation to transfer the Canal?

Or, will the members of the Congress take a closer look and consider America's interests first? Appendix U is a draft Act to Amend Public Law 96-70 (the Panama Canal Act of 1979)—not to transfer the Canal and other U.S. property—but to establish the fact that the 1977 Treaties are null and void, to remove all non-resident aliens from the Panama Canal Commission if they do not take oath or affirmation to support the Constitution, and, in effect, to reassert the in-force status of the 1903 Treaty. This draft Act is part of the record of the East hearing.

What can the U.S. President do? Dr. Breecher answered, in his testimony, that the first thing he can do, under his oath of office to preserve, protect and defend the Constitution, is to "remove the non-resident alien Panamanians from the Panama Canal Commission and the Deputy Administrator." He added:

What he cannot do, furthermore, is to quote the Panama Canal Treaties as his authority to do anything in the future. Otherwise, the President is perfectly free to do what he wants. He can submit a new treaty; he can, with or without the DeConcini reservation. He can declare the negotiations with Panama about the Treaties at an end. He can do absolutely nothing. That is up to the President. Legally, the position is, on the Panama Canal Zone, just as it was before the Treaties were signed, with one important exception—if the U.S. has given up rights by the legislation since then, only rights, that stands. We cannot get back—we can complain, but we cannot get back—that part of the Canal Zone which we have given up by legislation.[6]

The actions necessary to ratify the Treaties under international law were explained by Phillip Harman at the hearing:

No.1, Panama would have to withdraw its three paragraph long understanding from its instruments of ratification, thus making its text identical with the United States—Article 20.2 of the 1969 Vienna Convention.

No.2, if Panama did not do this, the U.S. President would have to submit Panama's understanding to the U.S. Senate for a two-thirds vote, as required by U.S. law. This is *Restatement of the Law (Second) of the United States Foreign Relations Law*, page 423.

No.3, if the U.S. Senate does not give consent to Panama's understanding, there would be no Treaties in international law. No doubt, the U.S. Senate would vote against Panama's understanding, as this understanding would nullify the DeConcini condition.[7]

Senator East understood the implications and their potential for future troubles. In his remarks at the June 23, 1983 hearing, he cautioned:

Now, we are told by the Government of Panama that we could not intervene even if we decided we wanted to, unilaterally. And in terms of Soviet and Cuban proxy activity down in that part of the world, I think we have not only lost something constitutionally; I think we have lost something of considerable value and merit in terms of the policy implications.

. . . .

I would submit, as a policy matter, it was probably interpreted, as I thought it would be at the time, as a sign of weakness and simply invited further Soviet and Cuban adventurism, which I think it has. I think it was a message that if we lacked the will and the vision and the capability to defend our own territory in our own hemishpere, the sky was the limit.[8]

VIEWS FROM PANAMA

Panamanian leaders have freely admitted irregularities in the Canal Treaties procedures, e.g., the failure of the U.S. Senate to consent to Panama's three paragraph counter-reservation, the failure of Torrijos to hold a second plebiscite in Panama, and the latent ambiguities in regard to U.S. defense rights and "head of line" privileges for U.S. warships. These were the main issues being contested from beginning to end—and in 1984, prominent Panamanians were, in effect, confessing wrong-doing by both sides.

Nonetheless, said Fernando Manfredo, the Panamanian Deputy Administrator of the Panama Canal Commission, during our interview in Panama on August 3, 1984, "Panama is always prepared to coordinate and cooperate with the United States for the protection of the Canal."[9]

Without exception our interviews with Mr. Manfredo, President-elect Nicolas Ardito-Barletta, and former Presidents of Panama, Demetrio B. Lakas and Marco Robles, produced expressions of willingness to make the Treaties work in the "new partnership," and assurances that there is "nothing to worry about." But, on specific points, most answers were vague, others evasive or not answered.

Mr. Manfredo did not understand the apprehensions of Americans in insisting on the DeConcini reservation, but then added,

DeConcini, you know, doesn't give the United States the right to take action to assure that the Canal remains open. . . . If there is unilateral action against the rule of Panama—no matter what the Treaties say—it will be resisted, not by the government of Panama but by the Panamanian people. . . . Dissatisfaction could cause the Panamanian people to commit an act of sabotage against the Canal. This is a real threat.[10]

Dr. Barletta, during our discussions in Panama, and earlier in his address before the National Press Club in Washington, also warned about a "dissatisfied Panamanian people."[11] Both Barletta and Manfredo, two prominent leaders, thus acknowledged potential violence unless the Panamanian people were satisfied with the way the Treaties were interpreted, i.e., they had to be pleased.

Former Presidents Lakas and Robles were likewise concerned about the "good will of the people." As for the U.S. rights under the DeConcini reservation (to defend or reopen the Canal), Mr. Lakas emphasized "cooperation at the time of the emergency," adding only, "We are working for a smoothly operating Canal."[12]

Mr. Robles agreed and expanded somewhat, "You can take your decision on your own opinion . . . but I do not like the DeConcini amendment because it gives the United States the right to move in troops. I agree with the whole treaty signed by Carter and Torrijos but none of the amendments. The U.S. Congress forced Carter to agree with the amendments . . . but I wouldn't sign that [the amendments] in the 1967 treaties with President Johnson."[13] Ardito-Barletta, the President-to-be, said, in August 1984, that Panama accepts the DeConcini reservation "grudgingly but we do not particularly like it."[14]

In regard to Panama's counter-reservation that voided U.S. defense rights, Mr. Manfredo, also a former Treaties negotiator, repeated his optimism, "We need good relations. That's the name of the game. It doesn't matter what the Treaties say or don't say." When pressed further about possible unconstitutional actions in the U.S. by not having Senate approval of these three paragraphs and in Panama by not having a second plebiscite, Manfredo tacitly admitted the point, "Yes, yes, in Panama it was not constitutional either because those amendments never went to a plebiscite . . . because [Torrijos] didn't want to take the risk."[15]

Barletta put his emphasis on "our mutual benefit," saying, "Panama is the first to want to defend the Canal." Lakas and Robles were non-committal, the latter admitting, however, "Panama wouldn't like U.S. intervention without our permission."

President-elect Barletta told his National Press Club audience about the need to widen the Canal channels and install another set of locks. The regular media glossed over these costly plans and no reporters' questions were heard as to who would pay the bills. We asked Dr. Barletta in Panama about this:

The two aspects are the main Canal and a new sea-level canal. To meet our responsibilities to operate and provide services to the world, we need to modernize and provide a third set of locks. We are working with Japan and the United States. As to who would finance these improvements, it all depends on how the study comes out.[16]

In our interview with Manfredo on August 3, 1984, the answer as to who would pay the bills was more direct:

I think the United States will have to pay for it. The Treaties provide that the United States has to maintain the efficiency of the Canal's operation . . . so the Canal will provide the same quality of service. It is the obligation of the United States to provide the same level of efficiency—and let me tell you something else: I think any improvements to the Canal are not the responsibility of Panama. It is up to the United States to maintain efficiency.[17]

The Deputy Administrator gave an estimated figure of \$400-600 million as the cost of improvements which he said the United States should provide. When asked if he thought that was really covered in the Treaties or was just the Manfredo interpretation, he did not hesitate, "No, it is very clearly stipulated in the Treaties and does not limit the United States as to the size of the investment." A similar statement had been made a few days earlier by President Jorge Illueca at ceremonies honoring the memory of Torrijos. Illueca insisted that such improvements should not be "contingent upon whether the necessary investment can be recovered prior to the year 2000."

Just how a half billion dollars *could* be recovered from an operation that is supposed to be non-profit was unclear, unless these funds were to come from the ever-bearing *Yanqui* money tree. As to what the Treaties "stipulate," the fact is, there is nothing in the two Treaties, or in the implementing legislation or agreements to suggest any such level of investment—merely that the United States "may" make improvements "as it deems appropriate," quoting from Article III of the Panama Canal Treaty.

We asked about emergency "head of line" privileges for U.S. warships, having in mind Panmanian negotiator Bethancourt's comment, "that is their problem with the other ships there." Barletta called this "another treaty provision," then cautioned, "Remember, we will be equal partners in operating the Canal."[18] Manfredo had no ready answer for this contingency, but said, "Well, with Panama . . . we'll comply with everything in the Treaties. We do not like it, but it is the law."

However, Deputy Administrator Manfredo's next answer took a different tack when he was asked if Panama could legally refuse U.S. action to reopen unilaterally a closed Canal:

Yes, but that depends on the prevailing circumstances. No country likes intervention on its territory. With or without the Treaties, if Panama recognized the action to be to its advantage, then Panama will support this "intervention"—but, if Panama concludes this action by the United States is not justified, then it will act against the United States—whether it's in the Treaties or not in the Treaties.[19]

Therefore, in this second response, Mr. Manfredo is saying Panama will be "selective" in deciding which Treaties provisions to observe. That is, Panama will comply when the Treaties are "to its advantage." A moment earlier, he had said, "We'll comply with everything in the Treaties."

The consensus among the Panamanian officials interviewed was simply that we have to get along and cooperate, and that we must not worry about what the Treaties say. Manfredo observed, "Those saying the Treaties are not legal are in the minority. 99% of the people haven't read them. I haven't since the drafting. What's important is good relations and operational efficiency. . . . I'm not concerned about fine print in the Treaties."[20]

Nonetheless, nearly all of our questions that related to the importance of contracts, even the "fine print," in resolving any disagreements were diverted into the perpetual and universal cure-all for the ambiguities in the Treaties: Use the "principles of mutual respect and cooperation." We heard this platitude many times in interviewing treaty-makers and their staffs, particularly when discussions closed in on specifics.

Indeed, the words, "mutual respect and cooperation," became prophetic after President Carter had first used them on September 7, 1977 at the Treaties-signing ceremonies in Washington.[21] Next, these identical words appeared in Panama's secret three paragraph counter-reservation that had been surreptitiously prepared at Carter's invitation to Torrijos when the latter was about to explode over U.S. rights.[22]

The Carter-Torrijos connection, therefore, was apparently welded with the flux of "mutual respect and cooperation" and both sides were intrigued with its usefulness. As with the new words, "sovereign integrity" that were introduced diplomatically for the first time in the leadership amendment, perhaps both sets of phrases were considered unassailable.

'NOT REALLY ACCEPTED BY PANAMA'

At the U.S. Embassy in Panama City, Mr. Ashley C. Hewitt, Jr., Political Counselor and number three man, told us that the Jorden book (*Panama Odyssey*) was the "Bible" on the Treaties.[23] The Deputy Chief of Mission and number two man, Mr. William T. Pryce, felt that the Panamanians "would abide by the 1977 Treaties with their own understandings and that the U.S. position was not really accepted by Panama."[24] The Ambassador, Everett E. Briggs, was in Washington on this date, August 2, 1984.

Mr. Hewitt's only "quotable" comment was:

I'm not going on record on anything, except: Panama accepts those documents they consider to be part of the Treaties. They do not accept those statements and documents they consider unilateral U.S. assertions.

Our questions about U.S. rights to move in to defend or reopen the Canal, under authority of the DeConcini reservation, were dismissed as "a straw man . . . not a real issue . . . a hypothetical case . . . a semantic problem . . . far-fetched . . . not a practical matter."[25] Incidently, these were almost verbatim the same "dismissals" used by Mr. Sherman Hinson (who previously had served in Hewitt's position in Panama) when we interviewed him in Washington on November 21, 1983.[26]

Mr. Hewitt indicated that these would be "policy matters" to be decided at the time an emergency arose. Moreover, alleged Hewitt, Panama had rejected Public Law 96-70 (the Panama Canal Act of 1979) that, said Hewitt, gave U.S. defense rights and "head of line" priorities to U.S. warships in emergencies. On the contrary, we should note, P.L. 96-70 has nothing to do with defense rights or "head of line" privileges. Public Law 96-70 is simply the U.S. law that implements the Treaties and it cannot be rejected by Panama. Although President Illueca, a few days earlier, had denounced this U.S. legislation as "unjust," the law is the guide.[27]

Nonetheless, one may ask, why should U.S. Embassy officials in Panama object to being quoted on public policy matters relating to the application of the very important Panama Canal Treaties, particularly since the Embassy will have the first responsibility to respond to any disagreements on the scene? Perhaps the answer would correspond to the one given at Senator East's hearing before the Subcommittee on Separation of Powers, when the State Department representative was asked, "Did the State Department ever ask Panama to withdraw their three paragraph statement from their instruments?" State's answer was, ". . . Since diplomatic consultations between governments are confidential, the Department must decline . . . to answer. . . ."[28] Using this criterion, State would never tell the public the secret of the three paragraphs of Panama's counter-reservation—unless the U.S. Congress decided to find out.

Our interview in Panama on August 3, 1984 with the Director of Public Affairs, Colonel William C. Hansen, U.S. Air Force, disclosed that the U.S. Southern Command would not be interpreting the Treaties, but would "stand on Embassy guidance." Both Hansen and Captain Jack Smith, U.S. Navy and Chief of Staff, felt there had been no problems with the Treaties. General Paul F. Gorman, U.S. Army, was "not available" for interview.[29]

Under the provisions of Article IV of the Panama Canal Treaty, a field training exercise, "Kindle Liberty," was conducted in February 1983 to test Canal defenses using combined U.S.-Panamanian military forces. This exercise involved some 10,000 military personnel, including 3,000 flown in from the United States and a battalion-sized contingent from Panama's National Guard. The Panamanian attitude was called "very positive."[30]

An appreciation of the value of the Canal itself and the engineering skill required to construct it may best be had by a transit of the waterway, for example, on a ship such as the Japanese motor vessel *Asuka*. One wonders how many of the politicians and negotiators ever made transits on board ship. Flying over the Canal may be just another flight—but from on board ship, one observes close up this monument to American sacrifice and national pride.

The 753-foot *Asuka* with a beam of 106 feet calls for skillful pilots, four of them, to guide her through the 110 foot wide locks chambers, using tugs and locomotives in a twelve hour passage that saw the 70,000 ton vessel lifted 85 feet above sea level at Miraflores and Pedro Miguel and then lowered 85 feet in the three-step locks at Gatun. This 51 mile run from Balboa on the Pacific side to Cristobal on the Atlantic had saved her some 8,000 miles and 33 days as opposed to the Cape Horn route. Her captain, Motoichi Shimoyama, a World War II Japanese Navy officer, was well aware of this, having transited the Canal more times than he could count.

A superb system of locks, lakes and personnel is the Panama Canal, carved out of the wilderness some seventy years earlier. A total of 413 million cubic yards of dirt and rocks were excavated for the 45-foot channels—enough diggings, if laid yard-to-yard, to reach from Panama City to the Moon and beyond. The eight mile long cut through the Continental Divide, 312 feet above sea level, took 168 million cubic yards—enough to circle the Earth four times, yard-to-yard. This Gaillard Cut cost the lives of hundreds of workers because of landslides and other accidents.

Our point is: If American territory and property are to be "surrendered," the value should be known. A higher value, however, must be placed on the Constitution—and on constitutional procedures.

'BIND HIM . . . BY THE CHAINS OF THE CONSTITUTION'

The loss in constitutional power, including the erosion of the system of checks and balances in the Constitution's provisions for the separation and limitation of power, was the background theme throughout the East hearing—indeed, it was this loss and erosion that made possible the Canal swindle. "In question of power, then," wrote Thomas Jefferson, "let no more be heard of confidence in man, but bind him down from mischief by the chains of the Constitution."[31]

The "chains of the Constitution" were loosened and the Canal got away. The Constitution was designed as a "first line of defense" for America's citizens and for the republic which it created. While its language is sententious, it is also marvelously clear. It belongs *to* the people, was written *for* the people, and gives the power of governance *to* the people.

When leaders in the national Congress, and the President, side-step the issue of invalid Panama Canal Treaties where the evidence is persuasive that such Treaties were produced by unconstitutional acts, and lament the lack of political will to investigate, are these Senators and other leaders also by-passing their oaths of office to defend the Constitution? Are they forgetting the history and intentions of the Constitution?

When the New York Convention was debating the federal Constitution in 1788, among the forms of government discussed were a limited monarchy, which was quickly discarded—then, a pure democracy, called "the most perfect government." But Alexander Hamilton promptly reminded the delegates of the tragedy of ancient Athens and its democracy where demagoguery turned the people into ungovernable mobs at the mercy of clever orators. When the people acted directly, they were weak and ineffective. He warned of tyranny, saying, "Sir, it is a truth sufficiently illustrated by experience, that when the people act by their representatives, they are commonly irresistible."[32]

The Constitution was accepted, and in 1956 Joseph Charles, author and historian of Jeffersonian democracy, wrote in one of his essays on the American political system, ". . . the second session of the first Congress . . . found the people of the whole country extraordinarily united in support of the new government."[33]

The members of the Congress are the representatives of the people, elected to serve the people and deriving their "powers from the consent" of the people. Above all, they are sworn to preserve the Constitution to the end that government will be of *laws* and not of *men*. Of course, these principles are basic and elementary, but are they sometimes glossed over for political expediency or for lack of political courage? Did this happen in "ratifying" the Panama Canal Treaties? In investigating their status and constitutionality?

The Preamble to the Constitution, the very first words, immediately guarantees that this is a government of the people, not of the national legislature or of the several States: "We the people of the United States . . . do ordain and establish this CONSTITUTION. . . ." The very first order of business, therefore, was to establish the Congress, composed of Representatives and Senators to act as agents of the people, and to be "bound by Oath or Affirmation" to protect the Constitution (Article VI).

Indeed, said James Monroe, in speaking of the Constitution, "The people, the highest authority known to our system and from whom all our instruction spring and on whom they depend, formed it."[34]

The evidence is substantial that President Carter and his State Department and treaty-handlers, as well as some U.S. Senators, may have deliberately by-passed the Constitution and international law in their zeal for ratified Treaties. Will American politics of the late 20th century condone further stonewalling and cover up, and eventually sweep the "legal mess" under the rug?

Alexander Hamilton, one of the most astute scholars on the Constitution, spoke to the by-passing of the "intentions of the people" in one of his "Federalist" essays. He was concerned that the legislative body would become the "constitutional judge of their own power," eventually "substituting their will to that of their constituents." Moreover, he wrote, the courts have a role in preserving the "intentions of the people" over the intentions of their agents in the Congress:

If it be said that the legislative bodies are themselves the constitutional judges of their own power, and that the construction they put upon them is conclusive upon the other departments, it may be answered, that this cannot be the natural presumption, where it is not to be collected from any particular provisions in the Constitution. It is not otherwise to be supposed, that the Constitution could intend to enable the representatives of the people to substitute their will to that of their constituents. It is far more rational to suppose, that the courts were designed to be an intermediate body between the people and the legislature, in order, among other things, to keep the latter within the limits assigned to their authority. The interpretation of the law is the proper and peculiar province of the courts. A constitution is, in fact, and must be regarded by the judges, as fundamental law. It therefore belongs to them to ascertain its meaning, as well as the meaning of any particular act proceeding from the legislative body. If there should happen to be an irreconcilable variance between the two, . . . the Constitution ought to be preferred to the statute, the intention of the people to the intention of their agents.[35]

The history of the Constitution and the intentions of its Framers have often been useful in applying and interpreting constitutional law. Nonetheless, in recent years, it has seemed that some jurists first "look for cases" instead of studying and applying this fundamental law. Hamilton's views expressed in *Federalist* No.77 interpose the courts between the people and the government in order to keep the latter within the limits of its authority. How is it working 200 years later?

For fifteen dollars in 1979 ($65 in 1985), any citizen of the United States could file a lawsuit in a federal court seeking relief from the government on specific grounds. He could sue the President, the Congress and the Supreme Court—all for one fifteen dollar fee. He could do it without a high-priced lawyer too—but he would not get to first base.

When California citizen Carl R. Hoffmann, Jr. filed his lawsuit on September 28, 1979—two days after the House of Representatives had approved the implementing legislation for the Canal Treaties—he got fast action from Judge Stanley A. Weigel's U.S. District Court of the Northern District of California. Or, to be more accurate, it was action from the substitute judge, Robert F. Peckham, and his clerk that Friday afternoon. The complaint was filed at 3:30 p.m. and the hearing completed by 5:15.

Mr. Hoffmann was suing to prevent transfer of the U.S. Canal Zone to Panama on October 1, 1979 because of illegal Treaties, and because the 1903 Treaty had not been abrogated and the United States still owned the property. The suit was against President Carter, Vice President Walter F. Mondale, the Supreme Court and the entire U.S. Congress. Hoffmann lost his case and the official decision, several weeks later, signed by Judge Weigel and Assistant U.S. Attorney Barg was based on the argument that Mr. Hoffmann had not moved for a temporary restraining order to maintain the *status quo* (a technicality) and that "October 1, 1979 has now passed and the Panama Canal has been transferred to the Republic of Panama."

The court accepted a fallacious argument. The Canal had *not* been transferred and *cannot* be transferred until the year 1999 in acordance with Section 1504 of the Panama Canal Act of 1979 which states," The Panama Canal . . . shall not be transferred to the Republic of Panama prior to December 31, 1999."

Obviously, the Judge and the Assistant U.S. Attorney did not look up the law but "looked for cases," citing two that did not apply to the question at hand. Moreover, instead of acting as an "intermediate body" for citizens to keep government "within the limits assigned to their authority," as envisioned by Hamilton, the court found for the government with no apparent effort to look up the fundamental law.

While, in fact, a part of the Canal *Zone* was transferred on October 1, 1979, several days after Hoffmann had filed his suit, the Canal and certain other properties were not. Even so, the fundamental law relating to Hoffmann's complaint was the failure to terminate constitutionally the 1903 Treaty by an act of the Congress, as indicated by Article VI of the Constitution, and as prescribed by paragraph 599 of *Jefferson's Manual of Parliamentary Practice*.

This *Manual* had been assiduously followed by previous Congresses until the congressional leadership apparently succumbed to the modern craving for legislative efficiency, or political expediency, or rule by concensus. Even so, paragraph 599 provides that ". . . an act of the legislature alone can declare them [treaties] infringed or rescinded."[36]

Did Judge Weigel or Mr. Barg look for the law—or look for cases? In his routine "order" for dismissal, the judge wrote, "The Court having considered everything relevant," but obviously he did not consider the fundamental law. Even so, very probably some other way would have been found to kill this lawsuit and to protect the President.

Mr. Carter's handling of the 1903 Treaty apparently set two records for him: illegal "termination" of two treaties by one President, the other treaty being the Mutual Defense Treaty with Taiwan. The other record was two cracks in the shield of the Monroe Doctrine by one President: helping install the Marxist regime in Nicaragua; and delivering the Canal to the pro-Communist Panamanian Government.

'TO HAUNT—LIKE THE GHOST OF BANQUO'

The loss of constitutional power resulting from the pressure of transferring the Canal was called the most serious issue of all, and one that will return to haunt future leaders. Professor Raoul Berger warned in his testimony before the Subcommittee on Separation of Powers in February 1978 that "this disregard to constitutional requirements in the proposed Panama Canal Treaties will haunt those who are closing their eyes to it down the years. . . . They will say they have a precedent."[37] Again, as with Judge Weigel, will these future leaders look up the law, or "look up cases"?

Judge Barrington Parker stated at the trial of Richard Helms, former Director of the Central Intelligence Agency, regarding the fundamental law versus "ill-conceived" precedents:

If public officials embark deliberately to disobey and ignore the laws of our land because of some misguided and ill-conceived notion and belief that there are earlier commitments and considerations which they must observe, the future of our country is in jeopardy. There are those employed in . . . this country . . . who feel that they have a license to operate freely outside the dictates of law. . . . Public officials at every level, whatever their position, like any other person, must respect and honor the Constitution and laws of the United States. [38]

On the basis of the exposed record of fraud, the United States is legally entitled to keep the Canal, in full sovereign rights and as U.S. property under the valid in-force Hay-Bunau-Varilla Treaty of 1903. Indeed, to give it to Panama would require special legislation enacted in accordance with Sections 1503 and 1504 of the Panama Canal Act of 1979.

But there is more. U.S. foreign policy and prestige would be enhanced tremendously with the world put on notice that Americans refuse to be cheated in international agreements. To be sure, such statesmanship would bring cries of condemnation and defiance from the Soviets and certain Third World leaders. They would be surprised surely; but, they would not have legal grounds for complaint. Moreover, reemphasis on the 1903 Treaty could be the most meaningful way to revive the Monroe Doctrine, the security shield of the Western Hemisphere for over one hundred and fifty years. In the early years, America was concerned with security rather than popularity—for, to a great extent, "Nations have no friends, only interests" (Benjamin Disraeli).

The true legal status of the United States must be reestablished in its historic role for the security of the trans-oceanic canal at the Isthmus of Panama. This necessity will not be going away. Neither will the need to modernize the existing Canal be going away. But the overdue improvements, if they are to be subsidized by the American taxpayers and other investors, will have to have security. And, U.S. sovereign rights and operational control would be essential before any outlay of American financing. The 1903 Treaty provides the security. And, the Terminal Lake-Third Locks Plan for modernizing the Canal offers potential for increased traffic, efficient operations and economic benefits for Panama and for the maritime community at large.

Why have United States leaders failed to protect American interests in the Western Hemisphere? Why has the Congress failed to give adequate support to El Salvador's efforts to oust the communists from that country? And the Nicaraguan patriots seeking to retake their country from the communist Sandinistas? Why is Cuba allowed to operate carte blanche as a conduit for South American drugs flowing into the United States in order to use the billions of dollars profit to buy armaments for the revolutionists in Central America? Why have America's legislators and other leaders soft-pedalled the Monroe Doctrine as anachronistic?

Is it ignorance of the threat to America? Complacency for the *status quo*? Or acquiescence to the communist advance?

If it is the ignorance of men and women in high places, Eric Hoffer, the political philosopher, speaks to ignorance: "Far more crucial than what we know or do not know is what we do not want to know" (1954).

If it is complacency, then Shakespeare wrote many times about this deadly attitude, for example: "The path is smooth that leadeth on to danger" (1593).

If it is acquiescence to the communist advance, then we live in weakness—apparently a weakness dominated by affluence, greed and self-interest in the good life, unhampered by the inconveniences and restrictions of national preparedness. Moreover, it has been said, "Not even a collapsing world looks dark to a man about to make his fortune."

Nonetheless, when the U.S. Senate agreed to treaties to place one of America's greatest strategic assets under an unpredictable government like

Panama, it consented to disaster in ways other than the weakness of U.S. rights to defend the Canal. By-passing international law and the U.S. Constitution were also involved. Primarily, however, it was the awesome power of the U.S. presidency, acting with impunity to renounce U.S. willingness to defend its interests in Central America, indeed in the Western Hemisphere.

Harry S. Truman told future CIA agents at an orientation briefing on November 21, 1952, ". . . the Presidential Office is the most powerful . . . in the history of this great world of ours" and not even the power of Genghis Khan, Augustus Caesar, Napoleon or Louis XIV could compare with it. "It is an office without parallel in the history of the world," he added.[39] Nonetheless, the Constitution provides a check to such power if there is the will to use it. "Only Congress itself can prevent power from slipping through its fingers."[40] In the case of the Panama Canal Treaties, constitutional power did slip through the fingers of a Congress slavish to a President obsessed with the correction of what he perceived to be an injustice: U.S. ownership of one of its greatest assets, the Panama Canal.

In 1788, Madison wrote Jefferson, "Wherever there is an interest and power to do wrong, wrong will generally be done. . . ."[41]

Most Americans are probably not aware that their Constitution has been copied, in whole or in part, throughout the world. Canada copied it in 1867; Australia in 1900; and even the Union of South Africa in 1909. France, Belgium and Switzerland adopted many of America's constitutional principles. Notably where these governments failed to follow the Constitution of the United States, their structures were generally weak and ineffective.[42]

Lord James Bryce (1838-1922), British jurist and statesman, wrote in 1888: "The Republic of the United States has not only presented the most remarkable instance of this type in the modern world, but has by its success become the pattern which other republics have imitated. . . ."[43]

However, British essayist and historian Thomas Babington Macaulay (1800-1859) was not impressed and wrote to an American friend in 1857: "Your Constitution is all sail . . . and either civilization or liberty must perish."[44] Perhaps Lord Macaulay gave insufficient credit to the unique system of checks and balances.

Some years later, in 1878, William Ewart Gladstone (1809-1898), four times Prime Minister of England, was complimentary. In comparing the British and American Constitutions, he said:

The one is a thing grown, the other a thing made . . . the one the offspring of tendency and indeterminate time, the other of choice and of an epoch. But, as the British Constitution is the most subtile organization which has proceeded from the womb and the long gestation of progressive history, so the American Constitution is, so far as I can see, the most wonderful work ever struck off at a given time by the brain and purpose of man.[45]

In the Foreword to Benjamin Waite Blanchard's treatise on the Constitution are these words by Russell Duane:

One of the most important purposes of a constitution is to protect the poor and weak and to guarantee that they shall enjoy the same rights as the strong.

. . . .

Without the provisions of a well-conceived constitution and wise laws, administered by just and impartial courts, civilization would be in constant jeopardy.[46]

The Constitution is America's greatest treasure. If it had been properly honored in handling the Panama Canal Treaties, the Canal very probably would not have been lost. Nonetheless, to those who did the job, surrender was obviously preferable to the wrath of a scorned President and the hysteria of Panama's masses.

In his speech to a joint session of the Congress on April 26, 1983, President Reagan warned, "The national security of all the Americas is at stake in Central America." Does this not include the Key to the Western Hemisphere, the Panama Canal, which is also the focus of the Monroe Doctrine?

In 1986, President Reagan either did or did not understand that the 1977 Panama Treaties are invalid under the procedures of both the Constitution and international law. He spoke forcefully against the dangers of these Treaties before they were accepted. Why has he been generally silent since? Has he been shielded? Our evidence, we believe, supports the following recommended actions:

—Determine the true legal position of the United States in regard to the 1977 Treaties.

—If the 1977 Treaties are found to be illegal or non-existent, proclaim that the 1903 Treaty, as amended, is still effective and that the 1977 Treaties are void.

—Negotiate a new treaty that protects the interests and security of the American people and the United States, and that retains sovereign rights over the Canal Zone.

—Based on a new treaty that provides U.S. control and rights of sovereignty, modernization of the existing Canal could begin without jeopardizing American investments or taxpayers' money.

It is important to establish the status of the 1977 Treaties and to inquire into the liabilities of those who took oaths of office to "preserve, protect and defend the Constitution."

President Ronald Reagan started America back towards greatness. He could become one of the all-time great Presidents if he were willing during his second term to attend to the threats against the Constitution, including oaths of office and unconstitutional procedures in treaty making.

The failure of President Carter and the U.S. Senate to produce irrefutably valid treaties has set the stage for future Americans to have no alternative but to use force to uphold America's legitimate interests in the Canal. Charges by Panama of misdeeds on the part of Teddy Roosevelt and the Frenchman, Philippe Bunau-Varilla, will be dwarfed in future history by denouncements of the Carter-Torrijos maneuvers.[47]

"It is more tolerable to be refused than deceived" (Publilius Syrus). America has been deceived. Will it also be refused?

The Constitution may be by-passed for a while. And invalid Treaties filed away temporarily. But not forever. Some day they will be back to haunt—like the Ghost of Banquo, invisible to most, but not to those who know.

Ronald Reagan voiced strong opposition to the Panama Treaties at this public forum in early 1978 in Denver, Colorado with the famous "Truth Squad." Later, he wrote, after the implementing legislation was passed, that "we might still . . . salvage something," as things heat up in Central America. Later, as President, he acquired power to "salvage something" but reneged even on the preliminary step of investigating the "flawed Treaties" — his words. (AP/Wide World Photos)

EPILOGUE

Americans were called Gringos when trying to give away the Canal, but by 1986 they became *Los Conojes del Norte* (Rabbits of the North), a Panamanian term of contempt because of perceived U.S. retreat. Other developments threatened the Treaties, even as State and Senate officials praised them.[1] In addition to invalid ratification, other problems included disagreements over the implementing legislation (Public Law 96-70); continuing political turmoil in Panama; and communist take overs in Central America, often aided by Panama and the new Treaties.

Panamanians named P.L. 96-70 Murphy's Law after U.S. Congressman John M. Murphy. President-elect Nicolas Ardito-Barletta claimed this law had eleven major "obstacles that . . . have been notorious," such as U.S. control over the Canal and free use of the operating areas.[2] Mr. Murphy had the foresight to preserve U.S. control even though choosing not to demand use of Article IV of the Constitution for disposal of the Canal Zone. Under authority of Article III of the Panama Canal Treaty, requiring creation of the Panama Canal Commission under U.S. law, Murphy and his House Committee on Merchant Marine and Fisheries deserve credit for establishing the various agencies for operating the Canal and protecting U.S. interests until the year 2000, all under the Secretary of Defense.[3] Apparently Article III permitted the only U.S. advantage that slipped by the negotiators.

GUARDIA 'UNWILLING TO ACCEPT' LOSS OF POWER

The power of the *Guardia* (Defense Forces) continues in Panama. In 1968 it used a military coup to oust President Arnulfo Arias; but in 1984 General Manuel Noriega simply had his men burn 13,000 ballots favoring Arias, who was running again, and fabricate 4,000 for *Guardia* candidate Barletta.[4] Previously Noriega had declared the *Guardia* "neutral." Untrue. He had told diplomatic sources he was unwilling to accept a "victory by Arias" and a subsequent loss of power.[5] In 1985 Noriega dismissed Barletta for investigating alleged *Guardia* misdeeds and installed his friend, Eric Arturo Del Valle. So much for democracy.

Noreiga's militancy is a matter of record. In 1973 he advised U.S. Ambassador John Scali, in Panama for a UN meeting, to vote "at the airport" if he intended to veto a resolution condemning U.S. colonialism. Scali voted at the council meeting. In 1978 Noriega's briefing for Senators Howard Baker, John Chafee and Jake Garn was threatening in tone, according to journalist Roger Fontaine.

Arias was bitter over the 1984 election "loss" by 1,713 votes (50.03% to 49.97%) and refused to be interviewed, saying, "Read the revisions and write what you think."[6] Later, aide Richard Gruber in responding to questions said that General Bolivar Vallarino had not plotted the 1968 coup against Arias and that *Guardia* officers met with U.S. intelligence officer Efrain Angueira during the night of the coup. This information was contrary to the account in William Jorden's book, *Panama Odyssey*. Nor, said Gruber, did Jorden talk with Arias about this.

Raul Arias de Para in *Anatomy of a Fraud: The 1984 Presidential Elections in Panama* (1985) wrote, "The election of Barletta was in fact . . . a vast all-pervading fraud . . . the inevitable consequence of the corrupt military regime in Panama since 1968." Prior to this fraud, Senator Daniel Inouye, D.-Haw., attached a rider to the 1984 Appropriations Bill (H.R. 492) to curtail aid to Panama if the *Guardia* interfered in the election. Candidate Ruben Dario Paredes, a former *Guardia* commander, complained of U.S. interference.[7] Nonetheless, the *Guardia* did interfere, generous U.S. aid did continue, and H.R. 492 was duly filed.

Barletta was an old timer in international politics. Ten years earlier, he had told Fidel Castro, "The Cuban process and the Panamanian process are the same."[8] Former President Carter and Secretary of State George Shultz attended Barletta's inauguration on October 11, 1984—exactly 16 years after the 1968 coup and with the *Guardia* still in control. The *Washington Times* editorialized, in part:

It is interesting to note that while Mr. Arias opposed the Carter-Torrijos Treaties,

Mr. Barletta helped negotiate them, after which he landed a cushy World Bank job in Washington. He also helped draft the laws which made Panama a haven for international banks, after which Torrijos got huge loans from those same banks. . . .[9]

TREATIES AID COMMUNIST ADVENTURES

Panama's involvement with communists in Central America did not delay implementation of the Treaties. Torrijos aided the Sandinista ouster on July 17, 1979 of Nicaragua's President Anastasio Somoza: On March 13 and 16, *Guardia* intelligence chief Manuel Noreiga provided two van loads of munitions for the Sandinistas. On May 11 Panama's puppet President Aristides Royo said, "If I am going to smuggle arms, . . . we have planes." Then, on May 30 a Soviet aircraft landed 200 battle-ready soldiers for transfer to the Sandinistas via Panamanian Air Force trucks.[10] Earlier, on the day the U.S. Senate approved the final treaty, Torrijos with his Sandinista associate, Tomas Borge, was ready with 20 guerrillas and *Guardia* troops to "blow up the Canal" should the treaty be rejected.[11]

The Panama Treaties dovetail with communist adventurism. With treaty guarantees of neutrality and Panamanian sovereignty in the Canal area, important changes followed: The Soviets use the old Navy hangers at Coco Solo in transshipping munitions to Nicaragua. Communist-bloc ships freely transit the Canal enroute to Corinto, Nicaragua with arms and tanks for the Sandinistas. When asked on August 3, 1984 about the Soviet *Nadezhda Krupskaya's* and Libyan *Maristella's* unhampered use of the Canal in hauling war supplies to destabilize Central America, Deputy Canal Administrator Fernando Manfredo said, "Yes, according to the Treaties, all ships get expeditious passage. They can declare dangerous cargo, then go through by the rules."

"By the rules" means that U.S. interests are subjugated by internationalization of the Canal. When Teddy Roosevelt planned the Isthmian canal, U.S. control and fortifications were absolute musts. Nothing less was considered. The Carter-Torrijos Treaties favor the communists. One recalls the Bryan-Chamorro Treaty (1914), terminated in 1972 and giving up 99 year leases for U.S. bases in Nicaragua. Henry Kissinger and the liberal senators who threw out this 1914 treaty also backed the 1977 Panama Treaties for surrendering the Canal.

The House of Representatives voted on September 26, 1979 to implement the Treaties. Most of those who voted that day to transfer the Canal voted again on May 24, 1984 (241 to 177) to deny U.S. aid to Nicaraguan patriots seeking to oust the Sandinistas, the latter a threat to the Canal's security. The Wrights, the Studdses, and the Markeys head the list; and year after year voters send them back to Congress.

Inside Panama, U.S. interests also suffer. On July 31, 1984 President Jorge E. Illueca announced that Fort Gulick and the School of the Americas, the latter a famous U.S. training facility for Latin American leaders, would be taken over by the *Guardia* on October 1, although the Treaties permitted delay. Illueca denounced U.S. colonialism and the Treaties implementing law (P.L. 96-70) as unjust. He demanded U.S. modernization of the Canal (at $400-$600 million) and warned of stringent law enforcement in Panama against Americans.

On October 1 the School of the Americas was closed, 1000 American Canal workers lost commissary and postal benefits, and 550 teachers and medical personnel were turned out of their housing in the Canal area. Mr. Manfredo noted "a loss of morale" along the tree-lined streets of the former Canal Zone, now patrolled by the *Guardia*.[12] And U.S. servicemen must wear civilian clothes when away from their posts. U.S. citizen employees of the Canal Commission, instead of being exempt from "all taxes" as provided by the Treaties, found themselves in 1986 embroiled in lawsuits against the U.S. Internal Revenue Service. [13]

'AS THE TERRITORIAL SOVEREIGN'

The basic treaty refers to Panama "as the territorial sovereign." Sovereignty was a nagging issue of the 1977 debates, and since the 1903 Treaty may still be valid, another look at sovereignty may be in order: Nowhere in the 1903 Treaty that transferred the Canal Zone to the United States do the words "rent" or "lease" appear. But "sovereignty" appears six times, "in perpetuity" seven times, and "grant" nineteen times. All evidence proves no intention of "renting" but a clear cut transfer of property "in perpetuity" and the exercise of sovereign rights by the U.S. to the "entire exclusion" of such rights by Panama.[14]

William Howard Taft confused the issue in 1904, saying that Panama "seems to preserve titular sovereignty," thus making the first move towards 80 years of appeasement. He was also wrong. Six all-embracing clauses in the 1903 Treaty (in Articles II, III, V, and XVIII) affirm and reaffirm U.S. possession "in perpetuity," thereby rendering any idea of "Panamanian sovereignty" meaningless and contradictory. That is, *both* contracting parties could not be sovereign, and Panama was specifically excluded from "any sovereign rights" by Article III.

The word "sovereignty" in the preamble of the 1903 Treaty simply established Panamanian *ownership*, a basic requirement in transferring property. Panama was 13 days old, and her right to sell the Canal Zone had to be established. Nowhere in the Treaty do any clauses reserve or affirm sovereignty or titular sovereignty to Panama. Many statesmen agreed, including President Reagan, former Ambassador Spruille Braden, Chief Justice Charles Evans Hughes, and Secretaries of State Elihu Root and John Hay. Senator Orrin Hatch, R.-Ut., called the 1903 Treaty "a final and absolute transfer of sovereignty in perpetuity."

U.S. ownership was absolute too: $10 million to Panama; $25 million to Colombia; $40 million to the French engineering company; and $4.8 million to individual land owners and squatters. No real estate in history was so thoroughly bought; it was paid for four times and disposed of by paying billions to another party to take it. The argument about a 99 year lease involved a concessionary contract (Article XXII) and had nothing to do with leasing property. The $250,000 annuity was for Panama's loss of revenue from the Panama Railroad.[15]

In perhaps the first judicial precedent alleging Panama's sovereignty, Judge Guthrie Crowe of the U.S. Court for the Panama Canal Zone ruled on July 8, 1963, in a suit brought by Gerald A. Doyle of the Panama Canal Company, that Panama's flag could legally be flown in the Zone. The judge failed to address the fundamental principle that a flag signifies sovereignty, saying instead that sovereignty was not the question. Neither did he recognize that the Supreme Court had ruled the Canal Zone U.S. territory and that the 1903 Treaty gave sovereign rights to the U.S. Later, Judge Crowe campaigned against the 1977 Treaties, saying, "There is no honor in appeasement." Had he forgotten his 1963 ruling that appeased the Panamanians?

In *Panama Odyssey*, William Jorden continued the fantasy about sovereignty and ownership, asserting that "Panama remained the sovereign power" and "the property was being restored to its rightful owners . . ." (p.675). The facts are as follows:

—The U.S. paid $4,728,889 for title to every tract of land and water in the Zone, disposing of 3,598 claims.[16]

—Article III of the 1903 Treaty granted sovereign rights to the U.S. "to the entire exclusion" of Panama. Without sovereign rights, Panama had no sovereign power.[17]

—American taxpayers were the rightful owners; asserting otherwise was pandering to the Panamanians who historically misrepresented sovereignty and ownership.

President Carter also ignored these facts, alleging in his June 23, 1976 speech before the internationalist Foreign Policy Association that the 1903 Treaty provided that "Panama should have sovereignty." He added, "I would never give up full control of the Panama Canal." The distinguished jurist Alfred J. Schweppe understood sovereignty and treaty power. Appendix V is one of his essays.

THE GOOD GUYS VERSUS THE BAD GUYS

Ambassador Jorden's *Panama Oyssey* pits the good guys who made the Treaties (the Carters, Kissingers, Linowitzes) against the bad guys who opposed the Treaties (the Reagans, Helmses, Moorers). It was the U.S. and Panamanian negotiators versus the "Canal Zone authorities and the U.S. military" (p.15).

At a Friday evening negotiating session in Washington, August 5, 1977, Jorden told Gabriel Lewis Galindo that Panama had been short-changed for 65 years, adding, ". . . we've made money and given you peanuts."[18] Untrue. Everything had been paid for; and the Canal operated at or below cost with "a net operating loss since 1973."

Omar Torrijos and diplomats of Colombia, Mexico, Venezuela, Costa Rica, and Jamaica joined the negotiators by telephone from Bogota, Colombia—with no qualms about interferring in business between the U.S. and Panama. Mexico's Jose Lopez Portillo and Jamaica's Michael Manley proposed that the U.S. not negotiate with a third country "for construction of another canal." President Carter wired the volunteers, "Tell General Torrijos that I accept, without taking out a single comma, the text of the proposals" (p.19). No one noted, however, that the U.S. constitutional system required "Advice and Consent" to this euphoria.

Jorden's bad guys included Representative John M. Murphy, D.-N.Y., who had insisted on U.S. rights in implementing the Treaties. Murphy stood accused of bribe-taking, said Jorden, while Torrijos stood in power "seven years later"(p.241). But this was a paradox: Torrijos ruled as a dictator, never accountable to voters or courts. Murphy had no such immunity. Other bad guys and their alleged misdeeds were Republican Congressmen Robert Bauman, a homosexual; George Hansen, improper financial disclosures; Richard Kelly, bribe-taking; Daniel Crane, sex with a female page; Democrat Charles Wilson, cocaine use.

The only miscreant among Jorden's good guys was Congressman Gerry Studds, criticized *not* for his homosexuality, as was Bauman, but for seducing a male page. Other good guys, i.e., Treaties supporters, included Democratic adventurers whose alleged misdeeds were not listed by Jorden, as follows: Edward Kennedy, Chappaquiddick and the death of Mary Jo Kopechne; Harrison A. Williams and John W. Jenrette, bribe-taking; Ronald V. Dellums, illegal drugs; Charles Diggs, mail fraud; Louis Stokes, drunk driving; Geraldine Ferraro, improper financial disclosures. Obviously there were serious indiscretions on both sides.

Mr. Jorden closed his interesting book with the observation, "God knows that small men, petty men, evil men will try to besmirch what has been done" (p.658). His odyssey omits the issues of constitutional and international law altogether—aberrations that "besmirch what has been done" and that endanger the American system of government.

'SOMEBODY'S GOT TO DO IT'—AND DID

President Carter, in taking on the politically unpopular Panama Treaties, told his wife, "Nixon didn't do it. Ford didn't do it. Everybody's putting it off. . . . Somebody's got to do it."[19]

Mr. Carter's Treaties relate to the scenario by T. Mac Long, National Youth Federation Adviser, as follows:

The U.S. paid France, Colombia, Panama and the private landowners for the U.S. Canal Zone, then built our Canal. A Communist dictator overthrew the elected Panamanian government. He borrowed so much money from such international bankers as the Marine Midland Bank that he could not even pay the interest. A director of that bank worked out a deal to turn over the Canal and the Canal Zone to the dictator and pay him to take it, the payments to be applied to repayment of his loans. The dictator agreed, but the U.S. Senate added a provision that in an emergency the U.S. could take over the Canal to keep it open. The dictator did not agree to the U.S. reservation, so there is no treaty.[20]

Admiral Thomas H. Moorer, former Chairman of the Joint Chiefs of Staff, wrote in 1980:

The Panama Canal Treaties of 1977 represent a profound misjudgment of the U.S. Government in the stream of history. . . . Recent history, especially that of Nicaragua, . . . conclusively shows that the real struggle on the Isthmus . . . is not between the U.S. and Panama, but between the U.S. and the Soviet Union in what informed leaders recognize as part of the war for the world.[21]

The late Maj. General Thomas A. Lane, a U.S. Army engineer with Canal Zone experience, predicted in 1974 that Marxist subversion would intensify with loss of U.S. sovereign authority and that the U.S. position would become intolerable:

The U.S. would be compelled to use force in Panama, or to withdraw and allow the Canal to be defended by another. . . .[22]

Hansen W. Baldwin, the historian and strategist, cautioned of complacency by the American public "until something happens, as it will."[23] And veteran Canal Pilot Leonard E. Bell warned of Treaties that incubate "one crisis after the other."[24]

President Carter and other American leaders of the late 20th century performed as follows:

—lost control of a strategic waterway,

—gave away a $10 billion asset and promised Panama $3 billion more ,

—by-passed the Constitution and international law in doing so,

—gave up rights to bases needed to defend the Canal and the U.S. Southern flank,

—lost guarantee of fast ocean to ocean movement of the U.S. Fleet,

—retreated from the Caribbean as the communists moved in,

—exposed the Canal to Soviet subversion and eventual take over,

—gave U.S. enemies equal access to the Canal,

—left a time bomb for future conflict with Panama,

—set an historical record in paying another nation to accept U.S. property that had already been bought four times legally,

—invited Americans to invest in a sea level canal and in improvements to a canal given to Panama,

—allowed Senators to participate in treaty negotiations,

—violated oaths of office to preserve the Constitution, and

—taxed Americans through direct appropriations, loss of Canal toll payments to the U.S. Treasury, and higher cost of goods caused by increased tolls on the Canal.[25]

RESTORATION OF CONSTITUTIONAL PRINCIPLES

A definite impression emerges from the evidence that has been offered, an impression of chicanery and loss of constitutional principles. Briefly, here is that image:

The Canal was sacrificed so Panama could pay her debts to the banks. The majority of the U.S. politicians, in Congress and in the Administration, were beholden in some manner to banking interests, and pleasing bankers had priority over voters or the Constitution. Voters were taken for granted, although 80% of them opposed the Treaties; they could be won back later, but bankers had long memories. The Establishment elitists trained Mr. Carter and believed they could safely by-pass the electorate.

A part of the scheme for surrendering the Canal included installing Omar Torrijos as Panama's dictator rather than working through President Arias's democracy. Efrain Angueira, the U.S. intelligence officer, aided in the plot; and it is difficult to believe that high Canal Zone officials did not acquiesce. Torrijos was selected over Martinez and Pinilla, both of whom would probably reject the chicanery.

Neither the Constitution nor international law were to stand in the way of bank debts that could be satisfied by a Panama-owned Canal. Clever manipulators circumvented these standards. A few well trained clones perpetrated this swindle of U.S. territory, and absolutely nothing may ever be done about it short of a war emergency take over—or an uprising of American voters demanding the restoration of constitutional principles, including either the legal ratification of the 1977 Treaties or their rejection.

Does Panama have the expertise and stability to operate and protect the intricate Canal system? No U.S. official with realistic experience and responsibility in Canal operation, especially in wartime when protection requires the combined U.S. military, naval, and industrial power, has been known to favor loss of U.S. sovereign rights over the Canal and its indispensable protective framework of the Canal Zone.

What shall be done? What if Panama as a sovereign nation asks Cuba, or the USSR, or Nicaragua to help operate the Canal and defend it? Would Washington rationalize such action as a treaty violation or as a part of the new world order in which U.S. interests must be adjusted for the common good?

The U.S. President should today immediately submit Panama's counter-reservation to the Senate for a two-thirds vote, as required by the Constitution (Article II) and the 1969 Vienna Convention (Article 2.1(d)), and as prescribed by the American Law Institute's *Restatement of the Law (Second)* (Section 136) and Charles G. Fenwick's *International Law* (pp.437-38).[26] President Carter did not ask the Senate to vote, obviously fearing rejection of Panama's proposal and thereby, the Treaties themselves.

If, at a future date, the Senate should vote on and not consent to Panama's counter-reservation, the 1977 Treaties would officially be invalid. The implementing legislation (P.L. 96-70) could then be repealed, subject to presidential veto. If P.L. 96-70 should be repealed, all Canal areas not already transferred would remain U.S. property and territory. Property already disposed of, however, could *not* be reclaimed. A new treaty would be indicated if transfer of the remaining property should be desired.

An alternative to the Senate two-thirds vote of approval would be Panama's withdrawal of her counter-reservation, thereby making both sets of Treaties identical.[27] If constitutional and international law standards are to be preserved, one of these alternatives is required—whether the Canal is transferred or not.

President Carter made 68 Senators a part of the Canal swindle by not assuring that they had consented to all parts of his Treaties. His successor to the presidency is obligated under his oath of office, the Constitution, and international law to ask the Senate's "Advice and Consent" to the disputed counter-reservation. He could also ask Panama to withdraw its contentious proposal. Or, the Senate itself could initiate action to determine the status of the counter-reservation and thereby, the validity of the Treaties.

WHAT DO LEGAL SCHOLARS SAY?

A number of jurists say that Panama's counter-reservation is *substantive*. Under the Constitution and international law, substantive material requires Senate approval. Professor Charles Rice of Notre Dame University wrote on November 26, 1984 to Phillip Harman:

I would regard Panama's counter-reservation as a substantive reservation. . . . If a case were presented in court, in which proper parties with standing raised the issue, it would be for the court to decide. . . .

I am not sure the Senate would have any jurisdiction to raise the issue at this time . . . . A possible argument could be that the Senate's consent was obtained by fraud and that therefore the Senate has a duty to reexamine the issue; or at least that the Senate has a duty to examine the allegations that its consent was achieved by fraud.

Legal scholars were asked four questions: (1) Was Panama's counter-reservation substantive? (2) Does it modify the DeConcini reservation? (3) Should the Senate have voted on it? (4) Who determines if a reservation is substantive?

The distinguished jurist, William M. Whitman, and Professor Richard Falk, Princeton University, answered "yes" to the first three questions, as did former Governor of New Hampshire Meldrim Thomson, also a constitutional lawyer, who added that the Senate determines whether a change is substantive. Appendix W contains Whitman's views.

Professor Hans Smit of Columbia had "little doubt that . . . the Panamanians will rely on what you call this reservation," i.e., it will be "invoked by them as if it were a true reservation." Jurist Charles Maechling called the reservation "substantive" and "inconsistent with the DeConcini reservation . . . if governments officially take their positions." Constitutionalist Seymour Rubin said "meaningful" to Panama's counter-reservation.

Dean Rusk, former Secretary of State, dismissed the issue as merely "theoretical." And Harold Maier of Vanderbilt University concluded that ". . . only a later dispute" can settle matters. Columbia's Professor Oscar Schachter took essentially the same position as the State Department, i.e., non-substantive. Several jurists declined to offer specific answers, including Luis Kutner who called the whole affair a communist coup, Carter blunder and Munich-style appeasement.

WHAT DOES PRESIDENT REAGAN SAY?

Before becoming President, Ronald Reagan warned that Panama could nationalize the Canal and that the UN Charter prohibited the use of force to prevent it. *President* Reagan understands this threat of expropriation and nationalization, and also the tendentious nature of the existing Panama Treaties. These points were clear in September 1979 when his friend, Dr. Donald M. Dozer, gave him a copy of the Dozer Memorandum

(Appendix N), proving that Article VI of the Constitution had not been used in terminating the 1903 Treaty and therefore, that the 1977 Treaties were "of no legal effect." Mr. Reagan indicated his concurrence about the "hangup" in his October 5, 1979 letter to Dr. Dozer:

I am afraid I have about "shot my bolt" on the Canal. I did some radio scripts (carried on 300 stations) about the hangup and have brought it to attention wherever I spoke around the country. Evidently, the press didn't pick those up.

. . . .

I'm very much afraid that what I said I hope wouldn't happen is happening, and that we are going to say—I told you so.

. . . .

I know how you must feel after your valiant fight. Maybe as things heat up in Central America and the Panamanian dictator shows his true colors we might still be able to salvage something.

Questions: If convinced of Professor Dozer's position, why did Mr. Reagan not go on national television to alert the public about unconstitutional Treaties? Why did he not use this issue in the 1980 presidential campaign against Mr. Carter, and why not in 1984 against Walter Mondale who had pushed the Carter Treaties? Is President Reagan willing to accept suspect treaties "as things heat up in Central America," quoting his letter to Dr. Dozer? Still quoting, does he believe "we might still be able to salvage something"—or might not?

The threat of nationalization is sufficient motivation to determine the status of the 1903 Treaty and the 1977 Treaties. The record of the June 23, 1983 hearing before the Senate Subcommittee on Separation of Powers is a proper starting point for the Senate Committee on the Judiciary, or other appropriate investigative body. If a serious effort is to be made, testimony under oath is a must, with a special counsel with subpoena powers to summon witnesses.

Sworn testimony is needed from the representatives of the American people, both elected and appointed, including but not limited to the following: President Carter and Vice President Mondale; Secretaries of State Vance, Kissinger and Rusk; Deputy Secretary of State Christopher; Assistant Secretary of State Rogers; Ambassadors Linowitz, Popper and Jorden; Senators Robert Byrd, Baker, Sarbanes, DeConcini, Biden, Brooke, Hatch, Helms and Laxalt; Representatives Crane, Hubbard, Murphy, and Hansen; National Security Advisers Pastor and Brzezinski; Legal Advisers Hansell and Kozak; and staff members who handled the Treaties for the Foreign Relations Committee and for the Senate leadership.

Such an inquiry would require political courage—a great deal more than formulating a record to gather dust on the shelf. Senator John East made a brave beginning with his lonesome Subcommittee, but it was only a beginning. Only an interested, strong-willed and impartial special counsel with subpoena powers could develop the true story of the Canal swindle and of the harried legislators manipulated into consenting to disaster. But, more than a story is needed. Where evidence supports probable wrongdoing, indictment and prosecution is the way to keep a nation of laws.

The "new diplomacy" is on trial—should be on trial. Will Americans accept a "diplomacy" that tramples upon the Constitution so that the Executive and Legislative Branches may circumvent the inconveniences of checks and balances in order to achieve their legislative and foreign policy goals—goals that would have been defeated in the case of the Panama Canal?

Since the days of the Treaties, the American mood has moved upbeat and positive, a new beginning. The time is right to let the President and Washington representatives know that the *status quo* on ambiguous and dangerous treaties is not acceptable.

APPENDICES

Appendix A

ROLL CALL: SENATORS VOTING TO SURRENDER THE PANAMA CANAL ON APRIL 18, 1978

John Sparkman, D-Ala.***
Mike Gravel, D-Alas.*
Dennis DeConcini, D-Ariz.
Dale Bumpers, D-Ark.
Kaneaster Hodges, D-Ark.**
Alan Cranston, D-Cal.
S.I. Hayakawa, R-Cal.***
Gary Hart, D-Colo.
Floyd Haskell, D-Colo.*
Abraham Ribicoff, D-Conn.***
Lowell Weicker, R-Conn.
Joseph Biden, D-Del.
Lawton Chiles, D-Fla.
Richard Stone, D-Fla.*
Sam Nunn, D-Ga.
Herman Talmadge, D-Ga.*
Daniel Inouye, D-Haw.
Spark Matsunaga, D-Haw.
Frank Church, D-Ida.*
Charles H. Percy, R-Ill.**
Adlai Stevenson, D-Ill.*
Birch Bayh, D-Ind.*
Dick Clark, D-Iowa*

James Culver, D-Iowa*
James Pearson, R-Kan.*
W. Huddleston, D-Kan.**
Russell Long, D-La.
William Hathaway, D-Me.*
Edmund Muskie, D-Me.***
Charles Mathias, R-Md.
Paul Sarbanes, D-Md.
Edward Brooke, R-Mass.*
Edward Kennedy, D-Mass.
Donald Riegle, D-Mich.
W. Anderson, D-Minn.*
Muriel Humphrey, D-Minn.***
John Danforth, R-Mo.
T. Eagleston, D-Mo.
Paul Hatfield, D-Mont.***
Howard Cannon, D-Nev.*
John Durkin, D-N.H.*
T. McIntyre, D-N.H.*
C.P. Case, R-N.J.**
H. Williams, D-N.J.***
Jacob Javits, R-N.Y.***
Daniel Moynihan, D-N.Y.

John Glenn, D-Ohio	George McGovern, D-S.D.*
H. Metzenbaum, D-Ohio	Howard Baker, R-Tenn.***
Henry Bellmon, R-Okla.	James Sasser, D-Tenn.
M.O. Hatfield, R-Ore.	Lloyd Bentsen, D-Tex.
R. Packwood, R-Ore.	Patrick Leahy, D-Ver.
Robert Morgan, D-N.C.*	Robert Stafford, R-Ver.
John Heinz, R-Pa.	Henry Jackson, D-Wash.***
John Chafee, R-R.I.	W. Magnuson, D-Wash.*
Clairborne Pell, D-R.I.	Robert Byrd, D-W.Va.
Ernest Hollings, D-S.C.	Gaylord Nelson, D-Wis.*
James Abourezk, D-S.D.	William Proxmire, D-Wis.

*Defeated in general election
**Defeated in primary election
***Retired or resigned
****Deceased

Note: 35 of these senators who voted to surrender the Panama Canal are no longer in the U.S. Senate for various reasons: Many attributed their defeat to their votes on the Canal Treaties. In 1978, 10 were defeated in the general election, 2 in the primary, and 4 retired. In 1980, 9 were defeated in the general election and 4 retired. In 1982, one was defeated, Howard W. Cannon, D.-Nev. In 1984, two were defeated, two retired and one died.

The same 68 Senators listed above also consented to the Neutrality Treaty on March 16, 1978.

Appendix A-1

ROLL CALL: REPRESENTATIVES VOTING TO IMPLEMENT THE PANAMA CANAL TREATIES ON SEPTEMBER 26, 1979

The following members of the U.S. House of Representatives voted to implement the Panama Canal Treaties (1977). The vote count was decisive, 232 to 188 with 196 Democrats and 36 Republicans agreeing to the Panama Canal Act of 1979 which became the second step required for the "surrender" of the Canal. The Canal could have been "saved" at that time by a House vote to reject the implementing legislation. In no wise was approval obligatory. This was an important part of the Constitution's unique system of checks and balances. Did the people's representatives know this?

An asterisk (*) indicates those no longer in the House. A dagger (†) identifies those switching from their September 20, 1979 vote. See additional explanation at the end of this listing.

Democrats (196)

Joseph Addabbo, N.Y.	Bill Alexander, Ark.
Daniel Akaka, Hawaii	Jerome Ambro, N.Y.*
Donald Albosta, Mich.	Ike Andrews, N.C.
	Frank Annuzio, Ill.

Thomas Ashley, Ohio*
Les Aspin, Wisc.
Les AuCoin, Ore.
Alvin Baldus, Wisc.*
Michael Barnes, Md.
Berkley Bedell, Iowa
Anthony Beilenson, Cal.*
Adam Benjamin, Ind.
Mario Biaggi, N.Y.
Jonathan Bingham, N.Y.*
James Blanchard, Mich.*
Corinne Boggs, La.†
Edward Boland, Mass.
Richard Bolling, Mo.*
William Boner, Tenn.
David Bonior, Mich.
Don Bonker, Wash.
Marilyn Bouquard, Tenn.†
Davis Bowen, Miss.*
John Brademas, Ind.*
John Breau, La.†
Jake Brinkley, Ga.*†
William Brodhead, Mich.*
Jack Brooks, Tex.
George Brown, Cal.
Bill Bulison, Mo.*
John Burton, Cal.*
Phillip Burton, Cal.
Bob Carr, Mich.
John Cavanaugh, Neb.*
Shirley Chisholm, N.Y.*
William Clay, Mo.
Tony Coelho, Cal.
Cardiss Collins, Ill.
John Conyers, Mich.
James Corman, Cal.*
William Cotter, Conn.*
Norman D'Amours, N.H.*
George Danielson, Cal.*
Thomas Daschle, S.D.
Mendel Davis, S.C.*
Ronald Dellums, Cal.
Butler Derrick, S.C.
Norman Dicks, Wash.
Charles Diggs, Mich.*
John Dingell, Mich.
Julian Dixon, Cal.
Christopher Dodd, Conn.*
Thomas Downey, N.Y.

Robert Drinan, Mass.*
Joseph Early, Mass.
Robert Edgar, Pa.
Don Edwards, Cal.
Allen Ertel, Pa.*
Billy Lee Evans, Ga.*
David Evans, Ind.*†
John Fary, Ill.*
Dante Fascell, Fla.
Vic Fazio, Cal.
Geraldine Ferraro, N.Y.*†
Joseph Fisher, Va.*
Floyd Fithian, Ind.*
James Florio, N.J.
Thomas Foley, Wash.
William Ford, Mich.
Harold Ford, Tenn.
Wyche Fowler, Jr., Ga.
James Frost, Tex.*
Robert Garcia, N.Y.
Richard Gephardt, Mo.
Robert Giaimo, Conn.*
Sam Gibbons, Fla.
Don Glickman, Kan.
Henry Gonzalez, Tex.
Albert Gore, Tenn.*
William Gray, Pa.
Frank Guarini, N.J.†
Tony Hall, Ohio*
Lee Hamilton, Ind.
Tom Harkin, Iowa*
Herbert Harris II, Va.*
Augustus Hawkins, Cal.
Bill Hefner, N.C.
Cecil Hefnel, Hawaii*
Kenneth Holland, S.C.*
James Howard, N.J.
William Hughes, N.J.
Andrew Jacobs, Ind.†
Edgar Jenkins, Ga.
James Jones, Okla.†
Ed Jones, Tenn.
Robert Kastenmeier, Wisc.
Dale Kildee, Mich.
Raymond Kogovsek, Colo.
Peter Kostmayer, Pa.
John La Falce, N.Y.
Raymond Lederer, Pa.*
William Lehman, Fla.

Mickey Leland, Tex.
Elliott Levitas, Ga.
Clarence Long, Md.*
Mike Lowry, Wash.
Stanley Lundine, N.Y.
Mike McCormack, Wash.*
Matthew McHugh, N.Y.
Gunn McKay, Utah*
Andrew Maguire, N.J.*
Edward Markey, Mass.
Robert Matsui, Cal.
Nicholas Mavroules, Mass.
Romano Mazzoli, Ky.
Daniel Mica, Fla.†
Barbara Mikulski, Md.
Abner Mikva, Ill.*
George Miller, Cal.
Norman Mineta, Cal.
Joseph Minish, N.J.
Parren Mitchell, Md.
John Moakley, Mass.
Toby Moffett, Conn.
Robert Mollohan, W. Va.
William Moorhead, Pa.*
John Murphy, N.Y.*
Austin Murphy, Pa.†
John Murtha, Pa.
Michael Myers, Pa.*
Stephen Neal, N.C.
Lucien Nedzi, Mich.*
Richard Nolan, Minn.*
Henry Nowak, N.Y.
James Oberstar, Minn.
David Obey, Wisc.
Richard Ottinger, N.Y.
Leon Panetta, Cal.
Edward Patten, N.J.*
Jerry Patterson, Cal.
Donald Pease, Ohio
Claude Pepper, Fla.
Peter Peyser, N.Y.*
Jake Pickle, Tex.
Richardson Preyer, N.C.*
Melvin Price, Ill.
Charles Rangel, N.Y.
William Ratchford, Conn.
Henry Reuss, Wisc.*
Frederick Richmond, N.Y.*
Robert Roe, N.J.

Dan Rostenkowski, Ill.
Edward Roybal, Cal.
Marty Russo, Ill.
Martin Sabo, Minn.
James Scheuer, N.Y.
Patricia Schroeder, Colo.
John Seiberling, Ohio
James Shannon, Mass.
Philip Sharp, Ind.
Paul Simon, Ill.
Neal Smith, Iowa
Stephen Solarz, N.Y.
Gladys Spellman, Md.*
Fernand St. Germain, R.I.
Edward Stack, Fla.*
Fortney Stark, Cal.
Tom Steed, Okla.*
Bennett Stewart, Ill.*
Louis Stokes, Ohio
Gerry Studds, Mass.
Al Swift, Wash.
Michael Syndar, Okla.
Frank Thompson, Jr., N.J.*
Bob Traxler, Mich.
Morris Udall, Ariz.
Al Ullman, Ore.*
Lionell Van Deerlin, Cal.*
Charles Vanik, Ohio*
Bruce Vento, Minn.
Doug Walgren, Penn.
Henry Waxman, Cal.
James Weaver, Ore.
Theodore Weiss, N.Y.
Charles H. Wilson, Cal.*
Timothy Wirth, Colo.
Lester Wolff, N.Y.*
Howard Wolpe, Mich.
Jim Wright, Tex.
Sidney Yates, Ill.
Robert Young, Mo.
Clement Zablocki, Wisc.
Leo Zeferetti, N.Y.*
Republicans (36)
John Anderson, Ill.*
Robin Beard, Tenn.*†
Douglas Bereuter, Neb.†
Ed Bethune, Ark.*†
William Broomfield, Mich.
John Buchanan, Ala.*

Caldwell Butler, Va.*
Barber Conable, N.Y.*
Silvio Conte, Mass.
Edward Derwinski, Ill.*
John Erlenborn, Ill.
Millicent Fenwick, N.J.*
Paul Findley, Ill.*
Hamilton Fish, Jr., N.Y.†
Edwin Forsythe, N.J.†
Bill Frenzel, Minn.
William Green, N.Y.
Harold Hollenbeck, N.J.†*
James Jeffords, Ver.†
James Johnson, Colo.*
Jim Leach, Iowa

Robert McClory, Ill.†*
Paul McCloskey, Cal.*
Stewart McKinney, Conn.
Marc Marks, Penn.*
Charles Pashayan, Cal.†
Joel Pritchard, Wash.
Carl Pursell, Mich.
Thomas Railsback, Ill.*
John Rhodes, Ariz.†*
Bill Royer, Cal.†*
Harold Sawyer, Mich.†
William Stanton, Ohio*
David Stockman, Mich.*
Bob Wilson, Cal.*
John Wydler, N.Y.†*

†These 25 Congressman had voted on September 20, 1979 to reject the Conference Report on the Panama Canal Act of 1979, the implementing legislation, but switched their positions for the final vote on September 26, 1979 after minor changes had been made and following intensive lobbying by the White House and comments by Congressman Robert Bauman, R.-Md. Frank Turberville, Jr. of the Canal Watchers' Educational Association sent separate letters to each of these 25 Congressmen asking what had caused them to switch their positions. No answer from anyone was received.

Appendix B

STATEMENT OF DR. CHARLES H. BREECHER BEFORE THE SENATE SUBCOMMITTEE ON SEPARATION OF POWERS, JUNE 23, 1983

Mr. Chairman, I make two flat assertions which I made under oath at the occasion of my deposition. First, the Panama Canal Treaties have not—I repeat, not—been ratified in international law, and they therefore did not go into effect on the 1st of October 1979, and are not in effect now.

The reason is very simple. In their respective instruments of ratification, the United States and Panama did not agree to the same text of the treaties. Instead, Panama first agreed to the treaties as the President of the United States had ratified them, pursuant to Senate advice and consent, and then added in both its instruments of ratification, unilaterally, something they called an understanding, on which Panama made its agreement to the treaties contingent.

This Panamanian understanding—in reality, a counter-reservation to both treaties, three paragraphs long—would, had it been accepted by the United States, have nullified the so-called DeConcini reservation under which the United States has permanently—and I repeat, permanently—the right to use independently—

and I repeat, independently—without Panamanian consent, or even against Panamanian opposition, military force in Panama to keep the Canal open and operating. Since the United States has not accepted this Panamanian so-called understanding, there are no treaties in international law.

My second point is that the Constitution unequivocally bars the President of the United States from appointing Panamanians, nonresident aliens—and I repeat, nonresident aliens—as members, administrators or deputy administrators of the Panama Canal Commission, a U.S. Government agency. This unsurmountable bar is expressed by the Constitution in the same pithy way as, for example, for infants, requiring that all executive officers shall bind themselves by oath or affirmation to support the Constitution. That is Article VI, section 3. A nonresident alien owing allegiance to Panama can obviously not swear that oath. Further, the Constitution provides that all civil officers can be removed from office in impeachment and for conviction of treason. . . .

Again, it is obvious that a nonresident cannot commit treason against the United States, so these provisions of the Constitution alone are an absolute bar to the President appointing nonresident aliens. . . .

Now, let me go back to the nonratification of the treaties—an issue of international law. Here, I want to make it absolutely clear that if there is one thing that is beyond any argument in international law, it is that to ratify a bilateral—and again I stress bilateral treaty—the parties must agree in their instruments of ratification to the same written text. Otherwise, there is no meeting of the minds, as required for ratification. There is no ratification if one party makes its agreement to the treaties contingent on any amendment, condition, understanding, interpretation, reservation, declaration, or whatever it wants to call it, that is not formally and verbatim accepted by the other party. . . . Note that Panama specifically makes its agreement to the treaties contingent on that so-called understanding.

Now, in paragraph 2, this Panamanian counter-reservation, is really a further proposed amendment to both treaties—it says in undisguised language that the DeConcini condition can be exercised in the spirit of cooperation with Panama only . . . the exact contrary of DeConcini. . . .

In paragraph 1, in the most camouflaged lawyers' language imaginable, Panama says flatly that the DeConcini reservation can be exercised only in self-defense, pursuant to Article 18 of the OAS Charter. The catch, of course, is that Article 18 has been amended in a very limited way in United States-Panamanian relations only by the DeConcini reservation.

I fail to see how anyone could claim that the United States has accepted that Panamanian so-called understanding. Where, may I ask? It is even more preposterous to say that these three paragraphs are just a correct factual statement which does not need acceptance. Saying that is demeaning to Panama, in my view, because why then did they put these three paragraphs in in three places?

It is demeaning to President Carter because if it were really a correct factual statement, the President could have just accepted it, maybe, in the protocol. It is an outright affront to the common sense of anyone if—that is a very big "if"—he has a full record and, may I add, if he cannot be bluffed all that easily.

. . . . .

There has not been a word of congressional or Executive Branch testimony on the nonratification issue. On the constitutional issue, there was testimony by a Justice Department attorney. . . . The so-called Foy memo repudiated a previous State Department position contained in a letter to Senator Roth in May 1978. . . .

That letter said that the Congress or a treaty could prescribe any, I repeat, any qualifications for Federal office, even foreign allegiance. Nonsense, of course, but the letter admitted at least that the members of the Panama Canal Commission were Federal officers.

. . . . .

Now, let me at the end, Mr. Chairman, to sum up in the simplest possible terms once more. What we have here on the documented record on nonratification is the worst fraud—I am very sorry, Mr. Chairman, I cannot use any other word, but if you wish, I shall substitute "swindle" or "hoax," in the words of another distinguished Senator—ever perpetrated on the U.S. Senate and on the American people.

That hoax was committed by pretending that in their respective instruments of ratification, the U.S. and Panama had agreed to the same treaty text, whereas, in reality, under the Panamanian instrument of ratification the U.S. could exercise the DeConcini reservation only on self-defense, pursuant to Article 18 of the OAS Charter, and in cooperation with Panama, the exact contrary of the DeConcini reservation, as contained in the U.S. ratification document of the Neutrality Treaty. Hence, no ratification, and the Treaties never came into effect. It is as simple as that.

What is more . . . we have three major published papers, what I call smoking guns, admitting U.S. Executive Branch complicity in the sorry affair: first, a speech by William D. Rogers, former Assistant Secretary for Latin American Affairs, . . . second, a letter by Ambassador David Popper, the man charged with the implementation of the Panama Canal Treaties, . . . and third, most startling, in President Carter's book at pages 172-74.

So much for the nonratification issue, and I challenge anybody to make any kind of argument that these treaties have been ratified. . . .

On the appointment of nonresidents . . . to U.S. civil office . . . this is the worst imaginable violation of the U.S. Constitution and of its privileges and immunities of U.S. citizens.

Now, this double fraud, which stares you in the face on the record, if you only had the record—it is, of course, a big "if"; nobody has it except the bureaucracy and somebody who really wants to go after it—has been perpetrated to date by what I can only call stonewalling.

Appendix C

EXCERPTS FROM TEXTS OF THE PROTOCOL OF EXCHANGE AND THE INSTRUMENTS OF RATIFICATION OF THE PANAMA CANAL TREATIES (1977)

The purpose of Appendix C, which directly relates to Dr. Breecher's statement in Appendix B, is to urge the reader to compare—*compare* the U.S. instruments with Panama's.

The following texts reveal the *differences* in the two sets of instruments, as well as an inconsistency in the Protocol of Exchange. It should be noted that every word and every paragraph of reservations, amendments, conditions and understandings are meticulously repeated *verbatim* in the instruments of ratification of both countries—*except* that Panama's three paragraph counter-reservation (identified in the margin of the page by the double vertical lines) was contained in both sets of Panama's instruments but *not* in the two sets of U.S. instruments.

Moreover, in the Protocol of Exchange, signed by U.S. President Jimmy Carter and Panamanian Head of Government Omar Torrijos Herrera, two paragraphs of Panama's three paragraph counter-reservation are also repeated *verbatim*. These are identified in the margin by the double vertical lines.

Panama's counter-reservation, called "the most substantive change . . . that can be imagined," was never voted on or consented to by the U.S. Senate. A consideration of the Protocol of Exchange, in which the Senate had no part, and a comparison of the two sets of instruments of ratification reveal that there was no meeting of minds between the United States and the Republic of Panama—and therefore, two sets of Treaties.

Sources of Documents: Department of State Bulletin, July 1978. Senate Debate on the Panama Canal Treaties: A Compendium of Major Statements, Documents, Record Votes and Relevant Events, prepared for the Committee on Foreign Relations, U.S. Senate, February 1979.

V. PROTOCOL OF EXCHANGE OF INSTRUMENTS OF RATIFICATION FOR THE PANAMA CANAL TREATIES, AND THE RELATED INSTRUMENTS OF RATIFICATION, JUNE 16, 1978

PROTOCOL OF EXCHANGE OF INSTRUMENTS OF RATIFICATION REGARDING THE TREATY CONCERNING THE PERMANENT NEUTRALITY AND OPERATION OF THE PANAMA CANAL AND THE PANAMA CANAL TREATY

The undersigned, Jimmy Carter, President of the United States of America, and Omar Torrijos Herrera, Head of Government of the Republic of Panama, in the exercise of their respective constitutional authorities, have met for the purpose of delivering to each other the instruments of ratification of their respective governments of the Treaty Concerning the Permanent Neutrality and Operation of the Panama Canal and of the Panama Canal Treaty (the "Treaties").

The respective instruments of ratification of the Treaties have been carefully compared and found to be in due form. Delivery of the respective instruments took place this day, it being understood and agreed by the United States of America and the Republic of Panama that, unless the Parties otherwise agree through an exchange of Notes in conformity with the resolution of the Senate of the United States of America of April 18, 1978, the exchange of the instruments of ratification shall be effective on April 1, 1979, and the date of the exchange of the instruments of ratification for the purposes of Article VIII of the Treaty Concerning the Permanent Neutrality and Operation of the Panama Canal and Article II of the Panama Canal Treaty shall therefore be April 1, 1979.

The ratifications by the Government of the United States of America of the Treaties recite in their entirety the amendments, conditions, reservations and understandings contained in the resolution of March 16, 1978, of the Senate of the

United States of America advising and consenting to ratification of the Treaty Concerning the Permanent Neutrality and Operation of the Panama Canal, and the reservations and understandings contained in resolution of April 18, 1978, of the Senate of the United States of America advising and consenting to ratification of the Panama Canal Treaty.

Said amendments, conditions, reservations and understandings have been communicated by the Government of the United States of America to the Government of the Republic of Panama. Both governments agree that the Treaties, upon entry into force in accordance with their provisions, will be applied in accordance with the abovementioned amendments, conditions, reservations and understandings.

Pursuant to the resolution of the Senate of the United States of America of March 16, 1978, the following text contained in the instrument of ratification of the United States of America of the Treaty Concerning the Permanent Neutrality and Operation of the Panama Canal and agreed upon by both agreements is repeated herewith:

"Nothing in the Treaty shall preclude the Republic of Panama and the United States of America from making, in accordance with their respective constitutional processes, any agreement or arrangement between the two countries to facilitate performance at any time after December 31, 1999, of their responsibilities to maintain the regime of neutrality established in the Treaty, including agreements or arrangements for the stationing of any United States military forces or the maintenance of defense sites after that date in the Republic of Panama that the Republic of Panama and the United States of America may deem necessary or appropriate."

The Republic of Panama agrees to the exchange of the instruments of ratification of the Panama Canal Treaty and of the Treaty Concerning the Permanent Neutrality and Operation of the Panama Canal on the understanding that there are positive rules of public international law contained in multilateral treaties to which both the Republic of Panama and the United States of America are Parties and which consequently both States are bound to implement in good faith, such as Article 1, paragraph 2 and Article 2, paragraph 4 of the Charter of the United Nations, and Articles 18 and 20 of the Charter of the Organization of American States.

It is also the understanding of the Republic of Panama that the actions which either Party may take in the exercise of its rights and the fulfillment of its duties in accordance with the aforesaid Panama Canal Treaty and the Treaty Concerning the Permanent Neutrality and Operation of the Panama Canal, including measures to reopen the Canal or to restore its normal operation, if it should be interrupted or obstructed, will be effected in a manner consistent with the principles of mutual respect and cooperation on which the new relationship established by those Treaties is based.

In witness thereof, the respective Plenipotentiaries have signed this Protocol of Exchange at Panama, in duplicate, in the English and Spanish languages on this sixteenth day of June, 1978, both texts being equally authentic.

For the United States of America:
JIMMY CARTER.
For the Republic of Panama:
OMAR TORRIJOS HERRERA.

U.S. INSTRUMENT—PANAMA CANAL TREATY

Jimmy Carter, President of the United States of America-   *To all to whom these presents shall come, greeting:*

Considering that:

The Panama Canal Treaty was signed at Washington on September 7, 1977; and

The Senate of the United States of America by its resolution of April 18, 1978, two-thirds of the Senators present concurring therein, gave its advice and consent to ratification of the Treaty, subject to the following:

(a) Reservations:

(1) Pursuant to its adherence to the principle of nonintervention, any action taken by the United States of America in the exercise of its rights to assure that the Panama Canal shall remain open, neutral, secure, and accessible, pursuant to the provisions of the Panama Canal Treaty, the Treaty Concerning the Permanent Neutrality and Operation of the Panama Canal, and the resolutions of ratification thereto, shall be only for the purpose of assuring that the Canal shall remain open, neutral, secure, and accessible, and shall not have as its purpose or be interpreted as a right of intervention in the internal affairs of the Republic of Panama or interference with its political independence or sovereign integrity.

(2) The instruments of ratification of the Panama Canal Treaty to be exchanged by the United States of America and the Republic of Panama shall each include provisions whereby each Party agrees to waive its rights and release the other Party from its obligations under paragraph 2 of Article XII of the Treaty.

(3) Notwithstanding any provision of the Treaty, no funds may be drawn from the Treasury of the United States of America for payments under paragraph 4 of Article XIII without statutory authorization.

(4) Any accumulated unpaid balance under paragraph 4(c) of Article XIII of the Treaty at the date of termination of the Treaty shall be payable only to the extent of any operating surplus in the last year of the duration of the Treaty, and nothing in such paragraph may be construed as obligating the United States of America to pay, after the date of the termination of the Treaty, any such unpaid balance which shall have accrued before such date.

(5) Exchange of the instruments of ratification of the Panama Canal Treaty and of the Treaty Concerning the Permanent Neutrality and Operation of the Panama Canal shall not be effective earlier than March 31, 1979, and such Treaties shall not enter into force prior to October 1, 1979, unless legislation necessary to implement the provisions of the Panama Canal Treaty shall have been enacted by the Congress of the United States of America before March 31, 1979.

(6) After the date of entry into force of the Treaty, the Panama Canal Commission shall, unless otherwise provided by legislation enacted by the Congress of the United States of America, be obligated to reimburse the Treasury of the United States of America, as nearly as possible, for the interest cost of the funds or other assets directly invested in the Commission by the Government of the United States of America and for the interest cost of the funds or other assets directly invested in the predecessor Panama Canal Company by the Government of the United States of America and not reimbursed before the date of entry into force of the Treaty. Such reimbursement for such interest costs shall be made at a rate determined by the Secretary of the Treasury of the United States of America and at

annual intervals to the extent earned, and if not earned, shall be made from subsequent earnings. For purposes of this reservation, the phrase "funds or other assets directly invested" shall have the same meaning as the phrase "net direct investment" has under section 62 of title 2 of the Canal Zone Code.

(b) Understandings:

(1) Before the first day of the three-day period beginning on the date of entry into force of the Treaty and before each three-year period following thereafter, the two Parties shall agree upon the specific levels and quality of services, as are referred to in paragraph 5 of Article III of the Treaty, to be provided during the following three-year period and, except for the first three-year period, on the reimbursement to be made for the costs of such services, such services to be limited to such as are essential to the effective functioning of the Canal operating areas and the housing areas referred to in paragraph 5 of Article III. If payments made under paragraph 5 of Article III for the preceding three-year period, including the initial three-year period, exceed or are less than the actual costs to the Republic of Panama for supplying, during such period, the specific levels and quality of services agreed upon, then the Panama Canal Commission shall deduct from or add to the payment required to be made to the Republic of Panama for each of the following three years one-third of such excess or deficit, as the case may be. There shall be an independent and binding audit, conducted by an auditor mutually selected by both Parties, of any costs of services disputed by the two Parties pursuant to the reexamination of such costs provided for in this understanding.

(2) Nothing in paragraph 3, 4, or 5 of Article IV of the Treaty may be construed to limit either the provisions of the first paragraph of Article IV providing that each Party shall act, in accordance with its constitutional process, to meet danger threatening the security of the Panama Canal, or the provisions of paragraph 2 of Article IV providing that the United States of America shall have primary responsibility to protect and defend the Canal for the duration of the Treaty.

(3) Nothing in paragraph 4(c) of Article XIII of the Treaty shall be construed to limit the authority of the United States of America, through the United States Government agency called the Panama Canal Commission, to make such financial decisions and incur such expenses as are reasonable and necessary for the management, operation, and maintenance of the Panama Canal. In addition, toll rates established pursuant to paragraph 2(d) of Article III need not be set at levels designed to produce revenues to cover the payment to the Republic of Panama described in paragraph 4(c) of Article XIII.

(4) Any agreement concluded pursuant to paragraph 11 of Article IX of the Treaty with respect to the transfer of prisoners shall be concluded in accordance with the constitutional processes of both Parties.

(5) Nothing in the Treaty, in the Annex or Agreed Minute relating to the Treaty, or in any other agreement relating to the Treaty obligates the United States of America to provide any economic assistance, military grant assistance, security supporting assistance, foreign military sales credits, or international military education and training to the Republic of Panama.

(6) The President shall include all reservations and understandings incorporated by the Senate in this resolution of ratification in the instrument of ratification to be exchanged with the Government of the Republic of Panama.

Now, therefore, I, Jimmy Carter, President of the United States of America, ratify and confirm the Panama Canal Treaty, subject to the aforementioned reservations and understandings, and on behalf of the United States of America undertake to fulfill it faithfully. I further hereby waive, in the name of the United States of America, the rights of the United States of America under paragraph 2 of Article XII of the Panama Canal Treaty.

In testimony whereof, I have signed this instrument of ratification and caused the Seal of the United States of America to be affixed.

Done at the city of Washington, this 15th day of June in the year of our Lord one thousand nine hundred seventy-eight and of the independence of the United States of America the two hundred second.

By the President:
JIMMY CARTER.
Acting Secretary of State:
WARREN CHRISTOPHER.

PANAMANIAN INSTRUMENT—PANAMA CANAL TREATY

Whereas the Panama Canal Treaty was signed in Washington on September 7, 1977, by the authorized representatives of the Government of the Republic of Panama and of the Government of the United States of America;

Whereas the Republic of Panama, by means of the plebiscite stipulated by Article 274 of its Political Constitution, ratified the aforementioned Panama Canal Treaty;

Whereas the Senate of the United States of America gave its advice and consent to the ratification of the Panama Canal Treaty with the following understandings and reservations:

(*Author's Note:* All 6 Reservations and all 6 Understandings that are in the preceding U.S. Instrument of Ratification to the Panama Canal Treaty are repeated *verbatim* in this Panamanian Instrument of Ratification—and in the interests of brevity are not being repeated here. The *difference* between the U.S. and Panamanian Instruments is the following Panamanian three paragraph counter-reservation, marked with double vertical lines in the margin.)

The Republic of Panama agrees to the exchange of the instruments of ratification of the Panama Canal Treaty on the understanding that there are positive rules of public international law contained in multilateral treaties to which both the Republic of Panama and the United States of America are parties and which consequently both States are bound to implement in good faith, such as Article 1, paragraph 2 and Article 2, paragraph 4 of the Charter of the United Nations and Articles 18 and 20 of the Charter of the Organization of American States.

It is also the understanding of the Republic of Panama that the actions which either Party may take in the exercise of its rights and the fulfillment of its duties in accordance with the aforesaid Panama Canal Treaty, including measures to reopen the Canal or to restore its normal operation, if it should be interrupted or obstructed, will be effected in a manner consistent with the principles of mutual respect and cooperation on which the new relationship established by that Treaty is based.

The Republic of Panama declares that its political independence, territorial integrity, and self-determination are guaranteed by the unshakeable will of the Panamanian people. Therefore, the Republic of Panama will reject, in unity and with decisiveness and firmness, any attempt by any country to intervene in its internal or external affairs.

The Head of Government of the Republic of Panama, availing himself of the powers granted by Article 277 of the Constitution, after having considered the aforementioned Panama Canal Treaty, hereby ratifies it and, in the name of the Republic of Panama, undertakes to comply with it faithfully. The Head of Government further hereby waives, in the name of the Republic of Panama, the rights of the Republic of Panama under paragraph 2 of Article XII of the Panama Canal Treaty and releases the United States of America from its obligations under paragraph 2 of Article XII of the Panama Canal Treaty.

In witness thereof, this instrument of ratification is signed by the Head of Government of the Republic of Panama.

Done at Panama City, Republic of Panama, this sixteenth day of June 1978.
OMAR TORRIJOS HERRERA.

U.S. INSTRUMENT—NEUTRALITY TREATY

Jimmy Carter, President of the United States of America
To all to whom these present shall come, greeting:
Considering that:

The Treaty Concerning the Permanent Neutrality and Operation of the Panama Canal (Neutrality Treaty) was signed at Washington on September 7, 1977; and

The Senate of the United States of America by its resolution of March 16, 1978, two-thirds of the Senators present concurring therein, gave its advice and consent to ratification of the Neutrality Treaty, subject to the following:

(a) Amendments:

(1) At the end of Article IV, insert the following:

"A correct and authoritative statement of certain rights and duties of the Parties under the foregoing is contained in the Statement of Understanding issued by the Government of the United States of America on October 14, 1977, and by the Government of the Republic of Panama on October 18, 1977, which is hereby incorporated as an integral part of this Treaty, as follows:

"'Under the Treaty Concerning the Permanent Neutrality and Operation of the Panama Canal (the Neutrality Treaty), Panama and the United States have the responsibility to assure that the Panama Canal will remain open and secure to ships of all nations. The correct interpretation of this principle is that each of the two countries shall, in accordance with their respective constitutional processes, defend the Canal against any threat to the regime of neutrality, and consequently shall have the right to act against any aggression or threat directed against the Canal or against the peaceful transit of vessels through the Canal.

"'This does not mean, nor shall it be interpreted as, a right of intervention of the United States in the internal affairs of Panama. Any United States action will be directed at insuring that the Canal will remain open, secure, and accessible, and it shall never be directed against the territorial integrity or political independence of Panama.'."

(2) At the end of the first paragraph of Article VI, insert the following:

"In accordance with the statement of Understanding mentioned in Article IV above: 'The Neutrality Treaty provides that the vessels of war and auxiliary vessels of the United States and Panama will be entitled to transit the Canal expeditiously. This is intended, and it shall so be interpreted, to assure the transit of such vessels through the Canal as quickly as possible, without any impediment, with expedited treatment, and in case of need or emergency, to go to the head of the line of vessels in order to transit the Canal rapidly'."

(b) Conditions:

(1) Notwithstanding the provisions of Article V or any other provision of the Treaty, if the Canal is closed, or its operations are interfered with, the United States of America and the Republic of Panama shall each independently have the right to take such steps as each deems necessary, in accordance with its constitutional processes, including the use of military force in the Republic of Panama, to reopen the Canal or restore the operations of the Canal, as the case may be.

(2) The instruments of ratification of the Treaty shall be exchanged only upon the conclusion of a Protocol of Exchange, to be signed by authorized representatives of both Governments, which shall constitute an integral part of the Treaty documents and which shall include the following:

"Nothing in the Treaty shall preclude the Republic of Panama and the United States of America from making, in accordance with their respective constitutional processes, any agreement or arrangement between the two countries to facilitate performance at any time after December 31, 1999, of their responsibilities to maintain the regime of neutrality established in the Treaty, including agreements or arrangements for the stationing of any United States military forces or the maintenance of defense sites after that date in the Republic of Panama that the Republic of Panama and the United States of America may deem necessary or appropriate.".

(c) Reservations:

(1) Before the date of entry into force of the Treaty, the two Parties shall begin to negotiate for an agreement under which the American Battle Monuments Commission would, upon the date of entry into force of such agreement and thereafter, administer, free of all taxes and other charges and without compensation to the Republic of Panama and in accordance with the practices, privileges, and immunities associated with the administration of cemeteries outside the United States of America by the American Battle Monuments Commission, including the display of the flag of the United States of America, such part of Corozal Cemetery in the former Canal Zone as encompasses the remains of citizens of the United States of America.

(2) The flag of the United States of America may be displayed, pursuant to the provisions of paragraph 3 of Article VII of the Panama Canal Treaty, at such part of Corozal Cemetery in the former Canal Zone as encompasses the remains of citizens of the United States of America.

(3) The President—

(A) shall have announced, before the date of entry into force of the Treaty, his intention to transfer, consistent with an agreement with the Republic of Panama, and before the date of termination of the Panama Canal Treaty, to the American Battle Monuments Commission the administration of such part of Corozal Cemetery as encompasses the remains of citizens of the United States of America; and

(B) shall have announced, immediately after the date of exchange of instruments of ratification, plans, to be carried out at the expense of the Government of the United States of America, for—

(i) removing, before the date of entry into force of the Treaty, the remains of citizens of the United States of America from Mount Hope Cemetery to such part of Corozal Cemetery as encompasses such remains, except that the remains of any citizen whose next of kin objects in writing to the Secretary of the Army not later than three months after the date of exchange of the instruments of ratification of the Treaty shall not be removed; and

(ii) transporting to the United States of America for reinterment, if the next of kin so requests, not later than thirty months after the date of entry into force of the Treaty, any such remains encompassed by Corozal Cemetery and, before the date of entry into force of the Treaty, any remains removed from Mount Hope Cemetery pursuant to subclause (i); and

(C) shall have fully advised, before the date of entry into force of the Treaty, the next of kin objecting under clause (B)(i) of all available options and their implications.

(4) To carry out the purposes of Article III of the Treaty of assuring the security, efficiency, and proper maintenance of the Panama Canal, the United States of America and the Republic of Panama, during their respective periods of responsibility for Canal operations and maintenance, shall, unless the amount of the operating revenues of the Canal exceeds amount needed to carry out the purposes of such Article, use such revenues of the Canal only for purposes consistent with the purposes of Article III.

(d) Understandings:

(1) Paragraph 1(c) of Article III of the Treaty shall be construed as requiring, before any adjustment in tolls for use of the Canal, that the effects of any such toll adjustment on the trade patterns of the two Parties shall be given full consideration, including consideration of the following factors in a manner consistent with the regime of neutrality:

(A) the costs of operating and maintaining the Panama Canal;

(B) the competitive position of the use of the Canal in relation to other means of transportation;

(C) the interests of both Parties in maintaining their domestic fleets;

(D) the impact of such an adjustment on the various geographical areas of each of the two Parties; and

(E) the interests of both Parties in maximizing their international commerce.

The United States of America and the Republic of Panama shall cooperate in exchanging information necessary for the consideration of such factors.

(2) The agreement "to maintain the regime of neutrality established in this Treaty" in Article IV of the Treaty means that either of the two Parties to the Treaty may, in accordance with its constitutional processes, take unilateral action to defend the Panama Canal against any threat, as determined by the Party taking such action.

(3) The determination of "need or emergency" for the purpose of any vessel of war or auxiliary vessel of the United States of America or the Republic of

Panama going to the head of the line of vessels in order to transit the Panama Canal rapidly shall be made by the nation operating such vessel.

(4) Nothing in the Treaty, in Annex A or B thereto, in the Protocol relating to the Treaty, or in any other agreement relating to the Treaty, obligate the United States of America to provide any economic assistance, military grant assistance, security supporting assistance, foreign military sales credits, or international military education and training to the Republic of Panama.

(5) The President shall include all amendments, conditions, reservations, and understandings incorporated by the Senate in this resolution of ratification in the instrument of ratification to be exchanged with the Government of the Republic of Panama.

Now, therefore, I, Jimmy Carter, President of the United States of America, ratify and confirm the Neutrality Treaty, subject to the aforementioned amendments, conditions, reservations and understandings, and on behalf of the United States of America undertake to fulfill it faithfully.

In testimony whereof, I have signed this instrument of ratification and caused the Seal of the United States of America to be affixed.

Done at the city of Washington, this 15th day of June in the year of our Lord one thousand nine hundred seventy-eight and of the Independence of the United States of America the two hundred second.

By the President:
JIMMY CARTER.
Acting Secretary of State:
WARREN CHRISTOPHER.

PANAMANIAN INSTRUMENT—NEUTRALITY TREATY

Whereas the Treaty Concerning the Permanent Neutrality and Operation of the Panama Canal was signed in Washington on September 7, 1977, by the authorized representatives of the Government of the Republic of Panama and of the Government of the United States of America;

Whereas the Republic of Panama, by means of the plebiscite stipulated by Article 274 of its Political Constitution, ratified the aforementioned Neutrality Treaty;

Whereas the Senate of the United States of America gave its advice and consent to the ratification of the aforementioned Neutrality Treaty with the following understandings, reservations, conditions, and amendments:

(*Author's Note:* The 2 Amendments, 2 Conditions, 4 Reservations, and 5 Understandings that are in the preceding U.S. Instrument of Ratification to the Neutrality Treaty are repeated *verbatim* in this Panamanian Instrument of Ratification—and in the interests of brevity are not being repeated here. The *difference* between the U.S. and Panamanian Instruments is the following Panamanian three paragraph counter-reservation, marked with double vertical lines in the margin.)

The Republic of Panama agrees to the exchange of the instruments of ratification of the aforementioned Neutrality Treaty on the understanding that there are positive rules of public international law contained in multilateral treaties to which both the Republic of Panama and the United States of America are Parties and which consequently both States are bound to implement in good faith, such as Article 1, paragraph 2 and Article 2, paragraph 4 of the

Charter of the United Nations, and Articles 18 and 20 of the Charter of the Organization of American States.

It is also the understanding of the Republic of Panama that the actions which either Party may take in the exercise of its rights and the fulfillment of its duties in accordance with the aforesaid Neutrality Treaty, including measures to reopen the Canal or to restore its normal operation, if it should be interrupted or obstructed, will be effected in a manner consistent with the principles of mutual respect and cooperation on which the new relationship established by that Treaty is based.

The Republic of Panama declares that its political independence, territorial integrity, and self-determination are guaranteed by the unshakeable will of the Panamanian people. Therefore, the Republic of Panama will reject, in unity and with decisiveness and firmness, any attempt by any country to intervene in its internal or external affairs.

The Head of Government of the Republic of Panama, availing himself of the powers granted by Article 277 of the Constitution, after having considered the aforementioned Neutrality Treaty, hereby ratifies it and, in the name of the Republic of Panama, undertakes to comply with it faithfully.

In witness whereof, this instrument of ratification is signed by the Head of Government of the Republic of Panama.

Done at Panama City, Republic of Panama, the sixteenth day of June 1978.
OMAR TORRIJOS HERRERA.

Appendix D
TEXT OF HAY-BUNAU-VARILLA TREATY (1903)

The United States of America and the Republic of Panama being desirous to insure the construction of a ship-canal across the Isthmus of Panama to connect the Atlantic and Pacific oceans, and the Congress of the United States of America having passed an act approved June 28, 1902, in furtherance of that object, by which the President of the United States is authorized to acquire within a reasonable time the control of the necessary territory of the Republic of Colombia, and the sovereignty of such territory being actually vested in the Republic of Panama, the high contracting parties have resolved for that purpose to conclude a convention and have accordingly appointed as their plenipotentiaries,—The President of the United States of America, John Hay, Secretary of State, and the Government of the Republic of Panama, Philippe Bunau-Varilla, Envoy Extraordinary and Minister Plenipotentiary of the Republic of Panama, thereunto specially empowered by said Government, who after communicating with each other their respective full powers found to be in good and due form, have agreed upon and concluded the following articles:

ARTICLE I

The United States guarantees and will maintain the independence of the Republic of Panama.

ARTICLE II

The Republic of Panama grants to the United States in perpetuity the use, occupation and control of a zone of land and land under water for the construction, maintenance, operation, sanitation and protection of said Canal of the width of ten miles extending to the distance of five miles on each side of the center line of the route of the Canal to be constructed; the said zone beginning in the Caribbean Sea, three marine miles from mean low water mark, and extending to and across the Isthmus of Panama into the Pacific Ocean to a distance of three marine miles from mean low water mark, with the proviso that the cities of Panama and Colon and the harbors adjacent to said cities, which are included within the boundaries of the zone above described, shall not be included within this grant. The Republic of Panama further grants to the United States in perpetuity the use, occupation and control of any other lands and waters outside of the zone above described which may be necessary and convenient for the construction, maintenance, operation, sanitation and protection of the said Canal or of any auxiliary canals or other works necessary and convenient for the construction, maintenance, operation, sanitation and protection of the said enterprise.

The Republic of Panama further grants in like manner to the United States in perpetuity all islands within the limits of the zone above described and in addition thereto the group of small islands in the Bay of Panama, named Perico, Naos, Culebra and Flamenco.

ARTICLE III

The Republic of Panama grants to the United States all the rights, power and authority within the zone mentioned and described in Article II of this agreement and within the limits of all auxiliary lands and waters mentioned and described in said Article II which the United States would possess and exercise if it were the sovereign of the territory within which said lands and waters are located to the entire exclusion of the exercise by the Republic of Panama of any such sovereign rights, power or authority.

ARTICLE IV

As rights subsidiary to the above grants the Republic of Panama grants in perpetuity to the United States the rights to use the rivers, streams, lakes and other bodies of water within its limits for navigation, the supply of water, or waterpower, or other purposes, so far as the use of said rivers, streams, lakes and bodies of water and the waters thereof may be necessary and convenient for the construction, maintenance, operation, sanitation and protection of the said Canal.

ARTICLE V

The Republic of Panama grants to the United States in perpetuity a monopoly for the construction, maintenance and operation of any system of communication by means of canal or railroad across its territory between the Caribbean Sea and the Pacific Ocean.

ARTICLE VI

The grants herein contained shall in no manner invalidate the titles or rights of private land-holders or owners of private property in the said zone or in or to any of the lands or waters granted to the United States by the provisions of any Article of this treaty, nor shall they interfere with the rights of way over the public roads passing through the said zone or over any of the said lands or waters unless said rights of way or private rights shall conflict with rights herein granted to the United States, in which case the rights of the United States shall be superior. All damages caused to the owners of private lands or private property of any kind by the operations of the United States, its agents or employees, or by reason of the construction, maintenance, operation, sanitation and protection of the said Canal or of the works of sanitation and protection herein provided for, shall be appraised and settled by a joint commission appointed by the Government of the United States and the Republic of Panama, whose decisions as to such damages shall be final and whose awards as to such damages shall be paid solely by the United States. No part of the work on said Canal or the Panama railroad or on any auxiliary works relating thereto and authorized by the terms of this treaty shall be prevented, delayed or impeded by or pending such proceedings to ascertain such damages. The appraisal of the said private lands and private property and the assessment of damages to them shall be based upon their value before the date of this convention.

ARTICLE VII

The Republic of Panama grants to the United States with the limits of the cities of Panama and Colon and their adjacent harbors and within the territory adjacent thereto the right to acquire by purchase or by the exercise of the right of eminent domain, any lands, buildings, water rights or other properties necessary and convenient for the construction, maintenance, operation and protection of the Canal and of any works of sanitation, such as the collection and disposition of sewage and the distribution of water in the said cities of Panama and Colon, which in the discretion of the United States may be necessary and convenient for the construction, maintenance, operation, sanitation and protection of the said Canal and railroad. All such works of sanitation, collection and disposition of sewage and distribution of water in the cities of Panama and Colon shall be made at the expense of the United States, and the Government of the United States, its agents or nominees shall be authorized to impose and collect water rates and sewage rates which shall be sufficient to provide for the payment of interest and the amortization of the principal of the cost of said works within a period of fifty years, and upon the expiration of said term of fifty years the system of sewers and water works shall revert to and become the properties of the cities of Panama and Colon respectively; and the use of the water shall be free to the inhabitants of Panama and Colon, except to the extent that water rates may be necessary for the operation and maintenance of sewers and water.

The Republic of Panama agrees that the cities of Panama and Colon shall comply in perpetuity with the sanitary ordinances whether of a preventive or curative character prescribed by the United States, and in case the Government of Panama is unable or fails in its duty to enforce this compliance by the cities of Panama and Colon with the sanitary ordinances of the United States the Republic of Panama grants to the United States the right and authority to enforce the same.

The same right and authority are granted to the United States for the maintenance of public order in the cities of Panama and Colon and the territories and harbors adjacent thereto in case the Republic of Panama should not be, in the judgment of the United States, able to maintain such order.

ARTICLE VIII

The Republic of Panama grants to the United States all rights which it now has or hereafter may acquire to the property of the New Panama Canal Company and the Panama Railroad Company as a result of the transfer of sovereignty from the Republic of Colombia to the Republic of Panama over the Isthmus of Panama, and authorizes the New Panama Canal Company to sell and transfer to the United States its rights, privileges, properties and concessions as well as the Panama Railroad and all the shares or part of the shares of that company; but the public land situated outside of the zone described in Article II of this treaty now included in the concessions to both said enterprises and not required in the construction or operation of the Canal shall revert to the Republic of Panama, except any property now owned by or in the possession of said companies within Panama or Colon or the ports or terminals thereof.

ARTICLE IX

The United States agrees that the ports at either entrance of the Canal and the waters thereof, and the Republic of Panama agrees that the towns of Panama and Colon shall be free for all time, so that there shall not be imposed or collected customhouse tolls, tonnage, anchorage, lighthouse, wharf, pilot or quarantine dues or any other charges or taxes of any kind upon any vessel using or passing through the Canal or belonging to or employed by the United States, directly or indirectly, in connection with the construction, maintenance, operation, sanitation and protection of the main Canal, or auxiliary works, or upon the cargo, officers, crew or passengers of any such vessels, except such tolls and charges as may be imposed by the United States for the use of the Canal and other works, and except tolls and charges imposed by the Republic of Panama upon merchandise destined to be introduced for the consumption of the rest of the Republic of Panama, and upon vessels touching at the ports of Colon and Panama and which do not cross the Canal.

The Government of the Republic of Panama shall have the right to establish in such ports and in the towns of Panama and Colon such houses and guards as it may deem necessary to collect duties on importations destined to other portions of Panama and to prevent contraband trade. The United States shall have the right to make use of the towns and harbors of Panama and Colon as places of anchorage, and for making repairs, for loading, unloading, depositing or transshipping cargoes either in transit or destined for the service of the Canal and for other works pertaining to the Canal.

ARTICLE X

The Republic of Panama agrees that there shall not be imposed any taxes, national, municipal, departmental, or of any other class upon the Canal, the railways and auxiliary works, tugs and other vessels employed in the service of the Canal, storehouses, workshops, offices, quarters for laborers, factories of all kinds, warehouses, wharves, machinery and other works, property, and effects appertaining to the Canal or railroad and auxiliary works, or their officers or employees, situated within the cities of Panama and Colon, and that there shall not be imposed contributions or charges of a personal character of any kind upon officers, employees, laborers and other individuals in the service of the Canal and railroad and auxiliary works.

ARTICLE XI

The United States agrees that the official despatches of the Government of the Republic of Panama shall be transmitted over any telegraph or telephone lines established for Canal purposes and used for public and private business at rates not higher than those required from officials in the service of the United States.

ARTICLE XII

The Government of the Republic of Panama shall permit the immigration and free access to the lands and workshops of the Canal and its auxiliary works of all employees and workmen of whatever nationality under contract to work upon or seeking employment upon or in any wise connected with the said Canal and its auxiliary works, with their respective families, and all such persons shall be free and exempt from the military service of the Republic of Panama.

ARTICLE XIII

The United States may import at any time into the said zone and auxiliary lands, free of custom duties, imposts, taxes or other charges, and without any restrictions, any and all vessels, dredges, engines, cars, machinery, tolls, explosives, materials, supplies, and other articles necessary and convenient in the construction, maintenance, operation, sanitation and protection of the Canal and auxiliary works, and all provisions, medicines, clothing, supplies and other things necessary and convenient for the officers, employees, workmen and laborers in the service and employ of the United States and for their families. If any such articles are disposed of for use outside of the zone and auxiliary lands granted to the United States and within the territory of the Republic, they shall be subject to the same import or other duties as like articles under the laws of the Republic of Panama.

ARTICLE XIV

As the price of compensation for the rights, powers and privileges granted in this convention by the Republic of Panama to the United States, the Government of the United States agrees to pay to the Republic of Panama the sum of ten million dollars ($10,000,000) in gold coin of the United States on the exchange of the ratification of this convention and also an annual payment during the life of this convention of two hundred and fifty thousand dollars ($250,000) in like gold coin, beginning nine years after the date aforesaid.

The provisions of this article shall be in addition to all other benefits assured to the Republic of Panama under this convention. But no delay or difference of opinion under this article or any other provisions of this treaty shall affect or interrupt the full operation and effect of this convention in all other respects.

ARTICLE XV

The joint commission referred to in Article VI shall be established as follows: The President of the United States shall nominate two persons and the President of the Republic of Panama shall nominate two persons and they shall proceed to a decision; but in case of disagreement of the Commission (by reason of their being equally divided in conclusion) an umpire shall be appointed by the two Governments who shall render the decision. In the event of the death, absence, or incapacity of a commissioner or umpire, or of his omitting, declining or ceasing to act, his place shall be filled by the appointment of another person in the manner above indicated. All decisions by a majority of the Commission or by the umpire shall be final.

ARTICLE XVI

The two Governments shall make adequate provisions by mutual agreement for the pursuit, capture, imprisonment, detention and delivery within the said zone and auxiliary lands to the authorities of the Republic of Panama of persons charged with the commitment of crimes, felonies or misdemeanors without said zone and for the pursuit, capture, imprisonment, detention and delivery without said zone to the authorities of the United States of persons charged with the commitment of crimes, felonies and misdemeanors within said zone and auxiliary lands.

ARTICLE XVII

The Republic of Panama grants to the United States the use of all the ports of the Republic open to commerce as places of refuge for any vessels employed in the Canal enterprise, and for all vessels passing or bound to pass through the Canal which may be in distress and be driven to seek refuge in said ports. Such vessels shall be exempt from anchorage and tonnage dues on the part of the Republic of Panama.

ARTICLE XVIII

The Canal, when constructed, and the entrances thereto shall be neutral in perpetuity, and shall be opened upon the terms provided for by Section I of Article III of, and in conformity with all the stipulations of, the treaty entered into by the Governments of the United States and Great Britain on November 18, 1901.

ARTICLE XIX

The Government of the Republic of Panama shall have the right to transport over the Canal its vessels and its troops and munitions of war in such vessels at all times without paying charges of any kind. The exemption is to be extended to the auxiliary railway for the transportation of persons in the service of the Republic of Panama, or of the police force charged with the preservation of public order outside of said zone, as well as to their baggage, munitions of war and supplies.

ARTICLE XX

If by virtue of any existing treaty in relation to the territory of the Isthmus of Panama, whereof the obligations shall descend or be assumed by the Republic of Panama, there may be any privilege or concession in favor of the Government or the citizens and subjects of a third power relative to an interoceanic means of communication which in any of its terms may be imcompatible with the terms of the present convention, the Republic of Panama agrees to cancel or modify such treaty in due form, for which purpose it shall give to the said third power the requisite notification within the term of four months from the date of the present convention, and in case the existing treaty contains no clause permitting its modifications or annulment, the Republic of Panama agrees to procure its modifications or annulment in such form that there shall not exist any conflict with the stipulations of the present convention.

ARTICLE XXI

The rights and privileges granted by the Republic of Panama to the United States in the preceding articles are understood to be free of all anterior debts, liens, trusts or liabilities, or concessions or privileges to other Governments, corporations, syndicates or individuals; and consequently, if there should arise any claims on acount of the present concessions and privileges or otherwise, the claimant shall resort to the Government of the Republic of Panama and not the United States for any indemnity or compromise which may be required.

ARTICLE XXII

The Republic of Panama renounces and grants to the United States the participation to which it might be entitled in the future earnings of the Canal under Article XV of the concessionary contract with Lucien N. B. Wyse, now owned by the New Panama Canal Company, and any and all other rights or claims of a pecuniary nature arising under or relating to said concession, or arising under or relating to the concessions to the Panama Railroad Company or any extension or modification thereof; and it likewise renounces, confirms and grants to the United States, now and hereafter, all the rights and property reserved in the said concessions which otherwise would belong to Panama at or before the expiration of the terms of ninety-nine years of the concessions granted to or held by the above-mentioned party and companies, and all right, title and interest which it now has or may hereafter have, in and to the lands, canal, works, property and rights held by the said companies under said concessions or otherwise, and acquired or to be acquired by the United States from or through the New Panama Canal Company, including property and rights which might or may in the future either by lapse of time, forfeiture or otherwise, revert to the Republic of Panama under any contracts or concessions, with said Wyse, the Universal Panama Canal Company, the Panama Railroad Company and the New Panama Canal Company.

The aforesaid rights and property shall be and are free and released from any present or reversionary interest in or claims of Panama, and the title of the United States thereto upon consummation of the contemplated purchase by the United States from the New Panama Canal Company shall be absolute so far as concerns the Republic of Panama, excepting always the rights of the Republic specifically secured under this treaty.

ARTICLE XXIII

If it should become necessary at any time to employ armed forces for the safety or protection of the Canal, or of the ships that make use of the same, or the railroads and auxiliary works, the United States shall have the right, at all times and in its discretion, to use its police and its land and naval forces or to establish fortifications for these purposes.

ARTICLE XXIV

No change either in the Government or in the laws and treaties of the Republic of Panama shall, without the consent of the United States, affect any right of the United States under the present convention, or under any treaty stipulation between the two countries that now exists or may hereafter exist touching the subject matter of this convention.

If the Republic of Panama shall hereafter enter as a constituent into any other Government or into any union or confederation of States, so as to merge her sovereignty or independence in such Government, union or confederation, the rights of the United States under this convention shall not be in any respect lessened or impaired.

ARTICLE XXV

For the better performance of the engagements of this convention and to the end of the efficient protection of the Canal and the preservation of its neutrality, the Government of the Republic of Panama will sell or lease to the United States lands adequate and necessary for naval or coaling stations on the Pacific coast and on the western Caribbean coast of the Republic at certain points to be agreed upon with the President of the United States.

ARTICLE XXVI

This convention when signed by the Plenipotentiaries of the Contracting Parties shall be ratified by the respective Governments and the ratification shall be exchanged at Washington at the earliest date possible.

In faith whereof the respective Plenipotentiaries have signed the present convention in duplicate and have hereunto affixed their respective seals.

Done at the City of Washington the 18th day of November in the year of our Lord nineteen hundred and three.

JOHN HAY [SEAL]
P. BUNAU-VARILLA [SEAL]

Appendix E

KISSINGER-TACK STATEMENT OF PRINCIPLES, FEBRUARY 7, 1974*

The Republic of Panama and the United States of America have been engaged in negotiations to conclude an entirely new treaty respecting the Panama Canal, negotiations which were made possible by the Joint Declaration between the two countries on April 3, 1964, agreed to under the auspices of the Permanent Council of the Organization of American States acting provisionally as the Organ of Consultation. The new treaty would abrogate the treaty existing since 1903 and its subsequent amendments, establishing the necessary conditions for a modern relationship between the two countries based on the most profound mutual respect.

Since the end of last November, the authorized representatives of the two governments have been holding important conversations which have permitted agreement to be reached on a set of fundamental principles that will serve to guide the negotiators in the effort to conclude a just and equitable treaty eliminating, once and for all, the causes of conflict between the two countries.

The principles to which we have agreed, on behalf of our respective governments, are as follows:

1. The treaty of 1903 and its amendments will be abrogated by the conclusion of an entirely new interoceanic canal treaty.

2. The concept of perpetuity will be eliminated. The new treaty concerning the lock canal shall have a fixed termination date.

3. Termination of United States jurisdiction over Panamanian territory shall take place promptly in accordance with terms specified in the treaty.

4. The Panamanian territory in which the canal is situated shall be returned to the jurisdiction of the Republic of Panama. The Republic of Panama, in its capacity as territorial sovereign, shall grant to the United States of America, for the duration of the new interoceanic canal treaty and in accordance with what the treaty states, the right to use the lands, waters and airspace which may be necessary for the operation, maintenance, protection and defense of the canal and the transit of ships.

5. The Republic of Panama shall have a just and equitable share of the benefits derived from the operation of the canal in its territory. It is recognized that the geographic position of its territory constitutes the principal resource of the Republic of Panama.

6. The Republic of Panama shall participate in the administration of the canal, in accordance with a procedure to be agreed upon in the treaty. The treaty shall also provide that Panama will assume total responsibility for the operation of the canal upon the termination of the treaty. The Republic of Panama shall grant to the United States of America the rights necessary to regulate the transit of ships through the canal and operate, maintain, protect and defend the canal, and to undertake any other specific activity related to those ends, as may be agreed upon in the treaty.

7. The Republic of Panama shall participate with the United States of America in the protection and defense of the canal in accordance with what is agreed upon in the new treaty.

8. The Republic of Panama and the United States of America, recognizing the important services rendered by the interoceanic Panama Canal to international maritime traffic, and bearing in mind the possibility that the present canal could become inadequate for said traffic, shall agree bilaterally on provisions for new projects which will enlarge canal capacity. Such provisions will be incorporated in the new treaty in accord with the concepts established in principle 2.

Henry A. Kissinger,	Juan Antonio Tack,
Secretary of State of	Minister of Foreign Affairs of
The United States of America	The Republic of Panama

*State Department Bulletin No. 9 (revised), January 1977, p.5. The Embassy of the Republic of Panama, Washington, D.C. publication, "The Agreement on Principles Between the Republic of Panama and the United States of America" (undated).

Appendix F
SIGNIFICANT DATES IN IMPLEMENTING THE PANAMA CANAL TREATIES

The official titles of the Panama Canal Treaties are:

1. *Panama Canal Treaty.* This treaty provides for the gradual transfer of the Canal from the United States to the Republic of Panama by December 31, 1999.

2. *Panama Canal: Permanent Neutrality and Operation,* called the "Neutrality Treaty." This treaty provides details for guaranteed neutrality and future operations of the Canal permanently.

The U.S. Senate consented to the second treaty (the Neutrality Treaty) first, i.e., approved the plan of operations before actually agreeing to transfer the Canal. Apparently, this was the most prudent *modus operandi,* psychologically and politically, for the Senate leadership, i.e., decide on U.S. rights before the actual "surrender" of the Canal.

The following is a chronology of certain significant dates:

February 7, 1974—Kissinger-Tack Statement of Principles, the forerunner of the Panama Canal Treaties of 1977, signed in Panama by U.S. Secretary of State Henry Kissinger and Panamanian Foreign Minister Juan Tack.

October 29, 1974—The first Linowitz Report (Commission on United States-Latin American Relations) recommended a new Canal treaty with Panama.

December 26, 1976—The Second Linowitz Report reinforced the first report and recommended "justice for Panama," a concept that was endorsed by the Council on Foreign Relations.

January 20, 1977—Inauguration Day for President Jimmy Carter who promptly assigned Ambassadors Ellsworth Bunker and Sol Linowitz to commence negotiations for new Canal Treaties.

August 10, 1977—Negotiators announced "agreement in principle" on the new treaties. Linowitz's 6 months appointment expired.

September 7, 1977—Both Treaties signed at Washington, D.C. by the Heads of Government with ceremonies.

September 16, 1977—Both Treaties transmitted by the President of the United States to the Senate (S. Ex. N, 95th Cong., 1st Session).

February 3, 1978—Both Treaties reported favorably by the Senate Committee on Foreign Relations (S. Ex. Rep. No. 95-12, 95th Cong., 2nd Session).

March 16, 1978—DeConcini reservation guaranteeing U.S. rights to defend and reopen a closed Canal agreed to by the Senate.

March 16, 1978—Senate gave advice and consent to ratification of the Permanent Neutrality and Operation Treaty subject to amendments, conditions, reservations and understandings.

April 6, 1978—U.S. Court of Appeals, District of Columbia Circuit, in a split decision, 2-1, rejected the *Edwards v. Carter* lawsuit to block transfer of Canal Zone property by the Panama Canal Treaties (1977), Judge George E. MacKinnon dissenting.

April 7, 1978—President Carter advised Panama's Omar Torrijos to issue his own "reservation about his understanding of what the Treaties mean on intervention," an action which later resulted in invalid Treaties.

April 18, 1978—Senate gave advice and consent to ratification of the second and final treaty, the Panama Canal Treaty, subject to reservations and understandings.

April 25, 1978—Panama's Foreign Ministry Communique repudiated six key amendments to the Treaties, including the U.S. defense rights under the DeConcini reservation.

June 15, 1978—Both Treaties ratified by President Carter subject to amendments, conditions, reservations and understandings.

June 16, 1978—Both Treaties ratified by Omar Torrijos, Head of Government of Panama.

April 1, 1979—Neutrality Treaty effective.

September 20, 1979—House of Representatives by a 203-192 vote did not agree with the Conference Report on the Panama Canal Act of 1979, the implementing legislation.

September 24, 1979—Both Treaties proclaimed by President Carter.

September 26, 1979—House of Representatives by a 232-188 vote agreed to the Panana Canal Act of 1979, the implementing legislation, after White Hosue lobbying and 25 Congressmen switched votes.

October 1, 1979—Both Treaties entered into force.

December 31, 1999—Panama Canal Treaty scheduled for termination.

Appendix G

EXCERPTS FROM ADDRESS OF DR. ROMULO ESCOBAR BETHANCOURT BEFORE THE NATIONAL ASSEMBLY OF PANAMA, AUGUST 19, 1977

(Dr. Bethancourt, the Head of the Panamanian Negotiating Team, delivered this emotional speech a few weeks after negotiations had ended in an attempt to prove to Panama's radicals and ultranationalists that the Torrijos regime had not "sold out." Any study of this inflammatory address proves instead the insuperable differences between the two countries in interpretations of the Treaties.)

The original [American] position was that to reach an agreement with Panama there would have to be a neutrality treaty and a military treaty. The military treaty would be made before the end of this century to be operative after the year 2000. This kept the negotiations stalled for a long time, because Panama opposed the enactment of a military treaty. Such a treaty would have implied two things: First, the continued U.S. military presence in Panama after the end of the present treaty [2000]; and second, the United States, as a great power, is a country frequently involved in wars in other parts of the world, and we did not want that, because of the existence of a military treaty, the future youth of our country to have to go fight in the American battlefields with the pretext that this related to the defense of the Panama Canal. This was a position that Panama maintained until the United States withdrew the idea of a military treaty. We were then able to negotiate a neutrality treaty alone.

With regard to the neutrality pact, the following situation arose: The United States asked if Panama would disagree with the idea of the canal being neutral. We told them we didn't, that on the contrary, a long-standing aspiration of Panama had been that the Panama Canal would be neutral. They said that they wanted the Panama Canal to be neutral and we said we entirely agreed with them. Differences then arose only in what they understood by neutrality and what we understood by neutrality. They proposed that Panama and the United States declare that the canal was neutral and that the United States would guarantee that neutrality. Panama was opposed to this concept. . . .

Another of the positions they presented was that Panama must agree to maintain the canal permanently neutral and permanently open. We told them that Panama could commit herself to maintain the canal permanently neutral because that was her wish. Panama has no interest in having anything other than a neutral canal, the Panama Canal, because otherwise the Isthmus of Panama could become a battlefield. But we said *Panama could not promise to maintain the canal permanently open* because of three circumstances that might arise. One, because of natural causes; we explained that an earthquake could take place, for instance, which would close the canal, and, in such a situation, Panama could not be under an obligation to keep it open. Another possibility was temporary disruptions—landslides could take place and the canal would have to be closed to carry out clean-up operations. *The third possibility was that the canal could become unprofitable for Panama; in such a situation, Panama could not be tied down to keeping open a canal which was not earning revenue.* They [United States negotiators] accepted the first two reasons—natural causes and temporary disruptions—but they did not accept the third reason, lack of profits. This too kept the negotiations stalled for a long time.

They argued that if the canal was not profitable, Panama could obtain money from the United States or the other countries that use the canal to keep it open. We told them that when the new treaty with the United States ended, we did not want Panama to be under either direct or indirect obligation to turn to the United States or any other country to request money to keep the canal open. . . .

The United States then proposed that there be a neutrality treaty between Panama and the United States and no one else. Because *they did not want for either the Russians, the Cubans or the Chinese—they said so exactly—to intervene in the neutrality of the Panama Canal.* Our position was that neutrality didn't make any sense if limited to two countries as a result of a treaty between the United States and Panama and that we opposed the other countries not having the right to join in that treaty. They changed their position and agreed to allow the countries of the American continent (except for Cuba), but no others, to join. We said no, that this was meaningless, because in case of a war between the United States and Russia or China, those countries not being a part of the neutrality agreement would be under no commitment to respect the canal or the Isthmus of Panama. That was another reason for long delays, until *they finally accepted the idea that all the countries of the world could join the neutrality treaty.*

. . . .

Another issue was preferential right of way through the canal for American warships. The Americans said that they had two problems. First, they had to please the Pentagon—they had to present it with something it liked so it would support the treaty; and second, that as they would be leaving Panama as soon as the treaty ended, they should be allowed at least that much, if nothing else, because they built the canal. We pointed out that we recognized they had indeed built the canal, but that writing in the neutrality pact that the United States warships would have preferential right of way over the rest of the vessels violated the neutrality treaty and that was contrary to the objective of the treaty we were negotiating. This was another cause for lengthy discussion and much analysis. They searching through their books and we searching through ours; they invoking their treaty writers and we invoking ours. This is how these discussions are carried out. Changing their position, *they asked for preferential right of way during times when the United States was at war—originally they wanted it in times of peace and war—and that this right be granted only when requested by the ship's captain. We said no—that wartime was the least appropriate moment to grant preferential passage rights since it would be a violation of neutrality.* After long discussions *they accepted that U.S. warships could not be granted preferential rights.*

. . . .

Later came a discussion on their proposal that the two countries commit themselves to upholding this neutrality under all circumstances. We said that if the phrase "under all circumstances" was included, two important exceptions would have to be made. *The first was that this would apply only so long as internal order was not involved, since these are problems for one country or our national guard to address; and second, in the case of an attack on the isthmus or the Panama Canal by a third country. This was cause for much discussion, and in the end, they preferred to leave out the phrase so that we would not include the exception.* We also pointed out that the neutrality pact must indicate clearly that after 31 December 1999 at 12 o'clock noon—or at 12 noon as [Edwin] Fabroga says or at 12 midnight as [Adolfo] Ahumada says—that from that date on, the American troops could not be in Panama. After much discussion, they said, "We don't like that phrase—that there can be Russian troops or Cuban troops." Then a proposal was made to change the phrase to read that from 31 December 1999 on only Panamanian troops could be stationed in Panama. We were in perfect agreement with this. They were happy, because they had been half-thinking that we are going to call in the Russians, and we were happy because one of our aspirations was precisely that our troops be the only ones here. . . .

. . . *Those are the facts of the matter so that with the neutrality pact, we are not giving the United States the right of intervention.* . . .

And, frankly speaking, they do not need this neutrality pact to intervene or not to intervene. They need it to present it to their Congress, to tell their Congress, "Look, we are giving the canal to those Panamanians, but we retain the right to watch over it so that they behave themselves." That's the truth. It's an internal political problem; they are trying to solve an internal problem with a Congress intensely opposed to these negotiations and one which, in addition, includes members who have not been elected by the American people but rather who have become members of Congress of their own accord—these are certain Panamanians living here and others in Miami. [Bethancourt refers here to exiles opposed to the Torrijos regime.]

. . . .

There was no way to reach an agreement on what they proposed. Panama's delegation wrote a proposal which met with general approval. Read word for word, it is more or less like this:

Article 3—The possibility of constructing a third set of locks or a sea-level canal.

1. The Republic of Panama and the United States agree that a sea-level canal could be important in the future or in the context of international relations.

Consequently, after its approval, the question of construction will be dealt with. There isn't even an option. The option relates only to studying the matter. We will sit down and analyze with the United States if it is feasible. If it is, the two countries will build it, maybe during the next ten or fifteen years. . . .

The ones who cannot prove that this treaty is better than the one of 1903, that perpetuity is better, will have the problem. That the two million dollars a year is better than what is proposed now. We don't care if they say that General Torrijos is a dictator; those who are opposed and say that we are not revolutionaries—let them grab their knapsack and their grenade and go prove it with deeds.

Appendix H

A LETTER TO PRESIDENT CARTER FROM FOUR FORMER CHIEFS OF NAVAL OPERATIONS

The President   June 8, 1977
The White House
Washington, D.C.

Dear Mr. President:

As former Chiefs of Naval Operations, fleet commanders and Naval Advisers to previous Presidents, we believe we have an obligation to you and the nation to offer our combined judgment on the strategic value of the Panama Canal to the United States.

Contrary to what we read about the declining strategic and economic value of the Canal, the truth is that this inter-oceanic waterway is as important, if not more so, to the United States than ever. The Panama Canal enables the United States to transfer its naval forces and commercial units from ocean to ocean as the need arises. This capability is increasingly important now in view of the reduced size of the U.S. Atlantic and Pacific fleets.

We recognize that the Navy's largest aircraft carriers and some of the world's super-tankers are too wide to transit the Canal as it exists today. The super-tankers represent but a small percentage of the world's commercial fleets. From a strategic viewpoint, the Navy's largest carriers can be wisely positioned as pressures and tensions build in any kind of a short-range, limited situation. Meanwhile, the hundreds of combatants, from submarines to cruisers, can be funneled through the transit as can the vital fleet train needed to sustain the combatants. In the years ahead, as carriers become smaller or as the Canal is modernized, this problem will no longer exist.

Our experience has been that as each crisis developed during our active service—World War II, Korea, Vietnam and the Cuban missile crisis—the value of the Canal was forcefully emphasized by emergency transits of our naval units and massive logistic support for the Armed Forces. The Canal provided operational flexibility and rapid mobility. In addition, there are the psychological advantages of this power potential. As Commander-in-Chief, you will find the ownership and sovereign control of the Canal indispensable during periods of tension and conflict.

As long as most of the world's combatant and commercial tonnage can transit through the Canal, it offers inestimable strategic advantages to the United States, giving us maximum strength at minimum cost. Moreover, sovereignty and jurisdiction over the Canal Zone and Canal offer the opportunity to use the waterway or to deny its use to others in wartime. This authority was especially helpful during World War II and also Vietnam. Under the control of a potential adversary, the Panama Canal would become an immediate crucial problem and prove a serious weakness in the over-all U.S. defense capability, with enormous potential consequences for evil.

Mr. President, you have become our leader at a time when the adequacy of our naval capabilities is being seriously challenged. The existing maritime threat to us is compounded by the possibility that the Canal under Panamanian sovereignty could be neutralized or lost, depending on that government's relationship with other nations. We note that the present Panamanian government has close ties with the present Cuban government which in turn is closely tied to the Soviet Union. Loss of the Panama Canal, which would be a serious set-back in war, would contribute to the encirclement of the U.S. by hostile naval forces, and threaten our ability to survive.

For meeting the current situation, you have the well-known precedent of former distinguished Secretary of State (later Chief Justice) Charles Evans Hughes, who, when faced with a comparable situation in 1923, declared to the Panamanian government that it was an "absolute futility" for it "to expect an American administration, no matter what it was, any President or any Secretary of State, ever to surrender any part of (the) rights which the United States had acquired under the Treaty of 1903," (Ho.Doc. No. 474, 89th Congress, p.154).

We recognize that a certain amount of social unrest is generated by the contrast in living standards between Zonians and Panamanians living nearby. Bilateral programs are recommended to upgrade Panamanian boundary areas. Canal modernization, once U.S. sovereignty is guaranteed, might benefit the entire Panamanian economy, and especially those areas near the U.S. Zone.

The Panama Canal represents a vital portion of our U.S. naval and maritime assets, all of which are absolutely essential for free world security. It is our considered individual and combined judgment that you should instruct our negotiators to retain full sovereign control for the United States over both the Panama Canal and its protective frame, the U.S. Canal Zone as provided in the existing treaty.

Very respectfully,
ROBERT B. CARNEY   ARLEIGH A. BURKE
GEORGE ANDERSON   THOMAS H. MOORER

Appendix J
LETTER OF INQUIRY TO SECRETARY OF STATE GEORGE P. SHULTZ

The following letter from Phillip Harman, Chairman of the Committee for Better Panama and United States Relations, was sent to the Secretary of State in regard to: (1) the State Department's unsatisfactory explanations of the Panamanian three paragraph counter-reservation and the unexplained date of June 16, 1978; (2) the apparent cover up and stonewalling; and (3) the apparent withholding of evidence from the Foreign Relations Committee at the time of the Treaties vote in 1978 and from the East hearing in the Subcommittee on Separation of Powers on June 23, 1983:

Hon. George P. Shultz   August 5, 1983
Secretary of State
Washington, D.C. 20520

Dear Mr. Secretary:

On September 18, 1975 just prior to the start of President Reagan's 1976 campaign for the presidency, I briefed him on Panama. It was his first briefing ever on that country and I found him extremely interested in what I had to say, and in particular about the 1968 gunpoint seizure of the country that could have a profound effect on the future security of the Panama Canal. I was pleased that he used the Canal issue in his 1976 campaign to expose this giveaway of America's most priceless asset and I believe it helped him in his 1980 campaign. I know Panama well having headed an anti-Communist task force in that country from 1956 to 1968 and also related to the founder of the Republic of Panama.

In regards to Senator East's hearing on June 23 concerning the legality of the 1977 Panama Canal Treaties, I have been trying for nearly a year to obtain from Mr. Davis R. Robinson, the Department's Legal Adviser, and also from Mr. Robert E. Dalton, the Assistant Legal Adviser for Treaty Affairs, copies of Panama's draft instruments of ratification that the Department gave in 1978 to the Senate Foreign Relations Committee for their review and comment before the Protocol of Exchange took place in Panama on June 16, 1978.

When the Protocol of Exchange did take place in 1978 and Panama's instruments were then made public, the instruments showed a three paragraph statement that was not in the U.S. instruments. At the hearing on June 23 it was proven conclusively by three witnesses, including myself, that Panama's statement in their instruments was a counter-reservation to the DeConcini Reservation that gives the U.S. the unilateral right to reopen the Canal if it is closed. Mr. Dalton, the Department's legal adviser at the hearing, stated in both of his oral and written statements that the State Department never received any objection from the Foreign Relations Committee about Panama's statement.

It is difficult, Mr. Secretary, to believe that among the 15 members of the Committee that not one member would say that Panama's three paragraph statement that was at the end of both of Panama's instruments contradicted the DeConcini Reservation and therefore it should be submitted to the Senate for a two-thirds vote *before the Protocol of Exchange took place in Panama on June 16, 1978*. Panama's statement clearly says that the U.S. can reopen the Canal if it is closed only with Panama's *cooperation*. Moreover, it makes the exchange of instruments contingent on this understanding of Panama's cooperation. President Carter must have known that if Panama's statement had been submitted for a Senate vote it would have been defeated as it nullifies the DeConcini Reservation; consequently, the Protocol of Exchange would not have taken place.

As I knew that Senator East was planning a hearing on the legality of the Canal treaties, and that I would be a witness, I wanted to see if the draft Panamanian instruments contained this three paragraph statement so it could be discussed at the hearing as well as being made a part of the written record.

Mr. Secretary, I wrote to Mr. Robinson's office as well as Mr. Dalton's office five different times from July 6, 1982 to April 30, 1983. I realized that they were not going to respond to my request. I never at anytime ever received a reply from their offices. Altogether there were *nine* requests before the June 23 hearing took place—five from my office and on my behalf four requests from Senators Baker, Helms, Cranston and former Senator Church.

After the hearing was over on June 23, I asked Mr. Dalton personally before he left the hearing room to please send me the draft copies of Panama's instruments along with the staff Committee's comments. The next day, June 24, I wrote to him reminding him about my request. I never heard from him until July 15 when I received in the mail an envelope from his office with no letter, only an unreadable copy of the draft Panamanian instrument of the Panama Canal Treaty as well as two unreadable copies of letters from Mr. Powell A. Moore, the Assistant Secretary, to Senators Baker and Cranston about the draft instruments. Not only was the material unreadable but he also failed to send me the other draft Neutrality Treaty instrument and the staff Committee's comments of the instruments.

The very day I received this material from Mr. Dalton, I returned the material to him requesting that readable material be returned to me by return mail as I wanted to submit this material to Senator East's Subcommittee to be inserted into the written record of the hearing. I sent Mr. Robinson a copy of this letter. As of today, August 5, I have never heard from Mr. Dalton nor Mr. Robinson. In a July 19 letter from Senator Baker he enclosed a copy of a letter that Mr. Moore had sent him about his request on my behalf for the draft instruments along with the two draft instruments. I sent this material to Senator East. So far, I have never received a copy of the staff Committee's comments.

Mr. Secretary, I lived in Washington for many years at various times since 1942 and although I have never worked for the Department, I have had numerous meetings with them; especially regarding Panama when I lived in Washington during the seventies. Therefore it surprised and disappointed me concerning the refusal by Mr. Robinson and Mr. Dalton to release Panama's draft instruments until after Senator East's hearing was over. Their actions as Department employees certainly reflects against the good name of the Department of State.

I would appreciate it very much, Mr. Secretary, if your office would give me an explanation as to why Mr. Robinson and Mr. Dalton withheld this pertinent material from me and various U.S. Senators that was important to be brought to the attention of Senator East for discussion during the hearing.

With kindest regards.

Cordially,
Phillip Harman
Chairman

cc: John P. East
    Howard H. Baker, Jr.
    Charles H. Percy
    Jesse Helms
    Alan Cranston
    Kenneth W. Dam
    Davis R. Robinson
    Robert E. Dalton
    Samuel T. Francis

Appendix K
TYPICAL STATE DEPARTMENT ANSWERS
RESPONSES OF ROBERT E. DALTON TO QUESTIONS OF PHILLIP HARMAN

Question 1. In the written statement of Mr. Robert E. Dalton, Assistant Legal Adviser for Treaty Affairs, on June 23, 1983 before the Subcommittee on Separation of Powers of the Committee on the Judiciary, he said the Department of State had close consultations with members of the Senate Foreign Relations Committee and also with the Senate leadership prior to the exchange of instruments of ratification regarding Panama's proposed instruments. Did the Department of State explain to the 15 members of the Committee as well as to the Majority and Minority leadership in the Senate about Panama's three paragraph statement in their instruments?

Question 2. Did the Department of State tell the Committee and the Senate leadership that the three paragraph statement did not modify the DeConcini Reservation?

Question 3. Who in the Senate leadership attended these consultations with the Department of State?

Question 4. On what date did the Department of State know for the first time about Panama's three paragraph statement?

Question 5. On what date or dates did the Department of State hold consultations with the Committee and the Senate leadership regarding Panama's instruments?

Question 6. During these consultations the Department of State had with the Committee and the Senate leadership, were they told by the Department of State there was no need for the President to submit Panama's three paragraph statement to the Senate for a two-thirds vote?

Answers 1 to 6. On June 23, 1983 Mr. Robert E. Dalton, Assistant Legal Adviser for Treaty Affairs, who appeared on behalf of the Department before the Subcommittee on Separation of Powers of the Committee on the Judiciary, said: "In the course of close consultations prior to the exchange of instruments of ratification, the Executive made Panama's proposed instruments available to the Senate leadership and to the Foreign Relations Committee".

The Department's participants in the consultations were Herbert J. Hansell, the Legal Adviser, and Curtis Cutter of the Bureau of Congressional Relations. Other participants in the meeting held to explain the draft instruments were members of the staff of the Foreign Relations Committee and of the staffs of the Majority leader and the Minority leader. The Department's understanding is that members of the staff of all 15 members of the Committee were invited to attend; however, not all those invited did, in fact, participate in the meeting.

Mr. Hansell took with him to the meeting the text of the draft instruments of ratification that it was expected would be exchanged and a draft protocol of exchange of the instruments of ratification. Mr. Hansell explained that the State Department thought that the recitations in those instruments were fully consistent with the requirements of the Senate as expressed in its resolution of advice and consent. Mr. Hansell added that he wanted to be certain that others who had been key participants in the advice and consent process shared that conclusion. In the course of the meeting members of the Foreign Relations Committee staff undertook to make the instruments available to members of the Committee.

Several days later the Department was informed by telephone that the Majority and Minority Leaders had no difficulty with the draft documents and that no member of the Foreign Relations Committee who had reviewed the documents had found any problems with the draft instruments. The Foreign Relations Committee staff proposed a technical change in the Protocol of Exchange; that change was incorporated prior to signature of the document.

Source: Hearing before the Subcommittee on Separation of Powers of the Committee on the Judiciary, U.S. Senate, 98th Cong., 1st Sess., on the Panama Canal Treaty—Constitutional and Legal Aspects of the Ratification Process, June 23, 1983, pp. 117-8.

Appendix L

SENATOR HELMS'S LAST MINUTE WARNING ABOUT PANAMA'S COUNTER-RESERVATION

Senator Helms's statement before the Senate on June 15, 1978 regarding Panama's understanding (three paragraph statement) in the instruments of ratification of the Panama Canal Treaties that modifies and alters the DeConcini Reservation:

Mr. President, when President Carter goes to Panama tomorrow to sign the protocol of ratification for the Panama Canal treaties, he will agree to a Panamanian understanding that has not yet been revealed to the American people. It is an understanding of potentially great significance to the defense of the canal; yet the American people will not have any inkling of its language much less its significance, until after the President has committed the United States to accepting it.

Moreover, there has been no debate or discussion of the matter in the U.S. Senate about the ramifications of this understanding, and no explanation to the Senate at large. It has been reported to me that the language has been held in the Foreign Relations Committee for a week, but no attempt was made to transmit the text to all Senators, nor even to those who were particularly active in the treaty debates. 124 *Cong. Rec.* 17790-91 (1978).

Appendix M

STATEMENT BY SENATOR DENNIS DeCONCINI ON HIS AMENDMENT, MARCH 16, 1978

Mr. DeConcini. Mr. President, I thank the Chair for his indulgence in calling the Senate to order.

For the last 3 months, I have argued that the treaties as drafted did not appear to contain sufficient safeguards for the United States. But I have also stated publicly that I believed a new treaty with Panama was essential; that history had bypassed the era of simple colonialism when large powers bullied the small. Until recently, I believed that it would be possible for the Senate to make some constructive amendments to the treaty that would satisfy the needs of Panama — but not at the sole expense of the American people. However, as every member of this Chamber knows, the administration was unwilling to accept the slightest changes in the text of the agreement.

Because of this recalcitrance, I suspect that a number of potential supporters of the treaty were lost. Together with Senator Ford, I offered a number of amendments to the treaty. When it became clear that no amendments would be accepted, I began to search for alternatives that would accomplish the desired objectives.

After extensive consultations with experts from the executive, Congress, and the academic community, I became convinced that it would be possible to achieve a clearer understanding of American rights and responsibilities under the treaty through the device of an amendment to the resolution of ratification in the nature of a condition precedent to American acceptence of the treaty itself. Such a condition will be binding on the Republic of Panama.

Therefore, I have recast my amendments in this form. I have assured the President that if my amendment No. 83 to the resolution of ratification is accepted by the Senate that I will vote in favor of the Neutrality Treaty. In turn, the President assured me yesterday in a meeting we had at the White House that he would accept and support my amendment. To the best of my knowledge, that is how things stand as of this moment.

I would like to stress that I am offering this amenmdment in the name of the people of Arizona. Like Senator Ford, I too have crossed my State and spoken personally to hundreds, perhaps thousands of concerned citizens. As a whole, my constituents do not approve of the Panama Canal treaties. However, they are willing to accept their necessity if American rights to insure open and free access to the canal are clearly spelled out. That is all my amendment intends—but that much at least is essential.

AMENDMENT NO. 83, AS FURTHER MODIFIED

Mr. DeConcini. Mr.President, I would like to call up my amendment No.83, as modified. I would ask, Mr. President, to further modify such amendment. A few of these changes are purely technical and drafting changes.

The Presiding Officer. The Senator will suspend until the clerk states the amendment.

Mr. DeConcini. Mr. President, I have the clarified drafted change amendment that I would ask the clerk to state.

The Presiding Officer. The clerk will state the amendment.

The second legislative clerk read as follows:

The Senator from Arizona (Mr. DeConcini) and Mr. Ford propose amendment numbered 83, as further modified, as follows:

Before the period at the end of the resolution of ratification, insert the following: "subject to the condition, to be included in the instrument of ratification of the Treaty to be exchanged with the Republic of Panama, that, notwithstanding the provisions of Article V or any other provision of the Treaty, if the Canal be closed, or its operations are interfered with, the United States of America and the Republic of Panama shall each independently have the right to take such steps as it deems necessary, in accordance with its constitutional processes, including the use of military force in Panama, to reopen the Canal or restore the operations of the Canal, as the case may be".

Mr. DeConcini. Mr. President, the changes are technical and draft changes. The one substantive change is to include the phrase "according to its constitutional processes," after the words "to take such steps as it deems necessary" and before the words "including the use of military forces."

I send to the desk a clean copy and I thank the Chair and the clerk for reporting same.

I also would like to ask that Senator Cannon, Senator Chiles, Senator Nunn, Senator Long, Senator Talmadge, Senator Paul Hatfield, and Senator Hayakawa be added as cosponsors.

The Presiding Officer. Without objection, it is so ordered.

Mr. DeConcini. The purpose of this amendment is quite simple, Mr. President. It is designed to establish a precondition to American acceptance of the Neutrality Treaty. That precondition states that regardless of the reason and regardless of what any other provision of the Neutrality Treaty might say or what interpretation it might be subject to, if the Panama Canal is closed, the United States has the right to enter Panama, using whatever means are necessary, to reopen the canal. There are no conditions, no exceptions, and no limitations on this right. By the terms of the amendment, the United States interprets when such a need exists, and exercises its own judgment as to the means necessary to insure that the canal remains open and accessible.

A good deal of the discussion involving the Panama Canal treaties has centered upon threats to the canal which might come from third parties—more specifically—the Communist countries. While this concern is certainly justified, I have been equally bothered by the possibility that internal Panamanian activities might also be a threat to the waterway, should we give it up. Labor unrest and strikes; the actions of an unfriendly government; political riots or upheavals—each of these alone or in combination might cause a closure of the canal. In February 1975, for example, there was a "sickout" which disrupted the efficient operation of the canal. Yet as I read the treaties, there does not appear to be any specific guarantee that a disruption of the canal arising out of internal Panamanian activities can be swiftly and adequately dealt with.

Although General Torrijos has brought a welcome degree of stability to Panama in recent years, it can be argued that the history of Panama is one of substantial political instability and turmoil. Under normal circumstances, the United States would not or should not comtemplate intervening in the internal affairs of another nation. However, there are extremely unique and special circumstances surrounding the relationship between the United States and Panama. Since the beginning of this century, the United States has exercised de facto sovereignty over the Panama Canal Zone, and has been responsible for the defense and operation of the canal. We have maintained this control over the canal for one very simple reason: The Panama Canal is vital to the security, economic and military, of the United States. This fact must be recognized in any treaty which contemplates a fundamental change in the American-Panamanian relationship.

The amendment contains a very specific reference to the use of miltary force in Panama. I believe these words are absolutely crucial because they establish the American right—which I am not convinced is adequately provided for either in the body of the treaty or the leadership amendment—to take military action if the case so warrants. It further makes it clear that the United States can take military action on Panamanian soil without the consent of the Panamanian Government.

The question of consent is also crucial. Since the main thrust of this amendment is directed toward situations in which the canal is closed because of internal difficulties in Panama—difficulties like a general strike, a political uprising, or other similar events, the consent of the Panamanians to take action would not make sense. If America is to have any rights at all under this treaty, it must have the right to act independently to protect the canal and to keep it open.

I believe that the question of an attack on the canal by a third party aggressor is adequately dealt with in the treaty. There seems to be little question that under such circumstances the United States does have the right to act with the Panamanians to protect and defend the canal. Thus, my concerns have centered around two problems. The first is the one expressed in the amendment now on the floor. The other is the question of a continued military presence.

We have just adopted an amendment by Senator Nunn that I had the privilege of cosponsoring. It provides that the United States and Panama may conclude an agreement providing for a continued American military presence in Panama after the year 2000. This change is important because it may be vital to both countries to provide for such presence while at the same time not disrupting the regime of neutrality that is established.

It was my desire, and the desire of Senator Nunn, to allow for a continued presence without a new treaty that would, by its very nature, call into question the regime of neutrality. It is much more appealing to have that right embodied in the very document that creates the regime of neutrality.

Therefore, I compliment the Senator from Georgia in his efforts to gain acceptance of the military presence reservation.

I hope the Senate will support the amendment I offer to the resolution of ratification providing for America's right to keep the canal open. I am also happy to announce that the President of the United States has endorsed this change, and has indicated that he believes it to be a constructive step in fulfilling the goals of the Neutrality Treaty.

I believe I speak for all Senators in stating that it is not our expectation that this change gives to the United States the right to interfere in the sovereign affairs of Panama. The United States will continue to respect the territorial integrity of that Nation. My amendment to the resolution of ratification is precautionary only; and it is based in the long history of American stewardship of the canal. It recognizes the very special relationship that the Panama Canal has to American security.

I certainly hope, Mr. President, that if this right is attached to the treaty it will never need to be exercised. Yet, it is important that the American people know that should the need arise, the United States has sufficient legal sanction to act.

Mr. President, I commend this change to my colleagues and urge their support.

Mr. President, I ask for the yeas and nays on this amendment.

(*Author's Note:* The amendment was agreed to by a vote of 75 to 23 and subsequently became Condition (1) to the Neutrality Treaty.)

Appendix N

MEMORANDUM: THE UNITED STATES CONSTITUTION AND THE PANAMA CANAL TREATIES

The negotiations between the United States and Panama which were initiated in 1965 by President Johnson and which resulted in the signing of two draft treaties by President Carter and General Omar Torrijos on September 7, 1977 were fatally flawed from the beginning in that they did not conform to constitutional requirements. At the outset of the negotiations President Johnson conceded to Panama that the 1903 treaty between the two countries "will be abrogated" and will be replaced by a "new treaty" which "will effectively recognize Panama's sovereignty over the area of the present Canal Zone." Speaking as head of the executive branch only, Johnson presumed to commit the United States to the abrogation of the 1903 treaty.

But the President's action was *ultra vires* and consequently of no legal effect, for the President alone is not given the power in the Constitution to abrogate treaties. The Constitution declares that "all treaties made, under the authority of the United States, shall be the supreme law of the land; and the judges in every State shall be bound thereby, anything in the Constitution or laws of any State to the contrary notwithstanding." Interpreting this article of the Constitution, Thomas Jefferson wrote in his Manual: "Treaties are legislative acts. A treaty is the law of the land. It differs from other laws only as it must have the consent of a foreign nation, being but a contract with respect to that nation. . . . Treaties being declared, equally with the laws of the United States, to be the supreme law of the land, it is understood that an act of the legislature alone can declare them infringed and rescinded."

Quite apart from the question as to the wisdom or the folly of the president's policy of negotiating with Panama, constitutional procedures were violated. At no time during the negotiations did Johnson or his successors in the presidency possess the power single-handedly to set aside the law of the land anymore than they could set aside a law duly passed by the Congress and signed by a president. A law of the land, including treaties, can be set aside constitutionally only by the procedure which requires the consent of both houses of Congress as well as the signed concurrence of the president. At no time from the beginning of the negotiations to the signing of the treaties was this requirement met. If the president wants a new treaty with Panama superceding the treaty of 1903, he can point to no power that exempts him from this explicit and prescribed constitutional procedure.

The treaty of 1903 between the United States and Panama therefore remains unabrogated and continues to be entitled as the law of the land for the United States governing our relations with Panama. Insistence upon this requirement is essential to preserve the principles of separation of powers and limitation of powers which are fundamental to our frame of government. The Constitution gives us a government of conferred, that is, delegated powers and requires that these powers interlock in certain respects between the three branches of government. It does not give the legislative power exclusively and completely to the Congress, nor the executive power exclusively and completely to the president, or the judicial power exclusively and completely to the courts. It makes no provision for the exercise of fiat power by any single branch of government. In the negotiation and ratification of treaties, for example, the president is not all-powerful; he cannot rule by decree.

During negotiations of the Panama treaties a case challenging the president's action was presented to the courts but was declared to be not "ripe" for decision. Since then the president has pursued the policy to the last stage through the exercise of claimed prerogatives alone and has carried his power to the point where, unless checked, a dangerous precedent will become embodied in our constitutional system. Already the Carter administration is following this course in its unilateral abrogation of the Mutual Defense Treaty with Taiwan without even replacing it with another treaty.

The question is now obviously "ripe" for judicial settlement. Because of the unconstitutional methods that have been followed by the executive, the new draft treaties should accordingly be held to be null and void and our relations between the United States and Panama remain based upon the treaty of 1903 which is still the law of the land.

The foregoing is based in part upon research brought to my attention by Mr. Carl R. Hoffmann, Jr., a member of this committee.

Donald M. Dozer, Chairman
EMERGENCY COMMITTEE TO SAVE
THE U.S. CANAL ZONE

September 17, 1979

Appendix O

JOINT RESOLUTION CONCERNING THE CLAYTON-BULWER TREATY

H.RES.250

IN THE HOUSE OF REPRESENTATIVES—MARCH 22, 1880—
read twice, referred to the select committee on interoceanic ship-canal,
and ordered to be printed.

Mr. Ellis introduced the following joint resolution:

JOINT RESOLUTION

Requesting the President to notify the Government of Great Britain of the abrogation of the Clayton-Bulwer treaty.

Whereas the President of the United States, in a message to Congress of date March eighth, eighteen hundred and eighty, declared and set forth in substance that it is the well-settled policy of the Government of the United States that any canal, water-way, or other means of communication to be constructed or opened across the Isthmus of Panama, or through the states of Central America, must be under the patronage and control of the United States; and

Whereas the special House committee on the proposed interoceanic canal have agreed upon a series of resolutions affirming in substance the declaration of the President's message of March eighth, eighteen hundred and eighty: Now, therefore,

Resolved by the Senate and House of Representatives of the United States of America in Congress assembled, That the President of the United States be requested to inform the Government of Great Britain that the convention of April nineteenth, eighteen hundred and fifty, between the Governments of the United States and Great Britain, commonly called and known as the "Clayton-Bulwer treaty", under which the Government of the United States admitted Great Britain to a joint protectorate with itself over any canal, water-way, or communication to be thereafter established over or through any of the states of Spanish America, between the Atlantic and Pacific Oceans, has ceased to be binding or obligatory on the United States.

Appendix P

CLAYTON-BULWER TREATY—
April 19, 1850

Art. I. The Governments of the United States and Great Britain hereby declare that neither the one nor other will ever obtain or maintain for itself any exclusive control over the said ship canal; agreeing that neither will ever erect or maintain any fortifications commanding the same, or in the vicinity thereof, or occupy, fortify, or colonize or assume, or exercise any dominion over Nicaragua, Costa Rica, the Mosquito coast, or any part of Central America; nor will either make use of any protection which either affords or may afford, or any alliance which either has or may have to or with any state or people, for the purpose of erecting or maintaining any such fortifications, or of occupying, fortifying, or colonizing Nicaragua, Costa Rica, the Mosquito coast, or any part of Central America, or of assuming or exercising dominion over the same; nor will the United States or Great Britain take advantage of any intimacy, or use any alliance, connection or influence that either may possess with any State or Government through whose territory the said canal may pass, for the purpose of acquiring or holding, directly or indirectly, for the citizens or subjects of the one, any rights or advantages in regard to commerce or navigation through the said canal which shall not be offered on the same terms to the citizens or subjects of the other.

Art. II. Vessels of the United States or Great Britain traversing the said canal shall, in case of war between the contracting parties, be exempted from blockade, detention or capture by either of the belligerents; and this provision shall extend to such a distance from the two ends of the said canal as may hereafter be found expedient to establish.

Art. III. In order to secure the construction of the said canal, the contracting parties engage that if any such canal shall be undertaken upon fair and equitable terms by any parties having the authority of the local Government or Governments through whose territory the same may pass, then the persons employed in making the said canal, and their property used, or to be used, for that object, shall be protected, from the commencement of the said canal to its completion, by the Governments of the United States and Great Britain, from unjust detention, confiscation, seizure or any violence whatsoever. . . .

Art. V. The contracting parties further engage, that when the said canal shall have been completed, they will protect it from interruption, seizure or unjust confiscation, and that they will guarantee the neutrality thereof, so that the said canal may forever be open and free, and the capital invested therein secure. Nevertheless, the Governments of the United States and Great Britain, in according their protection to the construction of the said canal, and guaranteeing its neutrality and security when completed, always understand that this protection and guarantee are granted conditionally, and may be withdrawn by both Governments, or either Government, if both Governments, or either Government, should deem that the persons or company undertaking or managing the same adopt or establish such regulations concerning the traffic thereupon as are contrary to the spirit and intention of this convention, either by making unfair discriminations in favor of the commerce of one of the contracting parties over the commerce of the other, or by imposing oppressive exactions or unreasonable tolls upon the passengers, vessels, goods, wares, merchandise or other articles. Neither party, however, shall withdraw the aforesaid protection and guarantee without first giving six months' notice to the other.

Art. VI. The contracting parties in this convention engage to invite every State with which both or either have friendly intercourse to enter into stipulations with them similar to those which they have entered into with each other, to the end that all other States may share in the honor and advantage of having contributed to a work of such general interest and importance as the canal herein contemplated. And the contracting parties likewise agree that each shall enter into treaty stipulations with such of the Central American States as they may deem advisable, for the purpose of more effectually carrying out the great design of the convention, namely, that of constructing and maintaining the said canal as a ship communication between the two oceans for the benefit of mankind, on equal terms to all, and of protecting the same; and they also agree that the good offices of either shall be employed, when requested by the other, in aiding and assisting the negotiation of such treaty stipulations; and should any differences arise as to right or property over the territory through which the said canal shall pass between the States or Governments of Central America, and such differences should in any way impede or obstruct the execution of the said canal, the Governments of the United States and Great Britain will use their good offices to settle such differences in the manner best suited to promote the interests of the said canal, and to strengthen the bonds of friendship and alliance which exist between the contracting parties.

Art. VII. It being desirable that no time should be unnecessarily lost in commencing and constructing the said canal, the Governments of the United States and Great Britain determine to give their support and encouragement to such persons or company as may first offer to commence the same, with the necessary capital, the consent of the local authorities, and on such principles as accord with the spirit and intention of this convention. . . .

Art. VIII. The Governments of the United States and Great Britain having not only desired, in entering into this convention, to accomplish a particular object, but also to establish a general principle, they hereby agree to extend their protection, by treaty stipulations, to any other practicable communications, whether by canal or railway, across the isthmus which connects North and South America, and especially to the interoceanic communications, should the same prove to be practicable, whether by canal or railway, which are now proposed to be established by the way of Tehuantepec or Panama. In granting, however, their joint protection to any such canals or railways as are by this article specified, it is always understood by the United States and Great Britain that the parties constructing or owning the same shall impose no other charges or conditions of traffic thereupon than the aforesaid Governments shall approve of as just and equitable; and that the same canals or railways, being open to the citizens and subjects of the United States and Great Britain on equal terms, shall also be open on like terms to the citizens and subjects of every other State which is willing to grant thereto such protection as the United States and Great Britain engage to afford.

JOHN MIDDLETON CLAYTON (SEAL)
WILLIAM HENRY BULWER (SEAL)

Appendix Q
HAY-PAUNCEFOTE TREATY—
November 18, 1901

TREATY TO FACILITATE THE CONSTRUCTION OF A SHIP CANAL

The United States of America and His Majesty Edward the Seventh, of the United Kingdom of Great Britain and Ireland, . . . being desirous to facilitate the construction of a ship canal to connect the Atlantic and Pacific Oceans, by whatever route may be considered expedient, and to that end to remove any objection which may arise out of the convention of the nineteenth of April, 1850, commonly called the Clayton-Bulwer treaty, to the construction of such canal under the auspices of the Government of the United States, without impairing the "general principle" of neutralization established in Article VIII of that convention, have ... agreed upon the following articles:

Art. I. The High Contracting Parties agree that the present treaty shall supersede the afore-mentioned Convention of the 19th April, 1850.

Art. II. It is agreed that the canal may be constructed under the auspices of the Government of the United States either directly at its own cost, or by gift or loan of money to individuals or Corporations, or through subscription to or purchase of stock or shares, and that, subject to the provisions of the present Treaty, (the said Government shall have and enjoy all the rights incident to such construction,) as well as the exclusive right of providing for the regulation and management of the canal.

Art. III. The United States adopts, as the basis to the neutralization of such ship canal, the following Rules, substantially as embodied in the Convention of Constantinople signed the twenty-eighth of October, 1888, for the free navigation of the Suez Canal, that is to say:

1. The canal shall be free and open to the vessels of commerce and of war of all nations observing these Rules, on terms of entire equality, so that there shall be no discrimination against any such nation, or its citizens or subjects, in respect of the conditions or charges of traffic or otherwise. Such conditions and charges of traffic shall be just and equitable.

2. The canal shall never be blockaded, nor shall any right of war be exercised nor any act of hostility be committed within it. The United States, however, shall be at liberty to maintain such military police along the canal as may be necessary to protect it against lawlessness and disorder.

3. Vessels of war of a belligerent shall not revictual nor take any stores in the canal except so far as may be strictly necessary; and the transit of such vessels through the canal shall be effected with the least possible delay in accordance with the Regulations in force, and with only such intermission as may result from the necessities of the service.

Prizes shall be in all respects subject to the same rules as vessels of war of the belligerents.

4. No belligerent shall embark or disembark troops, munitions of war, or warlike materials in the canal, except in case of accidental hindrance of the transit, and in such case the transit shall be resumed with all possible dispatch.

5. The provisions of this Article shall apply to waters adjacent to the canal, within 3 marine miles of either end. Vessels of war of a belligerent shall not remain in such waters longer than twenty-four hours at any one time, except in case of distress, and in such case shall depart as soon as possible; but a vessel of war of one belligerent shall not depart within twenty-four hours from the departure of a vessel of war of the other belligerent.

6. The plant, establishments, buildings and all works necessary to the construction, maintenance and operation of the canal shall be deemed to be part thereof, for the purposes of this treaty, and in time of war, as in time of peace, shall

enjoy complete immunity from attack or injury by belligerents, and from acts calculated to impair their usefulness as part of the canal.

Art. IV. It is agreed that no change of territorial sovereignty or of international relations of the country or countries traversed by the beforementioned canal shall affect the general principle of neutralization of the obligation of the High Contracting Parties under the present Treaty. . . .

JOHN HAY (SEAL)
JULIAN PAUNCEFOTE (SEAL)

Appendix R

WILSON'S PANAMA CANAL TOLLS MESSAGE

ADDRESS TO CONGRESS MARCH 5, 1914 (*CONGRESSIONAL RECORD*, 63d CONGRESS, 2d SESSION, VOL. LI, p.4313)

The Panama Canal Act of August 24, 1912 exempted vessels engaged in the coastwise trade of the United States from payment of the customary canal tolls. Great Britain protested that this exemption constituted a breach of the Canal Treaty of 1901, Article III, sec. 1; see Doc. No. 355. Congress yielded to the President's demand and required equality of charges on all vessels. Wilson's position on this question aroused general approval in the United States and Great Britain, and was instrumental in persuading Great Britain to follow Wilson's leadership in Mexican relations. See, R. S. Baker, Woodrow Wilson, Vol. IV, ch. viii.

Gentlemen of the Congress:

I have come to you upon an errand which can be very briefly performed, but I beg that you will not measure its importance by the number of sentences in which I state it. No communication I have addressed to the Congress carried with it graver or more far-reaching implications as to the interest of the country, and I come now to speak upon a matter with regard to which I am charged in a peculiar degree, by the Constitution itself, with personal responsibility.

I have come to ask you for the repeal of that provision of the Panama Canal Act of August 24, 1912, which exempts vessels engaged in the coastwise trade of the United States from payment of tolls, and to urge upon you the justice, the wisdom, and the large policy of such a repeal with the utmost earnestness of which I am capable.

In my own judgment, very fully considered and maturely formed, that exemption constitutes a mistaken economic policy from every point of view, and is, moreover, in plain contravention of the treaty with Great Britain concerning the canal concluded on November 18, 1901. But I have not come to urge upon you my personal views. I have come to state to you a fact and a situation. Whatever may be our own differences of opinion concerning this much debated measure, its meaning is not debated outside the United States. Everywhere else the language of the treaty is given but one interpretation, and that interpretation precludes the exemption I am asking you to repeal. We consented to the treaty; its language we accepted, if we did not originate it; and we are too big, too powerful, too self-respecting a nation to interpret with a too strained or refined reading the words of our own promises just because we have power enough to give us leave to read them as we please. The large thing to do is the only thing we can afford to do, a voluntary withdrawal from a position everywhere questioned and misunderstood. We ought to reverse our action without raising the question whether we were right or wrong, and so once more deserve our reputation for generosity and for the redemption of every obligation without quibble or hesitation.

I ask this of you in support of the foreign policy of the administration. I shall not know how to deal with other matters of even greater delicacy and nearer consequence if you do not grant it to me in ungrudging measure.

Appendix S

EXCERPTS FROM PANAMANIAN FOREIGN MINISTRY COMMUNIQUE ON CANAL TREATIES, APRIL 25, 1978

INTRODUCTION

When the Senate of the United States gave its advice and consent to President Carter regarding the Treaty Concerning the Permanent Neutrality and Operation of the Panama Canal, the Foreign Ministry issued two communiques (16 and 27 March) in which it said that the government would not express its judgment on the amendments, understandings, conditions and reservations approved by the Senate until the same body also arrived at its constitutional decision regarding the Panama Canal treaty.

On the 18th of this month the U.S. Senate gave its advice and consent to President Carter regarding the Panama Canal treaty with the reservations and understandings which will be analyzed in this communique.

With the completion of the Senate's proceedings in the United States, the Foreign Ministry, complying with orders from His Excellency President Demetrio B. Lakas and His Excellency Chief of Government Brig. Gen. Omar Torrijos Herrera, now undertakes to fulfill its duty of explaining to the citizenry the juridical scope of the resolutions of the Senate and setting forth its stand concerning the Senate's decision.

II. SIGNIFICANCE OF THE TERMS "AMENDMENTS," "UNDERSTANDINGS" AND "RESERVATIONS"

The above terms are used by the Senate in its resolutions of 17 March and 18 April of the present year. For this reason it is appropriate to express the meaning given to those terms by U.S. jurists.

Amendments

An amendment to a treaty is a formal change in the letter of the text negotiated by the parties.

Reservations

A reservation modifies or limits the substantive effect of one or more of the treaty stipulations. A reservation is a condition which adds something substantial to a treaty or eliminates something substantial from it. A reservation is a notification in the sense that the state making it will not implement the treaty except in accordance with that condition.

Understandings

The term "understanding" is used to describe a declaration which is not made with the intention of modifying or limiting any of the treaty stipulations. An understanding can clarify or interpret one or more of the treaty stipulations or incorporate a declaration of policy or procedure.

Declaration

The terms "declaration" or "communication" are used to express certain matters of policy or principle and in no way abrogate or change the rights or obligations stipulated in the treaty. Frequently those terms are used interchangeably with the word "understanding."

The legal meaning of a Senate declaration, regardless of its designation, depends entirely on its substance. A declaration which modifies, limits or changes the text of the treaty or its meaning is actually a reservation. A declaration which clarifies or explains or deals with a secondary matter does not change the treaty and consequently is not a reservation. Sometimes it can be difficult to distinguish clearly between an understanding and a reservation. One may gradually obscure the other and thus become a question which the two parties may decide for themselves.

(Source: Whiteman, Digest of International Law, Vol 14, pp 137-198)

The Vienna convention of 1969 on treaty law says in Article 19:

"Article 19. A state may formulate a reservation at the time of signing, ratifying, accepting or approving a treaty or adhering to it. . . ."

That same convention defines the term "reservation" in Article 2(1) D:

"D. 'Reservation' is understood to be a unilateral declaration, regardless of its name or designation, made by a state in signing, ratifying, accepting or approving a treaty or in adhering to it with the purpose of excluding or modifying the legal effects of certain dispositions of the treaty in its application to that state."

In formulating the draft to the convention, the commission of international law explained the word "reservation" in the following terms:

"13. A definition of reservation becomes necessary because the states, in signing, ratifying, accepting, approving a treaty or adhering to it, usually formulate declarations on the matter in which they understand some questions or on their interpretation of certain dispositions. Such a declaration can be a simple clarification of the position of the state or can be a reservation, depending on whether it modifies the application of the clauses of the treaty already approved or excludes it."

(Document of the United Nations, Supplement No 9 A/5209, p 8)

Although this Vienna convention has not entered into force, it is the product of the work of codification of public international law sponsored by the United Nations and reflects the present state of the development of the norms which regulate relations between those subject to international law.

We can assert that, regardless of the term used, what matters is if the condition, reservation, amendment or declaration made by one party to the other modifies or changes what has been agreed to by the plenipotentiaries. If that change has been made, it is unquestionable that the treaty has not been ratified but, rather, that a counteroffer has been made by one party which the other is at liberty to reject, modify or approve. Only if it approves the counteroffer is the consent or perfecting [perfeccionamiento] of the wish of both parties to obligate themselves realized.

III. RATIFICATION BY PLEBISCITE IN PANAMA

In the United States ratification is effected by the president with the advice and consent of the Senate. In Panama, in conformity with Article 274 of the constitution, ratification of the treaties concerning the canal is by plebiscite. The authority to ratify resides exclusively in the people, in each citizen who takes on the responsibility of a conegotiator. The executive branch is not responsible for ratification in Panama. Its role is limited to that of being a mere exponent of the popular will.

The plebiscite required by the constitution has already been carried out in Panama. The people of Panama expressed their desire to ratify, that is, to give their approval to, the government's negotiating effort in the plebiscite held on 23 October 1977....

V. THE DECONCINI RESERVATION AND THE PRINCIPLE OF NONINTERVENTION

. . . .

A clear Latin American contribution to the development of international law has been the formalization of the principle of nonintervention, which was codified for the first time in Article 8 of the conference [as published] on the rights and duties of states approved by the Seventh Pan-American Conference held in Montevideo in 1933. This rule states:

"No state has the right to intervene in the internal or external affairs of another."

President Franklin Delano Roosevelt's position was clearly expressed by the U.S. delegate in these words:

Declaration made by the U.S. commission upon signing the Convention on the Rights and Duties of States in Montevideo in 1933:

"Any observing person must clearly understand now that under the Roosevelt administration the U.S. Government is as opposed as any other government to interference with the liberty, sovereignty or other domestic affairs or processes of the governments of other nations."

. . . .

This principle or basic norm of international conduct was successfully introduced by Latin American jurists, including our Dr. Ricardo J. Alfaro, into the UN Charter, adopted in 1945, which in Article 2 (4) states:

"All members shall refrain in their international relations from the threat or use of force against the territorial integrity or political independence of any state, or in any other manner inconsistent with the purposes of the United Nations."

. . . .

Article 15 of the OAS Charter approved in Bogota in 1948: "No state or group of states has the right to intervene, directly or indirectly, regardless of the reason, in the domestic or foreign affairs of another. The foregoing principle prohibits not only action by the armed forces, but any other form of interference or attack on the character of the state and political, cultural and economic elements which constitute it." (Note: This article is identical to Article 18 of the OAS Charter amended by the Buenos Aires protocol in 1967.)

. . . .

But a hardly edifying spectacle was given when some U.S. senators, during the Senate debate on the Torrijos-Carter treaty, rudely used language which without a doubt indicated that, in their opinion, the United States has the "right to intervene" in Panama to preserve the neutrality and security of the canal.

This must be made very clear. The "right of intervention" does not exist; everything is to the contrary [todo lo contrario]. Intervention has been proscribed in international legal life. There may be interventions. These cannot be avoided, just as crime cannot be avoided, but such interventions can only be regressively engendered by colonialist and neocolonialist minds which still do not understand that the destiny of man is freedom.

During his speech in the Senate, Senator DeConcini used language which offended the dignity of the Panamanian nation and which is not consonant with the great advancements of humanity. He spoke of so-called rights of intervention which the peoples of the world, organized under the symbol of the United Nations, extinguished once and for all in a collective manner. However, Senator DeConcini also stated:

"This does not mean, nor should it be interpreted as, a right of the United States to interfere in the domestic affairs of Panama."

Any intervention violates the basic rule of self-determination.

. . . The U.S. Senate in its 18 April resolution stated:

Pursuant to its adherence to the principle of nonintervention, any action taken by the United States of America in the exercise of its rights to assure that the Panama Canal shall remain open, neutral, secure and accessible pursuant to the provisions of the treaty and the neutrality treaty, and the resolutions of advice and consent thereto, shall be only for the purpose of assuring that the canal shall remain open, neutral, secure and accessible, and shall not have as its purpose nor be interpreted as a right of intervention in the internal affairs of the Republic of Panama or interference with its political or sovereign integrity.

This Senate resolution renders indefensible the allegation that the Torrijos-Carter treaties grant the United States any right of intervention in Panama.

. . . .

Panama's political independence, territorial integrity and self-determination are guaranteed by the unshakeable will of the Panamanian people and the active solidarity of peoples of the world, in accordance with what was solemnly compacted in the UN Charter. On 26 November 1821 Panama declared its will to be free and independent. This decision was reaffirmed on 3 November 1903 and also on 9 January 1964 when the January martyrs who offered their lives pointed out the path of sacrifices as the price of liberation from the colonialist yoke. Therefore, the Republic of Panama rejects, in a united and decisive fashion, any attempt by any country to intervene in its internal affairs. This is not only a matter of international law but of the steadfast will of our people.

. . . .

VI. INTERVENTION IS REPUDIATED IN THE U.S. SENATE

The voices of great U.S. leaders were heard clearly as they repudiated any interpretation that an alleged "right" to intervene in Panama could be inferred. Senators Frank Church, Mike Gravel, George McGovern, Jacob Javits, Paul Sarbanes, Edward Kennedy and others stated that the era of intervention is a thing of the past. It is relevant to quote a portion of Senator Kennedy's statements:

"And it is quite fair that the government and people of Panama should aspire to end the foreign military occupation of their own territory, that they should aspire to recover full national control of all their territory almost 100 years after becoming independent."

. . . .

VII. AMERICA IN A STATE OF ALERT TO KEEP THE DOORS OF INTERVENTION FROM BEING REOPENED

As clear proof of all the American peoples' effective and affective solidarity with Panama in its struggle to free itself of every colonialist presence or vestige of colonialism in its territory, it is worthwhile to note the words of two prominent Latin American leaders.

Venezuelan President Carlos Andres Perez said the following on welcoming the President of the United States in Venezuela on 28 March of this year:

"With all this, Mr. President, the feelings of the Latin American people are interpreted in a fully optimistic manner but without being able to hide the sincere concern felt throughout Latin America in the face of any eventuality.

"Just as we joyously celebrated the U.S. bicentennial, we Latin Americans want to celebrate with the same fraternal rejoicing the ratification of the new treaties, the indication of a new era of friendship and cooperation between Latin America and the United States. This is the symbolic meaning of the new Panama Canal treaties."

. . . .

Colombian President Dr. Alfonso Lopez Michelsen let his eloquent voice be heard in the following terms:

"Let not the foot of a foreign power again be placed on the sacred soil of a Latin American country."

. . . .

VIII. GENERAL TORRIJOS SET THE PARAMETERS OF DIGNITY IN ORDER TO MAKE A DECISION

Despite the fact that the Foreign Ministry communiques expressed the government's decision to withhold judgment regarding the reservations introduced into the canal neutrality treaty, it is obvious that General Torrijos' statements to the press and his notes to the chiefs of state of the whole world and to President Carter indicated the government's dissatisfaction and concern regarding the interventionist nature of the so-called DeConcini reservation. . . .

And in his letter to President Carter, our chief of government said:

"However, I do wish to point out that this study will be based on the following concepts: Panama will consider unacceptable any reservation which offends the national dignity, which distorts or changes the objectives of the treaty or which is designed to prevent the effective exercise by Panama of sovereignty over all its territory, the turnover of the canal and the military withdrawal on 31 December 1999."

IX. ANALYSIS OF THE AMENDMENTS, RESERVATIONS AND UNDERSTANDINGS

The Foreign Ministry now proceeds, methodically, to analyze the amendments, reservations and understandings by which the U.S. Senate gave its advice and consent to the Torrijos-Carter treaties.

I. Amendments

A. At the end of Article IV, insert the following: "A correct and authorized statement of certain rights and duties of the parties under the foregoing is contained in the statement of understanding issued by the Government of the United States of America on 14 October 1977 and by the Government of the Republic of Panama on 18 October 1977, which is hereby incorporated as an integral part of this treaty, as follows:

"Under the Treaty Concerning the Permanent Neutrality and Operation of the Panama Canal (the neutrality treaty), Panama and the United States have the responsibility to assure that the canal will remain open and secure to ships of all nations. The correct interpretation of this principle is that each of the two countries shall, in accordance with their respective constitutional processes, defend the canal against any threat to the regime of neutrality, and consequently shall have the right to act against any aggression or threat directed against the canal or against the peaceful transit of vessels through the canal. This does not mean, nor shall it be interpreted as, a right of intervention of the United States in the internal affairs of Panama. Any United States action will be directed at insuring that the Canal will remain open, secure and accessible, and it shall never be directed against the territorial integrity or political independence of Panama."

B. At the end of the first paragraph of Article VI, insert the following:

"In accordance with the statement of understanding mentioned in Article IV above: The neutrality treaty provides that the vessels of war and auxiliary vessels of the United States and Panama will be entitled to transmit the canal expeditiously. This is intended, and it shall be so interpreted, to assure the transit of such vessels through the canal as quickly as possible, without any impediment, with expedited treatment, and in case of need or emergency, to go to the head of the line of vessels in order to transit the Canal rapidly."

A perusal of these two amendments reveals that they correspond exactly with the statement of understanding agreed upon by General Torrijos and President Carter on 14 October 1977. This declaration contains an authentic interpretation of the treaty of neutrality agreed upon by the signatories. It was released in Panama before the plebiscite and accepted by the citizenry in approving the Torrijos-Carter treaties.

. . . .

II. Reservations:

A. Subject to the condition which will be included in the instrument of ratification of the treaty which will be exchanged with the Republic of Panama, notwithstanding the provisions of Article V or any other provisions of the treaty, if the canal is closed, or its operations are interfered with, the Republic of Panama and the United States of America shall each independently have the right to take such steps as it deems necessary, in accordance with its constitutional processes, including the use of military force in Panama, to reopen the canal or restore the operations of the Canal, as the case may be.

This is what has commonly been called the DeConcini reservation. Obviously its scope departed from the Torrijos-Carter declaration because it eliminated the obligation of the United States not to intervene in the internal affairs of Panama and to respect the political independence and territorial integrity of Panama.

. . . .

As abominable as the DeConcini reservation were the baseless explanations of the same senator, who seeks to revive U.S. intervention in the internal affairs of Panama. Fortunately, the Senate approved the 18 April resolution, known as the Church amendment, which reaffirms respect for the principle of nonintervention in the internal affairs of the countries of America, which was reproduced above.

With this last Senate resolution, it is evident that the United States has reaffirmed its international commitments in light of the UN and OAS charters. With it the DeConcini reservation has been rid of its imperialistic and interventionist claws, and the enforcement of the principle of nonintervention has been reestablished. The specter of new interventions at the end of the 20th century, which rightly caused concern to all Panamanians, has been eliminated.

B. Subject to the condition that the instruments of ratification of the treaty shall be exchanged only on the conclusion of a protocol of exchange to be signed by authorized representatives of both governments, which shall constitute an integral part of the treaty documents and which shall include the following:

"Nothing in this treaty shall preclude Panama and the United States from making in accordance with their respective constitutional processes any agreement or arrangement between the two countries to facilitate performance at any time after December 31, 1999, of their responsibilities to maintain the regime of neutrality established in the treaty, including agreements or arrangements for the stationing of any U.S. military forces or maintenance of defense sites after that date in the Republic of Panama, that Panama and the United States may deem necessary or appropriate."

This is what is known as the Nunn reservation. It has been objected to in Panama with the argument that it is contrary to Article V of the neutrality treaty which stipulates:

"After the termination of the Panama Canal treaty, only the Republic of Panama shall operate the canal and maintain military forces, defense sites and military installations within its national territory."

The Foreign Ministry shares the national sentiment regarding the termination of U.S. military occupation. The Nunn amendment does not oblige Panama to negotiate an agreement on bases, much less to accept a treaty with this purpose. The obligation to negotiate is nonexistent and even if it did exist, the obligation to negotiate does not entail the commitment to sign a treaty. In 1970 Panama rejected the 1967 treaties without detriment to the commitment of the United States and Panama before the OAS to negotiate a treaty which would resolve the causes of conflict.

. . . .

Panama has no objection in conformity with the provisions of Paragraph 3 of Article VII of the Panana Canal treaty and once the provisions therein are fulfilled, to the burial of the remains of U.S. citizens under the shadow of their flag in Corozal Cemetery. The funeral rites which any civilized nation holds for those who have offered their lives is worthy of all our respect. This is not a matter of sovereignty or expression of the exercise of jurisdictional powers. The Panamanian flag will always be flown in a place of honor as unequivocal proof of its sovereignty.

. . . .

III. Understandings:

A. Paragraph 1C. of Article III of the treaty shall be construed as requiring, before any adjustments in tolls for use of the canal, that the effects of any such toll adjustment on the trade patterns of the two parties shall be given full consideration, including consideration of the following factors in a manner consistent with the regime of neutrality:

1. The costs of operating and maintaining the Panama Canal;
2. The competitive position of the use of the canal in relation to other means of transportation;
3. The interests of both parties in maintaining their domestic fleets;
4. The impact of such an adjustment on the various geographical areas of each of the two parties; and
5. The interest of both parties in maximizing their international commerce.

The Republic of Panama and the United States shall cooperate in exchanging information necessary for the consideration of such factors.

. . . .

E. The President shall include all amendments, reservations, understandings, declarations and other statements incorporated by the Senate in its resolution of ratification respecting this treaty in the instrument of ratification exchanged with the Government of the Republic of Panama.

This understanding is directed toward the President of the United States rather than Panama. Panama has no objection to this understanding.

RESERVATIONS AND UNDERSTANDINGS INTRODUCED BY THE U.S. SENATE INTO THE PANAMA CANAL TREATY

A. Reservations: 1. Pursuant to its adherence to the principle of nonintervention, any action taken by the United States of America in the exercise of its rights to assure that the Panama Canal shall remain open, neutral, secure and accessible, pursuant to the provisions of this treaty and the neutrality treaty and the resolutions of advice and consent thereto, shall be only for the purpose of assuring that the canal shall remain open, neutral, secure and accessible, and shall not have as its purpose nor be interpreted as a right of intervention in the internal affairs of the Republic of Panama or interference with its political independence or sovereign integrity.

This reservation is extremely important politically. With it the Senate dissipated the fears which had emerged throughout Latin America that the DeConcini amendment had revived gunboat and big stick diplomacy in this hemisphere. The

Senate has reaffirmed the U.S. commitment in multilateral pacts that are treaties—laws regulating not only life on the American continent but throughout the world. Intervention is not a right; it is an international crime. . . .

Panama experienced moments of patriotic indignation following the introduction of the so-called DeConcini reservation. Via diplomatic channels the national government firmly expressed its rejection of that amendment as something harmful not only to U.S. relations with Panama but its relations with the entire continent. President Carter and the Senate leaders quickly understood this. The Senate then pointed out that a major tenet of U.S. policy is its adherence to the principle of nonintervention. And this adherence also pertains to the neutrality treaty which is of an indefinite duration. It is necessary to stress that the Senate's definition of U.S. policy in this reservation covers both treaties, which are mentioned specifically in the reservation, so that there would not be the slightest doubt that the DeConcini amendment added to the neutrality treaty would not continue in force. . . .

And further, as the instruments drawn up by one or more parties regarding a treaty (Article 31 of the Vienna convention on treaty laws) are very important for the interpretation of treaties in international law, it is deemed pertinent to transcribe the letter that President Carter sent General Torrijos on 18 April:
"Gen. Omar Torrijos Herrera,
Chief of Government of Panama.

"Dear General Torrijos: "A few moments ago the U.S. Senate granted its consent to the second of the Panama Canal treaties that you and I signed in Washington in September of last year.

"The ratification of the new treaties opens a new era in U.S. relations not only with Panama but with all the nations of the hemisphere. Working jointly our two nations can set an example and encourage others in the Americas and elsewhere to work toward just and constructive international cooperation in the pursuit of common goals.

. . . .

"The patience and patriotism of the people of Panama during this lengthy process has been impressive and has earned the respect of the world. In recent months there have been moments when the outcome was uncertain and there were doubts as to whether the two treaties should be ratified. On our part, these doubts have been set aside.

"With its actions today the Senate has reaffirmed what was important in the treaties from the beginning: that the United States, while safeguarding its interest in a secure, open and accessible canal, does not intend to interfere in the domestic affairs of Panama, its government, its policies or its cultural integrity, nor in any way undermine its sovereignty or its political independence.

"These are the principles that we have always cherished as a nation. We have lived up to them in our relations with other American republics since President Roosevelt proclaimed his adherence to the principle of nonintervention in 1933. Those principles are consecrated as international rights in the UN and OAS charters. Therefore, it is appropriate that those principles, particularly the principle that no nation has the right to interfere in the domestic affairs of another, should be incorporated into the treaties and its related documents, including the Senate resolutions. When we meet to exchange the ratification documents we will be able to reiterate that this principle of nonintervention is clearly accepted by our two countries.

"Respect for the sovereignty and dignity of Panama and the United States must be the basis on which to establish the cooperation and mutual respect that will be decisive for the new kind of relationship that we are about to begin. I want to congratulate and thank you, General Torrijos, for the great courage and leadership you gave the people of Panama while our countries were negotiating this new relationship.

"I look toward the future with great hope and confidence. And, on the personal level, I hope and wish to visit Panama to reaffirm our personal friendship and this new relationship between our two countries.

"Sincerely,

Jimmy Carter."

In this letter, President Carter reaffirmed the U.S. commitment to refrain from intervention in Panama's internal affairs.

2. Notwithstanding any other provisions of this treaty, no funds may be drawn from the U.S. Treasury for payments under Article XIII, Paragraph 4, without statutory authorization.

Panama's right to receive the sums stipulated in Article XIII, Paragraph 4, is very clear. Now, if in order to meet its contractual obligations the United States must follow a domestic legislative procedure, Panama has no objection. What is important is for the United States to meet its obligations in Panama's favor. The domestic mechanism provided for in U.S. legislation is of no concern to Panama.

3. Any accumulated unpaid balance under Paragraph 4C. of Article XIII termination date of the treaty shall be payable only to the extent of any operating surplus in the last year of the treaty's duration, and that nothing in that paragraph may be construed as obligating the United States of America to pay after the date of the termination of the treaty any such unpaid balance which shall have accrued before such date.

This is a reservation which contains a correct interpretation of the treaty. Panama has always understood, and so explained to the citizenry at the time, that the budget containing revenues from and expenditures for the operation of the canal would be so drafted as to make the canal commission capable of paying to Panama the sum stipulated in Article XIII, Paragraph 4C. If for unforeseen reasons this sum were not paid in a certain year, Panama understands that the United States will make an effort to cover that sum in subsequent budgets. Paragraph 4C. is not symbolic or worthless. The two countries, in good faith, must give it practical content.

For this reason, Panama does not foresee the accumulation of unpaid balances in the year 2000. However, if they did exist, the United States would not be obligated to make such payment to Panama. In summary, there is a clear understanding between the U.S. Senate and the Republic of Panama in this area.

. . . .

5. The instruments of ratification to be exchanged by the United States and the Republic of Panama shall each include provisions whereby each party agrees to waive its rights and release the other party from its obligations under Paragraph 2 of Article XII.

. . . .

Paragraph 2A. Article XII represents a great concession made by Panama to the United States. Panama pledged not to build a canal or to permit a canal to be built in Panama for the duration of the treaty, that is until the year 2000, without the consent of the United States. Here there is a clear obligation on the territory of Panama which the United States cannot negotiate for 22 years.

Paragraph 2B. of Article XII places a limitation on the United States in its negotiating capacity. According to this article, the United States cannot negotiate for 22 years with third countries of America on the construction of a canal outside Panama, unless Panama frees it from that limitation.

. . . .

6. After the date of entry into force of the treaty, the Panama Canal Commission shall, unless otherwise provided by legislation enacted by Congress, be obligated to reimburse the Treasury of the United States of America as nearly as possible for the interest cost of the funds or other assets directly invested in the commission by the Government of the United States of America and for the interest cost of the funds or other assets directly invested in the predecessor Panama Canal Company by the government and not reimbursed before the date of entry into force of the treaty. Such reimbursement of such interest costs shall be made at a rate determined by the secretary of the Treasury of the United States of America and at annual intervals to the extent earned, and if not earned, shall be made from subsequent earnings.

. . . .

Aside from the fact that it is evident that the United States has been amortized bountifully, the knowledge of its revenue-raising capacity to cover the Panama Canal costs according to studies by experts contracted especially by U.S. authorities demonstrates that the policy on revenue and expenditures for the canal's operations can be established in such a manner that will satisfy the provisions of this reservation and the income which Panama hopes to receive according to Article XIII, Paragraph 4B. and C., without significantly affecting the volume of traffic. Therefore, this reservation does not alter what was agreed upon. To the extent that the United States does not violate the principle honoring the treaties in good faith, Panama cannot present claims to the United States.

The most significant point in Article XIII is that the canal will revert to Panama on 31 December 1999, free of debts. This remains unchanged and it is this great achievement which fills the hearts of all Panamanians with joy.

B. Understandings:

1. Nothing in Paragraphs 3, 4 and 5 of Article IV may be construed to limit either the provisions of Paragraph 1 of Article IV providing that each party shall act, in accordance with its constitutional processes, to meet any threat to the security of the Panama Canal, or the provisions of Paragraph 2 of Article IV providing that the United States of America shall have primary responsibility to protect and defend the canal for the duration of this treaty.

Here the Senate expresses an understanding that can meet no opposition in Panama. Paragraph 1 of Article IV was explained to Panamanian citizens just as it was outlined by the Senate. Paragraph 2 of Article IV grants to the United States

"... primary responsibility to protect and defend the canal." However, it is evident that, since the canal is on Panamanian soil, we Panamanians have the greatest interest in defending it. For that reason, the wisest course is for there to be close cooperation between the armed forces of the two countries for the protection of a canal that is of interest to them and to the world.

. . . .

3. Nothing in Subparagraph 4C. of Article XIII shall be construed to limit the authority of the United States of America through the United States Government agency called the Panama Canal Commission to make such financial decisions and incur such expenses as are reasonable and necessary for the management, operation and maintenance of the Panama Canal. In addition, toll rates established pursuant to Paragraph 2D. of Article III need not be set at levels designed to produce revenues to cover the payments to Panama described in Subparagraph 4C. of Article XIII.

This understanding is consistent with the treaty. During the debate which preceded the plebiscite, it was clearly explained that the United States would control the administration of the canal for 22 years by reason of its majority position on the Canal Commission. Article III, Paragraph 2D. gives the United States the power to "establish, modify, collect and retain tolls for the use of the Panama Canal, and other charges, and establish and modify methods of their assessment." The two parties agreed, in Article III, Paragraph 1A. of the Neutrality Treaty that the tolls would be ". . . just, equitable and reasonable, and limited to those necessary for safe navigation and efficient, sanitary operation of the canal."

When the text of Article XIII, Paragraph 4B. and C. was agreed to, it was evident from a study of the canal operations that the canal produces approximately $18 million annually which comprise the canal's operating revenues [costo de operacion]. The negotiators' understanding was that this figure would serve as a base to cover the payment to Panama of the $10 million guaranteed in Article XIII, Paragraph 4B. and the additional $10 million agreed to in Article XIII, Paragraph 4B. and C. these payments being considered as part of the canal's operating revenues. For this reason we are in agreement that the obligations derived from Article XIII, Paragraph 4B. and C. in favor of Panama can be covered without raising tolls and for this reason we agree with the Senate that it is not imperative to raise tolls to cover these obligations to Panama. By virtue of the principle of good faith which prevails in the observance of the treaties, Panama expects the United States to accommodate its policy on expenditures so that this article can be the means by which Panama receives a fairer retribution for its contribution to the canal work. To the extent that the Panamanian people are satisfied with the canal administration due to the products they derive from it, they will continue protecting their canal. But if a stingy spirit prevails, aggravating the injustice suffered by Panama since 1903, then a circle of friendship will not have been built around the canal but rather one of hatred, with possible grave consequences if a crisis occurs which the national government would be the first to deplore.

. . . .

Foreign Ministry Conclusions: The previous exposition permits the Foreign Ministry to declare that the Torrijos-Carter treaties with the Senate resolutions:

1. Do not offend the nation's dignity.—The unquestionable fact that the United States must leave the Isthmus of Panama at the latest by 31 December 1999

completes our process of independence and places in our hands the exclusive control of the canal for use as an effective lever for our economic and social development. Also, all prospects of an alleged and obsolete "right" of intervention have been dispelled since the Senate of the United States has reaffirmed in the Church amendment the contents of the Torrijos-Carter declaration, that is, that any action taken by the United States in connection with the Panama Canal ". . . shall not have as its purpose nor be interpreted as a right of intervention in the internal affairs of the Republic of Panama or interference with its political independence or sovereign integrity."

Nothing can reaffirm our national dignity more than the knowledge that there will be an end to the military occupation of the fatherland almost 100 years after the establishment of the republic.

2. The objectives of the treaty have not been distorted or changed.—The fundamental objective of the liberating negotiations was to agree in the treaty to a clear and categorical program for our liberation. For this reason it was a fundamental objective to agree to a definite date or deadline for the new treaty. What has been the ideal of all Panamanians was realized in Article II, Paragraph 2, of the canal treaty:

"2. This treaty will expire at noon, Panama time, on 31 December 1999."

Greater conciseness and precision cannot be conceived.

Nothing has occurred after the plebiscite which weakens or alters this clause.

. . . .

Other fundamental achievements of the negotiations are the abrogation of the 1903 treaty and its amendments (Article I) and the resumption by Panama of its exclusive jurisdiction throughout all national territory (Article XI). The amendments contained in the Senate resolutions have not tarnished these definitive achievements of our people.

3. Nothing will prevent Panama from effective exercise of its sovereignty throughout all its territory.—The position of the U.S. Government during the Senate debates was that the United States has no sovereignty in the Canal Zone. Carter has spoken firmly in defense of Panama's traditional thesis. This position has cleared this legal problem in the minds of the American people. In keeping with this position, Article XI establishes that Panama will resume total jurisdiction in the Canal Zone when the treaty enters into force. U.S. jurisdictional rights, the only thing it possessed in Panama, will end on that date. The Senate debate and the firm position of the Senate majority have reaffirmed Panamanian sovereignty, which will be exercised effectively by Panama when the treaty goes into effect, because this treaty eliminates the so-called Canal Zone government. The anachronism of two governments in a single territory, as was stressed with patriotic zeal by President Demetrio Basilio Lakas in a meeting with President Nixon in 1971, has been brought to an end.

4. Great national objectives have been achieved.—By virtue of the generational alpinism spoken of very properly so by the chief of government, all generations of isthmians have contributed their ideas, efforts and sacrifices. Each Panamanian has been a volunteer soldier in the common task of liberation. Beginning with the note by Jose Domingo de Obaloia and Eusebio A. Morales in 1904, which best expresses our legal arguments, up to the tragic event of the January

martyrs—22 Panamanian heroes offered their lives and gave an everlasting cry of Panama's wish to be sovereign and free—it can be said that Panama has sought to:

A. Abrogate the 1903 treaty;

B. Recover the patrimony constituted by Panama's geographic position and its isthmian configuration to exploit the most important natural resource given to it by God, that is, to exploit to its maximum transit operations of the canal, the railroad and ports under its exclusive control and administration;

C. Reincorporate the Canal Zone into the rest of the fatherland's territory;

D. End the U.S. civilian and military presence;

E. Place the canal under a system which will guarantee the transit of ships of all flags on equal conditions and isolate the canal from any public controversy; and

F. Train qualified personnel in technical matters to assume responsibility for the canal's administration to the fullest extent possible.

The Foreign Ministry can state with satisfaction that the fundamental objectives which were imbedded in the national soul have basically been achieved. Unfortunately, all of these objectives will not be achieved immediately. It involves a liberation program that will be completed in 22 years, because the treaty is the product of negotiations in which reciprocal concessions were made. All Panamanians would like this term to be shorter, but we were able to achieve only that which is established in the treaties, despite the titanic and persistent efforts of our negotiator.

. . . .

The Foreign Ministry has faith in the capacity for struggle of the Panamanians. It also has faith that with time the U.S. public will better understand Panama's reasons for insisting on an improvement in the terms of its contractual relationship with the United States. This will facilitate the future decisions of the U.S. Government in its relations with Panama. The North American people are a just people. Some of their leaders have shown courage, patriotism and a clear sense of history. The Torrijos-Carter treaties are evident achievements in our liberation struggle, but they are not the final phase.

. . . .

We are sure that we will climb the summit of perfecting our independence on 31 December 1999 without bringing anguish or mourning to the hearts of Panamanian mothers.

. . . .

We assume full responsibility for the acceptance of the treaties with the conviction, firmness and encouragement that patriotism and the dedication to the cause of Panama's liberation give us.

Panama and the United States have wanted and sought a friendly and peaceful solution. This was achieved after 14 years of intense negotiations in which Panamanian nationalism saw the flowering of its best ideas. It is now up to all Panamanians, architects and beneficiaries of the treaties, to enjoy these benefits in a climate of peace and national unity.

Panama, 25 April 1978, Foreign Ministry.

Appendix T
POST-TREATIES STATEMENTS OF OMAR TORRIJOS

The following is excerpted from the interview with the late Omar Torrijos conducted by Soler Serrano of the Spanish magazine, *Magazin,* as published in *La Prensa* newspaper, Panama on December 14, 1980:

Serrano: The Sandinista triumph. Will it be followed in the geopolitics of Central America?

Torrijos: Without doubt. Although they do not export the revolution, the example is imitated. El Salvador, Guatemala, Honduras will have a new political design.

Serrano: Is Panama vaccinated against this revolutionary germ because of the Yankee bases in your land?

Torrijos: Our vaccine is that for ten years we have had a series of changes by which no part of the Panamanian society is offended or deprived thereby not needing a violent situation to change it. (*Author's note:* Torrijos seized power from Major Boris Martinez after Martinez ousted President Arnulfo Arias in a military coup October 11, 1968. Thereafter, Torrijos or his surrogates continued in power.)

Serrano: (In reference to the Panama Canal Treaties of 1977) The later amendments introduced by the North American lobbyists with the excuse of justifying military intervention in certain cases . . .

Torrijos: In order to have intervention, there has to be a reason to intervene. If some day this intervention does arise, it will find a country that does not want to be intervened. And if the objective of the intervention is to defend the Canal, what they may get is the impossibility of traffic through it. But let's not be apocalyptical. The U.S. has already filled their quota of shame, and they know that the intervention will not be tolerated . . . nor is it a solution.

Appendix U
AN ACT TO AMEND PUBLIC LAW 96-70
(THE PANAMA CANAL ACT OF 1979)

AN ACT TO AMEND PL 96-70 AND FOR OTHER PURPOSES

WHEREAS :

1. The so-called DeConcini Reservation to the 1977 Neutrality Treaty authorizes permanently the use of U.S. military force in Panama, if necessary to keep the Canal open and operating, with or without the consent of the Panamanian Government and even against the Panamanian Government itself, and

2. The Panamanian Government unilaterally added in both its instruments of ratification to the Neutrality Treaty and the Panama Canal Treaty of 1977 a three paragraph long counterreservation, misleadingly called an "understanding," and

3. Such three paragraph long Panamanian counterreservation would have nullified the DeConcini Reservation and was not accepted by the United States, and

4. In consequence, the 1977 Treaties were not ratified and did not come into force, and

5. The U.S. Constitution does not allow the President to appoint or keep in office, if appointed, Panamanians, non-resident aliens, as members (misleadingly called Directors), D/Administrators or Administrators of a United States Government Agency, the Panama Canal Commission,

NOW THEREFORE :

Be it enacted by the Senate and House of Representatives of the United States of America in Congress assembled .

Sec. 1. That the Panama Canal Treaties of 1977 are null and void, and have been null and void ab initio, having never been ratified.

Sec. 2. Any reference to the Panama Canal Treaties of 1977 in the Panama Canal Act of 1979 and in any other law are hereby repealed and stricken from such law.

Sec. 3. The President shall immediately remove from office any Director, Administrator, Deputy Administrator or other officer of the Panama Canal Commission, a United States Government Agency, who refuses to bind himself by oath or affirmation to support the Constitution of the United States, as required by its Art. VI, Sec. 3 as a qualification to hold any civil office or public trust under the United States.

Sec. 4. Sec. 1102.(a) of the Panama Canal Act of 1979 is amended by striking the first two sentences, and replacing them by the following :

"Sec. 1102 (a). The Commission shall be supervised by a Board composed of five members, one of whom shall be the Secretary of Defense or an officer of the Department of Defense designated by the Secretary. The five members of the Board shall be citizens of the United States."

Sec. 5. The President is directed to submit draft legislation to the Congress, within 90 days after the enactment of this Act, as such legislation might be necessitated to carry out the provisions of this Act.

Sec. 6. The President shall advise the Republic of Panama expeditiously of the contents of this Act.

Sec. 7. Short Title : This Act may be cited as the . . .

Source: Statement of Phillip Harman, Chairman of Committee for Better Panama and United States Relations, before the Subcommittee on Separation of Powers of the Committee on the Judiciary, U.S. Senate, 98th Cong., 1st Sess., on the Panama Canal Treaty—Constitutional and Legal Aspects of the Ratification Process, June 23, 1983, pp. 162-3.

Appendix V

ALFRED J. SCHWEPPE: 'DON'T YIELD CANAL TO PANAMA'

(as published in The Seattle Times, September 16, 1977)

Congress in 1902 empowered President Theodore Roosevelt to acquire from

Colombia a strip of land across the Isthmus of Panama for a ship canal, if Colombia would grant "perpetual control" of the strip on reasonable terms, or, failing that, a comparable strip in perpetuity for an alternate route through Nicaragua.

A treaty for a 10-mile-wide zone was negotiated by the plenipotentiaries. But Colombia rejected the treaty in August 1903—although later on, when it was too late, Colombia wanted to accept it.

On November 3, 1903, Panama, a restless province of Colombia, started a revolution — bloodless, as it turned out. Roosevelt, to protect American citizens and prevent violence, kept Colombian troops at a distance with a show of gunboats and marines.

A NEW Panamanian government was formed, and a declaration of independence promulgated, on November 4, 1903. Two days later, Secretary of State Hay officially recognized the Republic of Panama.

On November 18, Hay concluded a treaty with the Panamanian representative on substantially the same terms and on the identical money terms previously offered to Colombia. Article I guaranteed the independence of Panama.

The treaty was ratified by the new government through parliamentary action on December 2. The United States Senate approved the treaty on February 23, 1904.

On May 25, Thomas Arias, secretary of the government of Panama, sent a note to the United States government:

The government of the Republic of Panama considers that upon the exchange of ratifications on February 26, 1904, of the treaty for the opening an interoceanic canal across the Isthmus of Panama, its jurisdiction ceased over the Zone.

THE U.S. under the treaty paid $10 million for the 10-mile-wide zone across the Isthmus, and an annuity of $250,000, increased in a 1955 treaty to $2.3 million.

In the 1903 treaty, the young republic granted to the U.S. complete sovereign rights in the Zone and renounced those rights for itself. The treaty describes the Zone as "lands granted" to the U.S. Panama has repeatedly stated that the Zone was "ceded."

The U.S. Supreme Court ruled in 1907 that the Zone had been ceded and that the U.S. had perfect title. The U.S., under Article VI and XV, through a joint commission, bought that part of the land that was privately owned, from the owners, and acquired title to it in fee simple.

Having first rendered the disease-infected strip habitable by a three-year sanitation program that conquered death-dealing yellow fever, the U.S. completed the canal in 1914, at a cost of $366,650,000. The first ship passed through on August 3, 1914.

UNDER THE 1903 treaty, the U.S. acquired the Zone from Panama, subject to whatever rights Colombia might still have. Colombia, not Panama, was the country aggrieved in 1903.

But Colombia made an amicable settlement, fully adjusting "differences growing out of the political events in Panama in November, 1903," in a treaty negotiated during the Woodrow Wilson administration and ratified in 1922, when Charles Evans Hughes was secretary of state.

Wilson, a man of high political morals, knew that although Roosevelt's moves could technically be considered legal, Colombia was seriously hurt in 1903 by the nearby presence of U.S. forces, the prompt recognition of the Republic of Panama, and the U.S. guarantee of Panama's independence in the treaty.

In the "friendship" treaty, Colombia obtained certain transit rights through the Canal Zone, "title to which is now vested entirely and absolutely in the United States." The U.S. paid Colombia $25 million for the loss of Panama, in return for Colombia's agreement to recognize Panama's independence.

COLOMBIA granted Panama full recognition in 1922 and settled the boundary between them. Acceptance of the $25 million put any legal question of our acquisition in the 1903 treaty permanently at rest, as well as any moral question.

In 1923, Hughes said:

It is an absolute futility for the Panamanian government to expect any American administration, no matter what it is, any President or any secretary of state, ever to surrender any part of these rights, which the U.S. has acquired under the treaty of 1903.

Congress in 1904 set up a government of the Canal Zone under the President, and in 1912 enacted a Canal Zone Code, updated as needed, covering all phases of government in the Zone.

The 1903 treaty was ratified by further treaties making adjustments in 1936 and 1955. Total U.S. investment in the Zone and the Canal is now about $7 billion.

BY THE guarantee in the 1903 treaty of Panama's independence, and the 1922 treaty with Colombia, Panama owes its continued existence to the U.S. The U.S. has put up all the money, done all the work, and taken all the risks.

Where would Panama be today except for the events of 1903? Probably still a part of Colombia, with either no canal or one negotiated with Colombia or Nicaragua.

One would suppose that Panamanians, if permitted to become aware of their history, would on their independence day, sing paeans of praise to the U.S., instead of falsely claiming oppression. Panama and its parental neighbor, Colombia, have derived tremendous benefits from the Canal, as has the rest of the world.

If the U.S. owes anything, it owes it to itself and to the world to keep the Canal open as long as it is useful. Until the Canal ceases to have this utility, it should not be turned over to Panamanian control.

One needs only to look at Egypt's discriminatory management of the Suez Canal after the U.S., in concert with Russia, prevented England and France from redressing the illegal seizure in 1956.

FORTUNATELY, under Article II of the Constitution, no renegotiation by the President of our treaty rights in the Canal Zone can be effective unless consent to ratification is given by two-thirds of the Senators present when the treaty is submitted by the President.

Property may be acquired or disposed of under the treaty power. It may also be disposed of by Congress.

Under Article IV of the Constitution, Congress has power to dispose of "property belonging to the United States." This would take a majority vote of both houses. Any money provisions in a treaty, to be effective, would have to be approved by both houses of Congress, where resides the sole power to make appropriations. All money bills originate in the House.

Hence the Canal Zone and the Canal will remain U.S. property until disposed of pursuant to the Constitution.

Appendix W

WILLIAM M. WHITMAN: ANALYSIS OF PANAMA'S COUNTER-RESERVATION

Mr. Phillip Harman   May 20, 1985
1860 Venice Park Dr., Suite 220
North Miami, Florida 33181

Dear Phil:

In response to your request I am enclosing my analysis of the four questions you asked in reference to Panama's reservations in the instruments of ratification of the 1977 Panama Canal Treaties. As indicated in the attachment, in my view the key to the problem lies in considering the reservation as a whole in the light of all the relevant factors including the history of diplomatic relations between the United States and Panama, the relationship of the relevant provisions of the charters of the Organization of American States and the United Nations, and the positions taken by the two Governments during the process of negotiation and ratification of the treaties.

So considered, the categorical answers to your four questions are:

1. In my opinion, Panama's reservation inserted in its instruments of ratification is substantive.

2. The second paragraph of the reservation, read with the other paragraphs, in the light of all relevant factors, alters and modifies Article IV of the Neutrality Treaty and rejects the DeConcini reservation.

3. In my opinion, under applicable U.S. law, the President had the obligation to submit Panama's reservation to the Senate for formal acceptance.

4. Under U.S. law, when a reservation is made by the other party to a bilateral treaty after the Senate has advised ratification, the President has the responsibility to determine whether the reservation is substantive requiring acceptance by the Senate.

The reasoning behind these answers is shown in the attachment. The issues raised by these questions and others arising from the ambiguities inherent in the 1977 treaties are complex and I am looking forward with great interest to the conclusions reached by your Committee's study.

With best personal regards,

Sincerely,
W. M. Whitman

NOTES

CHAPTER 1

1. Frederick J. Haskins, *The Panama Canal* (Garden City, N.Y.: Doubleday, Page & Co., 1913), p.148.

2. *Ibid.,* p.147.

3. Joseph Bucklin Bishop and Farnham Bishop, *Goethals: Genius of the Panama Canal* (New York: Harper & Brothers, Publishers, 1930), pp.208-9.

4. Miles P. DuVal, Jr., *And the Mountains Will Move* (Westport, Connecticut: Greenwood Press, 1969), pp.339-40.

5. Robert P. Griffin, U.S. Senator, R.-Mich., "The Panama Canal Treaties," speech before Economic Club of Detroit, March 20, 1978.

6. Ron Paul, U.S. Representative, R.-Tex., comments, *Congressional Record,* 96th Cong., 1st sess., vol.125, pt.13, pp.16128-9.

7. *Panama Canal Issues and Treaty Talks,* a study by The Center for Strategic Studies (Washington: Georgetown University, March 1967), p.vii.

8. Jon P. Speller, *The Panama Canal* (New York: Robert Speller & Sons, 1972), p.132-3.

9. Philip M. Crane, *Surrender in Panama: The Case Against the Treaty* (New York: Dale/Caroline Dale Books, 1978), p.36.

10. *Canal Record,* vol.IV, November 23, 1910, p.100, as quoted by Representative Daniel J. Flood, *Congressional Record,* 87th Cong., 2d sess., vol.108, pt.8, June 13, 1962, p.10422.

11. James T. Du Bois, U.S. Minister to Colombia, letter to Secretary of State Philander Chase Knox, September 30, 1921 (*sic.,* 1912), as quoted by DuVal, *Cadiz to Cathay* (Stanford University: Stanford University Press, 1947), pp.442-3.

12. T. Roosevelt, "How the United States Secured the Right to Build the Panama Canal," *Outlook,* October 7, 1911, p.318.

13. Theodore Roosevelt, letter to W.R. Thayer, July 2, 1915, as quoted by DuVal, *Cadiz,* pp.443-4.

14. Daniel J. Flood, "The Juridical Base of the U.S. Isthmian Canal Policy," *American Mercury*, January 1964, pp.22-3.

15. Charles H. Breecher, testimony before Subcommittee on Separation of Powers, Committee on the Judiciary, U.S. Senate, 98th Cong., 1st sess., hearing on the Panama Canal Treaties—Constitutional and Legal Aspects of the Ratification Process, June 23, 1983, pp.13-15.

16. *Ibid.*, p.17.

17. Zbigniew Brzezinski, *Power and Principle,* (New York: Farrar, Straus, Giroux, 1983), p.138.

18 Haynes Johnson, "Drama Pervaded Historic Roll Call," *The Washington Post,* first edition, March 17, 1978, p.1.

19. Jimmy Carter, former President of the United States, *Keeping Faith* (New York: Bantam Books, 1982), p.173.

20. Brzezinski, *Power* (see chap.1, n.17), p.138.

21. Johnson, "Drama" (see chap.1, n.18).

22. *Panama Canal, Permanent Neutrality and Operation Treaty,* Treaties and Other International Acts Series 10029 (Washington: Government Printing Office (GPO), 1977), Article IV.

23. Carter, *Faith* (see chap.1, n.19), p.170.

24. *Ibid.*, p.172.

25. *Webster's New World Dictionary of the American Language*, college edition, s.v. "fraud" (New York: The World Publishing Company, 1976), p.576.

26. *Congressional Record—Senate,* 95th Cong., 1st sess., vol.124, pt.7, April 10, 1978, p. 9569.

27. Carter, *Faith* (see chap.1, n.19), p.174.

28. *Panama Canal Treaty,* Treaties and Other International Acts Series 10030 (Washington: GPO, 1977), (a) RESERVATIONS: (1).

29. Carter, *Faith* (see chap.1, n.19), p.178.

30. Jeane Kirkpatrick, *Dictatorships and Double Standards* (New York: Simon and Schuster, 1982), p.23.

31. Charles Evans Hughes, address before American Bar Association convention, Minneapolis, Minn., August 30, 1923, as reported "Hughes Upholds Monroe Doctrine," *New York Times,* late city edition, Associated Press, August 31, 1923, pp.1-2.

32. "The Battle Blow by Blow," *Time,* October 18, 1976, pp.17-8.

33. Breecher, testimony (see chap.1, n.15), pp.82-83.

CHAPTER 2

1. Philip C. Clarke, "The Soviet Toehold in Panama," *The Washington Inquirer,* weekly newspaper, June 10, 1983, p.6.

2. Newsletter, Canal Watchers Educational Association, March 28, 1983; June 2, 1983.

3. Thomas H. Moorer, Admiral, U.S. Navy (Ret.), statement before the Subcommittee on Separation of Powers of the Senate Committee on the Judiciary, *Congressional Record,* 95th Cong., 1st sess., vol.123, pt.2, August 4, 1977, p.S13638.

4. Rudy Abramson, "Canal Debate Entangled by Technicalities," Norfolk, Va., *Virginian-Pilot and Ledger Star,* first edition, Los Angeles Times News Service, January 1, 1978, p.A1.

5. *Panamanian Instrument of Ratification—Panama Canal Treaty,* June 16, 1978, (b) Understandings, paragraph (6) and subsequent 3 unnumbered paragraphs, as published in "Senate Debate on the Panama Canal Treaties: A Compendium of Major Statements, Record Votes and Relevant Events," prepared for the Committee on Foreign Relations, U.S. Senate, 95th Cong., 2d sess., February 1979 (Washington, D.C.: GPO, 1979), pp.551-52. See also, *Panamanian Instrument of Ratification—Neutrality Treaty,* June 16, 1978, (d) Understandings, paragraph (5) and subsequent 3 unnumbered paragraphs; *ibid.,* "Senate Debate," pp.559-60.

6. *U.S. Instrument of Ratification—Neutrality Treaty,* June 15, 1978, (b) Conditions, paragraph (1); *ibid.,* "Senate Debate," p.553. See also, *Panamanian Instrument of Ratification—Neutrality Treaty,* June 16, 1978, (b) Conditions, paragraph (1); *ibid.,* "Senate Debate," p.557.

7. *U.S. Constitution,* Article II, Section 1.

8. *Panamanian Instrument of Ratification—Panama Canal Treaty* (see chap.2, n.5). See also, *Panamanian Instrument of Ratification—Neutrality Treaty* (see chap.2, n.5).

9. Breecher, testimony (see chap.1, n.15), pp.43-44.

10. Michael G. Kozak, Deputy Legal Adviser to Department of State, interview, November 21, 1983, in Washington, D.C.

11. Robert Dockery, former Foreign Relations Committee staff officer in charge of the Panama Canal Treaties, interview, November 15, 1983, in Washington, D.C.

12. James McClellan, former Chief Counsel to the Subcommittee on Separation of Powers of the Senate Committee on the Judiciary, interview, November 15, 1983, in Washington, D.C.

13. Breecher, testimony (see chap.1, n.15), p.45.

14. *Panamanian Instrument of Ratification—Panama Canal Treaty* (see chap.2, n.5). See also, *Panamanian Instrument of Ratification—Neutrality Treaty* (see chap.2,n.5).

15. "Dock workers strike at Panamanian ports," *The Miami Herald,* first city edition, January 22, 1982, p.1.

16. Phillip Harman, Chairman, Committee for Better Panama and U.S. Relations, testimony before the Subcommittee on Separation of Powers of the Senate Committee on the Judiciary, 98th Cong., 1st sess., June 23, 1983, p.144.

17. Harman, letter to *The Washington Post,* first city edition, October 1, 1979, p.13; letter to *The Washington Times,* city edition, September 9, 1983, p.11A.

18. Paul B. Ryan, *The Panama Canal Controversy* (Stanford, Cal.: Hoover Institution Press, 1977), pp.7, 13.

19. G.A. Mellander, *The United States in Panamanian Politics* (Danville, Ill.: Interstate Printers and Publishers, 1971), p.43, citing U.S. Department of State, report, "Relations of the United States with Colombia and the Republic of Panama" (Washington, D.C.: 1904), pp.51-62.

20. Philippe Bunau-Varilla, *The Great Adventure of Panama* (Garden City, N.Y.: Doubleday, Page, 1920), p.259.

21. Gerstle Mack, *The Land Divided* (New York: Alfred A. Knopf, 1944), p.489.

22. Denison Kitchel, *The Truth About the Panama Canal* (New Rochelle: Arlington House Publishers, 1978), pp.77-78.

23. Jules Dubois, *Danger Over Panama* (New York: Bobbs-Merrill, 1964), p.39.

24. Kitchel, *Truth* (see chap.2, n.22), p.80.

25. Edwin C. Hoyt, *National Policy and International Law, Case Studies from American Canal Policy* (Denver: Social Science Foundation and Graduate School of International Studies, University of Denver, 1967), p.39.

26. *Ibid.*

27. John W. Haizlip, "Panama Canal Defense—Influence of International Law," essay (Newport, R.I.: Naval War College, 1968), p.23.

28. Hoyt, *National* (see chap.2, n.25), pp.58-60.

29. U.S. Department of State, *Foreign Relations of the United States 1926,* vol.II (Washington, D.C.: GPO, 1941), pp.833-49.

30. Alfred J. Schweppe, "The Panama Canal Treaties," essay, printed in *Congressional Record,* 94th Cong., 2d sess., vol.122, pt.18, February 3, 1977, pp.22923-25.

31. *Treaties and Other International Agreements of the United States of America 1776-1949,* Department of State Publication 8642, compiled by Charles I. Bevans, vol.10, 1st ed. (Washington, D.C.: GPO, August 1972), pp.742-52.

32. Kitchel, *Truth* (see chap.2, n.22), pp.81-82.

33. Dubois, *Danger* (see chap.2, n.23), p.123.

34. Lester D. Langley, "The World Crisis and the Good Neighbor Policy in Panama, 1936-1941," *The Americas,* October 1967, pp.146-48.

35. Diogenes A. Arosema, ed., *Documentary Diplomatic History of the Panama Canal* (Panama City, 1961), pp.453-70.

36. Dubois, *Danger* (see chap.2, n.23), pp.181-82. See also, Hoyt, *National* (see chap.2, n.25), p.43.

37. Kitchel, *Truth* (see chap.2, n.22), p.84.

38. John J. Johnson, "United States—Latin American Relations: The Roots of Misunderstanding," *Current History,* vol.56, January 1969, pp.1-6, 53.

39. Dubois, *Danger* (see chap.2, n.23), pp.190-91: Some 100,000 people (one-eighth of the population) attended the rally. Present were all living ex-Presidents of Panama, except Arnulfo Arias.

40. *U.S. Treaties and Other International Agreements 1955,* vol.6, pt.2 (Washington, D.C.: GPO, 1956), pp.2273-89.

41. Ryan, *Controversy* (see chap.2, n.18), p.39.

42. This decision was first publicized at a press conference on December 1, 1959. Subsequently, only 3 out of 183 pieces of mail approved the President's action. See Department of State *Bulletin,* Publication 7081, vol.43, October 10, 1960 (Washington, D.C.: GPO, 1960), pp.558-59.

43. *Congressional Record—House,* 86th Cong., 2d sess., vol.106, pt.2, February 2, 1960, pp.1798, 1806, 1809. See also Appendix A-1 for tabulation of Congressmen voting to implement the 1977 Panama Canal Treaties.

44. *Ibid., Congressional Record,* pp.1806, 1809.

45. Department of State *Bulletin,* Publication 7307, vol.45, December 4,

1961 (Washington, D.C.: GPO, 1961), pp.932-33. Much of the "Flag Riot" results was confirmed by the former Assistant Secretary of State for Inter-American Affairs, Thomas C. Mann, in a telephone interview with the author, October 20, 1984.

46. Lawrence O. Ealy, *Yanqui Politics and the Isthmian Canal* (University Park, Pa.: Pennsylvania State University Press, 1971), pp.120-25.

47. *New York Times,* late city edition, March 22, 1964, p.44. See also, *Washington Post,* first city edition, March 22, 1964, p.44.

48. Thomas A. Bailey, *A Diplomatic History of the American People,* 9th ed. (Englewood Cliffs, N.J.: Prentice-Hall, 1974), p.895, n.3.

49. *Congressional Record—Senate,* 92d Cong., 1st sess., vol.117, pt.3, February 17, 1971, pp.2898-2900.

50. Atlantic-Pacific Interoceanic Canal Study Commission, final report, December 1, 1970, as reported by Senator Mike Mansfield, D.-Mont., in *Congressional Record—Senate,* 92d Cong., 1st sess., vol.117, pt.3, February 17, 1971, p.2899. See also, E.W. Tuttle, "Red Canal in Nicaragua?" *The Truth,* Fall 1983, p.8.

51. Strom Thurmond, U.S. Senator, R.-S.C., comments, *Congressional Record—Senate* (see chap.2, n.49), pp.2898-99.

52. Department of State *Bulletin* No.9 (revised) on "Current Policy," January 1977 (Washington, D.C.: GPO, 1977), p.5.

53. Hearings before the Subcommittee on Separation of Powers of the Committee on the Judiciary, U.S. Senate, on the Panama Canal Treaty (Disposition of United States Territory), 95th Cong., 2d sess., pt.4, March 11, 1978.

54. U.S. Supreme Court, *Wilson v. Shaw,* 204 U.S. 24 (1907). This 9-0 decision was written by Associate Justice David Josiah Brewer (1837-1910), one of the Court's all-time great jurists, and was agreed to by Chief Justice Melville Weston Fuller (1833-1910) and Justices Day, Harlan, Holmes, McKenna, Moody, Peckham and White.

55. *United States v. Husband R. (Roach),* 453 F.2d 1054 (5th Cir. 1971), *cert. den.,* 406 U.S. 935 (1972).

56. William D. Rogers, former Assistant Secretary of State for Inter-American Affairs, interview with author, November 14, 1983, in Washington, D.C.

57. Philip M. Crane, U.S. Representative, R.-Ill., interview, November 18, 1983, in Washington, D.C.

58. George V. Hansen, U.S. Representative, R.-Ida., interview, November 18, 1983, in Washington, D.C.

59. Sol M. Linowitz, Chairman, Commission on United States—Latin American Relations (New York: Center for Inter-American Relations), report, October 29, 1974, p.1.

60. Jon Basil Utley, "The Dodd-Linowitz Connection," *The Washington Inquirer,* weekly newspaper, May 20, 1983, p.6.

61. Linowitz, Commission report (see chap.2, n.59), p.23.

62. *Ibid.,* December 26, 1976, p.i.

63. Lewis A. Tambs, Professor of History, Oregon State University, "Soviet Threat to the Caribbean," published by the non-profit Americanism Educational League, Buena Vista, Cal., July 1983.

64. Simon Bolivar, "Letter to a Jamaican Gentleman, 1815," in J.F. Blanco,

Documentos para la Historia de la Vida Publica del Libertador de Colombia, Peru y Bolivia, p.340, as quoted by DuVal, *Cadiz,* p.421.

CHAPTER 3

1. John Reed, *Ten Days That Shook the World* (New York: Random House, 1935), pp.235, 321.

2. "Panama Protests Parly Exclusion," *New York Times,* late city edition, August 16, 1956, p.2.

3. Romulo Escobar Bethancourt, address before National Assembly of Panama, August 19, 1977, quoted by Crane in *Surrender* (see chap.1, n.9), pp.228-36.

4. Paul P. Kennedy, "30 Hurt in Panama in Rioters' Attempts to Enter U.S. Zone," *New York Times,* late city edition, November 30, 1959, pp.1, 12.

5. *New York Times,* editorial, August 5, 1962, p.32.

6. White House news conference, March 21, 1964, reported by *New York Times,* late city edition, March 22, 1964, p.44. See also, State Department *Bulletins,* January 9, 1965 and October 18, 1965. See also, National Security Action Memorandum No. 323, January 8, 1965, p.4.

7. Phillip Harman, letter to author, January 27, 1984. See also, Dean Rusk's testimony before Senate Foreign Relations Committee, hearings on Panama Canal Treaties, 95th Cong., 1st sess., pt.3, October 14, 1977, pp.519-23.

8. Rose Marie Aragon, testimony before the Senate Foreign Relations Committee, hearings on Panama Canal Treaties, 95th Cong., 1st sess., pt.3, October 12, 1977, p.257. As for the draft position paper, Colonel Robert D. Banning, Military Assistant for the Panama Canal, Office of Assistant Secretary of the Army, wrote, "... since it was a draft, it must have been destroyed some years ago...." (letter to Harman, July 27, 1981). Leopoldo Aragon, in a letter from Sweden to Phillip Harman in September 1977, wrote about the paper, but had immolated himself, in protest to the Treaties, before answering Harman's request for a copy.

9. Dean Rusk, former Secretary of State, testimony before Senate Foreign Relations Committee, hearings on Panama Canal Treaties, 95th Cong., 1st sess., pt.3, October 14, 1977, p.519.

10. Griffin, speech (see chap.1, n.5).

11. Amado Sanjur, former Chief of Staff, Panamanian National Guard, statement July 6, 1981, notorized on September 17, 1981 by Aline Goury, Miami, Florida. See also, Boris Martinez, former Chief of Staff, Panamanian National Guard, interview, *La Prensa* newspaper reporter (unnamed), Panama City, October 10, 1980, p.7. This meeting with Angueira was also confirmed by Ramiro Silvera, another former Chief of Staff of the Guard, in a telephone interview with the author on November 4, 1984.

12. Efrain Angueira, telephone interview with author, September 9 and 30, October 21, 1984. Personal interview, January 17, 1986, in Ft. Walton Beach, Florida.

13. Harman, *Panama's Arias Falls in Coup* (self-published), analysis, September 1981, p.3.

14. Robert W. Porter, Jr., General, U.S. Army (Ret.), telephone interview with author, October 6, 1984.

15. Covey T. Oliver, former Assistant Secretary of State, undated letter to Harman, quoted in Harman analysis (see chap.3, n.13), p.47.

16. Harman, analysis (see chap.3, n.13), p.18.

17. Sanjur, notorized statement (see chap.3, n.11).

18. William J. Jorden, former U.S. Ambassador to Panama, author, *Panama Odyssey* (Austin: University of Texas Press, 1984), p.132.

19. Boris Martinez, former Chief of Staff, Panamanian National Guard, interview with author, July 31, 1984, Miami, Florida.

20. Amado Sanjur, former Chief of Staff, Panamanian National Guard, interview with author, July 31, 1984, Miami, Florida.

21. Sanjur, letter to author, September 18, 1984.

22. Jorden, *Odyssey* (see chap.3, n.18), p. 131.

23. Martinez, interview (see chap.3, n.19). Martinez amplified these plans and the roles of Boyd and Garrido, interview October 19, 1984.

24. *Ibid.,* interview, July 31, 1984.

25. Chester L. Johnson, Maj. General, U.S. Army (Ret.), letter to Harman, March 18, 1983, passed to author by Harman.

26. Jorden, *Odyssey* (see chap.3, n.18), pp.137-38.

27. Martinez, interview (see chap.3, n.19). On September 30, 1984, Efrain Angueira was asked about this incident and said, "I cannot comment on that," apparently bound by his oath as intelligence officer.

28. *Ibid.,* Martinez interview (see chap.3, n.19). Sanjur confirmed the meeting at which Torrijos promised to curtail his drinking.

29. Jorden, *Odyssey* (see chap.3, n.18), pp.142-43. In one short paragraph, Jorden covers Martinez's downfall: the TV program, loss of support, forcible exile to Miami, refusal of new assignment, alleged get-together with Arias, explanation of the Inter-American Defense Board—but again omits particulars in this incident uncomplimentary to Torrijos.

30. Martinez, interview (see chap.3, n.19). This incident at the Panama City TV station was affirmed by Sanjur in our interview on August 31, 1984.

31. Sanjur, interview (see chap.3, n.20) and letter to author, September 14, 1984.

32. Sanjur, memorandum to author, August 11, 1984. Carl Perian, former Chief of Staff, House Committee on Merchant Marine and Fisheries, in a telephone interview with author, September 29, 1984, related another example of apparent deception for the sake of gaining support for the Treaties involving the other co-negotiator, Sol Linowitz, who told the Committee, in executive session on March 16, 1977, that the U.S. would control the Canal in perpetuity. When "leaked" to UPI reporter Juan J. Walte for publication, the Carter Administration and Panamanians were aghast. Then, "good soldier" John M. Murphy, the Committee Chairman, issued a waffling statement to get Carter off the hook and restore calmness for the moment.

33. "Noreiga reportedly suffers hysteria," *La Prensa,* November 1, 1985, p.1.

34. Fernando Manfredo, Deputy Administrator, Panama Canal Commission, interview with author, August 3, 1984 in Panama.

35. Sanjur, interview (see chap.3, n.20).

36. Ramiro Silvero, former Chief of Staff, Panamanian National Guard, telephone interview with author, November 4, 1984.

37. Cesar Napoleon Suazo, former Maj. General, Nicaraguan National Guard, interview with author, August 1, 1984, in Miami, Florida. General Suazo gave details: Somoza had directed him to provide an aircraft to fly Torrijos, Paredes, and Garcia back to Panama. He used Somoza's Aero Commander (Alfa Sierra Delta) for the flight on December 15, 1969 from Las Mercedes Airport (a Nicaraguan Air Base) to David, Chiriqui province. The plane was piloted by Red Gray, an American, who believed he was helping a fair cause. Lakas was not on this flight, but returned to Panama the next day.

38. Gorden Sumner, Lt. General, U.S. Army (Ret.), testimony before House Subcommittee on Panama Canal, Committee on Merchant Marine and Fisheries, hearing on Panama Gunrunning, 96th Cong., 1st sess., June 7, 1979, pp.124-28.

39. *Congressional Record,* 92d Cong., 1st sess., vol.117, pt.3, February 17, 1971, pp.2898-2900.

40. "New Dutch Contact Slated by Jakarta," *New York Times,* late city edition, Reuters News Agency, August 5, 1962, p.21. See also, Robert Trumbull, "Dulles in Tokyo Lauds Free Asia," *New York Times,* late city edition, Special to *Times,* March 18, 1956, p.39.

41. Other national organizations opposing dilution of sovereign rights: Daughters of the American Revolution, National Federation of Republican Women's Clubs, Navy League, and American Legion.

42. *Latin America,* weekly newspaper, Latin American Newsletters, Ltd., London, WR 73-48, November 30, 1973, pp.282-83.

43. State Department *Bulletin,* No.9 (revised) (see chap.2, n.52).

44. Jorden, *Odyssey* (see chap.3, n.18), p.222.

45. Isaac Don Levine, *Hands Off the Panama Canal* (Washington: Monticello Books, 1976), p.99.

46. Strom Thurmond, "For Perpetual U.S. Control over the Panama Canal," *New York Times,* late city edition, May 7, 1974, p.45.

47. Thomas C. Mann, former Assistant Secretary of State, letter to Captain Paul B. Ryan, quoted by Ryan, *Controversy* (see chap.2, n.18), p.105.

48. Winston Robles, Director of Panamanian Commission for Human Rights, testimony before House Committee on International Relations, hearings on Proposed Panama Canal Treaties, 95th Cong., 1st sess., October 11, 1977, pp.338-44.

CHAPTER 4

1. Carter, *Faith* (see chap.1, n.21), p.155.

2. Mr. Carter's first National Security Memorandum dealt with the Canal: "Presidential Review Memorandum/NSC 1," and was for action by Vice President Walter Mondale and the Secretaries of State and Defense.

3. Kevin P. Phillips, "The Canal and U.S. Patriotism," Norfolk, Va., *Virginian-Pilot,* August 26, 1977, p.A15.

4. *Arizona Republic,* December 6, 1975, p.1.

5. Linowitz, Commission report, October 29, 1974 (see chap.2, n.59), p.1.

6. *Congressional Record,* 95th Cong., 1st sess., vol.123, pt.4, February 22, 1977, pp.4805-07.

7. "National Security-Foreign Relations," *American Legion Bulletin* No.2-77, February 11, 1977, pp.3-4(A).

8. Reed Irvine, "Treaty Negotiator was Allende Agent," *Human Events,* January 21, 1978, p.12.

9. Jesse Helms, U.S. Senator, R.-N.C., address before the Senate, *Congressional Record* (see chap.4, n.6), p.4806.

10. Library of Congress, special report on Panamanian bank debts, made to Chairman, Senate Judiciary Committee, July 21, 1977.

11. U.S. Department of State, *Current Policy No.9,* Bureau of Public Affairs, November 1975.

12. Orrin Hatch, U.S. Senator, R.-Utah, "Panaman Canal Giveaway Violates Constitution," *Conservative Digest,* September 1977, pp.32-33.

13. John D. Blacken, Counselor, U.S. Embassy, Panama, address printed in *Congressional Record,* 94th Cong., 1st sess., vol.121, pt.23, September 25, 1975, pp.30312-15.

14. "Escobar Fuels Students," *Human Events,* September 10, 1977, p.3. See also, Ronald W. Reagan, testimony before Senate Subcommittee on Separation of Powers, hearings on Panama Canal Treaty, 95th Cong., 1st sess., pt.3, September 8; October 13, 28; November 3, 15, 1977, pp.7-16.

15. "New Deals for the Big Ditch," *Time,* July 25, 1977, p.27.

16. Graham Covey, "Carter Draws Line on Talks on Canal," *New York Times,* late city edition, Special to *New York Times,* August 2, 1977, pp.1, A9. See also, Covey, "U.S., Panama in Accord on Transfer of Canal by End of the Century," *New York Times,* late city edition, Special to *New York Times,* August 11, 1977, pp.1, 12A.

17. "Hemispheric Hotline Report," September 16, 1977, as reported by Representative Gene Snyder, R.-Ken., in *Spotlight,* weekly newspaper, October 31, 1977, p.8.

18. Abramson, "Canal Debate Entangled" (see chap.2, n.4).

19. Bethancourt, address (see chap.3, n.3).

20. Levine, *Hands Off* (see chap.3, n.45).

21. Donald M. Dozer, "State Department Determined to Give Away Panama Canal," *Human Events,* August 13, 1977, p.14.

22. Eduardo Abbot, report to Library of Congress, "Constitutionality of Canal Treaties," Section III, Conclusions, para.1, cited at hearings before Senate Subcommittee on Separation of Powers, 98th Cong., 1st sess., June 23, 1983, p.184.

23. "Capitol Briefs," *Human Events,* March 25, 1978, p.2.

24. "Now for the hard part," *Time,* September 19, 1977, pp.19-21.

25. Alfred J. Schweppe, letter to William F. Buckley, Jr., December 8, 1977, as quoted in Phillip Harman analysis, "Are the Panama Canal Treaties Invalid?" (self-published, 1978), January 1978, pp.19-20.

26. "Squaring Away on the Canal," *Time,* January 30, 1978, p.31. See also, Neil MacNeil, "The Wooing of Senator Zorinsky," *Time,* March 27, 1978, pp.12-13. See also, *Florida Sunvets,* editorial, October 1977, pp.4-5.

27. Kevin Phillips, "Carter's Legal Tricks," *Conservative Digest,* January

1978, p.21. See also, "Canal Pact Wording Resolved," Los Angeles Times News Service, Norfolk, Va. *Ledger-Star,* October 14, 1977, p.3.

28. James C. Roberts, "Summing Up the Anti-Canal Treaties Argument," *Human Events,* March 18, 1978, p.8. See also, *La Esprella de Panama,* Panamanian newspaper, September 10, 1977, p.1.

29. Griffin, speech (see chap.1, n.5).

30. "Inside Washington," *Human Events,* October 15, 1977, p.3.

31. "Text of Romulo Escobar Bethancourt's address before the National Assembly of Panama," *Matutino,* August 20, 1977, pp.1, 7. See also, Foreign Broadcast Information Services (FBIS) translation, August 29, 1977.

32. Bethancourt, quoted in "Senate Remains Skeptical About Panama Canal Treaties," *Human Events,* October 8, 1978, p.1.

33. Jorden, *Odyssey* (see chap.3, n.18). See also, John Wayne, letter, cited in *Congressional Record,* 95th Cong., 2d sess., vol.124, pt.4, pp.5361-63. See also, "Squaring Away," *Time* (see chap.4, n.26).

34. John H. Averill, "Both Sides Court Public as Canal Vote Nears," Los Angeles Times News Service, Norfolk, Va. *Virginian-Pilot,* January 22, 1978, p.1.

35. Julian M. Carroll, Governor of Kentucky, comments in introducing Secretary of State Cyrus Vance at Louisville, January 21, 1978, as reported by Averill, *ibid.*

36. Averill, *ibid.*

37. This is a direct quote from a tape recording of a conversation among Somoza, McAuliffe, and U.S. Ambassador William Bowdler on December 21, 1978, as noted by author Jack Cox in *Nicaragua Betrayed* (Boston: Western Islands, 1980), p.329. Somoza had begun taping all discussions with U.S. officials because of frequent leaks and misquotes.

38. *The Phoenix Republic,* January 1, 1978, p.1.

39. Sam Dickens, Colonel, U.S. Air Force (Ret.), former Chief of the Western Hemisphere Division of Plans and Policies, U.S. Air Force, interview with author, November 20, 1983, in Washington, D.C.

40. Thomas A. Lane, Maj. General, U.S. Army (Ret.), *The Breakdown of the Old Politics* (New Rochelle: Arlington House, 1974), p.213.

41. Hansen W. Baldwin, *Strategy for Tomorrow* (New York: Harper and Row, 1970), p.13.

42. Baldwin, review of *Swords and Plowshares* by Maxwell Taylor, *Intercollegiate Review,* Winter 1972-73, p.112.

43. Telegram, General David C. Jones, Chief of Staff, U.S. Air Force, to Commanders, as quoted in *Congressional Record,* 95th Cong., 2d sess., vol.124, pt.3, p.3808.

44. Baldwin, *Strategy* (see chap.4, n.41).

45. James C. Roberts, "A Fresh Look at Panama, the Canal and the Treaties," *Human Events,* February 18, 1978, pp.1, 5, 14.

46. Helms, comments, *Congressional Record,* 95th Cong., 1st sess., vol.123, pt.26, October 17, 1977, pp.33899-33900. See also, "Inside Washington," *Human Events,* January 7, 1978, p.3. See also, "Torrijos Linked to Narcotics Traffic," Associated Press, Raleigh, N.C. *News and Observer,* city edition, October 15, 1977, p.1.

47. Carter, *Faith* (see chap.1, n.19), p.166.

48. Hugh Sidey, essay, "Does Congress Need a Nanny?" *Time*, March 27, 1978, p.13.

49. Carter, *Faith* (see chap.1, n.19), p.174.

50. Helms, comments, *Congressional Record*, 95th Cong., 2d sess., vol.124, pt.8, April 18, 1978, p.10501.

CHAPTER 5

1. Clarence L. Barnhart, ed., *The New Century Cyclopedia of Names*, vol.2 (New York: Appleton-Century-Crofts, Inc.) s.v. "Alexandre Ledru-Rollin," p.2413.

2. John D. Lofton, Jr., "Baker Wiggles to No Position on Canal Treaties," *Human Events*, January 21, 1978, pp.5-6.

3. "Opening the Great Canal Debate," *Time*, February 20, 1978, p.19.

4. Lofton, "Baker Wiggles," (see chap.5, n.2), p.6.

5. Joseph E. Persico, *The Imperial Rockefeller: A Biography of Nelson A. Rockefeller* (Thorndike, Maine: Thorndike Press, 1982), p.105.

6. Kitchel, *Truth* (see chap.2, n.22), p.92.

7. *Ibid.*, pp.92-93.

8. The Hay-Herran Treaty of 1903 was with Colombia who balked in the hope of obtaining larger compensations from the United States. By the Spooner Act of 1902, the U.S. Congress, among other things, authorized the President to obtain land for a canal in Panama and to buy the assets of the Panama Canal Company.

9. Harman, testimony (see chap.2, n.16), pp.160-61.

10. Herbert J. Hansell, Legal Adviser to the Department of State, letter to Representative John M. Murphy, Chairman of the House Merchant Marine and Fisheries Committee, September 20, 1979, as published in hearing before Senate Subcommittee on Separation of Powers, June 23, 1983 (see chap.2, n.16), p.160.

11. John Sparkman, former Chairman Senate Foreign Relations Committee, letter to Harman, December 20, 1982, as published in hearing record, Senate Subcommitee on Separation of Powers, June 23, 1983 (see chap.2, n.16), p.160.

12. Harman, testimony (see chap.2, n.16), p.161.

13. *Ibid.*, p.160.

14. Hearing before the Subcommittee on Separation of Powers of the Senate Committee on the Judiciary, 98th Cong., 1st sess., on the Panama Canal Treaties— Constitutional and Legal Aspects of the Ratification Process, June 23, 1983, p.107. Hereinafter, this Subcommittee will be referred to as "East Subcommittee" or "East Subcommittee hearing," as appropriate.

15. *Ibid.*, p.117.

16. Robert E. Dalton, Assistant Legal Adviser for Treaty Affairs, Department of State, interview with author, November 22, 1983, in Washington, D.C.

17. Powell A. Moore, Assistant Secretary of State for Legislative and Intergovernmental Affairs, letter to Senator Alan Cranston, July 19, 1983, passed to author by Phillip Harman who obtained it from Senator Cranston.

18. Author's letter to Moore, December 19, 1983.

19. Phillip Harman, letter to George P. Shultz, Secretary of State, August 5, 1983, passed to author by Phillip Harman.

20. Griffin, former member Senate Foreign Relations Committee, letter to Harman, June 14, 1983, passed to author by Harman.

21. Harman, letter to Griffin, August 27, 1983, passed to author by Harman.

22. Carter, *Faith* (see chap.1, n.19), p.174.

23. Robert Pastor, former assistant to Zbigniew Brzezinski, the former National Security Adviser to President Carter, letter to the author, December 9, 1983.

24. *U.S. Instrument of Ratification—Panama Canal Treaty,* (a) RESERVA-TIONS: (1), as published in "Senate Debate on the Panama Canal Treaties: A Compendium of Major Statements, Record Votes and Relevant Events," prepared for the Committee on Foreign Relations, U.S. Senate, 95th Cong., 2d sess., February 1979 (Washington, D.C.: GPO, 1979), p.547.

25. William D. Rogers, former Assistant Secretary of State for Inter-American Affairs, address before the American Society of International Law, in Washington, D.C., April 28, 1979, as published in hearing record, East Subcommiteee (see chap.2, n.16), p.81.

26. Author's letter to Pastor, December 15, 1983.

27. Robert E. Dalton, Assistant Legal Adviser for Treaty Affairs, Department of State, testimony before East Subcommittee (see chap.5, n.14), p.107.

28. *Ibid.,* p.105.

29. Hansell letter to Murphy, September 20, 1979 (see chap.5, n.10).

30. Harman, testimony (see chap.2, n.16), p.397.

31. Hansell letter to Murphy, September 20, 1979 (see chap.5, n.10).

32. Four times, according to the record of the East hearing, Dalton stated that the Senate Foreign Relations Committee was shown Panama's proposed instruments of ratification and that no objections were made to the three paragraphs (pp.117, 118, 120 and 390). Dalton wanted to make an important point, but he and other State officials have never identified *to whom* the papers were shown and approved.

33. David H. Popper, former U.S. Ambassador, letter to Harman, June 5, 1982, as published in hearing record, East Subcommittee (see chap.2, n.16), p.384.

34. Breecher, testimony (see chap.1, n.15), p.93.

35. Dalton, testimony (see chap.5, n.27), p.103.

36. Breecher, testimony (see chap.1, n.15), p.142.

37. *Ibid.,* p.394.

38. Harman, testimony (see chap.2, n.16), p.161.

39. Breecher, testimony (see chap.1, n.15), p.11.

CHAPTER 6

1. "The Battle Blow by Blow," *Time,* October 18, 1976, pp.17-18.

2. Carter, letter to Senator Ted Stevens, R.-Alas., November 5, 1977, published in hearing record, East Subcommittee (see chap.5, n.14), pp.158-59.

3. Clements explained the roles of General Brown and Mr. Rogers in his letter

of October 26, 1984 to Harman, passed to author by Harman. Rogers served as adviser, while Clements and Brown did the negotiating with Torrijos.

4. Neutrality Treaty (see chap.1, n.22), Article IV.

5. William P. Clements, Jr., former Deputy Secretary of Defense, testimony before the Senate Armed Services Committee, 95th Cong., 2d sess., hearing on Defense, Maintenance and Operation of the Panama Canal, including Administration and Government of the Canal Zone, January 24, 31, February 1, 1978, p.209.

6. Clements, letter to Harman, February 1, 1978, passed to author.

7. Department of State *Bulletin,* No.2002, The Official Weekly Record of United States Foreign Policy, issued by the Bureau of Public Affairs (Washington, D.C.: GPO, 1977), November 7, 1977, p.631.

8. James B. Allen, D.-Ala., comments, *Congressional Record—Senate,* 95th Cong., 1st sess., vol.123, pt.27, October 19, 1977, p.34276.

9. "Canal Defense Accord Saves Treaty," Washington Post News Service, Norfolk, Virginia *Virginian-Pilot,* city edition, October 16, 1977, p.1.

10. Sol Linowitz as quoted by Rudy Abramson in "Canal Debate Entangled in Technicalities," (see chap.2, n.4).

11. *Neutrality Treaty* (see chap.1, n.22), proclamation (a), Amendment (1).

12. *Ibid.,* (a) Amendment (2).

13. Two articles in the conservative weekly, *Human Events,* reported details of Bethancourt's comments (see chap.4, n.32). Also, *Mututino,* August 20, 1977 (see chap.4, n.31).

14. Carter, *Faith* (see chap.1, n.19), p.173.

15. *El Panama America,* Spanish-language "sister paper" of *Panama American,* editorial, January 2, 1964, p.6.

16. Dubois, *Danger* (see chap.2, n.23), pp.241-42.

17. Ryan, *Controversy* (see chap.2, n.18), p.53.

18. "Panama's President Resigns," Norfolk, Virginia *Virginian-Pilot,* Associated Press, February 14, 1984, p.A4. It is apparent that de la Espriella resigned because he wanted clean elections and perceived that the Defense Force (National Guard) was ready to steal the May 6, 1984 election for the Guard's candidate, Nicolas Ardito Barletta. That was what happened.

19. Phillip Harman, Director of Information, Canal Zone Non-Profit Public Information Corporation, letter to the First Secretary of the International Court of Justice, January 28, 1977, passed to author by Harman.

20. A. Pillepich, First Secretary of the International Court of Justice, letter to Harman, February 9, 1977, passed to author by Harman.

21. *Star and Herald,* Panamanian newspaper, editorial, November 25, 1903, p.1.

22. *Wilson v. Shaw,* 204 U.S. 24 (1907).

23. *United States v. Husband R. (Roach),* 453 F.2d 1054 (5th Cir. 1971), *cert. den.,* 406 U.S. 935 (1972).

CHAPTER 7

1. "Elogia Torrijos a Fidel Castro," Diario las Americas, Spanish News Agency (EFE), Miami, Florida, September 11, 1977, p.1.

2. "Now For the Hard Part," *Time*, September 19, 1977, pp.19-21.

3. "Escobar Fuels Students," *Human Events* (see chap.4, n.14). See also, Kitchel, *Truth* (see chap.2, n.22), pp.122-23. See also, Crane, *Surrender* (see chap.1, n.9), pp.62-63.

4. "TANA Declares Reagan Guilty of Crimes," *La Prensa* newspaper, Panama City, Panama, December 3, 1983, p.2-D.

5. Helms address, *Congressional Record—Senate*, 95th Cong., 2d sess., vol.124, pt.12, June 5, 1978, p.16138.

6. Hansen interview (see chap.2, n.58).

7. *U.S. Constitution*, Article IV, Section 3 (2).

8. Johnson, "Drama" (see chap.1, n.18).

9. "Opening the Great Canal Debate," *Time*, February 20, 1978, p.19. See also, Griffin comments, *Congressional Record—Senate*, 95th Cong., 2d sess., vol.124, pt.6, March 16, 1978, p.7152.

10. Henry Clay Gold, "Senate Ratifies First Canal Pact," *Kansas City Times*, city edition, March 17, 1978, p.1.

See also, "U.S. Worried Over Panamanian Reaction," *New York Times*, late city edition, March 16, 1978, p.A1.

See also, Alan Riding, "Panamanians, Assured by Torrijos, Confident on Pacts," *New York Times*, late city edition, special to *New York Times*, March 16, 1978, p.A12.

See also, Riding, "Panamanians Reluctantly Indicate They Accept Pact's Reservation," *New York Times*, late city edition, special to *New York Times*, March 17, 1978, pp.A1, A12.

See also, Karen DeYoung, "Panama Hails Vote; Senate Reservation May Cause Trouble," *Washington Post*, final edition, Washington Post Foreign Service, March 17, 1978, p.A19.

See also, Riding, "Panamanian Aides React Angrily to Neutrality Pact Reservation," *New York Times*, late city edition, special to *New York Times*, March 18, 1978, p.A7.

See also, Dewey F. Bartlett, R.-Okla., comments, *Congressional Record—Senate*, 95th Cong., 2d sess., vol.124, pt.6, March 16, 1978, pp.7144-45.

11. Harman, testimony (see chap.2, n.16), p.166.

12. Griffin, comments, *Congressional Record—Senate*, March 16, 1978 (see chap.7, n.9), p.7139.

13. Popper, letter to Harman (see chap.5, n.33).

14. Griffin, Bartlett, comments, *Congressional Record—Senate*, March 17, 1978 (see chap.7, nn.9, 10), p.7428.

15. Carter, letter to Torrijos, March 15, 1978, as quoted by Helms in *Congressional Record—Senate*, 95th Cong., 2d sess., vol.124, pt.6, March 17, 1978, p.7432.

16. Helms, comments, *ibid*.

17. Torrijos, letter to Carter, March 15, 1978, as published in *Congressional Record—Senate*, March 17, 1978 (see chap.7, n.15), p.7433.

18. Jorge E. Illueca, Panamanian Ambassador to the United Nations, letter to Secretary General UN, March 28, 1978, as published in *Congressional Record—Senate*, 95th Cong., 2d sess., vol.124, pt.12, June 5, 1978, p.16147.

19. *Panamanian Foreign Ministry Communique on Canal Treaties*, Panama,

25 April 1978, Foreign Ministry, as published in *Congressional Record—Senate,* ibid., p.16159.

20. Bartlett, comments, *Congressional Record—Senate,* March 16, 1978 (see chap.7, n.10, Bartlett), pp.7145-46.

21. Harman, testimony (see chap.2, n.16), pp.197-98.

22. *Congressional Record—Senate,* 95th Cong., 2d sess., vol.124, pt.6, March 16, 1978, p.7142.

23. Brzezinski, *Power* (see chap.1, n.17), p.138.

24. Clements, testimony before the Senate Armed Services Committee, January 31, 1978 (see chap.6, n.5), pp.207-8.

25. Bartlett, comments, *Congressional Record—Senate,* 95th Cong., 2d sess., vol.124, pt.8, April 18, 1978, p.10485.

26. Green H. Hackworth, former Legal Adviser, Department of State, as quoted by Harman, testimony (see chap.2, n.16), p.189.

27. Harman, letter to Howard H. Baker, Jr., R.-Tenn., Senate Majority Leader, November 12, 1983, passed to author by Harman.

28. Lloyd M. Bentsen, U.S. Senator, D.-Tex., letter to Harman, November 29, 1983, passed to author by Harman.

29. Harman, testimony (see chap.2, n.16), p.199.

30. *Congressional Record—Senate,* 95th Cong., 1st sess., vol.124, pt.8, April 17, 1978, p.10280.

31. Hansell, letter to Murphy, September 20, 1979 (see chap.5, n.10).

32. Edward W. Brooke, R.-Mass., comments, *Congressional Record—Senate,* 95th Cong., 2d sess., vol.124, pt.8, April 17, 1978, p.10280.

33. Brooke letter to Carter, April 11, 1978; Carter letter to Brooke, April 17, 1978; both published in *Congressional Record—Senate,* 95th Cong., 2d sess., vol.124, pt.8, April 18, 1978, pp.10499-500.

34. Carter, *Faith* (see chap.1, n.19), p.174.

35. Hansell, testimony before the Senate Committee on Foreign Relations, 95th Cong., 1st sess., on the Panama Canal Treaties, September 26, 27, 29, and 30, and October 19, 1977, pp.215-16.

36. Harry F. Byrd, Jr., IND.-Va., comments, *Congressional Record—Senate,* 95th Cong., 2d sess., vol.124, pt.2, February 2, 1978, p.1918.

37. Helms, *Congressional Record—Senate,* June 5, 1978 (see chap.7, n.5), pp.16147-48.

CHAPTER 8

1. *Encyclopedia Americana,* International Edition, vol.3 (Danbury, Conn.: Grolier Incorporated, 1981), s.v., "Vasco Nunez Balboa," p.246.

2. Jean Descola, *The Conquistadors* (New York: Augusta M. Kelley, publishers, 1970), p.125, tr. Malcolm Barnes.

3. Samuel Crowther, *The Romance and Rise of the American Tropics* (Garden City, New York: Doubleday, Doran & Company, Inc., 1929), pp.13-14.

4. Harmodio Arias, former President of Panama, *The Panama Canal,* p.60, as quoted by DuVal, *Cadiz,* p.216.

5. William J. Jorden, U.S. Ambassador to Panama, testimony at hearings before the Committee on Foreign Relations, U.S. Senate, on the Panama Canal Treaties, 95th Cong., 1st sess., pt.1, September 26, 27, 29, and 30, and October 19, 1977, p.306.

6. *Congressional Record—Senate,* June 5, 1978 (see chap.7, n.5), pp.16156-63.

7. Aristides Royo, President of the Republic of Panama, letter to President Carter, January 8, 1980, as published, "Royo Terms Implementation Law 'Unacceptable' in Letter to Carter," *La Estrella de Panama,* Panama City, Panama, January 9, 1980, pp.A-1, A-12.

8. *Ibid.*

9. Harman, letter to former Ambassador David Popper, March 13, 1982, as published in hearing record, East Subcommittee (see chap.2, n.16), p.212.

10. Popper, Panama Canal Treaties negotiator, testimony before the Subcommittee on the Panama Canal of the Committee on Merchant Marine and Fisheries, House of Representatives, Sea-Level Canal Studies, 95th Cong., 2d sess., June 21, 27, 28, 1978, p.123.

11. Popper, letter to Harman, June 5, 1982 (see chap.5, n.33).

12. Helms, *Congressional Record—Senate,* 95th Cong., 2d sess., vol.124, pt.8, April 18, 1978, p.10500.

13. *Ibid.,* p.10501.

14. Carter, letter to Brooke, April 17, 1978 (see chap.7, n.33).

15. Helms, *Congressional Record—Senate,* 95th Cong., 2d sess., vol.124, pt.8, April 18, 1978, p.10501.

16. Charles I. Bevans, compiler, *Treaties and Other International Agreements of the United States,* vol.3, Multilateral 1931-1945, Seventh International Conference of American States, "Convention on Rights and Duties of States," signed at Montevideo, December 26, 1933 (Washington, D.C.: GPO, 1969), Article 8, p.148.

17. *Communique,* April 25, 1978, as published in *Congressional Record— Senate,* June 5, 1978 (see chap.7, n.19), p.16157.

18. *Ibid.,* pp.16157-58.

19. Breecher, testimony (see chap.1, n.15), pp.43-44.

20. Harman, letter to Richard Nixon, former President of the United States, July 23, 1982 was an example of the 150 letters that were sent to top-level officials and former officials in the U.S. government. A copy of this letter was passed to the author by Mr. Harman.

21. *The Review of the News,* commentary, July 16, 1980, p.3.

22. Popper, testimony before House Subcommittee on the Panama Canal, June 27, 1978 (see chap.8, n.10).

23. Carter, *Faith* (see chap.1, n.19), p.173.

24. *Ibid.*

25. *Ibid.,* p.174.

26. Dalton, testimony (see chap.5, n.27), pp.101-103.

27. *Ibid.,* p.102.

28. Staff Memorandum to the Senate Committee on Foreign Relations, *The Role of the Senate in Treaty Ratification,* 95th Cong., 1st sess., November 1977 (Washington, D.C.: GPO, 1977), p.3.

29. John R. Stevenson, Legal Adviser, Department of State, "Memorandum Concerning Reservations and Understandings to Treaties," March 22, 1971, as published in *The Role of the Senate in Treaty Ratification, Ibid.,* p.4.

30. Breecher, testimony (see chap.1, n.15), p.21.

31. *Ibid.*

32. Marjorie Whiteman, compiler, *Digest of International Law,* Department of State Publication 8547, vol.14, released September 1970 (Washington, D.C.: GPO, 1970), p.47.

33. Stevenson, "Memorandum Concerning Reservation" (see chap.8, n.29), p.4.

34. Carter, *Faith* (see chap.1, n.19), pp.174-75.

35. *Ibid.,* p.175.

36. William D. Rogers, address, "The International Uses of the Law," before the American Society of International Law, Washington, D.C., April 28, 1979, published by Judith R. Hall, editor, *Proceedings of the 73rd Annual Meeting of the American Society of International Law* (1979) (self-published, 1979), pp.294-99.

37. *Panama Canal Treaty,* as proclaimed, September 24, 1979 (see chap.1, n.28), (a) RESERVATIONS: (1).

38. David M. Maxfield, "Senate Backs Turning Over Canal to Panama," *Congressional Quarterly,* March 22, 1978, p.952.

39. *Neutrality Treaty,* as proclaimed, September 24, 1979 (see chap.1, n.22), (b) CONDITIONS: (1).

40. Rogers, address (see chap.8, n.36).

41. Baker, Senate Majority Leader, letter to Harman, January 4, 1983, passed to author by Harman.

42. Carter, letter to Stevens (see chap.6, n.2).

43. Baker, *No Margin for Error* (New York: Time Books, 1980), p.187.

44. *U.S. Constitution,* Article II, Section 2 (2).

45. "Opening the Great Canal Debate," *Time,* February 20, 1978 (see chap.5, n.3), p.19.

46. DuVal, *Mountains* (see chap.1, n.4), p.233.

47. Noel F. Busch, *T.R.: The Story of Theodore Roosevelt* (New York: Reynal & Company, 1963), pp.162-63.

48. Baker, *Margin* (see chap.8, n.43), pp.185-87.

49. *Ibid.,* pp.187-88.

50. Staff Memo, *Role* (see chap.8, n.28).

51. Lester S. Jayson, Supervising Editor, *The Constitution of the United States of America, Analysis and Interpretation,* 92d Cong., 2d sess., Document No.92-82, prepared by the Congressional Research Service, Library of Congress (Washington, D.C.: GPO, 1973), p.481.

52. P. Ford, editor, *Writings of Thomas Jefferson* (New York: 1895), pp.161-62, cited in *ibid.,* p.538.

53. Public Law 96, *U.S. Code Annotated,* vol.47, p.132. See also, 18 U.S.C. 953. For more information on the Logan Act, the reader is referred to the *Memorandum on the History and Scope of the Law Prohibiting Correspondence with a Foreign Government,* Senate Document Number 696, 64th Cong., 2d sess. (1917). The author was Charles Warren, then Assistant Attorney General. Further details concerning the observance of the "Logan Act" are contained in E. Corwin's *The*

President: Office and Powers, 1787-1957 (New York: 4th edition, 1957), pp.183-84, 430-31.

54. Staff Memo, *Role* (see chap.8, n.28), p.25.

55. *Ibid.*, p.27.

56. William R. Holmes, Parliamentarian, *Constitution, Jefferson's Manual and Rules of the House of Representatives* (Washington, D.C.: GPO, 1979), pp.109-287.

57. *Ibid.*, p.273.

58. George Washington, address to the House of Representatives, March 30, 1796, *Writings*, vol.35, p.3, cited and compiled by John Frederick Schroeder, *Maxims of Washington,* third printing (Mount Vernon, Va.: The Mount Vernon Ladies' Association, 1953), p.82.

59. Washington, letter to Henry Lee, October 31, 1786, *Writings*, vol.29, p.34, Schroeder, *ibid.*, pp.44-45.

60. Thomas James Norton, *The Constitution of the United States, Its Sources and Application,* Tower Book edition, 4th printing (New York: The World Publishing Company, 1943), p.117. Mr. Norton, one of the foremost constitutionalists America has produced, authored another book, *Undermining the Constitution—A History of Lawless Government,* warning that "clever, irresponsible men in every branch of government" are bypassing and ignoring the Constitution in the name of expediency and self-interest.

61. *Ibid.*

62. Charles A. Beard, editor, *The Enduring Federalist* (New York: Frederick Ungar Publishing Co., 1959), "Nature and Function of the Courts," Federalist 78, pp.333-34.

63. Baker, *Margin* (see chap.8, n.43) p.xxii.

CHAPTER 9

1. Henry A. Kissinger, former Secretary of State, testimony before the Committee on Foreign Relations, U.S. Senate, 95th Cong., 1st sess., pt.3, on the Panama Canal Treaties, October 10, 11, 12, 13, and 14, 1977, p.530.

2. Popper, letter (see chap.5, n.33).

3. Kissinger, testimony (see chap.9, n.1), p.530.

4. *Ibid.*, pp.525-7.

5. *Ibid.*, p.530.

6. Dean Rusk, former Secretary of State, testimony before the Committee on Foreign Relations, U.S. Senate, 95th Cong., 1st sess., pt.3, on the Panama Canal Treaties, October 10, 11, 12, 13, and 14, 1977, p.521.

7. Alfred J. Schweppe, attorney, letter to Bob Quartel, Answer Desk Coordinator, President Ford Committee, July 20, 1976. This letter was made available by Mr. Schweppe.

8. Rusk, testimony (see chap.9, n.6), p.521.

9. *Ibid.*, p.523.

10. Andy Ireland, U.S. Representative, D.-Fla., question to Messrs. Rusk and Kissinger at hearing before the Committee on International Relations, House of

Representatives, 95th Cong., 1st sess., on Implementation of the Panama Canal Treaties, September 14, 1977, p.142.

11. Rusk, testimony, *ibid.,* p.142.

12. Kissinger, testimony, *ibid.,* p.143.

13. Harold G. Maier, Professor of Law and Director of Transnational Legal Studies at Vanderbilt Law School, "United States Defense Rights in the Panama Canal Treaties: The Need for Clarification of a Studied Ambiguity," *Virginia Journal of International Law,* vol.24, Winter 1984, pp.287-322.

14. *Ibid.,* p.321.

15. *Ibid.,* p.318. Maier's interpretations seemed pro-Treaties, and errors of facts always favored the Panamanian positions.

16. Nicolas Ardito Barletta, President-elect of Panama, telephone interview with author, August 5, 1984, in Panama.

17. Manfredo, interview (see chap.3, n.34).

18. Department of State, *Bulletin* No.9 (revised), January 1977 (see chap.2, n.52), p.5.

19. McClellan, interview (see chap.2, n.12).

20. Harman, letter to Monroe Leigh, Legal Adviser to Department of State, September 30, 1975, as published in Harman's analysis, "Public Hearings on Constitutional Issues Concerned With the Panama Canal" (self-published), July 29, 1977, p.13.

21. Robert J. McCloskey, Assistant Secretary of State for Congressional Relations, letter to Senator Adlai E. Stevenson III, December 3, 1975, as published, *ibid.,* pp.17-18.

22. Harman, letter to McCloskey, December 10, 1975, as published, *ibid.,* pp.19-20.

23. Department of State, *Bulletin* No.9 (revised), January 1977 (see chap.2, n.52).

24. "Will Central America Survive Kissinger?" *Human Events,* July 30, 1983, p.8.

25. Gary Allen, *Kissinger,* (Seal Beach, Cal.: '76 Press, 1976), pp.45-6.

26. M. Stanton Evans, "On the Trail of Henry Kissinger," *Human Events,* September 10, 1983, p.7.

27. William D. Rogers, former Assistant Secretary of State for Inter-American Affairs, interview with author (see chap.2, n.56).

28. Robert O. Pastor, former assistant to Zbigniew Brzezinski, National Security Adviser to President Carter, telephone interview with author, November 13, 1983.

29. Michael G. Kozak, Deputy Legal Adviser to Department of State, interview with author, November 21, 1983, in Washington, D.C.

30. Robert E. Dalton, Assistant Legal Adviser for Treaty Affairs, Department of State, interview with author, November 22, 1983, in Washington, D.C.

31. Sherman Hinson, Panama Desk, Department of State, interview with author, November 21, 1983, in Washington, D.C.

32. Richard F. Starr, *Yearbook on International Communist Affairs* (Stanford, Cal.: Hoover Institution Press, 1976), pp.507-8.

33. East Subcommittee hearing (see chap.5, n.14), pp.100-121.

34. Dick Clark, former member of the Senate Foreign Relations Committee, interview with author, November 23, 1983, in Washington, D.C.

35. Robert P. Griffin, former Republican Senator from Michigan and former member of the Senate Foreign Relations Committee, telephone interview with author, November 16, 1983.

36. Steven D. Symms, U.S. Senator, R.-Ida., interview with author, November 18, 1983, in Washington, D.C.

37. Robert Dockery, former staff member of the Senate Foreign Relations Committee in charge of the Treaties 1977-78 for the Chairman, interview with author, November 15, 1983, in Washington, D.C.

38. *Ibid.*

39. Norvill Jones, former Chief of Staff of the Senate Foreign Relations Committee, interview with author, November 23, 1983, in Washington, D.C.

40. Richard McCall, former Deputy Staff Director of the Senate Foreign Relations Committee, interview with author, November 23, 1983, in Washington, D.C.

41. Kozak, interview (see chap.9, n.29).

42. Herbert J. Hansell, former Legal Adviser, Department of State, telephone conversation with author, November 18, 1983.

43. Kozak, interview (see chap.9, n.29).

44. East Subcommittee hearing (see chap.5, n.14), pp.100-121.

45. Hansell, letter to Murphy (see chap.5, n.10).

46. Breecher, testimony (see chap.1, n.15), p.43.

47. Herbert W. Dodge, former Foreign Service Officer, Department of State, testimony before Senate Subcommittee on Separation of Powers, June 23, 1983 (see chap.5, n.14), p.130.

CHAPTER 10

1. Charles A. and Mary R. Beard, *Basic History of the United States* (Philadelphia: The Blakiston Company, 1944), p.123.

2. *Ibid.*, p.127. See also, Gilbert L. Lycan, *Alexander Hamilton and American Foreign Policy* (Norman: University of Oklahoma Press, 1970), p.5.

3. U.S. Constitution, Article I, Section 8, Clause 17.

4. Norton, *The Constitution* (see chap.8, n.60), inside front cover.

5. *Ibid.*

6. Dodge, testimony (see chap.9, n.47), p.126.

7. Dodge, letter to East, May 8, 1983, passed to author by Dodge.

8. Breecher, testimony (see chap.1, n.15), p.46.

9. Dodge, testimony (see chap.9, n.47), p.130.

10. Washington, letter to Henry Lee, October 31, 1786, *Writings,* vol.29, p.34, cited in Schroeder's *Maxims of Washington* (see chap.8, n.58), pp.44-5.

11. Dodge, testimony (see chap.9,n.47), pp.130-31.

12. *Ibid.*, p.131.

13. Hearing record, East Subcommittee (see chap.5, n.14), p.152.

14. *Ibid.*

15. Breecher, testimony (see chap.1, n.15), p.33.

16. *Ibid.*, pp.34-5.

17. *Ibid.*, p.71.

18. Paul S. Sarbanes, U.S. Senator, D.-Md., comments, *Congressional Record—Senate*, 95th Cong., 2d sess., vol.124, pt.6, March 15, 1978, p.6958. See also, Helms, address, quoting Sarbanes, *Congressional Record—Senate*, 95th Cong., 2d sess., vol.124, pt.12, June 5, 1978, p.16141. See also, Charles G. Fenwick, *International Law,* 3d edition, (New York: Appleton-Century-Crofts, Inc., 1948), pp.437-38.

19. Adrian S. Fisher, Chief Reporter, *Restatement of the Law (Second): Foreign Relations Law of the United States* (American Law Institute, publishers. St. Paul: West Publishing Co., 1965), p.423. Associate Reporters were Covey T. Oliver, Cecil J. Olmstead, I.N.P. Stokes, and Joseph M. Sweeney.

20. Covey T. Oliver, Associate Reporter, *Restatement of the Law (Second), ibid.*, statement before Senate Committee on Foreign Relations, 95th Cong., 2d sess., pt.4, hearing on Panama Canal Treaties, January 19, 1978, p.97.

21. Oliver, letter to Harman, March 23, 1982, as quoted in hearing record, East Subcommittee (see chap.5, n.14), pp.154-55.

22. Carter, *Faith* (see chap.1, n.19), p.174.

23. Harold G. Maier, Vanderbilt Law School, letter to Harman, June 21, 1982, as quoted in hearing record, East Subcommittee (see chap.5, n.14), p.226.

24. Gerald Aksen, Chairman of the American Bar Association, Section of International Law and Practices, letter to Harman, March 31, 1982, as quoted in hearing record, East Subcommittee (see chap.5, n.14), p.266.

25. Rusk, letter to Harman, May 25, 1982, as quoted, *ibid.*, p.223.

26. Beth Crowe, Administrative Assistant to Herbert J. Hansell, letter to Harman, April 29, 1982, as quoted, *ibid.*, p.219.

27. Holmes, *Jefferson's Manual* (see chap.8, n.56), pp.274-75.

28. *Ibid.*, p.109. See also, Louis Henkin, *Foreign Affairs and the Constitution* (Mineola, N.Y.: Foundation Press, 1972), p.142.

29. Holmes, *Jefferson's Manual* (see chap.8, n.56), p.272.

30. Dozer, footnote to "State Department Determined to Give Away Panama Canal," *Human Events,* August 13, 1977, p.14.

31. Charles E. Rice, Professor of Law, Notre Dame University, letter to Carl R. Hoffmann, Jr., February 27, 1980, passed to author by Hoffmann.

32. Holmes, *Jefferson's Manual* (see chap.8, n.56), pp.274-75. See also, Henkin, *Foreign Affairs* (see chap.10, n.28), footnotes, pp.142, 168.

33. Alexander Hamilton, John Jay, and James Madison, "The Federalist No.75," *The Federalist* (New York: Random House, Inc., no publication date given), The Modern Library Series, p.486. See also, Norton, *The Constitution* (see chap.8, n.60), pp.114-15.

34. U.S. Constitution, Article VI. See also, David E. Engdahl, *Constitutional Power, Federal and State* (St. Paul: West Publishing Co., 1974), p.232.

35. William Roscoe Thayer, *The Life and Letters of John Hay,* vol.2 (New York: Houghton Mifflin Company, 1916), p.341.

36. William Proxmire, U.S. Senator, D.-Wis., citing Associate Justice Hugo L. Black in the *Congressional Record—Senate,* 97th Cong., 1st sess., October 26, 1981, p.S12098.

37. The following references are cited to clarify and illustrate the constitu-

tional procedures for abrogating treaties: Holmes, *Jefferson's Manual* (see chap.8, n.56), pp.274-75; Norton, *The Constitution* (see chap.8, n.60), p.115; Henry Steele Commager, editor, *Documents of American History,* fourth edition (New York: Appleton-Century-Crofts, Inc., 1948), Crofts American History Series, Dixon Ryan Fox, General Editor, Document No.177 on p.326, the Clayton-Bulwer Treaty (1850), and Document No.355 on p.200, the Hay-Pauncefote Treaty (1901), with texts and briefs on both treaties; *Congressional Record—House,* 46th Cong., 2d sess., March 22, 1880, p.1775 records the text of H. Res. 250 which was referred to the House Select Committee on Interoceanic Ship-Canal; Jayson, *The Constitution* (see chap.8, n.51), p.500; Alvin Josephy, Jr., *On the Hill: A History of the American Congress* (New York: Simon and Schuster, 1979), p.271; Charles A. Beard, *The Rise of American Civilization* (New York: McMillan Company, 1927), p.512.

38. *Congressional Record—House,* 46th Cong., 2d sess., March 22, 1880, p.1775.

39. Thayer, *Life and Letters* vol.2 (see chap.10, n.35), p.229.

40. President Wilson addressed a Joint Session of the 63d Cong., 2d sess., on March 5, 1914. This was his "Panama Canal Tolls Message" and it was printed as H. Doc. No. 813 in the *Congressional Record,* vol.51, March 5, 1914, p.4313. Wilson's action to bring the United States into compliance with Article III of the Hay-Pauncefote Treaty (1901) by removing toll-free privileges for vessels in the coastwise trade of the United States was honest and exemplary; and it conformed to the letter with that portion of the Treaty. Nonetheless, Wilson and the U.S. Congress could have refused under the authority of Article II which specified that the government which constructed the canal "shall have and enjoy all the rights incident to such construction. . . ." Toll-free passage would have been one way to "enjoy" the rights incident to construction. Other enjoyment comes to mind: Toll-free transits would have reduced the price of consumer goods for American taxpayers who had assumed the risks and provided the money to build the Canal, and who owned the Canal and the Canal Zone. Free-tolls could have aided hard-pressed U.S. registered merchant vessels to compete with foreign ships with the latter's lower wage scales. Free-tolls could have reduced the registry of U.S. ships under foreign flags and could have generated more loyalty to the American Canal and the need to retain U.S. control and sovereign rights. Nevertheless, President Wilson did the constitutionally correct thing. He did not rule by decree, but instead made a proper request to the Congress.

41. Norton, *The Constitution* (see chap.8, n.60), pp.114-15.

42. W. Taft, *The Presidency, Its Duties, Its Powers, Its Opportunities and Its Limitations* (New York: 1916), pp.112-13.

43. Jayson, *The Constitution* (see chap.8, n.51), pp.500-01, fn.7 on p.501.

44. *Ibid.,* p.502.

45. J. Terry Emerson, "The Legislative Role in Treaty Abrogation," *Journal of Legislation* (University of Notre Dame Law School, vol.5/1978), p.64.

46. Hansell, memorandum to Cyrus Vance, the Secretary of State, December 15, 1978, copy to author by Department of State letter, February 1, 1979.

47. Joseph Harding, "Unconstitutional," letter to editor, Norfolk, Va. *Virginian-Pilot,* final edition, October 26, 1979, p.6.

48. *Myers v. United States,* 272 U.S. 52, 293 (1920).

49. Kurt Andersen, "An Epic Court Decision," *Time,* July 4, 1983, pp.12-13.

50. Allen, Chairman, Senate Subcommittee on Separation of Powers, 95th Cong., 2d sess., Report on the Panama Canal Treaty and the Congressional Power to Dispose of United States Property (Committee Print), made to the Committee on the Judiciary, February 1978, pp.2-3.

51. Griffin B. Bell, Attorney General of the United States, letter to Vance, August 11, 1977, as quoted *ibid.,* pp.33-37.

52. Allen, Report on the Panama Canal Treaty, (see chap.10, n.50), p.44.

53. 22 Opinion, Attorney General 544, p.545 (1899). Also, see vol.2, J. Story, *Commentaries on the Constitution of the United States,* (4th edition, 1873) Section 1328, p.200: "The power of Congress over the public territory is clearly exclusive and universal. . . ."

54. Allen, Report on the Panama Canal Treaty (see chap.10, n.50), p.9.

55. *Botany Worsted Mills v. United States,* 278 U.S. 282, 289 (1929).

56. *Swiss National Insurance Co. v. Miller,* 289 Fed. 570, 574 (D.C.Cir. 1923). See also, Engdahl, *Constitutional Power* (see chap.10, n.34), pp.2-3.

57. Hansell, testimony before Senate Subcommittee on Separation of Powers, 95th Cong., 1st sess., July 20, 1977, p.4.

58. *Sioux Tribe of Indians v. United States,* 316 U.S. 317, 326 (1942).

59. Allen, Report on the Panama Canal Treaty (see chap.10, n.50).

60. *Ibid.,* p.8. Ralph E. Erickson at that time was Deputy Assistant Attorney General.

61. *Ibid.,* p.1.

62. *Panama Canal Act of 1979* (Public Law 96-70), 96th Cong., 1st sess., approved by President Carter, September 27, 1979 and published in "Weekly Compilation of Presidential Documents," October 1, 1979, Sections 1503, 1504.

63. Brown, *Jefferson's Manual* (see chap.8, n.56), para.283.

64. *Ibid.,* Rule XLII, para.938.

65. Peter W. Rodino, Jr., U.S. Representative, D.-N.J., "How Our Laws Are Made," Doc. No. 96-352, House of Representatives, 96th Cong., 2d sess. (Washington, D.C.: GPO, 1980), pp.42-44.

66. Mary Cohn, Almanac Editor, *Congressional Quarterly Almanac,* vol.35, 1979 (Washington, D.C.: Congressional Quarterly Almanac, Inc., 1980), "Panama Canal Implementing Bill Clears," pp.142-56.

67. John M. Murphy, D.-N.Y., former Chairman, House Committee on Merchant Marine and Fisheries, telephone interview with author, October 25, 1984.

68. President Carter's statement, September 27, 1979, made on signing H.R. 111 into law, quoted from Weekly Compilation of Presidential Documents of October 1, 1979. As enacted H.R. 111 is Public Law 96-70, approved September 27, 1979.

69. Murphy, interview (see chap.10, n.67). Since President Carter and the Congress did not use a Joint Resolution to abrogate the 1903 Treaty, as required by *Jefferson's Manual* and by Article VI of the Constitution, the 1903 Treaty remains in force—and the argument about self-executing 1977 Treaties vis-a-vis H.R. 111 would become academic.

70. Breecher, testimony (see chap.1, n.15), p.28.

71. *Foster v. Nielson,* 2 Pet. 253 (1829).

72. Murphy, opening remarks at the hearing on the New Panama Canal Treaty, 95th Cong., 1st sess., August 17, 1977, p.4.

73. Brown, *Jefferson's Manual* (see chap.8, n.56), paras.283-86.

74. Thomas P. "Tip" O'Neill, Jr., D.-Mass., Speaker, House of Representatives, comments, *Congressional Record—House,* 96th Cong., 1st sess., September 26, 1979, p.26335.

75. Oliver, letter to author, September 20, 1984.

76. Panama Canal Act of 1979 (see chap.10, n.62), Sec. 1102.

77. Breecher, testimony (see chap.1, n.15), p.49.

78. Panama Canal Treaty of 1977 (see chap.1, n.28), Art. III, 3.

79. "Section by Section Analysis of the Panama Canal Act of 1979," 96th Cong., 1st sess., Report 96-94, pt.2, April 11, 1979, p.41.

80. Robert A. McConnell, Assistant Attorney General, letter to Representative Carroll Hubbard, Jr., Chairman, House Subcommittee on the Panama Canal, 97th Cong., 2d sess., May 17, 1982, as published in Harman analysis, "Can Panamanians, non-resident aliens, be appointed to the Panama Canal Commission?" (self-published), October 1982.

81. *Foley v. Connelie,* 98 S.Ct. 1067 (1978).

82. *Reid v. Covert,* 354 U.S. 1, 40 (1957).

83. Brown, *Jefferson's Manual* (see chap.8, n.56), para.1004. See also, *Our American Government, What is it? How does it function? 150 Questions and Answers,* 1981 Edition, House Document No. 96-351, 96th Cong., 2d sess., May 9, 1980, p.14, para.44.

CHAPTER 11

1. Edward S. Ellis, *The Life of Colonel David Crockett* (Philadelphia: 1884), as quoted in "Message for Congress from Davy Crockett," *The Review of the News,* Nov. 14, 1979, pp.55-57. See also, Engdahl, *Constitutional Power* (see chap.10, n.34), pp.28-29.

2. DuVal, *James Monroe: An Appreciation* (Orange, Va.: James Monroe Memorial Foundation, 1982), pp.28-29. See also, Harry Ammon, *James Monroe: The Quest for National Identity* (New York: McGraw Hill Book Company, 1971), pp.487-88. See also, J. Reuben Clark, *Memorandum on the Monroe Doctrine,* Published by the Department of State (Washington, D.C.: GPO, 1930), pp.102-03. For another view of the Monroe Doctrine, see William I. Hull, *The Monroe Doctrine: National or International* (New York: G.P. Putnam's Sons, 1915), pp.107-29.

3. Levine, *Hands Off* (see chap.3, n.45), pp.38-40.

4. James Monroe, President's Annual Message to the Congress, Dec. 2, 1823, *Annals of Congress,* vol.18, pt.1, p.14.

5. Levine, *Hands Off* (see chap.3, n.45), p.49.

6. Clark, *Memorandum* (see chap.11, n.2), p.170.

7. Robert Seager II, *Alfred Thayer Mahan: The Man and His Letters* (Annapolis: Naval Institute Press, 1977), p.488.

8. Crowther, *The Romance* (see chap.8, n.3), pp.348-52, quoting part of the

Hughes lecture at Princeton University, May 9, 1928. See also, Clark, *Memorandum* (see chap.11, n.2), p.179.

9. John L. Martin, Chief, Internal Security Section, Criminal Division, Department of Justice, letter to author, July 30, 1984.

10. "Korean Plane Resolution," *Human Events,* Oct. 1, 1983, p.18. Senator Helms's amendment was the 7-part HJR 353, proposing sanctions against the USSR for destroying Korean civilian aircraft 007 on Sept. 1, 1983. The Senate tabled all 7 parts with votes ranging from 70-25 to 50-45.

11. Commodore Matthew C. Perry, address before the American Geographical and Statistical Society, March 6, 1856 (New York: D. Appleton and Company, 1956), p.28. See also, Samuel Elliot Morrison, *'Old Bruin': Commodore Matthew C. Perry, 1794-1858* (Boston: Little, Brown and Company, 1967), p.429.

12. Lawrence O. Ealy, s.v. "Panama Canal," *The Encyclopedia Americana,* International Edition, vol.21 (Danbury, Conn.: Grolier Inc., 1981), p.230.

13. *Selected Documents No. 6C,* Department of State, Bureau of Public Affairs, Dec. 1977, p.17 gives $561.5 million as the 1914 cost of the Canal and Canal Zone. See also, *U.S. Senate Debate 1977-78, Panama Canal Treaties,* prepared by Subcommittee on Separation of Powers, Senate Committee on the Judiciary, 95th Cong., 2d sess., Feb. 27-March 16, 1978, p.2949, which gives $993.1 million as the 1914 cost, including plant additions and supporting facilities, and $9.933 billion as the 1977 replacement value, including value of unused land in the Zone (Source: Panama Canal Company).

14. William F. Wright, "Transit through a troubled Canal," *The Washington Times,* city edition, Aug. 30, 1982, p.1A.

15. Harman, testimony (see chap.2, n.16), pp.168-69.

16. Douglas J. Bennett, Assistant Secretary of State for Congressional Relations, letter to Senator Helms, June 14, 1978, as quoted in hearing record of East Subcommittee (see chap.5, n.14), p.169.

17. Omar Torrijos, statement to reporter Serrano, as published in *La Prensa,* Panamanian newspaper, Dec. 14, 1980, p.1.

18. Bethancourt, address (see chap.3, n.3).

19. *Congressional Record—Senate,* 95th Cong., 2d sess., vol.124, pt.2, June 5, 1978, pp.16149-51.

20. *Ibid.,* p.16155.

21. *Ibid.,* p.16156.

22. Barry Goldwater, U.S. Senator, R.-Ariz., comment at hearing before Senate Committee on the Armed Services, 95th Cong., 2d sess., on Defense, Maintenance, and Operation of the Panama Canal, Jan. 31, 1978, p.238.

23. Harman, testimony (see chap.2, n.16), pp.178-99.

24. Julio Linares, professor of law, quoted, *ibid.,* p.186.

25. Cesar Quintero, Dean of Law, University of Panama, quoted, *ibid.,* p.180.

26. Harman, letter to Attorney Alfred J. Schweppe, Oct. 31, 1977, published in Harman, "Are the Panama Canal Treaties Invalid . . . ?" (self-published), Dec. 1977, pp.1-2. See also, Senator Bob Dole, R.-Kan., press release, Oct. 24, 1977, published in Harman's analysis, *ibid.,* p.7.

27. Schweppe, letter to Harman, Nov. 21, 1977, published in Harman's analysis, *ibid.,* p.17.

28. Schweppe, letter to William F. Buckley, Jr., Dec. 8, 1977, published in Harman's analysis, *ibid.*, pp.19-20.

29. "RP High Court Rejects Bid to Halt Plebiscite," Panama *Star & Herald,* Oct. 15, 1977, p.1.

30. McAuliffe, "The Panama Canal: Alive and Well and Setting Records," *The Retired Officer* magazine, Oct. 1982, pp.36-38.

31. Wright, "Transit . . .," (see chap.11, n.14), p.1A.

32. Maxwell D. Taylor, General, U.S. Army (Ret.), former Chairman, Joint Chiefs of Staff, testimony before Senate Foreign Relations Committee on the Panama Canal Treaties, 95th Cong., 1st sess., pt.3, Oct. 10, 1977, p.58. See also, "A Clash of Views Over Canal Security," *U.S. News & World Report,* Oct. 24, 1977, p.27.

33. Thomas H. Moorer, Admiral, U.S. Navy (Ret.), former Chairman, Joint Chiefs of Staff, testimony before Senate Foreign Relations Committee, *ibid.*, pp.6, 7, 27.

34. Moorer, "Comment and Discussion," Naval Institute Proceedings, June 1980, p.24.

35. George A. Makela, "A New Panama Canal?" *Civil Engineering/A.S.C.E. Proceedings,* April 1983, pp.58-61.

36. DuVal, "The Marine Operating Problems, Panama Canal, and the Solution," *A.S.C.E. Proceedings,* Feb. 1947, pp.161-74.

37. Duval, testimony before Subcommittee on Panama Canal, House Committee on Merchant Marine and Fisheries, on Sea Level Canal Studies, 95th Cong., 2d sess., vol.124, pt.21, June 28, 1978, pp.404-13.

38. Helms, *Congressional Record—Senate,* comments, 97th Cong., 2d sess., vol.128, pt.34, extension of remarks, March 30, 1982, pp.S3075-76.

39. East, comments before Senate Subcommittee on Separation of Powers, June 23, 1983 (see chap.5, n.14), pp.390-91.

40. Emerson Stone, Vice President CBS News, letter to Harman, Oct. 18, 1983, passed to author by Harman.

41. George Watson, Vice President ABC News, letter to Harman, Aug. 30, 1983, passed to author by Harman.

42. William Placek, Public Information NBC, letter to Harman, Sept. 16, 1983, passed to author by Harman.

43. Accuracy in Media Report, July 1, 1979.

44. The media attitude in ignoring charges of invalid Treaties and the evidence at the East hearing by former State Department treaty experts and a scholar on Panamanian legal procedures was in contrast to the wide coverage given every detail of the original ratification procedures in 1977-78. The major media contributed immensely to the adoption of the Panama Treaties.

45. "Canal Treaties Supported," *United Methodist Reporter,* Sept. 23, 1977, p.3.

46. William R. Cannon, "The Bishop's Corner," *Wesleyan Christian Advocate,* Feb. 23, 1978, p.3.

47. Thomas A. Lane, "Bishops Misled on Panama Issue," *The Wanderer,* April 10, 1978, p.6.

CHAPTER 12

1. East, comments before East Subcommittee (see chap.5, n.14), p.393.
2. *Ibid.*, p.391.
3. Breecher, testimony (see chap.1, n.15), p.94.
4. *Congressional Record—Senate,* 98th Cong., 2d sess., vol.130, March 19, 1984, p.S2824.
5. East, comments before East Subcommittee (see chap.5, n.14), p.400.
6. Breecher, testimony (see chap.1, n.15), p.79.
7. Harman, testimony (see chap.2, n.16), pp.148-49.
8. East, comments before East Subcommittee (see chap.5, n.14), p.392.
9. Manfredo, interview (see chap.3, n.34).
10. *Ibid.*
11. Barletta, interview (see chap.9, n.16).
12. Demetrio B. Lakas, former President of Republic of Panama, telephone interview, August 3, 1984, in Panama.
13. Marco Robles, former President of Republic of Panama, telephone interview, September 9, 1984, in Miami. A second telephone consultation with Robles took place on September 13, 1984.
14. Barletta, interview (see chap.9, n.16).
15. Manfredo, interview (see chap.3, n.34).
16. Barletta, interview (see chap.9, n.16).
17. Manfredo, interview (see chap.3, n.34).
18. Barletta, interview (see chap.9, n.16).
19. Manfredo, interview (see chap.3, n.34).
20. *Ibid.*
21. Jorden, *Odyssey* (see chap.3, n.18), p.454.
22. Carter, *Faith* (see chap.1, n.19), p.174.
23. Ashley C. Hewitt, Jr., Political Counselor, U.S. Embassy, Republic of Panama, interview, August 2, 1984, in Panama.
24. William T. Pryce, Deputy Chief of Mission, U.S. Embassy, Republic of Panama, interview, August 2, 1984, in Panama.
25. Hewitt, interview (see chap.12, n.23).
26. Hinson, interview (see chap.9, n.31).
27. Jorge E. Illueca, President of Republic of Panama, speech at Fort Amador, Panama, July 31, 1984, as reported by Foreign Broadcast Information Service (FBIS) "Daily Report," August 1, 1984, p.N1.
28. Hearing record, East Subcommittee (see chap.5, n.14), p.118.
29. William C. Hansen, Colonel, U.S. Air Force, Director of Public Affairs, U.S. Southern Command, Quarry Heights, Panama, interview, August 3, 1984, in Panama.
30. *Ibid.*
31. Norton, *The Constitution* (see chap.8, n.60), p.viii.
32. Henry Cabot Lodge, editor, *The Works of Alexander Hamilton,* vol.2 (New York and London: G.P. Putnam's Sons, The Knickerbocker Press, 1904), quoting Alexander Hamilton, "Speech on the Compromises of the Constitution," June 20, 1788 at Poughkeepsie, N.Y., p.52.

33. Joseph Charles, *The Origins of the American Party System* (Williamsburg, Va.: The Institute of Early American History and Culture, 1956), p.22.

34. Norton, *The Constitution* (see chap.8, n.60), p.1.

35. Hamilton, "The Federalist No.77 (Hamilton)," (see chap.10, n.33), p.506.

36. Holmes, *Jefferson's Manual* (see chap.8, n.56), pp.274-75.

37. Raoul Berger, Professor of Law, Harvard Law School, testimony before the Senate Subcommittee on Separation of Powers, quoted in the Allen Report, February 1978 (see chap.10, n.50), p.8.

38. David Wise, review of *The Man Who Kept the Secrets: Richard Helms and the C.I.A.*, by Theodore Powers, in *The New Republic*, November 13, 1979, p.36.

39. General Services Administration, National Archives and Records Service, Office of the Federal Register, *Public Papers of the Presidents of the United States, Harry S. Truman, 1952-53* (Washington, D.C.: GPO, 1966), p.1061.

40. Justice Robert H. Jackson (1941-54) in *Youngstown Sheet & Tube Co. v. Sawyer*, 343 U.S. 579, 654 (1952).

41. Norton, *The Constitution* (see chap.8, n.60), p.viii.

42. *Ibid.*, p.ix.

43. *Ibid.*

44. G. Otto Trevelyan, *The Life and Letters of Lord Macaulay, vol.2* (New York: Harper & Brothers, Publishers, 1875), p.409, excerpt from Macaulay's letter to H.S. Randall, May 23, 1857.

45. W.E. Gladstone, "Kin Beyond Sea," *Gleanings of Past Years*, vol.1 of 7 vols. (London: John Murray, Albemarle Street, 1879), p.212.

46. Russell Duane, in Foreword to Benjamin Waite Blanchard's *Your America—Its Constitution and Its Laws* (Philadelphia: J.B. Lippincott Co., 1936).

47. Harman, testimony (see chap.2, n.16), p.199.

EPILOGUE

1. The following individuals have commented favorably on the wisdom of the Panama Canal Treaties of 1977. The sources are indicated:

Robert C. Byrd, D.-W.Va., Minority Leader, U.S. Senate, comments, *Congressional Record—Senate*, 98th Cong., 2d sess., vol.130, March 19, 1984, p.S2842.

Alexander M. Haig, Jr., Secretary of State, letter to Robert C. Byrd, July 3, 1982, as quoted in *Congressional Record—Senate, ibid.*, and in response to Byrd's letter, June 28, 1982.

Robert O. Pastor, former assistant to National Security Adviser, Zbigniew Brzezinski, telephone interview with author, November 13, 1983.

Michael Kozak, Deputy Legal Adviser, Department of State, interview with author, November 23, 1983, in Washington, D.C.

Robert Dockery, former staff official of the Senate Committee on Foreign Relations in charge of the Panama Canal Treaties, interview with author, November 15, 1983, in Washington, D.C.

Richard McCall, former Deputy Staff Director, Senate Committee on Foreign Relations, interview with author, November 23, 1983, in Washington, D.C.

Margaret Hayes, Western Hemisphere Specialist for the Senate Committee on Foreign Relations, interview with author, November 19, 1983, in Washington, D.C.

Alison Rosenberg, Legislative Assistant for Foreign Affairs to Senator Charles Percy, R.-Ill., Chairman, Senate Committee on Foreign Relations, interview with author, November 21, 1983.

Sherman Hinson, Panama Desk, Department of State, interview with author, November 21, 1983, in Washington, D.C.

2. "Ardito-Barletta Discusses Canal Policy," *Critica* newspaper, Panama City, Panama, October 8, 1984, pp.2, 7.

3. *Panama Canal Treaty* (see chap.1, n.28), Article III, paragraph 3.

4. Mark Baille, "PRD 'Initiated Incidents'," *Latin* newspaper, Latin-Reuter News Service, Buenos Aires, Argentina, May 8, 1984, p.1. See also, Jay Millin, Sr., "Panamanians take to streets to protest presidential choice," *The Washington Times*, May 22, 1984, p.12A; "Electoral Tribunal Alternate Magistrate Resigns," *La Prensa* newspaper, Panama City, Panama, May 24, 1984, p.1A; "Signals from Panama," editorial, *The Washington Times*, May 25, 1984, p.11A; "Canal Watchers Educational Association Newsletter," Frank B. Turberville, Jr., publisher, Milton, N.C., June 6, 1984, p.1; Jay Mallin, Sr., "Panama election leaves a bitter aftertaste," *The Washington Times*, May 25, 1984, p.6A.

5. *Ibid.,* Baille, *Latin.*

6. Arnulfo Arias Madrid, former President of Panama, interview with author, October 19, 1984.

7. The Inouye rider was introduced by Senator Daniel K. Inouye, D.-Hawaii, who voted for the Treaties. General Paredes had retired from the Guard to run for President; but the new Guard commander Noreiga switched his support to Barletta, obviously concerned that Paredes's Guard connections might dilute Noreiga's own power.

8. "Barletta in Cuba," *La Estrella de Panama* newspaper, August 27, 1974, p.1. Barletta's observation about the "same objectives" for Cuba and Panama coincided with Torrijos's plan "to create a socialist democracy in Panama, friendly to, but deliberately independent of, the United States," according to author Graham Greene, a friend of Torrijos, in his book, *Getting to Know the General* (New York: Simon and Schuster, 1984), as reviewed by William Robertson, Book Editor, *The Miami Herald*, October 21, 1984, p.A5.

9. "Signals from Panama," *The Washington Times* (see Epilogue, n.4).

10. Luis Pallais, Vice President of Nicaragua, and Maxmilian Kelly, Secretary to the President of Nicaragua, testimony, hearings on Panama Gunrunning before the Subcommittee on the Panama Canal and the Committee on Merchant Marine and Fisheries, House of Representatives, 96th Cong., 1st sess., June 6, 7 and July 10, 1979, pp.27-35.

11. *Ibid.,* p.31, report of December 28, 1978 by Hugo Spadafora, former Panamanian Minister of Health, cited.

12. Thomas H. Brown, "Americans in Canal Zone witness great changes," Norfolk, Va., *The Virginian-Pilot*, Associated Press, October 1, 1984, p.A6.

13. "Agreement in Implementation of Article III of the Panama Canal Treaty," *Documents Implementing the Panama Canal Treaty,* Department of State Publication 8914, Inter-American Series 113, released September 1977, Article

XV, paragraph 2. See also, "Federal Income Taxes for Individuals," Internal Revenue Service Publication 17 (Washington, D.C.: GPO, 1983), paragraph 2. In 1983
former Panamanian President Demetrio Lakas, and former treaty negotiators Juan
Tack and Carlos Lopez Guevara signed statements confirming that "all taxes"
were exempt under Article XV(2). In 1985, after the I.R.S. lost the *Coplin v. U.S.*
tax case and after a $30 million U.S. grant made after a visit to Panama by Ambas-
sadors Bunker and Linowitz, Panama switched its official position in unsworn diplomatic notes asserting that Article XV(2) applied only to Panamanian taxes.

14. *Hay-Bunau-Varilla Treaty (1903)*, Article III.

15. *Ibid.*, Article XXII.

18. Dramatic proof was given by Doris McClellan, custodian and clerk of the
U.S. Court for the Panama Canal Zone, and by James C. Luitweiler, former Secretary of the Joint United States-Republic of Panama Land Commission, at hearings
before the Subcommitee on Separation of Powers of the Committee on the Judiciary, U.S. Senate, 95th Cong., 2d sess., pt.4, March 11, 1978, pp.5-16. Crates of the
original records of the land purchases were exhibited to the members of the Subcommittee. Miss McClellan is the daughter of the late Senator John L. McClellan,
D.-Ark., who co-sponsored many times with Senator Strom Thurmond, R.-S.C.,
Sense of the Senate Resolutions for retaining U.S. sovereign rights in the Canal
Zone.

As a matter of historical interest at this point, the first claim was paid to F.V. de
la Espriella, the great grandfather of Ricardo de la Espriella who in 1984 was
deposed as President by General Noreiga. Great grandfather de la Espriella was
also the first Foreign Minister of the new Republic of Panama in 1904 under President Manuel Amador, who had succeeded the leader of the separatist movement
from Colombia and Panama's President of the provisional government, Jose
Agustin Arango. Arango was a very humble man, refusing the presidency of the
new republic, saying, "My work is finished."

17. *Hay-Bunau-Varilla Treaty (1903)*, Article III.

18. Jorden, *Odyssey* (see chap.3, n.18), pp.2-3.

19. Sarah Booth Conray, "Rosalynn Carter: Politics and the Future," book
review, *The Washington Post*, April 25, 1984, p.D4.

20. "The Acid Test," *The American*, monthly newspaper of the American
Party, April 1984, p.4.

21. Thomas H. Moorer, Admiral, U.S. Navy, (Ret.), former Chairman, Joint
Chiefs of Staff, "Comment and Discussion," *U.S. Naval Institute Proceedings*,
March 1980, pp.93-94.

22. Thomas A. Lane, Maj. General, U.S. Army, (Ret.), comments, *Strategic
Review*, Winter 1974, p.4.

23. Hansen W. Baldwin, letter to author, April 20, 1984.

24. Leonard E. Bell, Senior Panama Canal Pilot, "Canal Employees Fought to
Save it, Now Struggle to Keep it Functioning," *The National Educator*, January
1982, p.14.

25. Thurmond, address before the Senate, *Congressional Record—Senate*,
95th Cong., 2d sess., vol.124, pt.8. April 18, 1978, p.10525.

26. The *Restatement* and Fenwick's *International Law* are among the most
cited secondary sources of the law:

Restatement of the Law (Second): Foreign Relations Laws of the United States (see chap.10, n.19), Section 136, p.423.

Charles G. Fenwick, *International Law,* 3d edition (New York: Appleton-Century-Crofts, Inc., 1948), pp.437-38. Fenwick states that "any change or amendment inserted by one party as a condition of ratification must be accepted by the other party if the treaty is to come into effect." Dr. Charles H. Breecher emphasized in his testimony before the East Subcommittee that changes, whatever they are called and whether considered substantive or not, have to be accepted by all parties to a treaty—and he called the Panamanian counter-reservation "the most substantive . . . that can be imagined."

Fenwick wrote that ratification "with the understanding" (p.438) places a specific interpretation on certain parts of the treaty—and that it is common practice to stipulate in advance such interpretations by means of "understandings." Panama ratified the Carter-Torrijos Treaties "on the understanding" that any U.S. measures to reopen or defend the Canal were subject to "mutual cooperation"—but this was not the "understanding" of the U.S. Senate upon consenting to the Treaties.

27. Article 20.2 of the 1969 Vienna Convention on the Law of Treaties states that "a reservation requires acceptance by all the parties."

BIBLIOGRAPHY

Abbot, Willis J. *Panama and the Canal.* New York: Syndicate Publishing Company, 1913.

Anguizola, Gustave. *The Panama Canal: Isthmian Political Instability from 1821 to 1977,* 2d edition. Washington, D.C.: United Press of America, 1977.

Beals, Charleton. *The Coming Struggle for Latin America.* New York: J.B. Lippencott Company, 1938.

Beard, Charles A. and Mary R. *A Basic History of the United States.* Philadelphia: The Blakiston Company, 1944.

Bishop, Joseph Bucklin. *The Panama Gateway.* New York: Charles Scribner's Sons, 1913.

Bishop, Joseph Bucklin and Farnham. *Goethals, Genius of the Panama Canal.* New York: Harper & Brothers Publishers, 1930.

Brzezinski, Zbigniew. *Power and Principle: Memoirs of the National Security Adviser, 1977-1981.* New York: Farrar, Straus, Giroux, 1983.

Bullard, Arthur. *Panama, the Canal, the Country and the People.* New York: The MacMillan Company, 1914.

Busch, Noel F. *T.R.: The Story of Theodore Roosevelt and his Influence on our Time.* New York: Reynal & Company, 1963.

Busey, James L. *Political Aspects of the Panama Canal: The Problem of Location.* Tucson, Arizona: The University of Arizona Press, 1974.

Carter, Jimmy. *Keeping Faith.* New York: Bantam Books, Inc., 1982.

Commager, Henry Steele. *Documents of American History.* New York: Appleton-Century-Crofts, Inc., 1948.

The Constitution of the United States of America.

Crane, Philip M. *Surrender in Panama: The Case Against the Treaty.* New York: Dale/Caroline Dale Books, 1978.

Crowther, Samuel. *The Romance and Rise of the American Tropics.* Garden City, N.Y.: Doubleday, Doran & Company, Inc., 1929.

Dozer, Donald M. *The Panama Canal in Perspective.* Washington, D.C.: Council on American Affairs, 1978.

DuBois, Jules. *Danger Over Panama.* Indianapolis: The Bobbs-Merrill Company, Inc., 1964.

DuVal, Miles P., Jr. *And the Mountains Will Move: The Story of the Building of the Panama Canal.* Westport, Connecticut: Greenwood Press, 1968.

—————. *Cadiz to Cathay: The Story of the Long Diplomatic Struggle for the Panama Canal.* Palo Alto, California: Stanford University Press, 1947.

—————. *James Monroe: An Appreciation.* Orange, Virginia: James Monroe Memorial Foundation, 1982.

—————. "Isthmian Canal Policy—An Evaluation." *U.S. Naval Institute Proceedings,* vol.81, no.3, March 1955.

Dye, Thomas R., Lee S. Greene, and George S. Parthemos, *American Government: Theory, Structure, and Process.* Belmont, California: Wadsworth Publishing Company, Inc., 1972.

Ealy, Lawrence O. *Yanqui Politics and the Isthmian Canal.* University Press, Pennsylvania: Pennsylvania State University Press, 1971.

Eisenhower, Milton. *The Wine is Bitter.* New York: Doubleday & Co., 1963.

Engdahl, David E. *Constitutional Power: Federal and State.* St. Paul: West Publishing Company, 1974.

Flood, Daniel J. *Isthmian Canal Policy Questions* (House Document No. 474, 89th Cong.). Washington, D.C.: Government Printing Office, 1966.

Forbes-Lindsay, O.H. *Panama, the Isthmus and the Canal.* Philadelphia: The John C. Winston Company, 1906.

Frank, Thomas and Edward Weisband. *Foreign Policy by Congress.* New York: Oxford University Press, 1979.

Geyelin, Philip. *Lyndon B. Johnson and the World.* New York: Praeger, 1966.

Gunther, John. *Inside Latin America.* New York: Harpers, 1940.

Harding, Earl. *The Untold Story of Panama.* New York: Athene Press, Inc., 1959.

Haskin, Frederic J. *The Panama Canal.* Garden City, New York: Doubleday, Page & Company, 1913.

Henkin, Louis. *Foreign Affairs and the Constitution.* Mineola, New York: The Foundation Press, Inc., 1972.

Hull, William I. *The Monroe Doctrine: National or International.* New York: G.P. Putnam's Sons, 1915.

Isaac, Rael Jean and Erich Isaac. *The Coercive Utopians: Social Deception by America's Power Players.* Chicago: Regnery Gateway, Inc., 1983.

Johnson, Lyndon B. *The Vantage Point.* New York: Holt, Rinehart & Winston, 1971.

Jorden, William J. *Panama Odyssey.* Austin, Texas: University of Texas Press, 1984.

Kirkpatrick, Jeane J. *Dictatorships and Double-Standards.* New York: American Enterprises Institute, 1982.

Kitchel, Denison. *The Truth About the Panama Canal.* New Rochelle, New York: Arlington House Publishers, 1978.

Lasky, Victor. *Jimmy Carter: The Man and the Myth.* New York: Richard Marek Publishers, 1979.

LaFeber, Walter. *The Panama Canal: The Crisis in Historical Perspective.* New York: Oxford University Press, 1979.

Lane, Thomas A. *The Breakdown of the Old Politics.* New Rochelle, New York: Arlington House Publishers, 1974.

Levine, Isaac Don. *Hands Off the Panama Canal.* Washington, D.C.: Monticello Books, 1976.

Liss, Sheldon B. *The Canal: Aspects of United States-Panamanian Relations.* Notre Dame: University of Notre Dame Press, 1967.

Lycan, Gilbert I. *Alexander Hamilton & American Foreign Policy.* Norman: University of Oklahoma Press, 1970.

McCullough, David. *The Path Between the Seas.* New York: Simon and Schuster, 1977.

Miner, Dwight Carroll. *The Fight for the Panama Route: The Story of the Spooner Act and the Hay-Herran Treaty.* New York: Columbia University Press, 1940.

Morrow, Jay J. *A Great People's Great Canal, Its Achievements, Its Perils.* Mount Hope, Canal Zone: The Panama Canal Press, 1923.

_____. *The Maintenance and Operation of the Panama Canal.* Mount Hope, Canal Zone: The Panama Canal Press, 1923.

Norton, Thomas James. *The Constitution of the United States: Its Sources and Application.* New York: The World Publishing Company, 1943.

Panama Canal Issue and Treaty Talks (Special Report Series: No. 3). Washington, D.C.: The Center for Strategic Studies, 1967.

Reed, John. *Ten Days That Shook the World.* New York: Random House, 1935.

Report on Events in Panama, January 9-12, 1964. Geneva: International Commission on Jurists, 1964.

Robinson, Tracy. *Fifty Years at Panama.* New York: The Trow Press, 1907.

Ryan, Paul B. *The Panama Canal Controversy: U.S. Diplomacy and Defense Interests.* Stanford, California: Hoover Institution Press, 1977.

Sibert, William L. and John F. Stevens. *The Construction of the Panama Canal.* New York: D. Appleton & Company, 1915.

Somoza, Anastosio as told to Jack Cox. *Nicaragua Betrayed.* Boston: Western Islands, 1980.

Speller, Jon P. *The Panama Canal: Heart of America's Security.* New York: Robert Speller & Sons, Publishers, Inc., 1972.

Veliz, Claudio. *Latin America and the Caribbean, a Handbook.* New York: Frederick A. Praeger, 1968.

Verrill, A. Hyatt. *Panama Past and Present.* New York: Dodd, Mead and Company, 1925.

U.S. GOVERNMENT
U.S. SENATE

Implementing the Panama Canal Treaty of 1977 and Related Agreements. Senate Report No. 96-255, 96th Cong., 1st sess., July 21, 1979. Washington, D.C.: U.S. Government Printing Office, 1979.

Senate Debate of the Panama Canal Treaties, A Compendium of Major Statements, Documents, Record Votes, and Relevant Events. Washington, D.C.: U.S. Government Printing Office, February 1979.

Panama Canal Treaties—Constitutional and Legal Aspects of the Ratification Process. Hearing before the Subcommittee on Separation of Powers of the Senate Committee on the Judiciary, 98th Cong., 1st sess., June 23, 1983. Washington, D.C.: U.S. Government Printing Office, 1983.

Panama Canal Treaties. Hearings before the Committee on Foreign Relations, United States Senate, 95th Cong., 1st sess., pt.3., October 10, 11, 12, 13, and 14, 1977. Washington, D.C.: U.S. Government Printing Office, 1977.

Panama Canal Treaties. Report of the Committee on Foreign Relations, U.S. Senate, with Supplemental and Minority Views on Executive N, 95th Cong., 1st sess., February 3, 1978. Washington, D.C.: U.S. Government Printing Office, 1978.

Panama Canal Treaty (Disposition of United States Territory). Hearings before the Subcommittee on Separation of Powers of the Senate Committee on the Judiciary, 95th Cong., 2d sess., pt.4, March 11, 1978. Washington, D.C.: U.S. Government Printing Office, 1978.

The Panama Canal Treaty and the Congressional Power to Dispose of United States Property. Report to the Committee on the Judiciary made by its Subcommittee on Separation of Powers, 95th Cong., 2d sess., February 1978. Washington, D.C.: U.S. Government Printing Office, 1978.

Panama Canal Treaty. Message from the President of the United States transmitting the Panama Canal Treaties, 95th Cong., 1st sess., September 16, 1977. Washington, D.C.: U.S. Government Printing Office, 1977.

The Role of the Senate in Treaty Ratification. A Staff Memorandum to the Committee on Foreign Relations, United States Senate, 95th Cong., 1st sess., November 1977. Washington, D.C.: U.S. Government Printing Office, 1977.

Panama Canal Treaty Implementing Legislation. Hearings before the Committee on Armed Services, United States Senate, 96th Cong., 1st sess., on S. 1024 to Implement the Panama Canal Treaty of 1977 and Related Agreements, and for Other Purposes, June 26-27, 1979. Washington, D.C.: U.S. Government Printing Office, 1979.

U.S. HOUSE OF REPRESENTATIVES

The Caribbean Basin Initiative. Hearings and Markup before the Committee on Foreign Affairs and Its Subcommittee on International Economic Policy and Trade and on Inter-American Affairs, House of Representatives, 97th Cong., 2d sess., on H.R. 5900, March 23, 25, 30; April 1, 27, 29; May 11; July 15, 1982. Washington, D.C.: U.S. Government Printing Office, 1982.

Constitution, Jefferson's Manual and Rules of the House of Representatives, House Document No. 95-403, 95th Cong., 2d sess., William Holmes Brown, Parliamentarian. Washington, D.C.: U.S. Government Printing Office, 1979.

How Our Laws Are Made, House Document 96-352, 96th Cong., 2d sess., presented by Representative Peter D. Rodino, Jr. Washington, D.C.: U.S. Government Printing Office, 1980.

Panama Canal Act of 1979, Public Law 96-70, September 27, 1979, 93 Stat. 452, 96th Cong., 1st sess. Washington, D.C.: U.S. Government Printing Office, 1979.

Panama Canal Briefings. Hearing before the Committee on Merchant Marine & Fisheries, House of Representatives, 93d Cong., 1st sess., April 13, 1973, Serial 93-8. Washington, D.C.: U.S. Government Printing Office, 1973.

New Panama Canal Treaty. Hearing before the Committee on Merchant Marine & Fisheries, House of Representatives, 95th Cong., 1st sess., on the Agreement in Principle with Respect to the Proposed Panama Canal Treaties of 1977, August 17, 1977, Serial No. 95-13. Washington, D.C.: U.S. Government Printing Office, 1977.

Panama Gunrunning. Hearings before the Subcommittee on the Panama Canal and the Committee on Merchant Marine & Fisheries, House of Representatives, 96th Cong., 1st sess., June 6, 7, and July 10, 1979. Washington, D.C.: U.S. Government Printing Office, 1979.

Our American Government: What is it? How does it function? House Document 96-351, 96th Cong., 2d sess., May 9, 1980. Washington, D.C.: U.S. Government Printing Office, 1980.

Sea Level Canal Studies. Hearings before the Subcommittee on the Panama Canal of the Committee on Merchant Marine and Fisheries, House of Representatives, 95th Cong., 2d sess., on H.R. 10087 and H.R. 13176, June 21, 27, 28, 1978. Washington, D.C.: U.S. Government Printing Office, 1978.

DEPARTMENT OF STATE

Documents Associated with the Panama Canal Treaties, Department of State Selected Documents, No. 6B, September 1977. Washington, D.C.: U.S. Government Printing Office, 1977.

The Meaning of the New Panama Canal Treaties, Department of State Selected Documents, No. 6C, December 1977. Washington, D.C.: U.S. Government Printing Office, 1977.

Texts of Treaties Relating to the Panama Canal, Department of State Selected Documents, No. 6A, September 1977. Washington, D.C.: U.S. Government Printing Office, 1977.

Panama Canal Permanent Neutrality and Operation Treaty between the United States of America and Panama, Treaties and Other International Acts Series No. 10029, U.S. Department of State, signed at Washington, D.C., September 7, 1977. Washington, D.C.: U.S. Government Printing Office, 1982.

Panama Canal Treaty between the United States of America and Panama, Treaties and Other International Acts Series No. 10030, U.S. Department of State, signed at Washington, D.C., September 7, 1977. Washington, D.C.: U.S. Government Printing Office, 1981.

MISCELLANEOUS

Background Documents Relating to the Panama Canal. Congressional Research Service, Library of Congress. Washington, D.C.: U.S. Government Printing Office, 1977.

Documents Illustrative of the Formation of the Union of the American States, prepared by H.H.B. Meyer, Library of Congress. Washington, D.C.: U.S. Government Printing Office, 1927.

Mickey Edwards v. James Earl Carter, No. 78-1166, United States Court of Appeals for the District of Columbia Circuit, decided April 6, 1978, on Motion for

Injunction Pending Appeal Motion for Summary Reversal, and Motion for Summary Affirmance (D.C. Civil 77-1733).

Storrs, K. Larry. *The 1977 Panama Canal Treaties, A Selection of Pro and Con Statements on the Major Issues,* prepared by the Congressional Research Service, Library of Congress. Washington, D.C.: U.S. Government Printing Office, 1978.

_____. *Panama Canal: Issue Brief Number IB74138,* prepared by the Congressional Research Service, Library of Congress. Washington, D.C.: U.S. Government Printing Office, 1976.

INDEX

Hatfield, Paul, 14, 75
Hart, Gary, 149
Hay-Bunau-Varilla Treaty (1903), 5-9, 18, 27-43
    passim, 48, 60, 65, 68, 72, 79, 87, 95-96, 133,
    135, 148, 150, 176, 180-181, 183, 201, 208-219
    passim, 229, 235-236, 255, 258, 267-268, 271,
    278-279, 285
Hay-Herran Treaty (1902), 96
Hay, John, 28-29, 96, 215, 279
Hay-Pauncefote Treaty (1901), 72, 214-215
Hayes, Rutherford B., 214-215, 218
Hazlitt, William, 135
Heinz, John, 149
Helms, Jesse, 67-68, 75, 89, 102, 122-123, 138,
    143, 161, 240, 242-243, 249, 257, 280, 285
Helms, Richard, 268
Helsinki Accords, 179, 187
Henkin, Louis, 212, 218
Heritage Foundation, 251
Hesburgh, Theodore, 44
Hewitt, Ashley C., Jr., 262-263
Hinson, Sherman, 191-192, 263
Hobart, Deming, 250
Hoffer, Eric, 269
Hoffmann, Carl R., Jr., 250, 267
Hollings, Ernest, 149
Hollings-Heinz-Bellmon Reservation, 146, 242
Holloway, James L., III, 82, 246
Honduras, 257
Hong Kong and Shanghai Banking Corporation,
    3
House Armed Services Committee, 49
House Committee on Merchant Marine and
    Fisheries, 57, 98, 111, 196, 224-225, 227, 275
House of Representatives, 11, 34-35, 40, 73, 139,
    145, 154, 163, 175, 183, 191, 199, 209-233,
    235-237, 255, 267, 277
House Subcommittee on Inter-American Affairs,
    50
House Subcommittee on the Panama Canal, 81,
    234-235
How Our Laws are Made, 223
Hubbard, Carroll, 81, 235, 257, 285
Huddleston, Walter, 149
Hughes, Charles Evans, 18-19, 29-30, 239, 279
Hull-Alfaro Treaty (1936), 31
Human Events, 188

Illueca, Jorge E., 133-135, 144, 261, 263, 278
Imperial Rockefeller: A Biography of Nelson
    Rockefeller, 94
Independent Lawyers Movement, Panama, 245
Inouye, Daniel, 149, 276
Institute of Pacific Relations, 163
Inter-American Committee of Alliance for
    Progress, 67
Inter-American Defense Board, 86
Inter-American Development Bank, 37
Inter-American Dialogue Group, 44

Internal Revenue Service (IRS), 243, 278
International Court of Justice, 127, 134-135, 181
International Law, 205, 245, 283
Ireland, Andy, 181
Irvine, Reed, 67
Isabella, 157
Isthmus of Panama, 1, 7, 20, 27, 39, 119, 135,
    157, 214, 221, 239, 241, 247, 269, 281

Jackson, Jesse, 239
Javits, Jacob K., 99, 162
Jefferson's Manual of Parliamentary Practice
    (Constitution, Jefferson's Manual and Rules
    of the House of Representatives (1979)), 40,
    72, 175, 209-215 passim, 222, 227, 229, 236,
    267
Jefferson, Thomas, 174-175, 209-210, 215,
    217-218, 227, 237, 264, 270
Jenrette, John W., 280
Jimenez, Humberto, 50, 57
Johnson Administration, 207
Johnson, Byron L., 35
Johnson, Chester A., 50, 55-56
Johnson, J. Bennett, 149
Johnson, Lady Bird, 75
Johnson, Lyndon B., 5, 9, 36, 38, 48, 51, 69,
    218, 240, 260
Joint Chiefs of Staff, 61, 76, 81-86, 126, 246
Jones, David C., 82, 86
Jones, Norvil, 193
Jones, Phil, 142
Jordan, Hamilton, 13, 88
Jordan, Jerry, 212, 218
Jorden, William J., 29, 34, 51-52, 55-56, 58, 79,
    111-118, 158, 172-173, 233, 257, 262, 276,
    279-281, 285
Judd, Walter, 34-35
Judge, Tom, 75
Justice Department, 68, 163

Kamenar, Paul Douglas, 212, 218
Karr, Alphonse, 129
Kastenmeier, Robert W., 35
Katzenbach, Nicholas deB, 44
Keeping Faith, 17, 105, 171, 206
Kelly, Richard, 280
Kennedy Administration, 207
Kennedy, Edward M., 132-133, 136, 149, 162, 280
Kennedy, John F., 35-36, 48, 186, 239-240
Kentucky Resolution (1798), 217
Khadafy, Muammar, 175
Khan, Genghis, 270
Kirbo, Charles H., 61
Kirkpatrick, Jeane, 40
Kissinger, Henry A., 40-43, 59-61, 66, 69, 75, 87,
    107, 178-188, 190, 195, 209, 224, 257, 277,
    280, 285
Kissinger-Tack Statement of Principles, 9, 19, 39,

Reader Comments

I have read your manuscript carefully. I agree. You have made your constitutional points emphatically. This is a timely, informative, courageous, historical contribution.
Alfred J. Schweppe, distinguished jurist, treaty expert.
American Bar Association

At the time I was inspecting the facilities in the Canal Zone and refining the estimated costs to the U.S. Army of nearly one billion dollars, Mr. Carter was telling the American people that the Panama Canal treaties were not going to cost the American taxpayers a single dime. Congratulations to you and your efforts to expose what is clearly one of the greatest frauds of our time as well as one of the least intelligent strategic decisions of any U.S. Administration since our founding.
John K. Singlaub, Maj. General USA (Ret.)
Former Chief of Staff, U.S. Army, South Korea

This book cuts through the confusion and the duplicity that have characterized the debate on this issue. With careful research and documentation, it lays to rest any lingering doubt as to the effect the Canal Treaties will have on the future security of our nation and our hemisphere. I only wish that those responsible for the Treaties had had the chance to read this book back in 1977. It might very well have changed the disastrous course of events.
Philip M. Crane
U.S. Representative, House Ways and Means Committee

It is good to see a book telling the truth about the military coup I carried out in Panama with the *Guardia Nacional* in 1968 against Dr. Arnulfo Arias.
Boris N. Martinex, Former Officer in Charge,
David Garrison, Guardia Nacional, *Panama*

This book presents to the American people the "other side of the story" which has been spiked by the media. Hopefully, it will contribute to clear understanding of the political problems we now face in those who want to continue the destruction of U.S. security in this hemisphere.
Gordon Sumner Jr., Lt. General USA (Ret.)
Ambassador at Large, Latin America

Captain Evans has undertaken the research that historians will find invaluable in explaining to future generations how President Carter succeeded in flouting the will of the American people in the Panama Canal giveaway.
Reed Irvine, Chairman, Accuracy in Media

The surrender of the Panama Canal is one of the sorriest chapters in our history. Americans should read the story of how we were trapped into this suicidal blunder, and weep.
Steven D. Symms,
U.S. Senator, Committee on Finance

The finest, most authentic book written about the tragic giveaway of the Panama Canal. With great force and unusual clarity, Captain Russell Evans describes the making of the illegal Treaties and their great cost to the American taxpayers.
Meldrim Thomson, Jr.
Former Governor, New Hampshire

Ever so often there comes an American patriot with the courage and integrity to speak the truth to his countrymen. Captain Evans renders that service in exposing the political intrigue that led to the giveaway of one of our nation's most strategic assets. He provides facts which the American people need to know — and, certainly, are entitled to know.
Jesse Helms, U.S. Senator
Committee on Foreign Relations

This incisive exposure contains a long overdue message relative to the blatant by-passing of the Constitution by the President and the Senate in surrendering the Panama Canal against the will of the American people and contrary to law and oaths of office.

C.M. Talbott, Lt. General USAF (Ret.)
Chief of Staff
Military Order of the World Wars

What a frightening story of deception and cover up! As a Panama Canal Pilot for 24 years, I was always so proud of my part in operating this strategic waterway built by American genius and sacrifice. Now, the know-how is being taken away, the operation is deteriorating, and the future is certainly beclouded.

John Wallace
Former Senior Panama Canal Pilot

I enjoyed reading this useful account of the Panama Canal Treaties debates. Anyone who wants to understand the source of fierce opposition to the Treaties would benefit from reading this book.

Orrin G. Hatch,
U.S. Senator, Committee on the Judiciary

The campaign for ratification, Captain Evans shows, was filled with deception and fraud. It is important that we understand what happened in 1978 so that it will never be repeated. This book will surely become a standard work on the subject.

Allan C. Brownfeld,
Analyst Editor, Lincoln Review

This book is a great research piece. The American people ought to know the facts that it contains.

William L. Dickinson, U.S. Representative
Committee on Armed Services

Sadly, the Panama Canal Treaties must remain a disgrace to American diplomacy. But *The Panama Canal Treaties Swindle* can alert the American people to the nature of the negotiations leading to the Treaties, and may thereby help to prevent further diplomatic tragedies. To leave the American people ignorant of what took place would compound that fraud.

John M. Fisher, President
American Security Council

Without reservation I recommend this important book. Nothing I have

read in recent years has so completely exposed the sick mentalities of some of those who climb to high places in Washington and then betray the most vital interests of the American people.
W. Cleon Skousen, distinguished jurist
Founder, The Freemen Institute